Psychology of the Consumer and Its Development

An Introduction

The Plenum Series in Adult Development and Aging

SERIES EDITOR:
Jack Demick, *Suffolk University, Boston, Massachusetts*

ADULT DEVELOPMENT, THERAPY, AND CULTURE
A Postmodern Synthesis
Gerald D. Young

THE AMERICAN FATHER
Biocultural and Developmental Aspects
Wade C. Mackey

THE CHANGING NATURE OF PAIN COMPLAINTS OVER THE LIFESPAN
Michael R. Thomas and Ranjan Roy

THE DEVELOPMENT OF LOGIC IN ADULTHOOD
Postformal Thought and Its Applications
Jan D. Sinnott

HANDBOOK OF AGING AND MENTAL HEALTH
Edited by Jacob Lomranz

HANDBOOK OF CLINICAL GEROPSYCHOLOGY
Edited by Michel Hersen and Vincent B. Van Hasselt

HANDBOOK OF PAIN AND AGING
Edited by David I. Mostofsky and Jacob Lomranz

HUMAN DEVELOPMENT IN ADULTHOOD
Lewis R. Aiken

PSYCHOLOGY OF THE CONSUMER AND ITS DEVELOPMENT
An Introduction
Robert C. Webb

A Continuation Order Plan is available for this series. A continuation order will bring delivery of each new volume immediately upon publication. Volumes are billed only upon actual shipment. For further information please contact the publisher.

Psychology of the Consumer and Its Development

An Introduction

Robert C. Webb

Suffolk University
Boston, Massachusetts

Kluwer Academic / Plenum Publishers
New York, Boston, Dordrecht, London, Moscow

ISBN: 0-306-46073-4

© 1999 Kluwer Academic / Plenum Publishers, New York
233 Spring Street, New York, N.Y. 10013

10 9 8 7 6 5 4 3 2 1

A C.I.P. record for this book is available from the Library of Congress

Printed in the United States of America

To Diane, for her unflagging support,
encouragement, and patience.

Preface

I wrote this book for a number of reasons. First, it arose from my perceived need for a volume that would address the many aspects of psychology in more depth than do the current consumer behavior texts. In teaching a course in consumer psychology for more than 15 years, I have been continually frustrated by having to use texts that were well designed for marketers, but not for psychologists. That is, they spend much of their pages on such topics as demographics and market segmentation—certainly important marketing considerations, but those that have little psychological interest. In their place I look more closely at classical conditioning and psychological needs, for instance. I hope the resulting book will be seen as a complement to the existing texts, rather than as a competitor.

Second, many of my students are marketing majors with very limited psychology background, and others are psychology majors with no marketing courses. I am attempting to write a book that will be of interest to both. At the same time, I hope to reach a general audience that is neither sophisticated in psychology nor in marketing, but who want to know more about the process of buying and using products and the attached process of advertising. These processes are so central to our culture that all of us are swept up in their forces, yet few understand the psychological principles on which they are based. We respond to advertising on an almost daily basis, but we have only a hazy idea of why. Our "buttons are being pushed" and we often do not realize it. We would all be better consumers if we were able to recognize false appeals and separate the real from the illusory. Thus, I have written this book at a level that does not require a special vocabulary in order to understand the psychological or marketing principles. For this reason, too, I have omitted discussion of research methods and statistical techniques.

I am aware that the more sophisticated practitioners of consumer psychology may feel that this volume is not written at a high enough level to be useful to researchers in the field. Many of the principles presented have additional abstruse theories attached that delve into esoteric details and predictions. The book, however, is meant to be taken as an introduction, not a handbook. One cannot treat all levels at once, yet even practitioners at the highest levels may find here ideas to enlighten their own work. I find marketing students who know very well how to appeal to consumers, but they would be better at their trade if they more fully understood the whys of their appeals.

A third reason for writing the book is to illuminate the need for research on the changes that take place in individuals as they grow and age in a consumer culture. Certainly, they become more sophisticated about the appeals to which they are subjected, and their needs change along with their economic fortunes. So far, we have seen little research to explore these changes. We may all guess at some of them, but my approach has been to stay with the empirical results—principles that have been experimentally demonstrated—rather than veering off into the uncertain world of speculation. This is not to say that speculation has no place, for it often provides the concept tested by research, but I have attempted to label speculation as such when it appears. This becomes particularly necessary in the area of adult development. The field is a relatively new one in psychology as a whole and its virtual absence in the consumer application is understandable. However, just as psychological research on this topic is growing rapidly, so should consumer research grow rapidly. For example, we need to go beyond the demographic approach, which simply finds what older adults buy, and explore how their psychological perceptions have changed—particularly because the percentage of older adults in society is rising dramatically. They need to be better understood, not simply more effectively sold to.

There are, of course, a number of people who have contributed to this effort in various ways. Particularly, I wish to thank Suffolk University for a sabbatical leave that allowed me to complete much of the manuscript, and Jack Demick, chair of the Psychology Department, who was completely supportive and encouraging throughout the long process. My thanks also to Kelly Fenton and Noreen Donovan who provided exceptional secretarial services and advice on the vagaries of the word processing program, and to Amy Martin who spent many hours finding and reproducing reference articles. I want also to voice appreciation for the hundreds of researchers who have so painstakingly contributed the basic knowledge on which the book is based. As all who come after, I owe them a tremendous debt. Many classes of students provided endless ideas and insights over the years. Finally, I must thank my wife Diane for putting up with my interminable hours on the computer on many weekends that might have been more sociably spent, and her unfailing support of the whole project.

Contents

CHAPTER 1

Introduction

The industrial revolution accelerated the nation's transition into a culture of consumers. Before that time, it was not uncommon for families to live on farms and to grow or make nearly all the things they needed. They often bartered and traded for the necessities they could not produce. Factory production changed all that. More and more people began to leave the farm, live in towns or cities, and buy whatever they needed. In a literal sense, we have always been consumers. We have always had to eat, but today, with most of the population either urban or suburbanites, we buy almost everything we use. This book is about the second meaning of consumer, the person who buys to use. Moreover, it is not directed solely at marketers, but to all of us, so that we can become better consumers, better in the sense of buying more wisely, not in the sense of buying more.

The automobile had a tremendous impact on the consumption process, but in actuality it was simply continuing a trend begun much earlier. It began with itinerant peddlers who traveled from town to town. They allowed rural and isolated communities to buy goods that were generally available only in large towns or cities. The mail order catalog expanded the opportunities manyfold, and nearly every imaginable product was available through its pages. With the coming of the automobile and of course the roads to drive it on, one could travel to more distant towns and bring home an item the same day, rather than waiting sometimes weeks for the mail order response. Merchants realized an expanded market at the same time and Main Streets flourished. When the interstates were built, malls began to appear; today they have all but replaced Main Street as the market for products. Malls have become what Main Street used to be, a place to hang out or windowshop, but our buying power has increased immensely over the years, and more is available in malls than there ever was on Main Street.

As goods became more widely distributed, prices went down and the variety of goods went up. No longer do we buy only what we need, save for an occasional trinket to soothe the soul. Today we are able to buy for a host of other reasons. We buy to cheer ourselves up when we are blue. We buy to stay in style and to express who we are. We buy to give gifts to others, in part also to express who we are. We buy to show our success and to indicate our status. When we buy, we can choose from immense variety. The market offers foods from all over the world and fresh flowers that may have been cut but a few hours ago on the other side of the globe. We can select from twenty varieties of coffee and more than a dozen cheeses. We also have at our disposal endless varieties of entertainment and sports from which we pick and choose. We can select a CD from thousands and play it on a sound system that can hardly be distinguished from a symphony hall. We can send instant messages to anywhere in the world virtually free. In short, we are almost overwhelmed by the possibilities and spend much of our lives considering and selecting what we will buy or do next. We have become a consumer society that Main Street was too small to hold.

Instead, Main Street has turned to services, such as dry cleaners, fast foods, insurance sales, and social agencies. The variety of services available to us has exploded nearly as much as the products. These are also a form of consumption. The family doctor has been supplemented by endless medical specialists. Lawyers too have proliferated. Today we seem to sue and be sued for the smallest grievance, and we have more lawyers per capita than any other country. Thus, we must also have insurance for every imaginable possibility—car insurance, house insurance, even trip insurance. We are so busy earning the money to pay for all this that there are legions of people who are in business to help us do things faster, better, safer, and with less effort. We can have help planning a party, doing our taxes, keeping fit, or walking the dog.

The automobile brought psychological as well as physical changes. When towns were small everyone knew each other, and people tended to form images of others in their town—whether good or bad. These images, formed early, would often stick for a lifetime. Not so when the car became common. Now one could leave the hometown behind and be in a new town in minutes. Here one became anonymous and now could choose the image of the moment. Now we were known only by our clothes and our car. We might live in poverty at home, but putting our money into a car and clothes, we could play the role of the wealthier classes in another place. Then, both clothes and cars took on a much more important role. Now we needed an appropriate set of clothes to express who we were in the new locale. Cars became both the means out of the old neighborhood and also an expression of who we were when we arrived.

Suburbia too reflected the new anonymity. For this reason, now, houses took on a new importance not only as places to live, but as public expressions to passersby of who we were, because they did not know us as they used to. Lawns became overly important and required hours of time seeding, rolling, fertilizing, and cutting. Pools for the backyard became symbols of status and appeared in large numbers even in New England, where their use was restricted to four months of the year. Once the children were grown, often the pool was seldom used again. House interiors too were important expressions of our status and interests for our new friends, and they triggered an equal measure of consumption. The carpet, sofa, drapes, lamps, and pictures all had to blend and make a coherent "statement" of who we were. In this new suburbia we began to measure our self-worth by our material possessions, because we knew very few people well enough to get past the superficial to who we really were. Today we hear a lot about the breakdown of the family, but our communities broke down before the family and took the extended family with them. It was a cost of mobility, while the benefit was consumption.

The material standard of living rose markedly, and the prices of goods went down. There was more money to spend. Adolescents who had little money and little to spend it on became a significant market segment. Consider this note from a recent *Boston Globe* article:

> American teenagers had a combined income of $105 billion last year—up $4 billion from the previous year. Where did all that money come from? In a survey of 2025 youngsters by Teenage Research Unlimited of Northbrook, Ill., 53% of those polled said they got money from their parents as needed, 47% said their cash came from gifts or occasional jobs, 32% had part-time employment, 30% got a regular allowance, and 11% had full-time jobs.
>
> What are the teens doing with all that money? Though 68% said they had savings accounts, not much appears to be making it to the bank. Of that $105 billion in income, $103 billion got spent. The boys spent an average of $70 a week—$6 more a week than the girls (Ciabattari, 1997, September 21).

All this buying power explains why so many ads are pitched to the adolescent market.

As the standard of living rose, a gradual change took place from selling goods that we need to selling ones that will enhance our image. We still buy colas because we like the taste, and many more products because they satisfy us directly, but now we are more interested in image and status items than we were. Not all of this is the result of the automobile, of course, because endless numbers of things were changing at the same time. Within a few years of the automobile, for example, another force became equally important and that was television. Now we are much more conscious of how other people dress and how they talk and behave. Although dramatic plots on television come and go, an attempt is usually made to make the characters believable by making them look like people everywhere, but their style of living is usually much more upscale than the norm. Generally, even when they are clearly not like people everywhere, as with the "rich and famous" and celebrities, we seek to emulate them. Thus, new fashions and styles are introduced rapidly, and viewers become quickly aware of changes and what they need to buy to keep up. Thus, television offers a perfect medium for creating image and status, and now we buy jeans not for fit and durability, but for the label on our fanny. We do not buy for the product's characteristics but for who was seen using it, and endorsements in some cases have become the major source of income for celebrities. As the Internet becomes more and more visual and more universal, this will become an equally important source of late fashion news.

Thus, the term "consumer" covers a tremendous amount of ground. Perhaps the most obvious aspect is the buying of products retail, but is there anything people do that cannot be considered a form of consumption? If we go to a concert, we are in a sense consuming the entertainment. In fact, we have probably paid a considerable sum to be there. If we go instead to the library, we are consuming the books, for they do wear out, and the newspapers, which anywhere else are generally discarded in a day or two. Are we not also consuming the knowledge in them? The knowledge does not wear out and is not used up by our use. On the other hand, the knowledge is really the reason for buying a book (unless it's entertainment), and someone was probably paid for putting the knowledge there. Money does change hands, even when it is something as abstract as knowledge that is being packaged. Knowledge is also the commodity that colleges and universities sell, and we know that large amounts of money change hands there.

What about travel? We are certainly consuming all kinds of services from travel agents to transportation and food and lodging, but are we consuming the view when we stop by the road to look at it? If we live nearby and see the view every day it is hard to think of looking at it as consumption, but it takes on a different nature if we have come a long distance and paid an airfare just to see it. Although the exchange of money is a characteristic of most consumption, we may also use the services of a nonprofit agency in which no money is charged. Such an agency exists to provide services, and thus is not fundamentally different from other agencies that do charge.

With the many kinds of consumption, can we formulate a definition of consumption out of it all? A fairly common one is that **consumption** is the evaluating, buying, using, and disposing of products and services. Thus the beautiful view, like knowledge, is not really consumption, but the delivery of it is. They are activities that may require me to engage in consumption to participate in them and are definitely a part of the consumption enterprise. If you take a moment to try to think of special cases, you may be able to find some instances that do not seem to fit the definition. Like all definitions, there are probably exceptions.

Because this book is about consumer psychology, we need to define that, too. **Consumer psychology** is the use of the principles of how people think, feel, value, and behave to understand the process of consumption. In a sense, the study of consumers would involve every aspect of psychology, because consumers are people first of all, the center focus of psychology. However, this would make the task too broad to be useful. Thus, we must limit our study to the aspects of people that are particularly relevant to their behavior as consumers, but the place where consumer psychology ends and the rest of psychology begins is arbitrary.

A division of the American Psychological Association is devoted to consumer psychology, but our universities and colleges do not yet have many classes in it. One publisher found only 22 courses in consumer psychology in the whole country. The reason may be that consumer psychology is usually considered synonymous with consumer behavior. There are many courses in consumer behavior, usually in schools of marketing, and there are a number of textbooks on that topic, but although the texts are often written by authors who have degrees in social psychology, the emphasis of their content is different. Their intent is to include considerable content on the techniques of marketing, often drawing from sources only marginally related to psychology. On the other hand, by widening the scope, a certain amount of depth is lost. It is my intention to delve more deeply into the psychological forces and to limit the scope, and consequently I have left out a number of topics that are usually found in books on consumer behavior—for instance, demographics and market segmentation, both very important to marketers. In their place, I have added more depth in the nature of the psychological forces that shape and control the consumer. However, in consulting the sources, I have drawn heavily from journals of marketing and advertising, which often investigate psychological problems, though their titles do not suggest it. The wider scope is appropriate for how-to-market books and courses, and anyone who is entering the marketing business should certainly know what is in them. But my approach here is more from the other side: why consumers buy. This content should also be of interest to all marketers, because ultimately one also needs to know more about the whys to modify and adapt techniques for new situations, new product lines, and new consumers. I intend this as a supplement to the other texts, not as a replacement, but it would be a mistake to think that the study of consumers and consumption is of interest only to marketers. Because it cuts across all the subgroups of psychology, consumer psychology serves to pull together considerable information from a variety of sources and to put it in a form more easily understood and remembered. Moreover, we are all consumers and thus have a natural interest in the topic.

Another content note here. Although organizations are also consumers, our interest here follows that of psychology in general and is in the individual, rather than in groups. There is considerable overlap, however, because even group purchases are usually made by an individual, and as such are susceptible to all the forces that influence other individual consumers. Moreover, although institutional buyers generally buy for others and usually use someone else's money as well, even individuals sometimes buy for others, for example, when parents buy for children or spouses buy for each other. Institutional buyers may also not be as close to the disposal problem as individual consumers are. It is individual concerns that have driven the demand for recyclable packaging and for environmentally safe products.

Our psychological survey has three parts. First we consider the role of cognition (the thinking part); second, we look at affect (the feeling part); and third we consider how they interact in the consumer (the behavioral part). We begin cognition with perception, specifically attention. Getting attention is also where the advertiser must start in putting an ad or commercial before the consumer. We also look at the perceptual process of drawing inferences and see that it is similar to drawing inferences from memory. Although perception is often regarded as a group of curious illusions, it has implications for the way packages are made, merchandise is displayed, and consumers' inferences are drawn. Reason is another important part of cognition, and it turns out that we do not usually think logically, but rather heuristically, that is, our conclusions are based on rules that usually work well for us but sometimes lead to mistakes.This means that our choices are heuristical as well, not logical.

Before going on to the discussion of affect, we consider the nature of the unconscious and the role it plays in our thinking. We look at the specific topics of subliminal advertising, Freud and his symbolism, and the impact of background music. Then we turn to the concept of affect, which generally means feelings, particularly the feelings of good and bad. We will see that much of affect is also unconscious but that it plays a central role in the whole process, underlying preferences, and often drives attention and cognition.

Affect and cognition interact in a number of ways. First, they combine to form attitudes, and thus are crucially important in persuasion and in advertising and marketing. They also interact in creating psychological needs and in our interpretation of the social forces that surround us, which in turn influence consumptive behavior.

Finally, we look briefly at the changes that come about in all of this as a function of age and development. However, this is the weakest aspect, because the information on how one develops into a consumer is thin indeed. Part of my interest in including it here is to draw attention to the sparsity of research in this area. There is, of course, considerable material on the way our needs and interests change as we go through the normal steps of life. We become interested in children's things when we have children, in home repair when we own a home. But this kind of change is neither profound nor psychologically particularly interesting. We do know that there are typically changes and concerns about health that appear with age, and we know there are progressive losses in the sensory systems. What we do not know is how our attitudes toward the consumptive process change as we age.

Predicting changes of a developmental nature are particularly difficult because the world is changing faster than we are. We are forced to assimilate technology, if we are to remain a member of society, but the adaptations necessary seem to accelerate decade by decade. People in their seventies today are not the same kind of people who were seventy in an earlier time. They are healthier, more active, and generally engaged in more productive lives than people of the same age 40 years ago, but these changes are more a function of our place in history than our particular age group. One can only guess at the changes in store for the future. The biggest challenge will probably come from the bioengineering field, and its impact on the consumer is likely to be tremendous. To understand the impact of the times on the person, the developmental effects must also be known. Perhaps this book will inspire some research on the topic.

Themes

A number of themes will appear and reappear as we go along, because they relate to material in more than one chapter. In general they represent psychological content areas of particular concern for the study of consumers. To call your attention to them, let me introduce them here. They constitute a set of forces that pervade our lives and fuel and direct much of our consumption.

The Need to Confirm Self-Worth.   We have already met anonymity previously. It stems from a number of social changes, including increased mobility, increased population, and loss of family support. Its impact threatens our sense of personal worth. This is one of our most powerful psychological needs, and so we respond to the threat in a variety of ways. We will see this force at work in the formation of attitudes, the making of decisions, and in the advertising appeals to which we are particularly sensitive. It changes its focus as we grow older, and we will consider this progression. In other words, we will consider it at some length and explain how it has its influence without our usually being aware of it, and it will reappear in several chapters.

Unconscious Versus Conscious.   The interplay between the conscious and unconscious is another aspect of consumer motivation that comes up in almost every chapter. It was Freud who called our attention to the unconscious just a hundred years ago. Since that time, particularly in the last 40 years, there has been considerable research on the question of the nature of the unconscious, so that today it seems far less magical than it did a century ago. We will see that perception, learning, memory, and motivation all have strong unconscious elements, but this does not mean that they are controlled by mysterious unknowable forces from the past. Rather, more often than not, these unconscious elements are quite predictable. Indeed, if most of our interactions with the world were not unconscious, our cognitive structure would be severely overloaded. However, the thought of our being controlled without our awareness is so unsettling that at times we have overreacted to the perceived threat. For example, Congress was asked to intervene when it appeared we could be made to buy soft drinks and popcorn in movie theaters without our conscious consent. We will look closely at that threat, though the evidence indicates that this type of unconscious control is not possible, because the incident illustrates the magical way the unconscious is regarded. We will try to remove the magic.

Cognition Versus Affect.   A third theme that occurs and recurs is the interplay between cognition and affect, as introduced previously. Generally, cognition is thinking, and affect is feeling. To begin with, this distinction has not yet been agreed upon by all the researchers in the area. They disagree on how big the province of cognition is and what the nature of affect is. Fortunately, most of the controversy is over definition rather than substance, but the topic has seen an immense amount of recent research, and the manner in which affect drives attention and other cognitive functions has only recently become clear. At the turn of the century, ads were nearly all written copy extolling the virtues of a product, that is, they were almost completely cognitive. Today they may have no copy at all, simply consist of a picture and a brand name, and are nearly all affect instead. We will look at the whole cognitive–affective relationship and how the consumer is an important piece of the mix, but the topic will be addressed in many places.

Individual Versus Community. Another theme that recurs is the conflict over our dual needs to be a member of the group but also to be an independent individual. Our culture puts a lot of emphasis on being independent and self-reliant. This was a natural outcome of the task of settling in an wilderness far from civilization, which of course happened first on the East Coast but moved relentlessly west. The classic Western movie depicted a land where people lived great distances from each other and were generally on their own in crisis situations. Movies were one force that kept the ideal current in our culture even into the twentieth century. The popularity of the Marlboro man, whose image of the rugged self-reliant male moved Marlboro cigarettes to the top of the pile for over 25 years, indicates that this ideal is still powerful today. On the other hand, we also want to be accepted by the group and even to be envied. Beer commercials, particularly, emphasize the social acceptance side of our motivation. Europeans often remark on the strength of the American trait of wanting to be popular. Thus we have a continual tension between wanting to be independent but wanting to be accepted. This tension comes out in our consumptive behavior when we buy what others are buying but then accessorize it to individualize it. Sometimes we move more one way and sometimes the other, but the polarity is nearly always there and will be reflected in the direction in which a particular purchase goes.

As the book unfolds, look for the interplay among these several themes.

CHAPTER 2

Attention and Awareness

MODES AND LEVELS

We start with attention because it appears from a common sense point of view that perceptual selection, which is really what attention is, should be the first step in the perceptual process. It is reasonable that the sensory inputs have to be selected first and then organized and interpreted, but we must start with a cautionary note, for that is not the way it generally works. We usually do not scan our world passively. Rather we scan looking for a certain bit of information, as in crossing a street, or enjoying a feeling state, as with a sunset. In other words, a preparative process, which is part of perception, has already taken place. We always respond to sharp, intense, or discordant stimuli, but the process is a spiral, and sensory inputs continuously alter the ensuing search, which then alters the inputs, round and round. Thus, while we are considering attention first, you will notice that the main variables controlling it are consequences of earlier perceptions and memories, and we are not really starting at the beginning, but jumping *in medias res*, as it were.

The task of advertisers, marketers, mail order companies, and museums is essentially the same, and starts with getting people's attention, whether to the ad being placed in front of them, the displays and packaging, the catalog, or the exhibits. This chapter considers the many aspects of getting attention.

Outward Versus Inward Modes

We need to start by considering the complexity of the process we call attention. The highest level of awareness is usually what we mean when we use the word attention. It is sometimes considered equivalent to consciousness. When we say we are conscious, we mean that we are processing at this high level. However, we can operate at two distinct modes at this level, and they sometimes cause confusion. The first mode is information gathering, turned outward, and the second is a ruminative mode, turned inward. Because these two modes generally compete with each other, instead of operating simultaneously, they should be considered alternative modes of the same high level of attention.

The outward mode, which is experienced as a focused concentration, involves searching for some information we need, or want, to know. From all of the inputs coming into the sensory monitor, it selects those that are of concern at the moment and disregards the rest. The disregarded inputs are not totally lost, however, for they continue to be monitored at unconscious levels for important changes, both affective and cognitive, as we shall see later.

On the other hand, many times our attention is operating in an inward mode instead. At these times we appear to be "lost in thought". We appear not to be "paying attention," but although it is true that our attention is not directed at the desired external stimulus, our attention system is not really shut down. Rather, it is simply using mostly memory inputs instead of sensory inputs. Attention turned inward takes attention away from attention turned outward and is more common than simply the absent-minded professor. For example, people engaged in conversation may be so absorbed that they notice very little of what is around them. Unfortunately, this often works at cross purposes with exhibit designers in museums and trade shows. Similarly, TV viewers often engage in conversation during commercials. The task in all these cases is to turn the viewers attention from inward to outward. A word of caution is in order here because the term "attention" has traditionally been used to refer only to the outward form. Thus, confusion may result if one does not carefully check the definition in the article one is reading.

Affective Versus Cognitive Modes

The two dominant elements operating in attention, affect and cognition, were introduced in the last chapter. Unlike the inward/outward competition, these elements do not always compete because to some extent they operate simultaneously. Affect concerns our feelings about something, particularly how much we like it. Affect may also be a reminder of its potential threat to us. It is a reminder because most things must be cognitively appraised when they appear for the first time, but once categorized by this appraisal, they become affectively tagged one could say. On subsequent meetings they operate without additional appraisal. In the outward mode, we detect the affect tag and attend to things with strong tags. Some stimuli thus trigger feelings, such as things that make us feel good, help us achieve a goal, or avoid pain. Consumer examples include food when we are hungry, and a brand that worked well in the past. We notice the food, not because of a cognitive appraisal that food is what I need now, but because the idea of food has become much more pleasant at the moment. We select a certain brand because we feel better about it than another.

Cognition, on the other hand, refers to the knowledge or factual side of attention. In the outward mode, it is exemplified by information gathering, for example, how to get from here to there, what to do now, or simply what is that over there. Consumer examples are someone who is looking for information about a product, perhaps with a particular application in mind, comparing information about specific brands, or asking friends for their advice.

The inward mode also has both affective and cognitive components. For instance, affect is the main component in rehearsing what we should have said to that rude clerk or imagining what will happen when someone discovers that embarrassing thing that we did. Inward cognition is dominant when we are trying to remember where we left our umbrella, comparing two products, or trying to determine the best value among several items.

The cognitive side certainly comprises an important side of consumer behavior, particularly with expensive items, but marketers have often spoken as if the typical consumer always gathers information and weighs it reasonably before making a decision. In actuality, that probably represents an ideal that seldom really happens. Consumers do act reasonably, but their reasoning is often affectively narrowed and driven. Affect may be more important than cognition in many, if not most, decisions, or they may work together. For example, affect may sensitize us to food, setting food as a motivational goal, whereas cognition enables us to know where to get it, outwardly by telling us where we are and inwardly by reminding us how to get to the cafe. More important to marketers, however, is our choice of cafes. Is affect or cognition working here? Probably both and it will take some time to explain how. Both elements must always be considered. Because of this, we will consider each in its own chapter, later on. Either element can get attention, but affect, probably because of its potential survival implications, can override cognition. Thus, in general, cognitions that have a strong affect get priority, absorb our attention, and dominate our thinking (Klinger, Barta, & Maseiner, 1980).

Conscious Versus Unconscious Levels

Attention and awareness are sometimes treated as synonyms, but this creates a problem for the concept of attention. It seems clear from the weight of evidence that we can respond to stimuli without being aware that we are. The response indicates that some level of my mind was aware, but the highest level was not. The highest level was, indeed, attending to something else. Thus, we would be led to conclude that we can pay attention to several things separately. In fact, this is probably the case, but this usage would cause the term attention to shift its meaning. What has happened is that our understanding of awareness has expanded in recent years, and attention and awareness are no longer seen as equivalent. Now attention is reserved by most writers for only those things of which my conscious, or highest, processor is aware. Lower levels of awareness have come to be categorized as unconscious and beyond our attention.

But do not go away, because there is a further distinction within the subconscious between those awarenesses of which I *can* become conscious and those awarenesses of which I *cannot* become conscious. Memories that I can call up and bring to consciousness have generally been called **preconscious**, after Freud, and sensations that are in the same relationship are known as **preattentional**. Memories that I cannot call up are called **unconscious**, whereas stimuli that do not reach my attention, but are still detected by a lower level, are called **subliminal**. To make it all the more confusing, all the levels of awareness seem to contain both affective and cognitive elements.

RESULTS OF INCREASED ATTENTION

When attention is aroused by one of the factors we are about to discuss, the result is a narrowing of focus and direction of attention toward that factor. For example, if a stimulus is personally relevant, it draws attention to itself and triggers a search for more information (Celsi & Olson, 1988). Essentially this is the whole purpose of attention. In fact, cognitive researchers in the field of information processing regard attention as a four-level measure of information-processing intensity not as a single state. This is based on the work of Craik and his colleagues, to which we will return in chapter 5. Briefly, Greenwald and Leavitt (1984) distinguish four levels of cognitive functioning that differ in the amount of attentional capacity they require. The lowest level, called **preattention**, uses little capacity and is equivalent to the monitor level. The

Table 1 The Four Levels of the Elaboration Likelihood Model of Cognitive Processing[a]

Level 1:	Preattention	Uses little capacity and is equivalent to the monitor level
Level 2:	Focal attention	"Uses modest capacity to focus on one message source, and to decipher the message's sensory content into categorical codes (object, name, word)"
Level 3:	Comprehension	Makes meaning out of the message
Level 4:	Elaboration	Does integration with the existing knowledge base, such as relating to self or future action

[a]Adapted from Greenwald and Leavitt, 1984.

second level is called **focal attention** and "uses modest capacity to focus on one message source, and to decipher the message's sensory content into categorical codes (object, name, word)." (p. 584) The third level, **comprehension**, makes meaning out of the message. Only at the fourth level, **elaboration**, does integration with the existing knowledge base, such as relating to self or future action, take place (Table 1).

To make this model relevant to the consumer field, Greenwald and Leavitt provide an example:

> Two musicians, husband and wife, are driving along a familiar stretch of highway. (No, this is not going to be a joke.) The radio is tuned to a classical music station. Between selections the station announces the sale of tickets for an upcoming concert in a nearby town, featuring one of the husband's favorite soloists. He discontinues the ongoing conversation and listens carefully. The concert announcement is followed immediately by an advertisement for some stereophonic audio equipment that they already own, and then an ad, which both of them have heard at least 20 times previously, for a soft drink. Further along, their conversation resumes and is uninterrupted by the advertisement of a sale at a clothing store ...
>
> The four hypothesized levels of audience involvement can be related to our ... description of two travelling musicians. Recall that the husband listened carefully to the advertisement of a concert by one of his favorite soloists. Perhaps he was thinking simultaneously about previous occasions on which he had heard this performer and about how to adjust his schedule to be able to go to the concert (elaboration). He may have continued to attend well to the immediately following advertisement for audio equipment (comprehension), but this ad may not have prompted elaboration, perhaps because it was not relevant to any future action. The next advertisement—a familiar soft drink commercial—may have been listened to (focal attention) because attention had not yet been diverted elsewhere, but the following ad—for a clothing sale—was ignored (preattention) ... (Greenwald & Leavitt, 1984, pp. 581 and 584).

Other researchers, for example, Burnkrant and Sawyer (1983), also working from an information processing viewpoint, consider that attention varies on a *continuum* of intensity rather than consisting of four distinct levels. Greenwald and Leavitt (1984) point out that the levels of attention also represent levels of increasingly durable effects on memory. The more attention one is paying to a stimulus, the more cognitive elaboration one is likely to do with the material. It is this elaboration that improves memory. For this reason we return to this theory in later chapters. For our purposes here we focus on the first two levels particularly.

The Preattentional Level

The nature of the lower levels of awareness is not yet completely clear, but, because their main function is to detect the presence of either affect or new cognitions within sensory inputs, I call them **monitors**.

Information Monitor.   Work in cognitive psychology has shown that we can scan for particular information we want to find, and in this case, we utilize a wide but indistinct sort of attentional net. Thus, we might be searching for a "t" in a matrix of "l's." This is cognitive preattention, and it seems to work even when we are not consciously searching but have simply been sensitized to a particular category of information. On the other hand, it may be that the way the attentional monitor knows what information to search for is that some of it has been brought out by a momentary increase in its affect. As a clarifying example, consider the way that food becomes the center of our detection system whenever we get hungry. Are we, at these times, simply detecting food stimuli because of their cognitive meaning, or are we detecting them because we want them more now and therefore they are arousing strong affect whereas before they were not? The latter case is often the better description. Besides, there is strong evidence that an affect monitor exists.

Affect Monitor.   The research in subliminal effects has shown that the affective and cognitive contents of a given stimulus are processed separately, and considerable evidence suggests the operation of a separate affect detector. For instance, studies, such as Coren (1984), report that what seems to be detected in most cases of subliminals is their affective, or emotional content. Zajonc refers to studies showing that affective content is processed faster than cognitive, so that we might actually be able to know whether we liked something, without being able to tell what it was (Zajonc, 1980; Zajonc & Markus, 1985). This is probably so because there is a very necessary distinction between the two classes of stimuli: pleasant/approach and painful/avoid. If we go back phylogenetically, we find that even the most primitive species can distinguish between approach and avoid, the dominant characteristic of affect. They do not, however, have any cortex, the site of higher level thinking. Thus, because our brains have evolved by adding more complex functions on top of the older ones, it makes some sense to expect that the detection of affect may be the function of a different, more primitive center of the brain rather than the cognitively oriented cortex.

It seems likely that when we detect affect alone without additional processing, we are close to what Freud described as the impact of the unconscious because there is no way to know from such information why it carries affect. It just makes us feel without knowing why. One possibility is that the monitor detects the affect and passes the information on to the higher center, but this center, possibly the verbalizer in the left hemisphere of the brain, does not know the source. Neurological results from patients, where two halves of their cortex are disconnected, have given considerable support to such an interpretation. Evidence from such neurological studies indicates that probably a number of independent processors operate in parallel and the left side verbalizer is given the task of integrating them all for communication to the outside world. In the so-called split-brain patients, if the verbalizer does not know the source of the anxiety, it rationalizes a plausible reason (Gazzaniga, 1985). Whether something like this also happens in the normal brain is not yet known.

Some subliminal effects work by presenting stimuli at too fast a rate for additional processing, so that only the affect is picked up. Note that detection on the part of these monitors is not consciously registered because it usually goes on while the higher level of attention is busy with something else. Thus, objects and words can have affective associations that are unrelated to their meanings. If a consumer were choosing between things that happened to differ in affect, it might well appear to an observer that the choice was based on cognitions, say verbal meanings, when it was actually based on affect. Even when we try, locating the source of an affective response may be hard.

Novelty Monitor.   Another type of low-level processor, even more controversial, seems to compare incoming sensory stimuli with programmed expectations, looking for mismatches. It could perhaps be called an expectation comparator or a novelty detector. It uses more complex information than affect, involves higher centers, and this is probably why it takes longer to operate. Any deviation detected from what is expected tells us that this is new information, and if strong enough, will interrupt the higher attention system for clarification, that is, it will "get our attention." The comic double take, for example, probably is a case where the person's higher attention, absorbed by something else, did not notice a change from the expected, or it would have reacted immediately, but a lower level noticed. A delay was introduced by the extra time it took for the low level monitor to override and alert the higher level. The delay makes it humorous. Of course, a change from expectation is novelty.

You probably have never considered all of your expectations, but you have a good many. For example, you do not expect the floor to move, and you expect the walls to stay in place. You expect the lights to stay on, and the room to stay quiet. Your sensory input monitor is programmed by your own experience to know what patterns to expect, and it matches the incoming pattern against that template of normality to detect anything unusual in the environment. All of these expectations sound like a heavy cognitive load, but most of your expectations come down to expecting no change. In other words, the monitor could simply make a match (probably about ten times per second), between conditions that have just existed and those that exist now, the pattern it is getting from the environment. When a mismatch occurs, the monitor signals change, and it calls the higher attention center in to check it out. This explains why the main characteristic of attention-getters is that they are a change from the expected.

To understand why changes from the unexpected are so important to us that we have a special monitor for them, we need to go back to the concept of information. Information is not only "what we want to know," but also can be referred to more specifically as "the locus of a particular change." Consider, for instance, that information about a figure comes from its contours, which are places where brightness changes from that of the background. Letters are special figures. When we read, our eyes, by moving, keep the letters changing so that we can derive information from them. If the letters stop changing, information transfer stops.

Motion of the eyes and also of the body is a major producer of localized change. Motion, initiated from within us, carries information about alterations in our relationship to our world. Initiated from the outside, motion gives us information about our world's alteration or about objects entering our environment from the outside. In short, information always involves some sort of change. Because perception is essentially an information-gathering system, it must be particularly sensitive to changes of all kinds. Our very survival depends on it.

There is also some interesting neurological support for a possible novelty detector. Weiskrantz (1986) reported a case of a neurological patient, DB, who received an operation to relieve severe migraine headaches. He was left blind in a part of his visual field. The curious thing was that he could still tell if a stimulus was presented to the area, and he could locate it, but he could not identify it. Weiskrantz calls this blindsight. More recently, the same researcher reported that such patients can report at above chance levels a match or mismatch between a stimulus presented to the blind area and one presented elsewhere in their visual field (Weiskrantz, 1990). This is strong support for separating the matching function from the identification function. It also suggests that the complex matching function is a cognitive element more than an affective one.

The low-level monitor may be the system developed to detect radical change from the expected, but this point is not certain. However, we know that we detect novelty, even if we do not know where and how the detection comes about. More on it in a moment.

Supporting Evidence. We have previously cited neurological supporting evidence, but there is also other evidence. One reason that it appears as though affect and novelty have their own monitors is that they continue to operate even in sleep, when our higher centers of attention are not functioning. We incorporate sounds and other stimuli into our dreams, and we respond to the alarm clock. It is important to realize that not just any stimuli will wake us up. They must be either intense and different from the ongoing surrounding stimuli, as in the alarm clock, or they must have affective significance, which informs us of their importance. If you sleep through an alarm, it may have become so familiar that it is no longer unusual, or you may be extra tired. Some theorists would say you did not really want to hear it, but that is hard to prove.

Other stimuli may be of very low intensity but wake us up because of their significant meaning, that is, their affect. Rabbits, for example, are supposed to wake up from the snap of a twig, when other sounds fail to rouse them, possibly because of the affective association with the approach of a predator. Mothers and fathers are likely to wake when their baby cries. Even silence wakes you, if it is a significant change from the norm. When I lived on an aircraft carrier, my bunk was just under the flight deck and was an extremely noisy place during flight operations. Soon I adapted to the noisy conditions but would be instantly awakened by sudden silence. It usually meant that a plane had gone into the water and one of my friends was in serious trouble. Even a change in a familiar sound may wake you. Once I knew a man who was the supervisor of a small manufacturing mill. He lived beside a brook which upstream was used to power the mill. His wife told me that any change in the sound of the brook would wake him in the middle of the night because it usually meant trouble at the mill.

In most of these examples, what the sleeper is really detecting is a change in a stimulus pattern that has affective meaning, that is, in the past some stimuli have been associated with affect or emotion, and this has given them special meaning. (Building these associational links is called conditioning, and we shall return to it.) Our low level monitor detects sensory changes of a simple nature, like alarms or lights, and also much more sophisticated affect-laden stimuli, such as the very subtle change in the sound of the water in the brook. We know that advertising with affective significance, that is, personal involvement, gets attention. The affect and change detectors may be the mechanisms that make it so.

The importance of these lower level monitors should be emphasized. Their presence means that at least some of the stimuli outside our attention span are received. Some of them will get our attention, but whether they are stored when they do not get attention is not clear. Our perception is likely to be biased by at least some of these preattentional stimuli, even though we do not realize it.

VARIABLES OF ATTENTION

Getting attention and holding it are important topics in the business of selling products. In trying to organize the seemingly endless factors that control the perceptual process of attention, we shall adapt the structure of McGuire (1976) who is oriented toward an information-processing model. Some of the major influences originate with the state of the perceiver, and others come from the stimulus itself. An interaction is always going on because there can be no perception without both aspects. For example, is the emotional appeal of a puppy a property of the viewer or of the stimulus? Clearly, it is both. At the risk of oversimplifying the interactions, let us look at the major factors.

Mainly-Perceiver Variables

Involvement.   Things get and hold our attention when we are involved with them. **Involvement** is essentially produced by personal relevance. Stimuli become attention-getters and holders when they are personally relevant. This happens in many ways, stemming from the individual's needs, value systems, experience, and expectations. Affect (or feeling state) is the system that signals us about this personal relevance, and we give it a whole chapter. Though affect is its main punch, involvement is so important to attention that we consider it here, but involvement does much more than simply get our attention. Through attention it directs the whole cognitive process. Thus, involvement must be put into several chapter slots and we will be bringing it back for encores later on. Here we consider the main forces that increase involvement and thereby increase attention.

Affective Tags. We saw previously that affective material presented outside awareness may quickly capture our conscious attention (Nielson & Sarason, 1981), so that a monitor system for affect is likely. Emotional needs of the moment can control our attention and cause us to focus on emotion-related cues, while ignoring others. We saw previously that emotion can cause us to turn inward and partially or completely block our outwardly oriented mode. Here we look at the implications of the fact that affect can become attached to almost any stimulus.

Because we are not innately programmed, as goslings are to fear hawks, we must learn what things are dangerous. The **affective tagging** of past events allows us to do this, and we remember that in the past they have caused us pain, fear, anxiety, sorrow, or some other unpleasant emotion. Ego-threatening stimuli (threats to self-worth) are also likely to fall into this same category and become tagged with unpleasant affect.

The stronger these affective/emotional cues are, the quicker their associated stimuli get our attention. It is quite likely that dangerous stimuli get our attention in this way. For example, one study found that dangerous species in a zoo attract attention more strongly than non-dangerous species. In fact, the more dangerous they are perceived to be, the more strongly they attract (Bitgood, Patterson, & Benefield, 1986). These authors also found that although attracting power increases, holding power does not, a good indication that these two indexes are not the same thing. The likely reason is that when we focus on the dangerous animal, we eventually notice that it is in a cage and not a real danger. As the affect drops, so too does the attention-getting power.

Similarly, many stimuli become tagged with pleasant affect. Most sexual stimuli are attention-getters, possibly because of their previously enjoyable connections, though the possibility of innate mechanisms for recognizing some sexual stimuli has been proposed. The common use of sexual images in advertising depends on this strong ability to get attention. Sexuality may be focused on relationships, for example, when a couple is portrayed as deeply involved with each other, or on physical qualities, for example, when a woman in a bathing suit is used to sell car polish.

Beauty also has attracting power, not just human beauty, but also beauty of place, objects, and animals. Bitgood et al. (1986) found a strong positive relationship between attracting power and the perceived beauty of zoo animals. Reptiles were an exception. They strongly attract in spite of their ugliness, possibly because of their perceived dangerousness. The other exception they found was elephants. In this case it probably was their unusual size that attracted because they too are generally rated low on the beauty scale. Danger and beauty stimuli and also many other stimuli, likely work by creating affect, which serves to remind us of our relationship to these stimuli.

Identification.   Illuminating a potentially important component of involvement, David Ogilvy, one of the most successful of advertising executives, says, "When I worked for Dr. Gallup, I noticed that moviegoers were more interested in actors of their own sex. People want to see movie stars with whom they can identify. The same force is at work in advertisements." (Ogilvy, 1985, p. 79) In other words, faces are attracting not just because they are pretty, but because they have a special meaning for us—we can **identify** with them. We may want for ourselves the qualities they represent, or we may feel they are similar to ourselves, but in either case we can relate our own condition to theirs. For application in the promotional field, notice sometime how many magazines in your supermarket have a picture of a woman's face on the cover (nearly all, every month). Yet these magazines are pitched almost exclusively to women, not men. This is clearly not sexual attraction, but identification. Women identify with women, as Ogilvy says. Similarly, Nelson (1986) reports that children are more likely to learn when the model is a child than when it is an adult. Children identify with children.

The power of applied identification is well understood in the advertising field. The clearest example is the Marlboro man. This has been the most effective ad series of all time. The image of independence and rugged masculinity rapidly brought Marlboro cigarettes from an obscure woman's cigarette to the largest selling brand, and the ad has run unchanged for 25 years (Ogilvy, 1985). The appeal is strongest for adolescents because they are particularly vulnerable to identification processes. It is masculine because males buy more cigarettes than women, and the company wanted to change its image to a masculine one. The power of the ad is clearly its ability to offer a powerful figure for adolescent males to identify with and emulate.

An exception may exist for older consumers. A number of studies have found that older people have a self-perceived reference age (cognitive age) that is younger than their chronological age. Thus, the elderly often identify more with models ten to fifteen years younger than with models their own age because they do not view themselves as getting old. See Stephens (1991) for a good review of this literature.

The process of identification is of concern to advertising, and also probably to nearly every exhibit of any kind, including art museums and arboretums. Worts (1992) has written of the importance of the identification in an art museum, and related it to involvement. He distinguishes two levels of identification, personal and as a group member. He writes,

> It is worth noting that both aspects of identity—the personal and the relationship to a collective—seem to be dependent on some sense of relevancy. If the person does not feel the experience has relevance to him/her, then there is little meaning that is made from the experience. (pp. 157–158)

Similarly, Schroeder (1993), reporting the results of a visitor survey to identify favorite vistas in an arboretum, writes,

> ... Arboretum users associated their favorite settings with walking, contact with nature, and memories of people, places, and past events in their lives. This indicated that arboretum settings are not experienced simply as aesthetic scenes to be viewed in a stationary, detached way, but these settings help people feel connected with the processes of nature and with their natural and historical heritage. (p. 13)

In other words, scenes with which they can identify. Further research on identification has wide application.

Human Interest. The power of human interest, long recognized as the essential ingredient in news stories, may derive in part from identification because it often describes material with which people reliably identify. But human interest also includes strong affect, such as joy or sorrow, and frequently elements of relationship. The combination of forces is powerful and common, and thus it rates its own category. Drama, mystery, romances, and soap operas are all largely based on human interest. Sports, too, have an element of human interest and are even more appealing when at some point we have participated in them ourselves. Museum exhibits about the Oregon Trail in its anniversary year increased their effectiveness by focusing on facts and figures and also on what the people were going through, what the children did all day, how they dealt with loss, and why they were there in the first place.

The supersuccessful documentary on the Civil War, produced by Ken Burns, was almost entirely made up of actual letters of real people. If you saw it, you know it was certainly involving and had high human interest.

Advertising reveals a wide variety of human interest themes because advertisers have been very good at finding and using such themes. Babies, for example, have dependable human interest. They were used in advertising much more in the 30s and 40s than in more recent years, but they continue to have appeal. A study by Bitgood, Patterson, and Benefield (1986) found that when baby animals are present in zoos, the holding power of the exhibit doubles. Note that here the baby animal is the exhibit, so that it holds attention as well as gets it. When babies are used only to get attention, they may distract from the message because of their strong affective appeal, a process we discuss in a moment. Cute children have strong universal appeal, as do many relationships. When I have had pictures rated for affective content, babies and children are consistently rated with the highest positive affect.

Enhanced Self-Worth. Identification, reflecting our need for a favorable identity, is one of a number of needs that come under the heading of ego needs. We devote an entire chapter to consideration of these forces. We introduce them briefly here because ego forces are a major source of involvement. They are based mostly on the need to feel some importance or worth in life, so the general rule is that anything which works in the direction of increased personal importance should be more involving. The core values in the preceding section can be seen as outcomes of the way one's culture defines personal worth. This is probably why we take our society's core values so seriously. More on this later.

Use of ego needs can often be seen in advertising, as when McDonald's persuades us with, "You deserve a break today," but enhancing personal worth goes far beyond the realm of advertising. The impact of service personnel on the customer is largely a matter of this principle. If customers are made to feel unimportant or demeaned, they feel anger and resentment, whereas if they feel welcome and respected, they feel pleasure. Thus, for example, cordiality and graciousness on the part of staff make customers feel more important and would be predicted to cause them to regard the whole company more favorably. Clean and well-maintained buildings and grounds likely have a similar effect. Conversely, ignoring customers while you work on something else is communicating the message that they are not as important as what you are doing now. In this situation, customers should at least be recognized and an apology offered for the wait. Personnel should be trained to realize the importance of their behavior, whether they are simply sales clerks or receptionists. Interacting with the public is never easy, and those who do it for a long time seem to forget its importance.

Cultural Appeals. Other appeals that effectively produce involvement are culturally based and reflect values that the main culture values. A number of lists of American core values that have particular relevance to the consumer field have appeared. We shall look at them in more detail in chapter 11, but one example by way of illustration uses the strong American pride in freedom: a General Motors ad shows a car on the open road, with a hawk soaring above, and the heading says, "It's not just a car, it's your freedom." The use of such themes strike a positive chord in the typical American viewer that heightens their sense of personal involvement and increases attention.

Persisting Interests. The influence of persisting interests on attention is similar to but more personal than cultural appeals. They form such an important part of us that McQuire gives them a separate listing. In short, "people tend to notice aspects of the environment that are relevant to those aspects of the world they value highly." (McGuire, 1976) For example, automobile buffs notice an antique car more quickly, whereas gardeners may notice the flowers around it. When things are personally relevant, we notice more quickly, and we stay with them longer. Any particular hobby sensitizes us to the sources of relevant information or supplies, and we remember those sources better than someone who has no interest in that hobby. Similarly, with endless other interests, such as political issues, religious orientations, or job-related information. Because it is inefficient to advertise to only part of a readership, special interest magazines for nearly every conceivable interest have become popular. Many of them, being primarily advertising vehicles, are thin on articles and content, but they get subscribers because of the pull of the special topic, so that even the ads hold interest.

Transient Need Satisfaction. Appeals in the category of transient need states are not as permanent and enduring as those we have discussed so far. Some needs come and go. McGuire (1976) says, "People are more likely to notice aspects of their environment that are relevant to the satisfaction of their current needs." This heightened awareness of certain stimuli, called **perceptual vigilance**, is clearly based on increases in affect. In other words, we look for stimuli that satisfy our aroused need, and it follows that stimuli in this category is particularly involving. For example, Schiffman (1971) found that 30% of households, where at least one member was restricting salt intake, tried a new reduced salt product, whereas only 6% of other households did. In the example introduced previously, you can feel the attention-directing power of your transient need state, if you thumb through some ads for food when you are particularly hungry. Similarly, you should not go shopping at the supermarket when you are hungry, because you are likely to notice and buy more food-related impulse items.

Perceptual vigilance can be used by marketers, because by calling attention to a need, we momentarily increase it, and then we can expect increased attention to a product that offers to satisfy that need. Many ads work this way, both on the level of physical needs (where they are called problem identification) and on the level of psychological needs (where they are ego-related). Consider a few examples, and notice how our attention is directed by the mention of a particular need (including some we were not aware of) to the product that alleviates the need:

> Conair Cordless Curlers: "No Appointment Necessary."
>
> NutraSweet: "Big taste. No waist." (Accompanied by picture of a slim model)
>
> Easy Spirit Shoes: "Looks like a pump, feels like a sneaker." (Women playing basketball in pumps in the background)
>
> Toyota Camry cars: "Low maintenance relationship." (Couple in background)
>
> Topol toothpaste: "This is a smoke stain from one cigarette. If you think it looks disgusting here, imagine how it looks on your teeth."
>
> DAP glazing compound: "You're only as good as your materials."
>
> Kimber diamonds: "Diamonds are forever. That's a long time to live with a mistake."
>
> Johnson & Johnson dental floss: "If you fail this simple test, you could lose your teeth."
>
> Churchill's Bio-zone septic system additive: "Don't wake up to a nightmare!"

In each case, our involvement in a picture is increased by a verbal question or statement that calls attention to the personal relevance, just in case you failed to notice it. Then a product is offered to solve the problem or need, and the reader has been motivated to read further for more information. Interactive exhibits use this principle when they employ flip cards that ask a leading question and require you to lift the cover to find the answer. The question creates a need for the answer, and we become involved in looking for it. Interactives of all kinds apply a variation of the same thing. In other words, when interacting, we have to pay attention, that is, we have an increased need for information to direct our motor activity, if nothing more. One caution here. If people feel they are being manipulated, they may resent it, but they can simply stop interacting. Children are less likely than adults to feel manipulated, perhaps because they are more used to being controlled by adults.

Another use of transient need states has importance for stores, malls, and museums. Many transitory needs of the viewer become strong distractors from shopping or viewing exhibits. It can work against marketers when strong extraneous needs pull one away from an intended object. For example, museum studies have shown that fatigue, satiation with exhibits, and the exit-pull of a nearby door, all reduce the attracting and holding power of an exhibit (Bitgood, Patterson, & Benefield, 1986). Thus, exhibits viewed first are viewed longer than later ones (Falk, Koran, Dierking, & Dreblow, 1985).

Being aware of the distracting needs and eliminating them can increase the viewer's involvement. For example, articles have appeared over the years urging museum staff to provide places to sit, things to lean against, convenient rest rooms, and sources of food, to name just a few. When you are hungry, food stimuli attract attention. If they are part of your exhibit, that may be good, but if they are next door in the cafeteria, your exhibit will suffer. Generally, increasing the comfort of shoppers and visitors frees their psychic energy to attend to the exhibits or to shopping. Stores generally ignore these aspects, apparently considering only the expense of maintaining rest rooms, not the gains that result from shopper comfort. In fairness it should be pointed out that restrooms are often so scarce that a store may find it is running the facility for the whole neighborhood. Americans seem particularly averse to providing public, well-staffed restrooms, though malls have them. Malls are also beginning to offer more places to sit amid pleasant surroundings. Although it is true that the goal is to move customers through the stores, if you let them rest once in awhile, they may stay longer.

Moods

Freud made the point, not generally disputed, that we have only so much "psychic energy" to use at any given time. Freud was referring to the dominant role played by emotionality: fears, angers, doubts, and anxieties of all kinds. Emotional conflict can take so much energy and absorb so much of our attention that a person cannot even function. At a lower intensity, if we are anxious, worried, or even strongly concerned about something, emotion dominates our attention system and leaves us less energy to devote to more constructive forms of thinking. Anxiety makes outside cues lose their importance, unless they concern the source of anxiety, and we turn our attention inward. In such a state it is harder to attract our attention because we become very selective about the kind of information we are interested in.

Moods, generally, have an impact on our attention process. People in a good mood tend to be turned outward and looking for "instrumental opportunities," whereas those in a negative mood tend to turn inward and increase their self-focus (Morris, 1992). To insure that the viewer has a better chance of receiving the message, it is in the advertisers' interest to advertise to people who are in good moods. This explains why producers of serious shows and those which may have a depressing aspect find sponsors hard to get. Conversely, because comedy produces good moods through humor, it becomes thereby the perfect medium for advertising. No wonder we have so many sitcoms.

Humor. Humor tends to be based on the unexpected twist, or an ironic surprise, as we have seen in the comic double take. This is why jokes are never as funny the second time. They are no longer unexpected. Advertising frequently uses humor, but expectation works two ways here. Humor is expected, but what form it will take is unexpected. We have learned to expect the unexpected. Many television commercials, for example, are set up on a standard format. A humorous situation is introduced or set up, the commercial message is delivered next, and finally a short humorous tag line finishes it off. We tend to wait through the commercial to hear the humorous conclusion. We have seen the format so often, we know that a tag line will be along.

Not all advertisers agree on the value of humor, but most agree it is not sufficient by itself. It gets attention, but like all attention-getters must lead to better message assimilation, or it is not doing its job. As Torin Douglas, writing from the advertiser's point of view, comments:

> Humor softens the sales blow and puts the audience in a relaxed and warm frame of mind, in which it is more prepared to listen and accept what is being said. Nevertheless, it is rarely enough for an advertiser simply to amuse its target audience and hope to reap the sales benefit.... In most cases, humor—like music—must be linked to other creative techniques in order to have any effect ... (Douglas, 1984, p. 131)

In other words, Douglas is pointing out that mood by itself is not enough for sales effectiveness.

Experience

We spoke previously about the probability of monitors for particular information and novelty. Here those concepts return, and we discuss them in the context of the nature of the stimuli rather than the operation of the brain.

Information Content. Since the early 60s when information theory appeared, we have seen a number of attempts to measure the information content of messages or stimuli. The problem, however, is that information is both a function of the receiver and the message. For example, a foreign word carries very little information to one who does not speak the language, but a great deal to one who does. In addition, information depends on whether its message content is already known by the receiver. For this reason, it makes sense to list information content under the heading of perceiver variables.

The presence of potential information is an attention-getting situation, but it is difficult to measure. Berlyne (1960) operationalized some aspects of information content and found that complexity and uncertainty, along with novelty and surprise, are predictors of attention paid to a stimulus. Morrison and Dainoff (1972) confirmed that subjects spend more time looking at slides of print ads when they are visually complex. Berlyne predicted an inverted U-shaped function for all these variables, such that attention would decrease again as a stimulus became too high on these dimensions, so that, moderate levels are optimal. All four dimensions are, of course, aspects of information and also decrease with familiarity, probably because over time each exposure to a stimulus, in an exponential function, leaves less information to be derived. Thus, novelty too may get its power from the information or potential information it carries.

Expectations. Selection of input is guided by our expectations. "Our background knowledge for a situation seems literally to guide our eye movements when we examine a picture ... and in general to guide our attention." (Schwartz & Reisberg, 1991, p. 358) After reviewing a number of studies, Houston, Childers, and Heckler (1987) concludes that, generally, when people get information that differs from their expectations, it gets their attention better and gets processed to a higher level than information that meets their expectations. The famous Volkswagen ad "Think small" probably got much of its attention-getting power from the sharp contrast with the common, and therefore expected, American theme, "Think big." Note that information counter to our expectations includes novelty. However, expectations seem to go beyond novelty because they direct attention and they also structure what we see.

For completeness, one form of expectations should be noted in passing. This is an increase in attention from classical conditioning procedures. In a well controlled study, Janiszewski and Warlop (1993), showed that classical conditioning results in increased attention paid to the conditioned stimulus in a lab condition that approximated real television commercials, but we will postpone a more complete discussion until that chapter.

Novelty. By definition, novelty is unfamiliar, and thus it represents new information. At first we tend to think of novelty as a stimulus variable, but it is not, for like other informational aspects, it depends solely on the past experience of the viewer. Usually we do not pay much attention at all to what we see. Rather we are simply confirming what we already know. Thus we can walk down a street while we rehearse an upcoming meeting. We interpret things in the familiar way, as long as the stimuli are not markedly different from what we expect, because we are not really attending to them completely. When the difference between the present and the expected is great enough, however, we notice. It gets our attention. Commercials that follow a standard format become predictable. We do not expect them to differ from those we have seen in the past. To get our attention they must be different somehow. This discrepancy from expectation is known as "novelty." When the discrepancy is great enough, it becomes "surprise." As we have seen, these two aspects were confirmed early by Berlyne (1960) as attention-getting.

Novelty generally requires attention to identify the novel stimulus, because being new, it has not been affectively tagged and it could be a threat. The very fact that it is unexpected indicates the necessity of classifying it cognitively and affectively. Olney, Holbrook, and Batra (1991) confirmed that, as Berlyne predicted, novelty demonstrates an inverted U-shaped function with interest. In other words, as novelty gets too high, we lose interest.

The creation of novelty must be the first rule of advertising. Mac-Innis, Moorman, and Jaworski (1991) found references to a number of novelty-increasing strategies in advertising, These included unusual cinematography, different commercial formats, large numbers of scenes in an ad, sudden voice changes, sudden silence, and ads that open with surprise or suspense. One could probably extend this list indefinitely, because there is tremendous pressure to keep inventing new ones. Humor, for example, is a form of novelty and certainly takes unlimited forms.

Habituation. Advertisers have long been aware of the role that novelty plays in attracting attention, but it is a fleeting thing and dissolves before us. Novel patterns, presented several times, soon lose their novelty. This process, called **habituation**, involves becoming accustomed to a repetitive stimulus pattern. Habituation is a form of learning, and, like the other attention processes, it aids survival. It serves to keep perception focused on the new information by removing all of the unchanging stimulation that no longer contains new information. Actually, "new information" is redundant, because in perception, if it is not new, it is not information. Remember, information is change, and when there is no more change, there is no more information. (An exception is the pain system, which is apparently the only sensation that does not adapt. In this case, pain continues to have meaning, something is still wrong, and adaptation would not aid survival.)

We do not know how habituation works exactly, but it is probably by the gradual change of the templates of expectancy, so that when the monitor compares the incoming signals to its program, now it finds them expected, rather than novel. How the process works aside, habituation has some real world implications. It means that advertisements that use novelty to get attention may lose their effectiveness as they are presented over and over. Fortunately, however, though habituation works against marketers, at the same time two things are working for them.

First, the target group is continuously changing. David Ogilvy, one of the long-time successful advertisers, says, "You aren't advertising to a standing army; you are advertising to a moving parade," and he reports finding that in the case of magazine advertisements, they remain effective through at least four repetitions (Ogilvy, 1985, p. 20). Ads may not be repeating as much as one might believe. Rosser Reeves, one of the most respected of advertising people, emphasizes this point when he reports that fifteen years of data from studying ad campaigns that spend more than $ five million a year show that in spite of all the expense, "seven out of ten people are not even aware of having seen the advertising at all." (Reeves, 1961, p.98) (We should point out that his data go back to the earliest days of television, and the results might be quite different now.)

The second principle countering habituation from repetition is that although repetition makes attention weaker, it makes learning stronger (as we shall see in chapter 8). Thus, what you lose in attention-getting power, you may pick up in memory power. Both of these factors probably contribute to the reason why Reeves' experience also indicates that you cannot have too much repetition of a good ad (Reeves, 1961).

Complex Habituation. Habituation may take place to quite elaborate stimulus relationships over long time periods, because we habituate to specific stimuli and also to their patterns and meanings, though these are sometimes quite complex, that is, we adapt to both the amount and meaning of stimulation. For example, perhaps we have been getting up at the same hour every day, going to work, coming home, going to bed, getting up, so that every day is the same and we are bored. If you look closely, you see days in which there is some variety but not enough to flip the coin to novelty, and when you back off and look at the whole week, you see that the everyday changes are so predictable that they form their own unchanging pattern. Although mornings differ from evenings, every morning is like all the other mornings. We sense this long term lack of change, and we get bored.

James Gibson, who spent a lifetime studying perception, said that humans are "information-seeking" systems, and it is a central part of our nature (Gibson, 1966). Boredom is the feeling of having too little change or information, and it motivates us to look for more. A bored person is likely to go looking for excitement (which boosts information transfer) and to take risks (which increase the importance of the information). It is our information-seeking nature that makes variety the spice of life. It may be that considerable buying behavior results simply from attempts to relieve boredom.

We can habituate to type as well as amount of stimulation, as another example will illustrate. My uncle lived in an apartment in Brooklyn that faced a fire station. Every night the engines would go out, sirens blaring, sometimes three or four times. I had a hard time sleeping there, but my uncle, illustrating habituation very nicely, would say in the morning, "Oh, did they go out last night?" One summer he came to visit us in the country, and the tables were turned. This time, it was he who could not sleep, because of the "incessant chirping" of the crickets. Of course, I had not noticed them at all. The point here is that when inputs do not change, even though their cycle of repetition is fairly long sometimes, our perceptual process of habituation removes them from our consciousness. This is why novelty is so important.

Certain predictions follow from the habituation principle. One would predict that as people become more sophisticated viewers of television, having seen thousands of television commercials, a certain sameness will set in, and they will all begin to seem alike. One might also predict that the advertiser's job of attracting attention will get harder as the viewing audience becomes more sophisticated. Fortunately for marketing, there are always new consumers coming along.

Successive Contrast.   In some ways successive contrast could be considered a type of habituation, but the effect is so unique that it deserves its own label. The idea is that stimuli that have been present a long time and even sometimes strong stimuli that have been present just a short time can often change our perception of new stimuli. It is not that you do not notice things anymore, as would be the case with habituation, but rather that they seem different. The perception of the new stimulus tends to be distorted in the direction opposite to the accustomed one.

For example, after looking out from a moving train for some time, when the train stops at the station, it appears to be moving backward just a bit because the scenery seems to move in the opposite direction from that to which we have adapted. The same process takes place in "the waterfall effect." After staring at a waterfall for a minute or more, when we look away, things appear to be rising. Similarly, things may sound loud to someone used to silence but quiet to someone used to loud noise.

More social examples are also available. For example, in one study male students who had just watched an episode of the popular TV serial, "Charlie's Angels" (which featured three beautiful women), rated a woman's photograph as less attractive than did a control group who did not see the show (Kenrick & Guitierres, 1980). In another study, men who had just seen a slide of Farrah Fawcett (one of the three beautiful women in the previous study) rated another woman's yearbook picture as less attractive than did men who had not seen the slide. This particular contrast effect has been labeled the "Farrah Factor." (Tedeschi, Lindskold, & Rosenfeld, 1985) Contrast effects may also be a factor between a commercial and the show in which it is embedded, or between a commercial and those that precede or follow it.

MAINLY-STIMULUS VARIABLES

Some stimulus dimensions, or characteristics, have particular prepotency in perception. When stimuli stand out, they are called salient, which means they are more noticeable than others. Their effectiveness will always be altered somewhat by the particular viewer's state, because as we have said, effects are always an interaction. But some effects are universal enough to be considered separately. Here we look at just what the dominant causes of salience are.

Stimulus Properties

Intensity. This principle is quite simply that stronger stimuli get our attention compared with less intense stimuli, and they get our attention more quickly, that is, "we are more likely to notice loud noises than soft ones and bright lights more than dim ones." (McGuire, 1976) TV commercials often seem louder than the program they interrupt, though the advertisers say it is not really so. The fact that they would get attention better if they were louder, makes us continue to be suspicious.

Vividness. A major contributor to salience is called **vividness**. Three characteristics that make a stimulus vivid are proposed by Nisbett and Ross (1980). They find that a stimulus is vivid: (a) if it is emotionally interesting (for example, a plane crash is inherently more vivid than a normal flight); (b) if it is image-provoking (for example, a detailed description of a particular accident is more vivid than the statistics about it); and (c) if it is proximate in a sensory, temporal, or spatial way (for example, an accident in your local airport is more vivid than an accident elsewhere) (Examples are provided by Fiske & Taylor, 1991, p. 254).

Size. Attention-getting power varies with size, but with decreasing returns. "In print media, attention increases ... in proportion to the square root of the ad's area. Thus to double its attention-attracting power, the size of the advertisement would have to be quadrupled." (Loudon & Della Bitta, 1984, p. 429)

Museums often try to have one big item such as a dinosaur or railroad steam locomotive, to attract visitors. It will generally be the thing remembered longest and most favorably by visitors. Research shows that, generally, the larger an exhibit, the greater its holding power (Bitgood et al., 1986). The large item is also likely to be the thing they return to see again and creates a comfortable feeling of familiar space for returning visitors. Such an item is particularly important when exhibits are changed often, to help the museum preserve its sense of continuity and identity. Operating on the negative side, however, is the tendency for large dramatic pieces to draw attention away from the rest of the exhibit. Size as an attention-getter is illustrated by the many roadside attractions that were popular in the 30s and 40s. Some of these are still in use, for example, the 40-foot-tall giant milk bottle built in 1934 that now marks the Boston Children's Museum or the giant steer that still calls attention to the Hilltop Steak House on Route 1 north of Boston.

Color. Color ads are generally twice as memorable as black and white ads (Ogilvy, 1985). Bright colors, particularly the primaries, are well known as attention-getters. Red is so effective it is used to call attention to danger, as in stop signs. Similarly, it is effective in packaging products as an attention-getter. The most popular colors in the dominant American culture are red, white, and blue, but so many packages are likely to appear in these colors today that their attention-getting power has been reduced. Choosing less popular colors means balancing increased attention-getting (because of novelty), and potential loss of appeal (because of color unpopularity).

Faces. Facial recognition is so important to us that a special center in the brain has evolved whose sole function is recognizing faces. We also read faces and determine a great deal of information about people from their facial expressions. By far the most important thing we read there is in the evaluative dimension, that is, liking and disliking, which are, of course, forms of affect. The process is very rapid, and physical attractiveness plays a major role in this assessment (see Hatfield & Sprecher, 1986). Attractive people are much more likely to be liked, and this evaluation spills over into most other judgments. Attractive children are judged less harshly by adults than unattractive children (Dion, 1972). Unattractive defendants are likely to get longer sentences than attractive ones, and crimes against attractive victims are likely to bring longer sentences than those against unattractive victims (Landy & Aronson, 1969). In one study, pictures of people who were previously rated attractive and unattractive were given to subjects to rate on a list of characteristics having nothing to do with physical attractiveness. Attractive people were rated highest on nearly all characteristics. (Dion, Berscheid, & Walster, 1972). The reasons for this "halo effect" is probably the need for cognitive consistency, as we shall see in chapter 4. It certainly is one reason why pretty faces are used to sell products. One interesting note, however, is that faces enlarged bigger than life size repel readers (Ogilvy, 1985).

Celebrities' faces are often used to draw attention to an ad or to sell magazines, but their drawing power is not the same for all groups. Men's magazines (unless they are of the variety that specifically display pictures of women, like Playboy) generally feature masculine objects on their covers, rather than people at all. A person, if included, is usually incidental to the action, rather than central.

Attention-getting is only part of the advertising task, of course. Brand recognition and sales are the ultimate goals. The attractiveness of faces helps in attention-getting but not necessarily in brand recognition. Warah (1986) reported a study in which ad retention was compared for two groups, one who saw ads that included a picture of a person, and the second who saw the same ads with no person. When a person was included, subjects were more likely to remember having seen the ad, but they did not remember the brand name any better. There was no connection in these ads between the person and the product. Thus the presence of a face may have allowed the brain to use its facial recognition capability in recalling the ad, but because no connection was made to the brand, facial recognition did not aid recall of the brand.

Special Stimuli. As strong as faces and people are in attracting attention, they may lose out to other special stimuli, for example, food, particularly when you are hungry. While gauging readership of food ads, the ad research agency Starch INRA Hooper noted that the more the ad focused on people rather than food, the worse it did at holding readers' interest. "... Humanity only detracts from the purely and powerfully visceral appeal of food" ("Forget the people," 1992). In other words, well-presented food sells itself. I wanted to include a picture of this happening, but when reproduced in black and white most of the affect in food disappears.

Motion. It has long been known that motion is a very powerful attention-getter. After studying visitor behavior in zoos, Bitgood and his colleagues reported that any kind of motion increases the holding power of nearly all exhibits. In fact, they have measured this increase in zoos and find that "no matter what the species and across many types of behaviors, almost any kind of animal activity doubles the holding power of the exhibit" (Bitgood et al., 1986, p. 2). Shop owners are well aware that motion in a store window is very effective in attracting attention. Dyment, a producer of displays, produced a "tipping can" display for supermarket promotions of Pepsi, in which a six-pack tips over, seems to fall off the shelf, and then straightens up again. The addition of this motion to their display reportedly increased sales in a test market by 12 cases per display. (*Sales and Marketing Management*, 1983, cited in Mullen & Johnson, 1990).

An empirical test of the effectiveness of motion in displays was undertaken by the Olympia Brewing Company. The company was interested in examining the potential benefits of point-of-purchase motion displays (those with movement generated by the display) versus static displays (those without movement). These two types of displays were installed in both food and liquor stores in two California cities. After a four-week period, motion displays generated nearly twice the sales of the static display in liquor stores and nearly three times the sales in food stores (Engel et al., 1986, p. 210).

Ease of Viewability

Generally, people will view a display or an exhibit longer, if they can see it easily. Impediments to viewing include distance, obstructions, and barriers (Bitgood et al., 1986). For the same reason, Ogilvy warns advertisers to avoid hard-to-read copy. He says,

> Good typography *helps* people read your copy, while bad typography prevents them doing so..... Professor Tinker of Stanford has established that capitals retard reading. They have no ascenders or descenders to help you recognize *words*, and tend to be read *letter by letter*. Another way to make your headlines hard to read is to superimpose them on your illustration. Another mistake is to put a period at the end of headlines. Periods are also called full stops, because they stop the reader dead in his tracks.... Yet another common mistake is to set copy in a measure which is too wide or too narrow to be legible. People are accustomed to reading newspapers which are set about 40 characters wide.... The more outlandish the typeface, the harder it is to read ... Sanserif faces ... are particularly difficult to read.... [Avoid] copy set in reverse—white type on a black background. It is almost impossible to read ... (Ogilvy, 1985, pp. 96–97).

Ogilvy learned from experience and research what makes people read advertisements. In the same reference he has ten more rules for making long copy more easily read. Many of the same principles also apply to the field of exhibit labeling (see Serrell, 1983).

BETWEEN-STIMULUS VARIABLES

Stimulus Competition

Competition from Sheer Numbers. When a stimulus is all by itself, it gets undivided attention, but when other stimuli are there, competition takes place. The more stimuli, the more competition. Competing signs lose much of their effectiveness in the sign-clutter of commercial strips so common to American cities. Stimulus competition doubtless contributes to the reason commercials perform better when they appear during a program rather than in the clutter of other commercials and announcements at program break. Another reason is probably that, when several commercials are strung together with a station break, there is time to leave the room for food and other necessities. Thus commercials lose their effectiveness from competition with other commercials but also from competition with other quite different stimuli, as we discussed previously under transient need states. Exhibit competition is reported by Bitgood et al. (1986) who found that when two strong exhibits were opposite each other, they markedly reduced the attracting power of each other.

Competition from Affect. The character of the competing stimuli may be more compelling, so that it is not just their numbers which competes, but also their nature. We noted earlier that affect-arousing stimuli get attention. This means that distractors are also particularly strong when they are affect arousers. This principle was demonstrated by Erdelyi and Appelbaum (1973) who found that the presence of strong affectively arousing distracting stimuli, either negative or positive, disrupted the processing of other information. This is known as **dimensional dominance** and is generally a form of affective competition. It may set two parts of an exhibit or advertisement against each other and reduce their effectiveness. For example, advertisers report that although beautiful women definitely increase attention-getting in ads, they may totally distract from the message, so that the actual effectiveness of the ad is very low. For example, the advertiser Reeves reported that when a beautiful woman vocalized a message in several ads, no one heard the message, because the woman was so distracting (Reeves, 1961).

Similarly, the use of celebrities as endorsers may distract from the product being sold. Ogilvy says he stopped using celebrity endorsements in his ads because "readers remember the celebrity and forget the product" (Ogilvy, 1985, p. 83). Empirical confirmation of this observation is available in a study by Krugman (1967) in which he found that the audience produced fewer ad-related thoughts when the ads were set in a program of celebrity interviews, than when they were set in less interesting material.

Because of their arousal of strong affect ("Aren't they cute!"), children and young animals are also potential distractors, when they are used only to get attention and have no relationship to the message. Actors know that when they play a scene with a child or an animal, they are very likely to be "upstaged" and not noticed. In fact, children and animals can severely disrupt the whole flow of a play unless they are carefully built in and can operate the same way in commercials or ads. For example, in one Kraft ad, a squinting child is holding up some flowers and dominates the ad. Only by reading the copy do we find a tenuous relationship between attractor and product. The child pulls attention away from the brand name. The brand name is so small and in the lower righthand corner that one wonders if the ad is really selling much salad dressing.

The challenge for advertisers, as for exhibit designers, is to find clever ways to build strong affectively involving attractors, such as these, into the commercial or exhibit itself, so that they become an integral part of the message. Notice how in the clever series of ads promoting milk, the image of Larry King himself incorporates the message, so that the viewer is not pulled away from it (Figure 1). Remembering him, you remember the ad and the product. A commercial which also does this particularly well is by Michelin. This ad makes the point that the brand is safer and will protect the child better than the competition, simply by using the slogan, "because so much is riding on your tires." Thus, the child is part of the meaning of the verbal message and is strongly connected to the product image by putting the child right in the middle of the tire. Thus, rather than a distractor, the commercial effectively uses the strong affect aroused by the image of the child to hold attention and to communicate its message.

Position Preferences.   The fact that our language is read from left to right probably creates some position preferences. For example, Melton (1933) discovered that people tend to turn to the right when they enter exhibit halls, that is, we scan from left to right and tend to move off in the direction we are facing when done scanning. In another early study, Melton found that 80% of the visitors to an art museum turned to the right and started viewing on the right-hand wall. More than 60% of them never viewed the left-hand wall at all (Melton, 1935).

We also have a preference for stimuli at eye level, which makes that shelf in a supermarket particularly good for product visibility. Products for children, for example, sugar coated cold cereals, are usually put on the bottom shelf, where they have low visibility for adults, but high visibility for children. Aisle ends are also more visible than the middles, and some stores are now breaking up long aisles with shorter ones arranged at angles to each other. Although this arrangement creates better product exposure, it is harder to learn your way around, and some items may be missed because they were never passed. On balance, it seems to increase product exposure. One supermarket reported that after they had eliminated the long aisles, people thanked them for carrying so many more types of products. In fact, they had not added any.

Stimulus Contrasts

Whether a stimulus attracts attention at a given time may be a function of its contrast with the other stimuli. This form of contrast is called **simultaneous contrast**. The term "simultaneous" as it is used

After 40 years in
broadcasting, I've got
my finger on the nation's
pulse. So take it from
me. Drink fat free milk.
Studies suggest that a
healthy diet rich in lowfat
dairy products may help
lower the risk of high
blood pressure.
Listen to the King and
drink up, America.

MILK
Where's *your* mustache?"

Figure 1. The famous milk mustache, seen here on Larry King, works well because the mustache combines the product with the celebrity in the viewer's memory. (Reproduced by permission of the National Fluid Milk Processor Promotion Board.)

here means that the effects are going on while you are actually perceiving the stimulus. This distinguishes these effects from "successive" contrast, introduced previously, in which the effects occur because of stimuli that are no longer present. Simultaneous contrast involves two processes, attention getting and quality change. A sound may get attention simply because it differs from all the other sounds (increased attention-getting), or it may change its very nature because of the presence of other stimuli (quality change).

Quality changes happen in a variety of ways, all involving a change in the perceived nature of the stimulus. This can be in intensity, for example, where objects appear to be brighter if their surrounding background is made darker. Similarly, a given sound appears louder in a quiet room than in a noisy room. A normal conversational intensity in a church or library may seem like a shout and draw attention for this reason. The perceived change may also be in size, so that objects appear larger if they are displayed with small objects rather than big ones.

Color Contrasts. Colors against other colors change their apparent hue, so that, for example, a red circle against a green background looks very different from the same red circle against yellow. I have seen a customer in a fabric shop trying to match a scrap of blue fabric to another. She tried to isolate a bit of the color to get the exact match. When she got it home, however, she may well have been disappointed because the blue will have changed its character, and the store lighting will doubtless be blamed. Lighting can change colors dramatically, but in this case it was the other colors in the pattern which caused the change. Colors must be matched as they will be used, with the other colors present, not in isolation. It is a harder task, however, because it is so subjective. We try to make it easier by isolating color, but in the process we miss the match completely. Dry goods merchants would have happier customers if they took the time to educate them gently about color.

Butchers use simultaneous contrast in their display cases. The bright green strips in between the cuts of meat make the meats look redder, because the colors are complements of each other. The other day I saw a meat case where the intermediate strips were a pale peach color, and the meat looked pale and unattractive. Generic products are packaged in black and white to distinguish them clearly from brand products, but probably to make them seem less appealing as well, so that they will not compete as strongly. On the other hand, black and white can also be used for strong contrasts, so that the whole image becomes more striking.

Solo Effects. Contrast effects are often more important than the color itself. White socks worn by a stage actor generally pull attention completely away from the action and dialogue, and are a strong taboo. A spot of color in a black and white picture can be a strong attention-getter. Figure 11 (p. 262) shows an example of this, but the effect has been lost by the black and white reproduction. In the original the grape in the middle is a yellowish-green, whereas all of the Certs are their natural white. The spot of color is a strong attention-getter. For the same reason, though color is generally more attention-getting, one black and white ad in a color magazine would probably attract extra attention. In other words, it is not just the color, but the contrast.

We want to make the point here that the presence of other stimuli may also change the qualitative nature of the stimulus. Taylor, Fiske, Etcoff, and Ruderman (1978) showed that when a person is black in an otherwise all-white group or is female in an otherwise all-male group, viewers' perceptions of them changed radically. For example, solo members in discussion groups were judged to have been more active and influential, and their responses were better recalled than those of others. Note that the solo stimulus here draws more attention and is also changed perceptually. This particular change of perception is called the **solo effect**.

CHAPTER 3

Inferences of Organization and Meaning

INFERENCES OF ORGANIZATION

The process of cognition usually begins with perception because perception involves registering outside stimuli and also drawing many kinds of inferences from them. We want to consider the inference process carefully because it underlies the process of gathering information about products. One of the oldest questions in psychology asks how we get from seeing to perceiving. It might seem that these are the same thing, but they are really quite different. Seeing is the process in which the eye reacts to the light that reaches it. The eye sees variations in brightness, possibly color, in endless arrays of shape and form. Perception, on the other hand, uses the same bits and pieces, but now their arrangements produce a level of meaning, such as "Jimmy playing his tuba marching by with the band." The process of seeing is called sensation, whereas the process of understanding what is seen is called perception. Notice that it is not necessarily understanding correctly, but simply some understanding, some meaning, that makes it perception.

This seemingly subtle distinction between sensation and perception has real importance for understanding the consumer. The meaning that things have, particularly products, is crucial to the way people react to them as consumers. Everyone who passes a store window or sees a magazine ad, sees the same thing, but how it registers in their minds, that is, how it will be perceived, is another thing altogether. It is clearly the perception that matters, and it depends on several factors.

The relationship between sensation and perception sounds pretty simple until it turns out that what we perceive may not be there at all and what we should see is overlooked entirely. The many optical illusions you may recall from Introductory Psychology are meant to illustrate this principle exactly. Things are not always what they seem, but if you come away from such demonstrations with only the message that the eye can sometimes be fooled, you have missed the point. Rather than seeing this as a sometime relationship, you should understand it as a window on the normal way the system works most of the time. In fact, it is the only way the system works. Optical illusions are not unusual exceptions. They are proofs of the normal. They show that perception is an active, information-seeking process, not passive as was once thought. Nearly always we actively add meaning to what we are sensing, and thus perceive more than what is present in front of us.

In other words, much of what we perceive is really inferred, not always in a completely logical way, but certainly as an extension beyond the sensations. In this process of inference the sensations are organized, constructed, interpreted, and selected. In this chapter we consider the first two of these four aspects of perception. Note, however, that all four are closely interrelated and cannot really be neatly divided into separate categories. Note also that memory plays an active role in each step. Memory and perception are involved in reciprocal roles so that memory changes perception, but then perception is stored as a memory, which in turn affects future perception. Because of this tight reciprocal spiral, it is hard to know where to begin. We shall start with organization because some elements of this process operate without the need for memory inputs.

PERCEPTUAL ORGANIZATION

Background

Two main philosophical viewpoints on the nature of perception existed at the turn of the twentieth century. One view, going back primarily to the seventeenth century British philosopher, Thomas Hobbes, maintained that we are born with blank minds and everything that eventually gets in it comes first through the senses. The second view, going back to the late eighteenth century philosopher Immanuel Kant, argued that we have predispositions to organize incoming sensory experiences according to relationships of time and space.

The two opposing positions were put to the test in the first decades of the twentieth century by a group of German psychologists who came to be known as the gestaltists. (A "gestalt" roughly translates as "the whole perception taken at once.") The results of their experiments strongly supported the Kantian view. They showed that incoming visual sensations are automatically organized by the perceptual process, so that relationships among them are perceived, often more strongly even than the separate units.

Relationships are strange because they are abstracts. For example, we see A and we see B, and at the same time perhaps we see that A is above B, that is, how A and B are related. Maybe we also see that A is bigger than B, or rougher or heavier or redder. Comparisons of this sort are relationships, and they obviously do not exist apart from their associated objects. But notice that seeing that A is a bit rougher than B is different from the way you see A when it is by itself. Your attention is drawn to a particular feature, and you are evaluating. Every item in a store window is affected by its relationship to the other objects there and to the window in which it is displayed. Items on a supermarket shelf are seen in relation to each other. Although complex, some of these relational effects have been spelled out.

Gestalt Laws

The gestaltists based their view on solid empirical research and sorted out the manner in which perceptual organization takes place (Kohler, 1929, 1947). Their laws have been so widely accepted that they are now in every introductory textbook. Originally there were about twenty principles, but they are often distilled down to five or six, because it was shown that many of them are special cases of the others. Let us start with figure ground.

Figure Ground. The most basic organizational tendency the gestaltists uncovered was the sorting of visual experience into figures and backgrounds. Figures are seen as areas enclosed by a contour, but not always. Sometimes the contour encloses a space and is seen as a hole, rather than a figure. The important principle is that the part that is perceived as a figure gets our attention, and the rest is seen as background and given little attention. Complex images must be sorted into their figure-ground components before any sense can be made of the scene, and color and contour are the most important determinants of this organization.

The **figure-ground tendency** applies directly to marketing. The task of sales is always to make the product stand out from the background. For example, the product in an ad must be seen as the subject, and not the background, because the figure is much more likely to be remembered.

Among the sea of competitors on the shelf, your product must stand out, and this is accomplished somehow by making it seem clearly different. It is the difference that causes the product to be perceived, while the competitors become background. Thus, advertising often focuses on some desired attribute which the product has and that others do not have that makes it unique. If it does not stand out, it blends with the background of all the others, remains indistinct, and something else becomes the figure.

Music is similarly distinguished, in this case between foreground and background music. "They differ primarily in that foreground music includes original artists and lyrics, whereas background music uses studio musicians playing instrumental." (Yalch & Spangenberg, 1990, p. 57). Foreground music uses more cognitive resources and may distract from a simultaneous message because it acts much like a figure in getting attention. Background music works more affectively (i.e., from feelings) and has its main impact through the mechanism of mood. It can have a powerful effect on mood, as in movies and television, even though we may not consciously be aware of it (see Bruner, 1990).

One other example of figure ground at work is found in a natural history museum. A display case of a hundred moths or ninety-eight rocks may very well be passed by, in part because no figure is present. Their numbers and similarity cause them all to be perceived as background, and thus they do not get attention. Advertisers generally want their product to be seen as a figure. Notice in the ad for Naturalizer shoes (Figure 2) that the product is first seen as background, and attention goes to the people who become the figure. It is only when you find out what the ad is selling that you look for the product and it becomes figure. The gamble they take is that many viewers may not care enough to find out. This effectiveness depends on the viewer being curious enough to look for the product and also being aware that Naturalizer is a type of shoe. The ad certainly scores high on human interest, but we do not know whether it sells shoes.

Similarity. The Gestaltists found that we tend to look for similarities in what we see, and we tend to group several figures together on the basis of the similarities we find. They called this tendency the **law of similarity**. In fact, it is this tendency that forces a figure to be unique to stand out. In other words, we do more than simply noting individual items that come before us. We actively search them for similarities and perceptually group the items on the basis of the similarities we find, all without knowing we are doing it.

Figure 2. In most ads designers attempt to make the product the figure, but here the people become the figure and the product is background. Once you read the brand, you tend to go back to the picture and reconfigure it to make the shoe become the figure. This does not occur, however, if you do not know that *Naturalizer* is a brand of shoe, and you may remain mystified as to the product. (Reproduced by permission of Brown Group, Inc.)

As we go about sorting, we tend to use the most salient characteristic, probably color or shape. Real differences may not be visible, so that their salient qualities cause them to be grouped together. Indeed, such grouping may lead us to overlook important differences of less salient characteristics. For example, this is what unhappily occurs in racial prejudice. In marketing, it means that the house brand looks the same as the nationally advertised one because the salient characteristics are carefully designed to look as similar as is legally possible. Even though we may know better on an intellectual level, our automatic level is working, and we tend to perceive them as essentially the same (Loken, Ross, & Hinkle, 1986). Perceptually we group them together because they appear so similar. No one actually tells us that the two products are the same. They do not have to because they know that our power of inference will draw us to that conclusion. Then, the next step follows that if they are really the same, it makes sense to buy the less expensive one, which is the house brand. The process is not really a conscious one, and our lack of awareness makes it all the more powerful. Much advertising is devoted to combating the natural tendency to regard all members of a group as similar. Notice in the ad for Oldsmobile Silhouette (Figure 3), for example, how General Motors carefully points out what makes their product different, just so that you will not think it is simply another minivan. Because the name is new and fairly small, one may not register that this different van is a type of Oldsmobile. On the other hand, someone who found the feature attractive will probably seek out the brand name.

As we become familiar with more members of a group, the group becomes too big to be useful. We look for more subtle similarities and begin to organize at a new level. This is the process by which we develop taste. For example, when we start out as wine drinkers, about all we know is that there are red, pink, and white wines. We learn that red goes with meat and strong dishes, and white goes with fish and light dishes. Later, we are able to sort further among the reds and distinguish Burgundy, Chianti, and Beaujolais. Eventually, with continued experience, we may be sorting by vineyard and year. In other words, we sort by more and more subtle characteristics as we become more familiar with the group. Notice how perception is being stored in memory and returns to alter future perceptions. Thus, the perceptions of the same bottle of wine will be totally different for an expert compared to a novice. Perception is as much in the mind as it is in the world. A museum curator will not perceive an exhibit the same way as a naive visitor. This means that marketers must be aware of the level of sophistication of their customers.

Figure 3. In this ad *Oldsmobile* identifies a problem (activating a sliding door when your hands are full) and offers a product to solve it. The feature distinguishes their van from many similar vans. (Reproduced by permission of General Motors Corporation.)

Proximity.   A third way by which the gestalt psychologists found that our system organizes is summarized in their **law of proximity**. This says that figures close together tend to be perceived as a group, regardless of how similar they appear to be.

Proximity does more than this, however. Having perceived objects as a group because of their proximity, we tend to perceive them as similar in some way, that is, in all groups their similarities are emphasized rather than their differences. Previously we saw that similarity in one dimension produces the perception of similarity in others. Here we see that perceptual similarity may also be produced by close position. Thus the principles of similarity and proximity work together.

As a common example, consider the newspaper picture of a smiling politician next to a headline announcing a scandal. We become angry because we infer that the politician is treating the scandal as a joke, that is, we assume they are from the same moment because they are placed together. The picture probably came from the file and was taken sometime ago before the scandal even broke. This is one way by which magazines and newspapers quietly, but powerfully, editorialize. Remember too that magazines and newspapers are products that need to be sold.

As a marketing application, consider your perception when a retailer places a dozen brands of margarine side by side in the supermarket cooler. We tend to see them all as very similar, because they have similar shapes and they are in close proximity. Retailers probably do not care which brand the customer buys, but the manufacturers do care, and they must find some way to counteract the principle and make their product stand out (become a figure). This is why they may choose a package color that is very different from the others. Changing the package shape would help even more. Of course, if it is too different, it will not fit with the others, will be shelved elsewhere, and may be totally overlooked by a consumer looking here for margarine.

The laws of similarity and proximity may have even more far-reaching implications. In our culture we tend to express our individuality in our consumer products, particularly in our clothes. But consider the process itself for a moment. Why does my wearing particular clothes communicate something about me? It is probably an extension of the same laws of proximity and similarity. The law of proximity is operating when we assume that the meaning of the individual is the same as the meaning of the clothes they are wearing, because they have been put together. We tend to think (and are probably mostly correct) that poor clothes are worn by poor people, rich clothes by rich people, exciting clothes by exciting people, and dull clothes by dull people.

But is this always true? Intellectually we know that this consistency may not always hold, but our perception operates on the principle of the most likely case. Thus, our perception may force similarities, and we perceive them where none actually exist. Hence, I will be known by my clothes and indeed by all the products that surround me. The tendency operates to produce cognitive consistency to which we shall return in a moment.

The catch is, of course, that the meaning of clothes keeps changing. Today, what signifies "cool" or "stylish", tomorrow will signify "out of touch" or "old-fashioned." We have to keep buying new things to stay ahead of the changing meaning. We do not have to look for a vast corporate conspiracy in changing fashions. It is just in the nature of the process.

Simplification

It is not known how our psyches came to be built so that we categorize by similarity and proximity. Simplification is the best guess. The idea received some support when the concepts of information theory were advanced in the 1950s. Things which can be grouped together need less information to recall or reproduce later. For example, if you know that B is right beside A, then knowing where A is will also give you the position of B with very little extra information. Without knowing their relationship to each other, however, you would need to know the specifics of both positions. Thus, the laws that the gestaltists discovered may have evolved to allow the brain to reduce the information load. However, although simplification is intuitively sensible, it is often hard to define and measure.

A possible by-product of simplification is that things are sometimes perceived as having some of the qualities of the category into which they are placed when in fact they do not have them. This means that members of the category may be perceived as having similar characteristics, which obscures to some extent the differences each has. We have seen this operating to the advantage of the house brand, but it also happens in other places. For example, consider what happens when you go into a store that proclaims itself a discount store. You tend to perceive all of the items as priced lower and will probably not check them all. In fact, many of the items, particularly those with which you are not so familiar, may very well be priced higher than usual, but once having dealt with the question of price in your mind, you put it aside and focus on other things. Most of the time it works, it saves time and energy and

certainly simplifies day to day decisions. But retailers use these principles to their advantage.

MEMORY ORGANIZATION

The general outlines of memory are organized much as perceptions
are. For example, Schwartz and Reisberg point out that we improve
memory by imposing order on it:

> In general, when we understand something, we find the principle or princi-
> ples that hold it together, the rules that provide the unity behind the diversity.
> If no organization can be found, we invent one, imposing an order on the
> materials. Once this is done, it's this organized whole that enters memory, an
> organized unit, rather than diverse and separate materials.... It is easy to
> show that subjects spontaneously use organizing schemes to help them
> remember, without special instruction to do so and without extraordinary
> motivation (Schwartz & Reisberg, 1991, pp. 325–327).

Is this a perceptual level or memory? It is usually hard to tell. The ways
we look for and impose order in memory are virtually the same as those
we use in perception. For example, we form groups at both levels.

Forming Categories

Expectations. The role of expectations "goes under a variety of
other names such as **perceptual set**, familiarity, context, or availability."
(McGuire, 1976) Generally, we assign meaning to a stimulus on the basis
of its expected characteristics, rather than on the basis of what exists in
reality (Lindsay & Norman, 1977). The old saying is, "We see what we
expect to see," but it would be more accurate to say, "We perceive what
we expect to perceive." Expectations originate with experience, so they
could be considered a subcategory of past experiences, but expectation
is a more active concept than the rest of experience. The experiences that
create our expectancies are not simply filled and waiting for the appropriate stimuli to call them forth. Rather, they are already in use structur-
ing the framework and background for the selection and interpretation
process.

The essence of set is that we structure stimuli in accordance with
preset categories. Perception is a constructive process. We construct in
accordance with categories of meaning of which we may not be consciously aware but which are set up by the context of our environment.
As an example, consider this demonstration:

In one soft drink test several years ago, cups labeled "Diet" and "Regular" were both filled with the same regular soft drink. Even though the cups contained the same drink, those labeled "Diet" were rated less favorably than those identified as "Regular." Indeed, many of those who consumed the contents of the "Diet" cup complained about a bitter aftertaste. The expectation created by the label was powerful enough to alter substantially consumers' perceptions of the product (Engel, Blackwell, & Miniard, 1986, p. 221).

The subtle way in which set can be created is illustrated in another study. Subjects were asked to memorize a number of word pairs, including "ocean-moon." After completing this task they were asked to name a detergent. Having studied "ocean-moon," though it was only one pair among several, subjects showed increased likelihood of giving "Tide" as their response compared to the control group whose list of pairs did not include "ocean-moon." Note, however, that although "nearly all subjects could recall most of the word pairs, subjects almost never mentioned a word pair cue as a reason for giving a particular target response." (Nisbett & Wilson, 1977, p. 243). Instead they made up logical reasons such as, "My mother uses Tide." Set can have effects on perception and also on memory, where more elaborate forms of perceptual set are known as scripts and schemas.

Clustering. **Clustering** is one variant of the way we form categories in memory. This involves grouping memories together because of similarities, but this is not being done in the perception stage, but after the material is already stored. It can be seen in a study done in the field of learning. A subject is given a list of words to remember, and some of the words fall into similar categories. For example, the list might have several modes of transportation, several fruit, and several types of clothes, presented to the subject in a random order. Having learned the list the subjects are asked to recall it at some later time. Schwartz and Reisberg (1991) report that "subjects are likely to report back one category of items ..., then pause, then report back one of the other categories, and so on." (p. 327) In other words, at some point, the subjects' minds unconsciously organized the material into categories to aid memory.

As an example of memory principles, consider what happens when we decide to purchase laundry detergent. We may buy the same one as always, in which case habit has taken over and no decision is really being reached. On the other hand, maybe our usual brand is not available, or we disliked it last time. Now we have to decide from a group of detergents that come to mind. One brand may come to mind, or perhaps several from which we pick one, and this group is called the "evoked set." The task of the marketer is to insure that when the group "laundry detergents" comes to consumers' minds, the marketer's brand is included. Then it has a chance of being chosen. If people do not think of it when they think of the group, how can they select it? Thus, the task of the marketers is to make their products stand out in memory when a particular category is called up. Identifying what the product is or does will help do this, as will repeated advertising. Of course, consumers may simply wait until they get to the store and look at those available on the shelf. This process reduces the demands on memory, but the one they want may not be there. If it is not in their evoked set, however, they will not miss it.

Remembering the Category, Not the Item. Just as perceiving their relationship makes remembering about A and B simpler, so our minds work similarly when we remember that all matches are basically the same except that each brand has a minor difference. Thus we have to store only the characteristics of matches in one place and not repeat them in another new place with every new brand. Storage is simplified and reduced, and brand differences are lost. General characteristics are stored with every experience with any brand and thus become stronger than the details. Because the details of individual brands of matches are hard to remember, we end up unable to distinguish between the different brands. Can you even name a brand of matches? We forget their uniqueness and remember what they all share in common because these commonalities define their category.

What all this means for marketing is that in categories in which all members are pretty much alike (e.g., beer, cigarettes, perfume, jeans, matches, etc.) image becomes vital. In other words, when no real differences exist, they must be invented. Otherwise, how will your product stand out? Image becomes more important than substance, and promotion becomes more important than product characteristics. Image sets the product apart within its category when its own characteristics do not.

Schemas **Schemas** are basically complex categories, which include a host of related attributes, beliefs, and even expected actions along with a simple concept. The notion of the "schema" was introduced by Bartlett (1932) and Piaget (1936) and is commonly used to refer to mental structures that have a dynamic or relational aspect to differentiate them from simple concepts (Nisbett & Ross, 1980). For example, "upon deciding on the basis of a particular animal's appearance that it is a 'dog', one makes the inferential leaps that it is trainable, capable of loyalty, able to bark, and likely to chase cats, but is unlikely to climb trees, purr, or wash its coat." (Nisbett & Ross, 1980, p. 33) Thus, schemas are clusters of associations often built by experience, though sometimes built simply for recall, around our simple concepts.

Compare, for example, two schemas you probably have built from experience, one evoked by the name Nieman–Marcus and the other by K-Mart. You are aware that an extensive picture comes to mind with each of these, possibly including what the interior of the store looks like, what the sales clerks are like, which products you can expect to find there, and what the price range is likely to be. Mandler (1982) found evidence to support the idea that we form schemas of television commercials, based on distilling commonalities from the huge number we have seen, and that an incongruity between this schema and a new commercial is the basis for increased attention.

Sometimes we create associations to aid memory, and these too constitute schemas. For example, Tulving (1962) gave subjects lists of unrelated words to learn. He presented the same lists several times but always in a different order. What he noticed was that subjects would recall the same clusters of words each time, as though they had been linked together in some unique way. Note, however, that these are not words with similarities but are simply unrelated words. They do not stay unrelated, however. In other words, subjects were spontaneously organizing material as it was stored to make retrieval easier. Perhaps they would be linked with a story line, for instance, the *girl* with the *hat* rode in the *truck* in the *trees*. The story line becomes the schema or structure used in recall. Tulving showed how basic this process is to perception and memory.

Considerable evidence from the fields of memory and learning indicate that what we remember is not always what happened. Rather we seem to carry in our minds a framework which is generally true, but in remembering we add details, sometimes details from other similar events, so that we end up with a memory that is a composite. Schwartz and Reisberg (1991) point out that there is good and bad in the schemata process. On the good side we do not need to look at all the details in each event to recognize it because we utilize our past experience. This makes us faster and more efficient, particularly in problem solving. On the other hand, the bad side is that we often distort or do not even notice what does not fit our schemata. Thus, we will remember according to our prejudices and preconceptions, because if our understanding of a situation is faulty, then our memory is too. Set and schemata are particularly important for marketers because what we expect of a product has a lot to do with how we ultimately evaluate it.

Schemas are also important under the heading of "image." If I create a luxurious image for my product, then it is remembered as having luxurious characteristics, even though it really does not. Those mental pictures, or schemas, shape what you hear about the product, what you associate it with, and even distort your memories (and perceptions) in their direction. They shape how you react to what you experience in the product or find in a store. This is the power of image and why companies are willing to spend money to develop it.

Scripts   When schemas are more extensive and involve action over time, they are known as **scripts**. Doubtless you have already encountered this word as meaning a program of action and dialogue, such as actors use in plays or movies. The concept here is similar, but it is not written down or formal. Rather it is a memory and expectation of a sequence of actions that is triggered by a particular concept or word. The common example is of a "restaurant script" which includes scenes of "entering," "ordering," "eating," "paying," and "exiting," but all places of business, from malls to museums, have scripts. In other words, we generate expectations that can be very complex. We expect things to progress in a certain order, we expect to be treated in a certain way, and we expect to have a certain experience.

Disruption of our expectations can have consequences for sales. For example, a local fast food lunch restaurant developed a good business in which the procedure was essentially cafeteria style. Customers came in, took a tray, proceeded down a counter, ordered their sandwiches, soup or whatever, put them on their trays, paid at the end of the counter, and took their trays to tables. Customers formed a script for this particular restaurant. But now the management decided to extend their day into the dinner hour and to change the format after four o'clock. Now customers were to go to tables, order from menus, and waitpersons would bring their meals. The change seemed to have no real reason because the restaurant was still designed in the cafeteria style with a long counter, now to be unused by customers. Moreover, it was clear that customers were still applying their cafeteria scripts. Customers consistently continued to come to the counter, only to be told, sometimes only after standing there awhile, that the setup had changed. They often appeared annoyed. The staff were clearly tired of pointing this out and began to sound irritated. Customers felt manipulated and sometimes angry. Not only did there seem to be no reason for the change, it was clearly going to take longer to get their meal, and, since a waitperson had to be tipped, it was going to be more expensive. Waitpersons caught in the middle had to explain repeatedly, apologize, and hope the customers' anger did not translate into lower tips. The problem was a clear example of customers using an old script no longer appropriate, and, ignored by management, the situation went on creating ill will and did not improve for many weeks. I felt so manipulated the last time I was there that I have never gone back.

Scripts also involve expectations about the way products operate. Products are usually evaluated against an internalized standard set by our expectations, and the nature of these expectations is of considerable importance to marketers. Customer scripts must be considered when, for example, a company changes the way its product is to be used, say, from soaking in to spraying on. Following their scripts, customers are very likely not to read the label, because they expect it to be like it was or like the other products in its class. Thus they may be disappointed or angry when it does not perform well. They will probably never know why and simply buy something else.

Personas. Another type of schema commonly used in our inferential process is that called **persona** by Nisbett and Ross (1980), after the name for the cast of characters in a play, the dramatis personae. The authors write that

> personas are essentially people stereotypes that are shared within the culture or subculture (the sexpot, the earth mother, the girl next door, the redneck, the schlemiel, the rebel without a cause) ... the big ox.... In each instance the persona constitutes a knowledge structure which, when evoked, influences social judgments and behaviors. Once the principle features or behaviors of a given individual suggest a particular persona, subsequent expectations of and responses to that individual are apt to be dictated in part by the characteristics of the persona (Nisbett & Ross, 1980, p. 35).

Movie stars tend to get personas, particularly when they are cast repeatedly in similar roles. Clint Eastwood comes to mind as a clear example. When these stars undertake to sell products, it is their persona to which we respond. But Nisbett and Ross are saying that we all get personas, and we all know this because we spend so much effort on our image. Clothes are chosen to make a statement, and cars are chosen to express who we think we are or who we wish to be seen as. We choose products to match our desired personas. Hence, advertising often suggests that its product will create a particular persona for its user. Personas are another form of the same process of forming categories and then responding to the category.

Transfer of Affect from Category

The notion of categories was extended further by Fiske (1982) who showed that the way we feel about a category transfers to people and things placed in it. Fiske called this "schema triggered affect," and it works this way. If the present situation reminds us, even unconsciously, of a memory situation (a schema), we are likely to respond to the present situation on the basis of the feeling (affect) attached to the situation in the past. Thus, as soon as we categorize a product, it picks up affect from the category itself. For example, all brands of sports cars benefit from the advertising of any brand in the category because if we come to like sports cars in general better (that is, the category), then we will automatically like the members in it better. In order not to help the competition while we advertise our brand, sharp differences must be drawn, so that the consumer will find it harder to put both brands in the same category. Again, image is the means of creating differences.

Effects of Prior Knowledge

An important aspect of category formation is the amount of one's prior knowledge, or how much information one brings to the situation. It seems like a simple concept, but like most, when you start working on it, it becomes more complex. Just how you measure prior knowledge turns out to be difficult and important. Brucks (1985) has divided this somewhat sophisticated research area into three groups: (1) uses some objective test measure of what they in fact know (**objective knowledge**); (2) uses a measure of a person's own perception of how much they know about a product class (**subjective knowledge**); and (3) uses a measure of their usage experience with the class (**user history**).

Unfortunately, the three measures of knowledge sometimes give conflicting results. To summarize without getting too far into it, objective knowledge (what you really know) leads to more efficient information search because it allows consumers to ask the right questions, explore a greater number of product attributes, and eliminate inappropriate questions. Just thinking you know does not allow this. We retain information better when we already have a category to put it in, and we also become more efficient in knowing what else we need to know. Thus, it will be easier to add new information to products which we already have heard about or may have already used. This means that even advertising brand name alone, with no information about product, will make future ads better remembered. Later information already has a hook ready to hang it on and an easier situation than having to create the hook at the same time.

Subjective knowledge (what we think we know), on the other hand, leads to more confidence, more reliance on what you know, and probably less dependence on salespeople. But, in fact if your perception of what you know is faulty, then this confidence may not lead to a better decision. User history may give a picture different from the other measures, because even though you use it, you may not be learning about it. For example, you may not know or may not pay attention to the brand name at the time of use. Or worse yet, you may have been mistaken about the brand.

There are also studies that categories used in the recent past tend to create a channel for current thinking. This a form of perceptual set. Fiske and Taylor (1991) cite no less than twelve studies that support this principle. In other words, perceptual set is likely to call up a particular schema when there are a number possible. Categories used frequently and information encountered early in a communication both create a set and influence later information. Thus, image is a set creator.

Application

Positioning. **Positioning**, making sure in which category consumers place the product initially, is crucially important. Positioning applies all the principles of perceptual organizing, grouping, and affective transfer and is a matter of creating a meaning for a product in the consumer's mind. Once it has a meaning, this categorizes it, and consumers no longer attempt to place it. Rather it picks up meanings and feelings from other products in the group.

It is difficult to change a product's positioning. For instance, if the manufacturer finds some new use for the product, it may be very hard to get consumers to see it ever in a new category. In other words, once we organize a perception, that organization tends to stay with us and is sometimes very difficult to overcome because it goes into memory in that form and things come out of memory as they go in. Thus, the crucial part of positioning a product is its initial placement in a particular group.

For example, if people do not like buttermilk and I present them with a new buttermilk, saying that I think they may like because it does not taste like other buttermilks, they are likely to reject it without even tasting it. They are applying the affect of the category. If it truly does not taste like buttermilk, then I had better not call it buttermilk. People will form false expectations from that label, so that I will lose either way. Those that dislike buttermilk will avoid it, and those who like buttermilk will be disappointed.

As another example, consider the classic case of baking soda. A number of years ago, baking soda was seen as simply a product used in baking. It had few other uses, and therefore sales were somewhat limited. The Arm and Hammer company decided to broaden the potential market and reposition its product as a product which could also be used to remove refrigerator odors. The company realized it would have to undertake an intensive advertising campaign to change the basic perception of baking soda. It was attempting to put the product in a new category and change the mind-set of consumers, so that they would think of baking soda for this new task, while before they would not. The advertising campaign to do this was successful, and sales rose markedly. People simply had never thought of baking soda as a refrigerator deodorizer. A more recent example is seen in ads by the Clorox company in which they are attempting to position their product as something other than simply a laundry whitener and sanitizer. The heading reads, "The first thing to put under your tree is a little Clorox bleach," and the copy tells of a number of less well known uses for the product. In Figure 4 we are encouraged by Kellogg Company to see *Rice Krispies Cereal* as a baking ingredient.

Note that there can be a danger in this process because a new meaning may weaken or replace the old one. In the case of Arm and Hammer, it did not, probably because the old use was so well known and because there were not many competing products for the old use. Had there been, they would have run a high risk of losing the old market while attempting to add the new, for after all, who wants to add a refrigerator deodorizer to their cake? In such a case, a catchy new name to distinguish the new product from the old may have been required.

Brand Extension.   **Brand extension**, the use of the single company name for all of its products, is another place where positioning is important. The more different products a brand name covers, the vaguer its meaning becomes. For example, Colgate markets shaving cream and hand soap under the same name as its well-known toothpaste. The more Colgate is advertised as a toothpaste, the harder it is to think of Colgate when you shop for shaving cream. However, losses in individual product lines may be offset by greater familiarity with the brand name because of the additional advertising from other product lines. More on this later.

INFERENCES OF COMPLETION

As we have just seen, our perceptual process groups together the visual bits and pieces we are seeing and in the process infers similarities because they share some characteristics or because they are close to each

Figure 4. Kellogg Company in this example is positioning *Rice Krispies Cereal* as a baking ingredient. Ambiguity as to whether it is the mother or the child who is the potential talk of the 4th grade may increase the attention. (Reproduced by permission of Kellogg Company.)

other. Now we turn to the ways by which perception actually adds to the bits and pieces, inferring the presence of parts not actually sensed. The gestalt principles of figure ground, closure, and goodness of figure are examples of the way in which the perceptual system actually completes figures and fills in missing information. Even at this simple level, inference is going on, so that the perceived pieces can be completed into meaningful units and interpretation of their significance drawn.

As you might expect, we do the same thing in memory. We rarely actually remember details. We remember general outlines and later when we recall, we add reasonable details again. Of course, we think we are remembering the details clearly, but generally we are not. Because memory affects perception and what we perceive, we remember. It becomes artificial to keep the two processes separate, and for the rest of this chapter we will not try to keep them apart. Perceptions are altered in the completion process, so that we have a sense of a whole reality, but it is our memory and experience that is doing the filling in. Let us see how it works.

VISUAL CONSTRUCTION

More Gestalt Laws

Figure Ground Revisited. As we discussed previously, the gestaltists discovered that the most primitive visual process and the first to occur when a stimulus was encountered, was the differentiation of a stimulus pattern into a figure and a ground. Visual figures tend to be produced by a space enclosed by a contour, and ground tends to be defined by the space around the figure. An important thing about them, however, is that they are not opposites. Background is seen as having a distinctly different nature than figures. Background does not simply fill the space around figures, so that they share a contour, as in two dimensions, but rather it is perceived as actually extending behind the figure and on beyond the frame of a picture. Thus, the contour is part of the figure, in fact defines it, and the background has no contour.

These differences in the perception of figures and backgrounds reveal a basic and powerful process. Part of the perception is being constructed. It is not in the sense data at all. We perceive extensive background to be there, even though we are sensing only a small part of it. It turns out that a great deal of what we visually perceive is not really seen but is still understood to be there. In other words, perception is often a matter of what we understand to be, rather than what we see. Let us look at other examples.

Closure, Good Continuation, and Goodness of Figure.   The gestalt **law of closure** says that when part of a familiar figure is missing, we will fill it in, and we will probably not even realize it was missing. The gestaltists demonstrated this by using a simple circle with a segment missing, but it is a principle that we encounter hundreds of times a day without realizing it. Every time we see an object standing behind another, we perceive that the occluded object is complete. If a bicycle is leaning against the back side of the tree, we do not perceive that the middle portion of the bicycle is missing. Instead, we perceive that the bicycle is whole. Later, we may not actually recall against which side of the tree the bicycle was leaning, and we certainly will not recall that part of it was missing. Of course, none of it really was missing, so our perception serves us better than our eyes. We inferred the meaning of the parts, that a whole bicycle was present. The meaning, like all of the Gestalt laws, serves to keep us in touch with reality in a way that pure sensory awareness would not.

One aspect of the perceptual tendency to fill in information is that the system uses the information available to make the simplest prediction of what the missing piece will be. If you see a headlight and a part of a fender projecting from behind a wall, you perceive that a car is parked behind the wall. You would be startled to find on rounding the corner that the parts were propped up by themselves. You would also be surprised to find them attached to a boat. Thus, the perception constructed is clearly not random. It is predicted by the part. The gestaltists expressed this in the law of good continuation and the law of goodness of figure. They were criticized for using the term "goodness" which seems to have no adequate definition. They defended the term, however, asserting that it will be the figure most familiar to the viewer in that context. It remains clearly demonstrable, though hard to define. In fact, "good continuation" is a perceptual tendency employed in the art of camouflage. When used cleverly, we see shapes that are not there and fail to see shapes that are there.

Applications

Part for the Whole.   The application of the principle of perceptual construction to marketing is readily seen in advertising, where the part is often used to suggest the whole. For example, to create the impression of luxury, one might choose to build a scene around an expensive automobile parked in front of a French chateau. It is sufficient to show only a part of the automobile, for we perceive that the rest is there, just out of sight. When choosing parts to stand for wholes, one must be sure to use a part that is unambiguous and commonly known, or the perception created may not be the one desired. For example, the familiar grillwork of the Rolls Royce is fairly universally understood as meaning luxury, whereas the grill of some other expensive car might not because it might not be distinctive enough to be recognized as part of an expensive automobile. Similarly, we do not need to see all of the chateau to know what is there. Simply, the ornate doorway will do. From the car and the doorway, we infer a whole lifestyle of elegance and luxury as a background against which to position a product. From proximity then we will infer that the product is luxurious and of high quality, and no one has verbally said so. Many ads are built on this principle. In fact, inference is much more powerful than direct statement because it comes less consciously from our perception and has the feel of reality, rather than contrivance. It is tapping into our affect rather than our cognition. The inference produced by the use of a part for the whole is apparent in a recent ad for Capri cigarettes. The ad uses associations already established for the brand name in the romance of the Isle of Capri and extends them to a whole luxurious style of life by using carefully chosen details that surround the model. She is dressed in a long gown and is looking over a courtyard bordered by an Italianate marble colonnade. All of these associations are illusion because it really is just another cigarette. Perhaps the users hope that the illusion will raise their own image, or maybe they will simply feel differently about themselves when they smoke this brand. Still illusion, but then, much of life is illusion.

Recently, Peracchio and Meyers-Levy (1994) investigated an aspect of perceptual construction that has further implications. They looked at pictures used in advertising that are ambiguous in some way, usually because they are severely cropped and an important part is missing. Such pictures tend to keep attention longer to decide what the picture is about. They cite a Faier and Unger (1987) study that found that 44% of ads contain ambiguities or instances in which information is unresolved or incomplete. For example, a woman holding a Diet Coke is cropped so that only the face below the nose is visible. They found that the resolution of the ambiguity by the viewer produces positive affect. There is greater positive affect transfer (to the ad and product) when the ambiguity concerns some aspect of the informational claims in the picture, than when it has no connection to these claims. A form of ambiguity appears in a Speedo ad in which the diver appears transparent, but her swimsuit is not. The uncertainty created probably increases the holding power of the image considerably.

Redundancy.   The same idea of filling in what is missing has also appeared in communication work where it is called **redundancy**. It is the verbal counterpart of the gestalt work with visual figures. When parts of words are missing, we may not even notice it because the remaining parts are sufficient. For example, if we miss the vowel in a word, we can usually still understand the word, as in the license plates that read, "PHNTM", or "MPULSV". Or again in the Christmas ad for J&B Scotch, remarking that Christmas just is not the same without the J&B, the copy reads, "ingle ells, ingle ells". Other examples not only require supplying missing letters, but more complex translations from visual to auditory forms, as in, "CUL8R". There is redundancy in sentences too, particularly familiar ones. If there were not, the television game show Wheel of Fortune, in which contestants try to guess a familiar phrase or saying, as letters are gradually filled in, would not be possible. Postal addresses use state names and zip codes, although the zip code generally includes information about the state. With the redundancy there is a better chance of deciphering illegible hand writing or of correcting errors. Redundancy means that we can understand each other even over noise, and radio transmissions can be understood over static. In each case we are constructing the whole from the part. Ads and commercials use redundancy when the picture and the verbal message communicate the same thing. In this case it improves the transfer of brand information.

AUDITORY CONSTRUCTION

Verbal Examples

We tend to think of written words as visual, but they are only partly so because we "hear" and see written words. Ries and Trout:

> When words are read, they are not understood until the visual/verbal transla-
> tor in your brain takes over to make aural sense out of what you have just
> seen.... headlines, slogans, and themes should be examined for their aural
> qualities. Even if you plan to use them in printed material only.... Messages
> would "sound better" in print if they were designed for radio first. Yet we
> usually do the reverse. We work first in print and then in the broadcast media
> (Ries & Trout, 1986, p. 90).

Thus even written words are more auditory than visual, but the process of filling in is still there. Tannen, a psycholinguist, notes that "Much—even most—meaning in conversation does not reside in the words spoken at all, but is filled in by the person listening." (Tannen, 1990, p. 37) Fiction, particularly, uses the perceptual process of construction for its very essence. We visualize a scene from a few carefully chosen words of description. The more colorful the writing, the more vivid the imagery, and the more exciting the tale. Radio drama was based almost completely on this process. Most of the story was supplied by the listener, and the dialogue provided carefully chosen clues, as for example, "The door is open. I'm going in." The listener supplies the mental picture from the clue. In general, suggestion is more powerful than the complete picture or story because the hearers fill in what in their experience is most appropriate, and the perceived whole is tailored to each hearer differently. Thus, the partly concealed form is more sexy than complete nakedness.

Applications of perceptual construction in radio and television commercials are endless. Almost every one depends on the process, but one minor and unusual application is worth mentioning in passing. Wendy's restaurants ran a now famous series of ads which featured the line, "Where's the beef?" to emphasize the small size of their competitor's hamburger. Later in the series, the last word was omitted, apparently to add involvement by having the listener fill it in. Whether it increased the effectiveness of the ad is not disclosed, but certainly many people filled in the word.

Sound Effects

Old-time radio dramas also offered countless examples of another type of construction at work, sound effects. Sounds of all kinds enabled the listener to visualize the action. For example, the sound of footsteps was enough for us to picture a person walking. Street noises and we pictured a street. The whinnying horse and the pounding of hoofbeats were obligatory in all westerns. In written dramatic fiction even the description of sounds allows us to vividly imagine them. "A stair creaked behind him" almost is enough for us to hear the sound and react as if we did. All of this works, of course, because that is what we do everyday in getting around our world. Sounds have meanings, and we respond to those meanings.

Music too provokes specific images and moods, and one must be aware of these musical images to match them to any message that may accompany them. If they do not match, then perception of the message suffers. (See more on music in chapter 13.)

INFERENCES OF MEANING

Perceptual Interpretation

Completion and interpretation differ in that completion adds elements that are not there, whereas interpretation adds meaning to parts that are there. The two processes generally interact and happen together, so that they usually cannot be separated. In fact, it may be impossible to complete a meaningful percept, if the parts cannot first be interpreted. In other words, we are pulling meaning out of a stimulus, and we are also putting meaning in. It is important to bear in mind, however, that the way information is added is not random. It is triggered and predicted by the sensory image.

Psychology has investigated many examples of perceptual interpretation. In any perception information comes from two sources, the visual images themselves, and memory, which adds meaning to the images based on our past experience with them. We are indebted to James Gibson for revealing the richness of sensory information that is contained in visual images themselves. These bits of information, called cues, are details of contour, brightness, color, lighting, texture, or placement, which convey information about the objects in the image. In Gibson's view, called an ecological theory, memory plays no part in perception, and all perception comes from these cues (Gibson, 1950).

However, the overwhelming weight of evidence favors the opposing, or constructivist theory. The constructivist view does not necessarily negate Gibson's idea of the role played by cues, but goes further and adds memory as a major source of perceptual influence. Gibson may have been right for simple perceptions, but for complex perceptions his view was incomplete and unable to explain the evidence. Experience gives the cues added meaning and allows them to be used in more complex ways. Symbols, for example, come to have tremendous meaning, and people are willing to die for what they represent. But the meaning is not in the symbol itself. Rather it is clearly in the memory of the observer. In this section, under the heading of interpretation, we look at how the perceptual process makes sense of visual cues and by putting them together, interprets the meaning of the image.

Nonverbal Interpretation

Unstated Extensions. A picture that accompanies an ad may cause the viewer to infer that qualities in the picture are also found in the product, even though no one says so. For example, Mitchell and Olson (1981) presented an ad with a beautiful sunset in one condition and no sunset in another, and the verbal message was simply "Brand I Facial Tissues are Soft." The presence of the sunset created beliefs that the tissues came in more attractive colors. In this case the color concept seems to have been remembered as part of the product. This tendency toward faulty memory can be exploited in advertising as a means to deception as we shall see in the next chapter.

Symbols. Most objects have symbolic meanings, and behavior, too, takes on symbolic connotations, as in the case of rituals. Symbols can also call up schemas and scripts. Thus the luxury car symbolizes a whole luxurious lifestyle. Note carefully, however, that the meaning of symbols is not in them, but in the mind of the users, that is, symbols are a function of prior learning. Their meanings must be agreed upon by the sender and receiver to communicate without error and are thus open to misinterpretation when cultural backgrounds vary to any marked degree.

Notice how this is a natural extension of the perceptual processes of construction and interpretation. Most stimuli in our visual world allow us to fill in information that is missing because we know what the stimuli mean. Parts stand for wholes perceptually, and this is just what a symbol does. It stands for a larger concept. Like the rest of perception, symbols can stand only for what we know they mean. Thus it is crucial to understand that cultures, subcultures, and groups have their own meanings which they symbolically represent, perhaps with the same symbol that has a different meaning in another culture.

Marketing is filled with nonverbal symbol usage on many levels. Simple usage of symbols occurs in company and brand logos. More complex usage is found in advertising, where moods and feelings are created by representative scenes or objects. Putting effects into neat pigeon holes is not always possible. When, for example, does an image become a symbol? Simple images carry all manner of affect and subtle meanings, and some of them can have real marketing impact. Consider this recent example. W. J Deutsch & Sons imports a brand of chardonnay wine labeled Georges Duboeuf. William Deutsch told writer Katharine Whittemore (1996), "The label used to show a little purple thistle the French call a *chardon*. In France, that was fine, but over here sales were not too exciting. My daughter Susan suggested changing the image to a sunflower. Sales skyrocketed more than fivefold." (p. 52) The sunflower clearly carries a strong positive affect that enhances the product. Other levels of symbolization occur in expressing status and using status symbols to communicate cultural categories or to enhance the owner's sense of self-worth. We deal with some of these in later chapters.

The symbol that a company uses as a trademark for quick identification is called a **logo.** They are sometimes made up of the corporate letters arranged in a novel way. Others also involve additional symbols. For example, to suggest speed, wings, fins, or the cartoonist's speed lines have all been employed. Just as in brand and product names, we infer a considerable amount of information from the impression that the logo creates. For example, Masten (1988) showed that the same name in different type faces was rated differently on quality, value, and preference measures. Perhaps the most important element conveyed in a logo is the feeling of being up-to-date or outmoded. In general, logos have become increasingly simple and more abstract over the years (see Morgan, 1987). Styles continually change, and thus logos must be continually updated to remain modern looking. The trick is to make them look more up-to-date without losing the image that has been attached to them. Gradual changes are generally necessary.

Social meanings also change, and a benign symbol may suddenly be politically incorrect. For example, the school mascot logo of the University of Massachusetts was changed in 1972 from an Indian to the Minuteman, a Revolutionary War figure carrying a musket because of increasing sensitivity to the social implications of the Indian logo, particularly for Native Americans. Then in 1993, the Minuteman too came under fire for being white, male, and armed, whereas, a group of protesters maintained, UMass was diverse, nonsexist, and a community that practices peace (Arnold, 1993). Proctor and Gamble used a moon and stars symbol for more than 150 years, but the meaning underwent a change and they had to abandon it. Morgan explains:

> In 1982 the design became the focus of a bizarre rumor that the company was involved in devil worship. Because an artist had chosen a field of thirteen stars as a patriotic gesture more than a century ago, one of the country's oldest trademarks was suddenly singled out as a satanic symbol. After three years of battling the false stories without finding a way to silence them for good, the company decided in 1985 to drop the mark from its products (Morgan, 1987, p. 184).

When symbols do not mean the same thing to everyone and meanings change with time, it seems doubtful whether a symbol can be found that appeals to everyone.

Symbolic Systems. Early twentieth century writers like James, Veblen, Jung, and Freud wrote of unconscious mechanisms, and unconscious symbolism. It remained for Ernest Dichter to apply these approaches to the consumer realm. Although Dichter invokes Freudian sexualism in many cases, he also invoked the analyses of other writers. For example, consider his analysis of banks reported by Packard. His particular interest was in the paradox of the great growth of loan companies in spite of the fact most banks offered personal loans at lower interest and were more lenient in accepting people for loans. His conclusion was that the loan company's big advantage over the bank was its lower moral tone, that is, that loan companies are perceived as less austere and more friendly than banks. He wrote:

> The bank's big handicap ... is its stern image as a symbol of unemotional morality. When we go to a banker for a loan, he points out, we are asking this personification of virtue to condescend to take a chance on us frail humans. In contrast, when we go to the loan company for a loan, it is we who are the virtuous ones and the loan company is the villain we are temporarily forced to consort with.... We shift from feeling like "an unreliable adolescent to feeling like a morally righteous adult. The higher cost of the loan is a small price to pay for such a great change in outlook." (Packard, 1957, pp. 56–57)

In contrast to the Freudian based sexual significance that Dichter often freely invoked elsewhere, his symbolism here covers other psychological concerns, such as self-image and self-worth. The bank has come to symbolize moral righteousness because this is the image bankers have created for themselves to project the essential feeling of security. Unfortunately, the empirical validation of Dichter's approach, Freudian or otherwise, is lacking. It was not always possible to tell whether he was right in his analysis or not, and advertisers grew disenchanted with it because they were unable to show that it helped sales. More detail on this approach, particularly the connection to Freud, later. The power of image, however, has never been in question.

In the early 70s, Wilson Bryan Key, who followed and perhaps attempted to "expose" Dichter, published a book called *Subliminal Seduction* in which he claimed that symbolisms of all kinds are found in advertisements and that they are effective in making us buy products. He echoed the earlier writers by claiming it was all unconscious. The book created considerable interest but did not establish the effectiveness of the subliminal, or even of the subattentional as most of it turns out to be. His argument, an apt example of faulty reasoning, generally proceeds in this way: (1) these ads must be effective because they are expensive, and advertisers wouldn't pay for them if they didn't work; (2) there are hidden symbols in them; (3) the symbols must be what is making them effective; and (4) Freudian or Jungian interpretations explain why.

Note how in the following "explanation" Key's reference to the Jungian notion of archetypes imparts a tone of authority. He has just pointed out that in a magazine ad for Chivas Regal scotch, the white wrapper partially removed from the bottle forms the head of a dog, if you turn the magazine sideways. He writes,

> The dog (especially subliminal dogs) appears to provide an unconscious stimulus for the purchase of alcohol. Traditionally in our culture the symbolic archetype of the dog has meant affection, companionship, courage,

devotion, and fidelity. Faithful love and friendship are frequently mentioned as basic qualities of the dog symbolism in medieval Christian art. A white dog is a happy omen. Presumably these symbolic archetypal meanings are buried in the unconscious of all of us. The dog is one of the richest and most complicated of animal archetypes—especially in North America where, as people have become more and more alienated from each other, they have developed an increasing emotional dependency upon dogs ... (Key, 1973, p. 99).

Key is outdoing even Dichter here, but unfortunately there is no controlled study to test the correctness of his symbolic interpretation any more than Dichter's. Without such studies, many interpretations are possible, and we cannot know which situation applies. For example, readers may or may not be aware of this particular symbolic meaning of dogs. They may be aware of this or other symbolic references to dogs, but that may have no relevance to this ad. The meanings may indeed be relevant to this ad but do not affect sales. Without research controls, interpretation becomes simply speculative assertion. Symbol usage necessitates an agreement between voicer and hearer as to the meaning of the symbol. Without this agreement, communication is not taking place. Hence, Key may be aware of all kinds of meanings in advertising symbols, but if the consumer is not aware of them, no meaning is being transferred.

Symbols continue to be found in nearly all ads because nearly every object has symbolic and literal meanings, and many of them are placed there intentionally. But, whether a particular symbol has the supposed effect on the viewer, whether the reason for an effect is in fact the theoretical one claimed, and whether it sells products as a consequence, all remain matters for research to be demonstrated convincingly. Yet they continue to be used.

Quality Appraisal.   In choosing products, and particularly those new or unknown, various perceptual cues are often used to determine the quality of the item. These perceptual cues are details in the product or the environment and in this case we use them to infer quality. We probably have few alternatives, but sometimes they work and sometimes they do not. Olshavsky (1985) summarizes the variety of such cues:

The most frequently researched surrogate or index of perceived quality is price. But other cues that have been identified are country of origin, brand name, manufacturer's reputation, brand familiarity, popularity of brand, and certain intrinsic product cues such as package design, size (for example, of hi-fi speakers), length of warranty, materials used (for example, wood versus plastic), style (for example, of car), odor (for example, of bleach or stockings), and design (exterior or interior) of a retail structure. Store image may also serve as a cue to the quality of a brand and vice versa (Olshavsky, 1985, p. 9).

The process of inferring quality remains subjective and proves difficult to simplify. Desirable attributes clearly differ across product categories and even within category. For example, "thickness is related to high quality in tomato-based juices, but not in fruit-flavored children's drinks. The presence of pulp suggests high quality in orange juice but low quality in apple juice." (Zeithamel, 1988, p. 7) Ultimately, this means that one has to research the question product by product, but research has produced some attributes which seem to cross many categories. For example, contributors to the impression of store quality include store reputation, store characteristics (such as pleasant atmosphere, cleanliness, spaciousness, who the other shoppers are), service aspects (such as salespeople who are more knowledgeable, helpful, personal, and younger—for a college-aged sample), and, of course, attributes of products (such as well-made, desired brand, good variety, and, for clothes, natural fibers, classic style, unique designs, and good fit) (Gutman & Alden, 1985). These attributes might influence the perception of all goods sold in a given store.

There are many potential perceptual cues, but not everybody evaluates these cues in the same way. For instance, Morgan (1985) points out that quality is not perceived in the same way by marketers and consumers. In a study for GE product developers, manufacturers, marketers, and consumers were asked to list attributes that define quality. There was a surprising amount of disagreement among the groups. The only attribute they all listed was reliability. Consumers also listed appearance, cleanability, ease of use, features, safety, and workmanship. Only on reliability did consumers agree with marketers, who listed cost/price, delivery, performance, product information, service, and unit consistency instead. Consumers showed only slightly better agreement with product developers, differing except for appearance and reliability.

Consumers showed better agreement with manufacturers than with marketers, agreeing on five out of seven attributes. In spite of this, however, Morgan found a "quality-perception gap" between manufacturers and consumers. As evidence he quotes a Fortune survey of chief executive officers of the largest U.S. companies which found that only 13% believed quality was declining. At the same time a study of 7000 consumers found that 49% believed quality was declining. Although reliability was the attribute all agreed was important for quality, another study showed that 50% of manufacturers believed reliability had improved, but only 20% of consumers agreed (Morgan, 1985).

Verbal Interpretation

Language. We begin with a review of the nature of language. The topic is vital to anyone who writes copy and attempts to influence others. It is particularly relevant for those who communicate across cultures, as marketers abroad. Language, of course, is a special case of our ability to use symbols, and it is an elaborate symbol system. First our quick review.

Experience. The experiences we have as we grow up tend to be quite like those of our neighbors. This commonality of experience is what we mean when we speak of a cultural group, and it is why cultural groups tend to have similar perceptions. Perhaps we can illustrate just how culture shapes perception by considering the example of language. Take the word "cow," for instance. It seems as though there is a lot of meaning in that word, but in fact there is very little. Even the dictionary definition is not in the word. If it were, we would not need the dictionary. What if I look it up? Then, do I put the meaning into the word? No, I put the meaning into my brain. Moreover, even though I know what cows are, I probably cannot tell you what the dictionary says about cows without looking the word up because I did not learn what a cow is from a dictionary. I learned it from first-hand experiences with cows and from vicarious experiences in reading. At first, someone must have told me, "That is a cow," but later on I added considerable knowledge by myself. For example, I used to bring cows in from the pasture as a child, and I can still picture their slow, methodical walk, their bony hips and swishing tails. I can remember the warm smell of the barn at milking time, the cows' placid eyes, and their fat, rough tongues. All these memories and hundreds more are connected to the word "cow," so that the word has come to have a lot of meaning for me.

Now suppose I speak to someone else and I use the word "cow." Does all this meaning that I understand cram itself into the word "cow" and leap across the intervening space on the vehicle of my voice? Of course not. What happens is that the word "cow" is a signal to the listeners to go into their memory banks and retrieve what they have stored there under the symbol "cow." If they have stored experiences similar to mine, then they will understand me as I intended. On the other hand, if they have very different experiences filed there or very few at all (perhaps they are deprived urbanites who have grown up in the city and have never seen a cow), they may understand something a bit different from what I intended. In fact, because of this personal component, two listeners may interpret my words totally differently.

When two people come from different cultures, then they have different experiences, and it means that they have less common ground by which to communicate. One psycholinguist comments, "when speakers from different parts of the country, or of different ethnic backgrounds, talk to each other, it is likely that their words will not be understood exactly as they were meant." (Tannen, 1990, p. 13) The more cultures differ between speaker and listener, the more miscommunication is likely to happen, because the more our memory-filed experiences are likely to differ. For instance, if you grew up in India where cows are sacred, what would the word "cow" mean to you then? I am not sure I can even guess. I do not know because it is not in my experience. Because they use the same language, speaker and listener may think they are communicating, when, in fact, they are not. Testing messages carefully with local listeners is clearly essential when marketing across cultures.

Connotation.   It is important to notice that words communicate a dictionary level of meaning, their denotation, and also additional meanings related to when they are used, subtle nuances of connotation. For instance, to refer to someone as a "cow" in English implies that the person is fat, slow and passive, while in French, to call a person a "vache," French for cow, implies instead that the person is mean and nasty. In general, English words, compared to French, contain far more additional meanings of connotation produced by subtle variations in context, inflection, or emphasis. That is why French is generally preferred as an international negotiating language. The point was expressed by Joseph Conrad, whose native language was Polish, but who was considered a master craftsman in the way he used English. He said he wrote originally in French to get the meaning down but translated his own work into English before publication to add richness and depth. The point for English speakers is, "Watch your connotations."

Metamessages.   Tannen points out that messages, whether verbal or nonverbal, carry additional meaning which she calls **metamessages**. By this she means "information about the relations among the people involved, and their attitudes toward what they are saying or doing, and the people they are saying or doing it to" (Tannen, 1990, p. 32). For example, a person who says, "Here, let me do that," may intend the message, "I want to be helpful," but may also be communicating, "You can't do it right," and "I am more competent than you." Just what metamessages are communicated depends particularly on the relative status of the people involved, and also on the tone of voice, facial expressions at the time, gestures, and the total context. Tannen stresses that much of the misunderstanding that takes place between the sexes is the result of different interpretations of messages. Women focus more on community, whereas men focus more on status. For example, women often hear an invitation to more intimate talk and an exchange of feelings in a statement, whereas men hear a request for information or advice on solving a problem. Thus women are frustrated when men offer a solution and then turn away, and men do not understand why their advice was asked for, if the woman is not interested in hearing it. The communication of metamessages may be an important element in phrasing advertising directed at men or women, but this is a relatively unexplored area in research.

Detailed study of connotation and metamessages is beyond our scope here but would be well worth the time for anyone who deals primarily in communication. For Americans in international trade especially, the lessons of language need to be emphasized. Although the United States is made up of many cultures, we are isolated from other countries much more than Europeans, and we are less aware of the subtle difficulties in using language. Our isolation can make us ignorant of foreign cultures and deaf to foreign advice.

Inference from Names.   Names are particularly rich with connotation. Hahari and McDavid (1973) conducted a study on the inferences drawn from first names. They asked fifth grade teachers to grade some essays actually written by fifth graders. They found that when essays were perceived as having been written by boys with the names Elmer or Hubert they were scored significantly lower than when perceived to have been written by David or Michael. They found the effect in experienced teachers, but not in college sophomores, which suggests that the teachers picked it up from their experience. It is not just personal names which carry connotation and produce inference. Names of products, brands and companies also do.

Brand Names.   In their excellent book on positioning, Ries and Trout provide many examples of effective and ineffective name selection from the marketing world. We shall draw on their work for much of what follows. Their findings are applications of the inferential process on which so much of perception is based, that is, we infer a considerable amount about a company or product after simply seeing or hearing the name. From a good brand name we infer that a new product with the same brand will also be of good quality. This is, of course, why brand names have such tremendous value, but Ries and Trout maintain that competition has become so fierce that brand names are no longer sufficient. The product name should also be a trigger to call a particular product to mind. It is no longer a battle of brands but also a battle of names.

A product name should tell what the product's main benefit is to position the product in the mind as the one product which does this particular task. Names which do not allow the hearer to infer anything are far less powerful. For example, Taster's Choice is a much more effective name than Maxim for an instant coffee. Maxim was supposed to trigger associations with Maxwell House, who produced it, but the connection is weak. Even if it does remind one of Maxwell House, it depends on the brand name Maxwell House already having the meaning "quality coffee" in the mind of the shopper. Taster's Choice, on the other hand, suggests quality coffee with no other connections necessary. We picture a panel of experts tasting all the instant coffees and selecting this as the best. We infer that a panel has selected it, but nobody says so. Ries and Trout maintain that this is the main reason why Taster's Choice was outselling Maxim 2 to 1, even though General Foods, who owns Maxim, invented the process and was the first on the market (Ries & Trout, 1986).

Today, the principle is more important than ever because of the increased information overload with which we are beset. Some of the brand names they singled out as particularly effective are DieHard batteries, Head and Shoulders shampoo, Intensive Care skin lotion, Close-Up toothpaste, and Shake'n Bake chicken treatment. The names are unique, so that they stand out from the competition, and they also tell what the product does, which creates an instant image in the mind the first time we hear it. This makes them more memorable. In contrast, they single out Breck One and Colgate 100 as particularly meaningless (Ries & Trout, 1986).

These authors also advise against the practice of extending the company name to cover each new product, a system used by Colgate, for example. You may gain something if the company name already means quality, but you may lose even more because the product is indistinct and lost in a group. To dominate a market, the product must be seen as uniquely better and must stand out from its competitors. In other words, Colgate tends to mean toothpaste, and confusion arises when it is applied to other products. Because the name does not bring these other products to mind, they lack a trigger in the mind of the consumer. On the other hand, Head and Shoulders brings to mind a specific product that has a specific attribute and thus is more powerful.

Kraft has found the best of both approaches in naming its new low-fat frozen dinners "Eating Right," while it retains the Kraft brand name, small but prominently displayed. This particular line of products illustrates another point about names of this sort. There may become so many, all creating a similar image though with different names, that similarity begins to set in, and their individual effectiveness is reduced. Now we have "Healthy Choice," "Healthy," "Right for Lunch," and "Eating Right." They all state what their main attribute is, but because the category has grown, the individuals no longer stand out.

Company Names.   Company names that are simply letters have no meaning either and are also poor triggers. Some initials are perceived as standing for a longer company name and so have meaning in that way. The best is example is IBM, short for International Business Machines, as everyone knows. IBM took on meaning because there were few such labels when it was established, and it stood out. But now, when there are many, there is less opportunity to establish the meaning of new combinations, and new initials are harder to recall. For more recent companies, the initials may not stand for anything meaningful. Sometimes this occurs because the company expands its function and the old name is no longer appropriate. Trying to retain some of their identity, they simply shorten the name to letters. For example, few remember that TRW originally meant the Thompson Ramo Wooldridge Corporation, but even if you do know this, does any image come to mind? So the company has engaged in a considerable effort to give its letters some meaning. The clever use of the word "TomoRroW" in their advertising helps tie the company into images of high tech and future growth, but can anyone tell what they do?

Other companies with less clever promotional schemes, like CPC, MEI, and AMP are fighting perpetual anonymity instead of establishing image. Ries and Trout tested the effect:

> We conducted a survey of both "name" and "initial" companies using a Business Week subscriber list. The results show the value of a name. The average awareness of the "initial" companies was 49 percent. The average awareness of a matched group of "name" companies was 68 percent, 19 percentage points higher (Ries & Trout, 1986).

Ries and Trout make another psychologically interesting point. They point out that a company name has a different meaning depending on your point of view. Names should be chosen from the consumer's point of view but are often chosen from management's. Colgate, as we have seen previously, is an example. Another they provide is from Cadillac. "Cadillac" to GM management means a production division. Therefore, producing cars of different types under that name makes sense. Hence, they produced Cimarron as a small, efficient, less expensive model. On the other hand, to the consumer "Cadillac" means big, luxury car. Thus, the name Cimarron produced confusion in the consumer from a contradiction of meaning. It cannot be seen as small and less expensive, while at the same time being seen as large and expensive. Thus, the consumer either inflates the value of Cimarron or deflates the value of Cadillac to resolve the apparent discrepancy. Either interpretation will ultimately hurt Cadillac sales. Thus, Cimarron was not well positioned. Sales were not strong, and it was dropped in 1988. Of the two meanings, management and consumer, that in the mind of the consumer is the important one, because it influences sales. In sum, brand names are more powerful if they are short, different, have a clear meaning, and are chosen from the consumer's point of view (Ries & Trout, 1986).

CHAPTER 4

Cognition, Reasoning, and Choosing

The topic of information processing is immense. It is often construed to include perception, learning, and memory. A distinction has been drawn between information processing (which is assumed to be cognition) and an affective choice mode (Mittal, 1988). We can see this in advertising where two appeals based either on cognition or on affect have developed. The predominately affective approach is called "value-expressive" after Katz (1960) and involves image more than function. It taps into psychological needs that people have, particularly self-image that we explore in chapter 10. The more cognitive approach is usually termed "utilitarian," again after Katz, and involves the presentation of information about product benefits and attributes. Which approach is the more effective depends on a number of factors we shall consider, but primarily on the type of product and the attention or involvement of the audience (Johar and Sirgy, 1991).

In general agreement with this division, we consider cognition in this chapter and affect in the next one, although, as Mittal has pointed out, it is impossible to separate them in actual product selection. Even with this separation, it is not possible to summarize all of the cognitive effects.

As an indication of the enormity of the problem, recall from the attention chapter that cognition can take place inwardly without paying attention to stimuli. For example, inward cognitive activities might include thinking about how a product would serve our purpose, trying to remember what the last brand we used was called, or remembering what we came to the store for. Cognition can also be outward, interacting with stimuli. The outward mode is exemplified when we are looking for information about a product, reading a label, or comparing features. We may be trying to determine the best product to use, gathering information about the attributes of several brands, or asking friends for their advice. Cognition without our awareness is more difficult to characterize and remains controversial (see Reber, 1993).

Rather than summarize the vast literature on memory and cognition, we have chosen to be very selective and to focus on selected aspects that are most relevant to the consumer field. In this chapter we look at parts of the learning/memory system in which the most fruitful research has been done.

GENERAL PRINCIPLES OF MEMORY

An earlier model, which has not been entirely dismissed by any means, describes the learning process as a series of three boxes. These are sensory memory, short-term memory and long-term memory. Information was conceptualized as moving from box to box, and rehearsal is the main device for keeping things active long enough to be permanently stored. Simply keeping the input active long enough was considered adequate for learning to take place.

Levels of Processing Theory

With the research of Craik and his colleagues in the early 70s (e.g., Craik & Watson, 1973, Craik & Lockhart, 1972), it became clear that rehearsal by itself was not sufficient to transfer information into long-term storage. Rather, the mechanism of transfer had to do with the level of processing that the material was given. Simple rehearsal became known as "maintenance rehearsal," and the type of rehearsal necessary for memory to take place was called **elaborative rehearsal**. This "elaboration" involved making connections between the new information and old memories already stored, that is, memory is organized and things are filed according to meanings. Then, meaning becomes understood as connections, associations with other material. The more connections to existing knowledge, the better our understanding. In other words, what elaborative rehearsal apparently does is to establish the associational links that allow for later retrieval. Without those links, it is a bit like looking for a card that has been randomly placed in a card file. It cannot be found.

It became clear, however, that elaboration is not a simple level, a level we either reach or fail to reach, as in the older boxes model, but rather varies with the amount of time and effort devoted to it. One can do a lot or a little elaborating. Thus, material can reach the elaborative level and still not be as well stored and retrieved as other material. One of the distinctions, for example, is between recognition and recall measurement. Recognition shows that much material that had little elaboration is still stored in long-term memory. It is not accessible to recall, however, apparently because not enough retrieval associations were made at the time of storage. Measurement by a recognition task, in other words, may show considerable memory, whereas measurement by a recall task does not. Clearly, however, material that can be recalled is more useful than material that can be only recognized because it can be manipulated and combined with other material in memory without the outside prompting that recognition takes. These additional associations are, indeed, what we know as "understanding." Elaboration, in other words, should not be seen as a single state, either it is done or it is not, but rather as a continuum in which more or less elaboration can be done. The more elaboration, the deeper the processing, and the better the understanding and recall later.

A study by Rogers, Kuiper, and Kirker (1977) supplies strong support for the role that increased elaboration plays in processing. Solso (1995) provides a concise summary:

> ... they asked subjects to evaluate a list of forty adjectives on one of four tasks hypothesized to vary in depth, or semantic richness. Included were structural, phonemic, and self-reference tasks. Typical cue questions were as follows:
>> Structural task; Big letters? (Adjective presented in the same size of type as the rest of question or twice the size.)
>> Phonemic task: Rhymes with? (Word did or did not rhyme with presented adjective.)
>> Semantic task: Means same as? (Word was or was not synonymous with presented adjective.)
>> Self-reference task: Describes you?
> As in the Craik and Tulving study, it was assumed that words more deeply coded during rating should be recalled better than those words with shallow coding. After the subjects rated the words, they were asked to free-recall as many of the words they had rated as possible. Recall was poorest for words rated structurally and ascended through those phonemically rated and semantically rated. Self-reference words were recalled best (pp. 171–173).

This study also illustrates how easily affect slips in to direct cognition. The affect in that simple reference to self was enough to influence recall, apparently by increasing the amount of elaboration. As we see in the next chapter, affect in the form of involvement is one of the main sources of motivation for elaboration.

Words Versus Images

It is clear from the literature that words and pictures are not processed in the same way. Images are processed primarily by the right side of the cerebral cortex and are perceived rapidly and all at once. In fact, the right hemisphere is often spoken of as a simultaneous processor. Verbal material, on the other hand, is processed primarily in sequence in the left hemisphere, that is, sounds and letters have no meaning until put together with other sounds or other letters to form words, sentences, and paragraphs. Hence, the left hemisphere is spoken of as a sequential processor. Words and images have different impacts on memory and on attitudes. We return to the attitudinal implications in the next two chapters. Here we want to consider the effects on memory.

Pictures Aid Memory. In general, pictures are remembered better than words (Alesandrini, 1982). More recently, Macklin (1994a) found no difference in audio and visual information presented separately to preschoolers. The reason for the discrepancy is probably the difference between recognition and recall as measurements. Pictures are certainly easier to recognize, but information presented in picture form may not fare better than information presented verbally. Macklin was testing recall of information and concluded that comprehensibility is the critical factor.

Because of their superior recognizability, ads which contain a picture are recognized better than ads without. John and Cole (1986) reported that this is true for the elderly and younger adults. Macklin (1994b) also found that pictures aid memory when they accompany verbal material.

Three factors probably contribute to this effect. Kiselius (1982) argued that pictures lead to greater elaboration and supported her claim by showing that sentences of brand information are recalled better when they are accompanied with a picture than when they are not. She assumes, not unreasonably, that since more verbal material is recalled, more elaboration must have gone on. Because pictures are easier to remember, it is likely that they help trigger the recall of the more difficult material to which they are attached. The association that forms this trigger must have been elaborated, though perhaps at a very low level.

A second explanation would argue that it is not necessarily more elaboration but more efficient elaboration. Pictures are generally complex assemblages of stimuli all of which have meaning already. If they did not, the picture would not be recognized. Words, on the other hand, tend to be more simple, and because they are processed sequentially, a number of words are required to convey the same information that is in a picture. The saying, "one picture is worth a thousand words" reflects this difference. Thus, in a short time pictures can be expected to generally tap into much more already-stored information, and this may be what makes them easier to recognize. In other words, tapping into a picture, taps into more meaning. This is essentially a cognitive advantage. Consistent with this interpretation, Kieras (1978) found that pictures stimulate thoughts, and thoughts preserve features about the object.

A third factor is affect content. Pictures are very effective at transmitting affect because affect is part of the "already-stored" information into which pictures tap. It may be that they are remembered better, therefore, because they carry affect in addition to cognitive information. Neither of these latter explanations require more elaboration, just more effective elaboration. In other words, if I establish a link to a concept that already has many other associations, this is a more efficient link than that to a relatively isolated concept.

A study by Mitchell and Olson (1981) illustrates both cognitive and affective qualities. We will use the summary of Edell and Staelin (1983):

> Each subject saw four advertisements, each for a different brand of fictitious facial tissue. The advertisements contained only one element (a picture or a verbal claim) and the brand name. Subjects saw the advertisements between two and eight times. The verbal claim was "Brand I Facial Tissues are Soft." The pictures were of a "fluffy kitten," a "spectacular sunset over an ocean," and "a presumably neutral picture of an abstract painting." In this instance the ad containing the drawing of a kitten ... was found to yield more favorable beliefs that the brand was very soft and came in more attractive colors than was the verbal message without a picture. Moreover, the overall brand attitude for the facial tissue advertised using the kitten picture was found to be more positive (p. 46).

The change in beliefs that Mitchell and Olson found is cognition, and the change in the overall brand attitude is affect. Both were produced by adding a picture to the verbal message about the brand. The remembrance of a "fluffy kitten" is clearly packed with both cognitions and affect in a way that the word "soft" by itself is not. Soft is general, in that there are many kinds of soft: soft water, soft lights, soft music, and each is a different sense system. Kittens are very specific, in that their softness is one of touch, and is the one the advertiser wants to connect to tissues. The picture, being seen first, tunes the cognitions to interpret the words consistently. In other words, the kitten picture directs elaboration more efficiently.

Picture "Framing."   Edell and Staelin (1983) did their own study to understand this relationship better. (The term "framing" will have a second meaning later in the chapter.) As used here, **framing** means the restatement in a verbal form of the pictorial information. A phrase or sentence that accompanies a picture calls attention to the aspect of the picture that is intended in the ad. For example, when the phrase "Soft as a sunset," frames (occurs with) a picture of sea, surf, a beach, lovers, and sunset, it calls our attention to the sunset, rather than all the other things present, and by making a connection between the softness of the product and the affect of the scene, pulls us back to think about the product. Without the frame, the picture may very well distract from brand information processing and draw us away from the written content. Confirming this, Edell & Staelin found that subjects produce fewer thoughts related to the brand, and thus, less brand information, when pictures are unframed. "The number of items recalled about the ad was smallest for verbal ads (with no picture), followed by the unframed picture, and then the framed picture." (p. 55) The authors caution that these were new not known brands. In the latter case, the brand name alone may provide its own framing, because so much is already known about it.

Picture-Message Congruency.   In general, when two channels of information carry the same message, there is increased processing of the message. On the other hand, if the channels are discrepant, then the message suffers. For example, Kellaris, Cox, & Cox (1993) found that if the nonverbal message of music differs from that delivered verbally by the message, the message retention suffers. On the other hand, Houston, Childers, & Heckler (1987) found that memory is better for ads in which the picture and the words are discrepant. This seems to happen only in ads which are interactive, that is, in which the picture portrays some attribute of the brand and the verbal part presents a different attribute. In other words, both sources are still related to the brand. They hypothesize that the picture is likely to be attended to first and that it will establish an expectancy for the verbal part. When that expectancy is not fulfilled, there is an increase in elaborative processing to resolve the discrepancy. Both sources contribute to information about the brand, however, so that this is not the same situation in which the verbal part is about the brand and the picture is not.

Uniqueness

There is general agreement that unique things are easier to remember. Memory research has shown that the unusual item is remembered better than the others in a list, a phenomenon called the Von Restorff effect (Lutz, 1994). In chapter two we discussed that novelty increases attention, and it should not be surprising that it also increases memory. For example, the various novelty-producing techniques reported by MacInnis, Moorman, & Jaworski (1991), and noted in chapter two, generally increase recall of ads, and increase attention.

The same principles are at work in more complex social situations. For example, the schema that people evoke in a given situation is likely to be that which distinguishes them from others (Fiske & Taylor, 1991). In other words, we are known by our dominant characteristic. When we see Michael Jordan, we think of him as a basketball player, even though he also has other roles, such as a promoter of social goals, products, or businesses, and even a baseball player. Similarly, a given image or a brand name can call up a number of schemas, depending on the moment, but the most unique schema tends to be called up first. When a Tylenol bottle was used to deliver poison to someone, Tylenol became remembered for that incident for years, in spite of their millions of other uneventful sales. Similarly, Exxon is still remembered for the Valdez oil spill, and "Wrong Way" Corrigan was not remembered for his many runs in the right direction.

INFERENCES OF REASONING

Logic

Ever since Aristotle worked out the rules of the syllogism, there has been a tendency, even a desire, to perceive ourselves as essentially logical thinkers. With the advent of the study of cognition in the 50s, however, there has been a growing body of studies that indicate that, although we may think logically sometimes, most of the time we violate the rules of logic in favor of other principles. For instance, many times we tend to ignore logic when our beliefs and prior knowledge conflict with logical conclusions. This tendency may be considered reasonable if it is free of contradictions (see Dawes, 1988), but it cannot be considered logical, because logic involves a very specific application of rules to reach conclusions. In popular discourse we find that the terms reasonable and logical are often used as synonyms, but they are not actually the same.

Deductive logic is a system of rules that enable drawing true conclusions from true propositions. If your starting propositions are true, the rules guarantee that your conclusion is also true. This is a classic example of the common syllogistic form that may date from the days of Aristotle:

> All men are mortal.
> Socrates is a man.
> Therefore, Socrates is mortal.

However, we will bypass an introduction to logic here and go on to processes that are more important to us. As Reber (1993) expresses it:

> During the 1970s ... it became increasingly apparent that people do not typically solve problems, make decisions, or reach conclusions using the kinds of standard, conscious, and rational processes that they were more or less assumed to be using.... The important insight was that, when people were observed making choices ... the rational and the logical elements were often missing. (p. 13)

Departures from Logic

Many times we are not able to evaluate the truth of propositions or premises and hence cannot know the truth of the conclusion, regardless of the logic. This severe limitation of logic may be one reason why we end up bypassing logic so often. Other reasons are summarized by Solso (1991), and we shall follow his analysis here.

Form.   We often tend to follow the general impression of the argument rather than its logical content. Hence, if both premises are positive, we tend to accept a positive conclusion. Begg and Denny (1969) tested and confirmed this tendency and found that this principle is operating: only when at least one premise is negative is a conclusion negative. A study by the Consumer Product Safety Commission of people buying toys for young children age two illustrates this principle in practice. Forty-four percent said they would buy a item labeled "recommended for 3 and up", but only 5% would buy it if it were labeled "not recommended for below 3—small parts." (Gest, 1992) This study suggests that when a warning is positive, as in the first form, the resulting behavior is likely be positive, regardless of what is said. In this particular case, where the purchases were for very young children, the desired behavior for these consumers was negative, and it was brought about in a larger number of cases by the negative warning. Note that this is a two-edged sword, for although the desired behavior of those buying for children under three is negative, the desired behavior for those buying for children over three is positive, and the negative warning would doubtless reduce their buying behavior somewhat. Manufacturers clearly have a decision to make here.

The study has a flaw, however, in that the two messages do not differ in only one aspect, but in two so that these two variables are confounded. The negative message, in other words, is not only negative, but also adds an explanation, "small parts." It might well be the case that people heed it more, not because it is negative, but because there is a rationale for their expected behavior. A number of studies in the human factors field show that when reasons are given, people are more likely to comply. Because of the design we cannot be sure which factor, or perhaps both, contributes to the different behavior.

Imagery.   When syllogistic statements are high in imagery and relatedness, they are solved significantly better than other forms (Clement & Falmagne, 1986). In other words, we are better able to manipulate concepts, just as we are better able to remember them, when they represent real objects or the relationship between real objects because imagery, one of our most powerful aids, is much harder with abstracts. For example, try to picture "running" without picturing the runner.

The lesson from this principle is that if you want people to follow your reasoning, make it as concrete as possible. For example, consider how parables do this. We find it hard to communicate the abstract "love," but people can abstract it for themselves, if you give them a number of concrete examples that contain it. We say in effect, "Find the commonality in all these stories," and people can do that, as we discussed in the last chapter. In fact, ads often lead us to abstract a commonality without knowing. For example, in successive beer ads, we see images of similar social occasions, and we abstract out of these the constant elements, beer, good-fun, and lively social times with friends. The strong imagery short-circuits our logic and we conclude that these constants, beer and good times, usually go together, and even indeed that beer causes the good times. The strong images seem to shift our thinking from "sometimes" to "most of the time," yet no one actually says this.

Misunderstanding Premises.   Ceraso and Provitera (1971) identified misunderstanding of premises as a major source of errors in syllogistic reasoning. For example, "All A are B" is understood (incorrectly) to mean that A and B are equivalent, that is, that "All B are A" is also true when, of course, there could logically be many B that were not A. We are led to do this in advertising. For example, what is implied by the statement, "The most beautiful women in the world wear Lejaby?" It is ambiguous as to whether all of these women or only some of them wear this brand. We are supposed to read it as all, and thus it is a form of "All A are B." But then do we not compound our error by inferring that all women who wear Lejaby are beautiful ("All B are A"), though logically, the most ugly women could also wear it? And even if all the most beautiful women do wear it, there is no necessary causal connection stated, so that wearing it may be coincidental to their beauty, rather than a contributor as we are likely to infer. Statements, such as these, work because our faulty logic leads us to make false inferences predictably.

We see a similar error frequently used to advantage in advertising when the phrase "There is none better than A" is taken by readers to be equivalent to "A is better than all others", when it could equally well mean (and probably does mean), "There is no difference between A and all the others."

Further misunderstanding may lurk in the terms "always" and "never" because they are typically not used precisely in popular discourse. "Always" as used in popular speech means "frequently" or "very often", as in, "You always slam the door!" Similarly, "never" tends to mean only "seldom", or "not often enough," as in, "You never say thank you for anything!" Thus, it would not be surprising to find that these words lead to misunderstanding when required in logical thinking. We perceive them to mean "sometimes" instead of their precise literal meanings.

Conflict with Previous Knowledge.   When a logical conclusion runs counter to what we already know, then we tend to choose a conclusion that is consistent with what we know and ignore the logic. We choose consistency with previous knowledge over consistency of argument. Solso provides an example:

> All men are moral.
> Hitler is a man.
> Therefore Hitler is moral (p. 419).

Most people would reject this conclusion, though it follows logically from the premises. The error has a common sense appeal, for if we already know that something is the case and our minds are made up, why spend the time and effort to derive it logically, and why spend time looking for an error in the logic? Similarly, subjects tend to accept the conclusion of an invalid syllogism if the conclusion is consistent with their own attitude (Janis & Frick, 1943). Uneducated people particularly tend to ignore logical argument in favor of concrete everyday knowledge (Cole & Scribner, 1977).

Trusted Source. Just as we tend to ignore logic when it conflicts with our own attitudes or knowledge, so we ignore logic in favor of authorities or appeals in which we believe, probably to maintain cognitive consistency. As Baron (1988) points out, it makes sense to believe authorities because they can be assumed to know more than others on particular topics. The assumption can, of course, be wrong. However, we believe known authorities and also people we like. For example, my grandmother had great faith in The Philadelphia Inquirer. I can remember her stout assertion that "It must be true, or they wouldn't print it." Others place their faith in the roles that actors play, particularly when they dress as doctors. Consider that during the five years when Robert Young played Dr. Marcus Welby on television, the actor received more than 250,000 letters asking him for medical advice (Levin, 1990).

Attacks on speakers, instead of against their arguments (called ad hominum arguments), are really attempts to use this tendency. Because it is hard to trust an argument from a speaker we do not trust, if we can make the speaker seem untrustworthy, then the speaker's argument will be discounted. These errors are not necessarily unreasonable, but simply not logical.

If we do not always use logic, then what is it that enables us to get along in the world as well as we do? The answer is heuristics, and we turn to these now.

Heuristics: Alternatives to Logic

Most of the short cuts we take in our reasoning process are the result of experience. When a short cut works for us, we tend to try it again when the situation returns. These short cuts and rules-of-thumb are called **heuristics**. Many of the mistakes we make in logical thinking are in fact heuristics that enable us to think faster and still be correct a fair portion of the time. They do not always work, but we seem to accept this in return for their much faster operation and reduced cognitive effort. Let us look at some marketing-related examples.

Size Means Value. A commonly used shopping heuristic is that "the larger size is a better value." With the advent of unit pricing, it became clear that this heuristic is not always true. Yet it is also clear that many people ignore the information provided by unit pricing and still buy the larger, even when they are sometimes actually penalized for doing so. For these people, the utility of the heuristic as a time-saver may be outweighing the inconvenience of taking time to check. Others, of course, may be willing to spend more to reduce the amount of packaging material.

Another way this heuristic appears is in the packaging of individual products. They are often packaged to look as though they contain more than they do. Taller bottles, for instance, look as though they hold more than short ones, and if the prices also differ, then it may be difficult to evaluate the better buy. Furthermore, if the product in each bottle were the same, then it would make sense to choose the larger, but often the larger amount is less efficient than the smaller. House brand detergents are sometimes more watery and thus require one to use more each time for the same results. In this case a smaller amount at the same price might in fact be a better value.

Sales Volume Means Quality.   A second shopping heuristic is that "larger volume of sales means products are better quality." Solso (1991) calls this the "majority must be right" appeal, and claims it as the basis for phrases like, "Ten million Americans use 'Zapo' deodorant, so it must be good," or the familiar advertising boast that "X is the best selling brand." (p. 420) Examples are not hard to find. For instance, the headline in a Ford Taurus ad says, "We made it the best Taurus ever. You made it America's best-selling car. Again." Notice that this ad is reinforcing the connection by inferring that the high quality made it the best selling.

High volume of advertising (as opposed to sales) also communicates the implication of high quality (Zeithamel, 1988) perhaps because we equate advertising volume with sales volume. Hence, when we are in doubt, we are likely to choose the brand we have seen advertised the most.

Price Means Quality.   A third shopping heuristic shows up in our tendency to think that "higher priced items are of better quality." Applying this heuristic is usually far quicker than asking friends, going to the library to consult Consumer Reports, or sometimes simply reading the labels. This means that, faced with uncertainty about products and wanting high quality, we tend to buy the more expensive item. Ogilvy (1985) confirms this tendency and gives us an unusual example. He writes, "In a study of the causes of inflation, the French Government cut thousands of cheeses in half and put them on sale. One half were marked 37 centimes, the other 56 centimes. The higher-priced cheese sold faster. Customers judge the quality of a product by its price." (p. 164)

Just when we use this heuristic is complicated, however. Zeithamel (1987) found that it is not always used and the tendency differs with individuals, with product category, and with the amount of other quality-indicating cues available. When other perceptual cues to quality, such as brand name or store image, are available, they may be chosen instead as cues more reliable than price. Being in a hurry reduces our ability to process other cues, and this may be when we are most likely to fall back on price.

How often is this heuristic true? Certainly not always. Zeithamel (1987), having reviewed the research, concludes that the relationship between price and objective quality is often low, absent, or even negative. Still, the research is not complete, and doubtless there are areas where it holds.

DISTORTIONS OF INFERENCE

Errors of Probability Assessment

The research team of Kahneman and Tversky have been the most influential in uncovering the process by which people judge probabilities. Nearly every event in the world is predictable only at a level of probability. Almost nothing happens with complete certainty. That the sun will come up tomorrow has a very high probability, so high I can regard it as certain. On the other hand, whether I will be around to see it has a decidedly lower probability, but still fairly high, I hope. On the other hand, how high a probability would you ascribe to the question of whether an electric can opener will work without fail for five years? We ascribe such probabilities whenever we buy a product, so that the process holds particular interest in the consumer field. Kahneman and Tversky have inspired considerable research on the difficult question of how we evaluate probabilities when making decisions. It turns out that we are not very good at it and often make mistakes. We look at some of them now.

Representativeness Heuristic. In chapter 2 we discussed the perceptual tendency to categorize things according to qualities in which they are similar. Tversky and Kahneman (1974) found that having done that, then we judge their probability of occurrence by how well they seem to represent the larger class. They called this tendency the **representativeness heuristic.** For example, we judge that the sequence of a tossed coin HHHHHTTTTT belongs to the class of highly structured things and thus is not likely to happen by chance alone. At the same time, we judge that the sequence HTTHHTHTHT looks like randomness and therefore is likely to occur by chance. But the likelihood that these two sequences occur is actually identical. In other words, we judge by a class, rather than the case, not checking to see if the case matches the class in the significant respects.

We can begin to get a sense of the importance of this heuristic in an example from Dawes (1988). He points out that "characteristics access schemas, which in turn access other characteristics (all through association)." (p. 69) His example goes like this. An admissions committee notes that an applicant has misspelled a word and without thinking perhaps labels the applicant dyslexic. Then, they compound the error by concluding that the person has other characteristics of dyslexics, for instance, difficulty in school, and reject the applicant from their academic program. Difficulty in school does not logically follow from a single misspelling. The error is that there is a much larger group of people who also misspell and who are not dyslexic. We overlook it because misspelling does not seem to be very representative of them. In other words, misspelling seems to represent the class called dyslexics better than it represents nondyslexics. Thus, the committee judged that it is highly likely that a misspeller is in the class dyslexic, even though misspelling a single word matches the characteristics of the class nondyslexic just as well.

A second error is also involved. The class nondyslexic is so much bigger than the other class that it makes membership in the class nondyslexic actually much more likely. The probability error of not taking the size of the classes into account is called ignoring the base rate. Incidentally, we are not dealing here with the third error, that not all dyslexics have difficulty in school. That is yet another issue.

Consider an example from the consumer world. Take the term "imported." There are individuals who buy only imported wine because they feel that this term guarantees quality. The term has come to represent the class of good wines so strongly that they forget there is a bigger class of imported wines that are not particularly good at all. The term itself tells you nothing about quality, just as the misspelling of a word also tells you very little about the individual. If the class of poor imported wines is bigger than that of imported good wines, which it probably is, then by using the term "imported" alone, you are more likely to get poor wine than good.

Availability Heuristic. In general, when people reason, they are likely to assume that things that come to mind readily are more common occurrences than things that do not. This tendency was labeled the **availability heuristic** by Tversky and Kahneman (1973), using the term "available" to mean that something comes readily to mind. As we have seen in both attention and attribution theory, numerous factors influence how readily things come to mind. For example, most people think that death by murder is more likely than death by suicide, probably because murders are more widely publicized (Combs & Slovic, 1979). Availability changes our perception of probability.

The principle of availability is introduced into advertising by repetition. Repetition in advertising does not really convey much information to the listener. Assuming that an ad is heard clearly and understood the first time, what information is gained by hearing it again? Although not much information is gained, however, a lot of availability is gained. Repetition aids memory, and a second factor, called recency, becomes important. Things you have heard more recently are remembered better than things heard longer ago. Because repetition means that it will have been a shorter time since the listener heard the brand name, it will be better remembered. Both of these factors mean that a repeatedly advertised brand name will come to mind more easily than another.

Then, the availability heuristic predicts that the brand that comes to mind readily tends to be regarded as more likely to occur. In other words, it is the availability heuristic that makes heavily advertised brands seem more widely used. Putting this with our shopping heuristic, that "Better selling products are generally better in quality," means that we perceive that the repeatedly advertised brand has better quality from simply hearing it many times. This is one of the little known values of advertising.

Perhaps the same thing happens with in-store displays. Because these displays are present when many shopping decisions are made, they have tremendously increased availability at just the right moment. Products thus displayed can be expected to be judged as more common brands and hence of better quality.

Word-of-mouth is an important way we form attitudes about things. It may be that the judgments and attitudes of friends become so important to decision making because they are so available to our minds. Thus, "Mary says" may in our minds become "everyone says" because of the availability heuristic.

Yet another way that the availability heuristic appears is in our construction of causal scenarios (Tversky & Kahneman, 1973). A causal scenario occurs when we imagine ourselves engaged in a sequence of events leading from a particular situation to a particular outcome. We base our estimate of the likelihood of the outcome by the ease with which the causal scenario was brought to mind, the ease with which we can picture ourselves doing it. For example, if you can easily imagine yourself becoming an accountant with all the intervening steps that entails but cannot imagine yourself doing all the things necessary to become a world class tennis player, then you will judge the likelihood of becoming the accountant as higher than that of becoming the tennis player.

Gregory, Cialdini, and Carpenter (1982) put the notion of causal scenarios to the test, and their data supported the availability hypothesis. They had subjects read scenarios in which a person is arrested. Half the subjects were also to imagine it happening to themselves. Those with the imagining component judged that the likelihood of such an event happening to themselves was higher than did the controls.

These researchers then went further to see if the likelihood of happening also translates to actual behavior. They found out that indeed it can, as shown by their follow-up study. Two groups were created. One, the information-only group, heard passages like the following:

> CATV will provide a broader entertainment and informational service to its subscribers. Used properly, a person can plan in advance to enjoy events offered. Instead of spending money on the babysitter and gas, and putting up with the hassles of "going out," more time can be spent at home with family, alone, or with friends (p. 95).

The second group, the imagination group, on the other hand, heard passages like the following instead:

> Take a moment and imagine how CATV will provide you with a broader entertainment and informational service. When you use it properly, you will be able to plan in advance which of the events offered you wish to enjoy. Take a moment and think of how, instead of spending money on the babysitter and gas, and having to put up with the hassles of "going out," you will be able to spend your time at home, with your family, alone, or with your friends (p. 95).

Of the imagination-group subjects, 47.4% later subscribed to the CATV service, while of the information-only-group, only 19.5% did, a huge 27.9% difference (Gregory et al., 1982). We know that the request to imagine aids memory, and it apparently influences behavior as well.

Anchoring and Adjustment Heuristic.   The strategy of judgment called the **anchoring and adjustment heuristic** involves two steps. First, an arbitrarily chosen reference point (called the anchor) strongly influences estimates of value. Second, adjustments are made away from the anchor toward the true value, but the adjustments are generally insufficient (Slovic & Lichtenstein, 1971).

In one test of this principle, Davis, Hoch, and Ragsdale (1986) found that people were not accurate in predicting the buying preferences of their spouses for 20 new product concepts. They concluded from their analysis that people anchor on their own preferences and then adjust, often inappropriately, for their spouse. Anchoring on their own preferences is an appropriate strategy because, on average, spouses are more similar to each other than to other people, but 42% would have been more accurate in their estimates of their spouses preferences, if they left it at that. In trying to adjust their anchor point, they made their estimates worse. "Only 53% of the subjects outperformed a hypothetical forecaster who simply predicted the average sex-specific preference for each of the products." (p. 33) The authors suggest that the "anchoring and adjustment strategy would appear to underlie most of our predictions about other people, whether they be spouses, best friends, colleagues, or for that matter, complete strangers (such as the 'average' consumer)." (p. 35) We like to think of ourselves as average and typical, but, in fact, we are often not.

Northcraft and Neale (1986) sought to try out the concept of anchoring and adjustment in a real-world setting and chose the purchasing of residential real estate. They chose this "product" because the fair market value is not objectively determinable and a bidding process is used to arrive at the property's actual selling price. Their findings were consistent with the use of the anchoring and adjustment heuristic, in which the listing price serves as the anchor. Groups, which are given the same information except for a different listing price (that is, anchor), produced estimates that were significantly biased in the direction of the anchor.

The same tendency is exploited by auctioneers who begin the bidding by saying, "Who'll open the bidding at 300 dollars?," and retailers who tag their shirts with, "Compare at $27.00." Rachlin (1989) argues that the principles of anchoring and adjustment are also the reason why first impressions of people are so hard to change. He points out, "we form initial impressions of an individual on the basis of immediate evidence and often do not adjust that impression sufficiently ... by considering later-arriving facts." (p. 61) To refer back to an earlier term, first impressions seem to make instant "personas," and these are highly resistant to change. One possible reason may be that impressions are affectively based when first made, and the adjustments are cognitive. Anchors may also tap into this second evaluation system.

Framing Heuristic: Gains Versus Losses. Tversky and Kahneman (1974) showed that the way a proposition is worded makes a difference in how its probability is assessed. They called this the **framing heuristic**. It is a second meaning of the term "framing" we encountered earlier. There it meant a picture setting the meaning for words, whereas here it is the order of words setting meaning. One of their examples will illustrate the principle. Imagine that the U.S. is preparing for the outbreak of an unusual Asian disease that is expected to kill 600 people. Two alternative programs have been proposed. Assume that the exact scientific estimate of the consequences of the programs is as follows:

If Program A is adopted, 200 people will be saved.
If Program B is adopted, there is a one-third probability that 600 people will be saved and a two-thirds probability that no people will be saved.

When the question "Which program would you adopt?" was put to their group of university students, 72% chose Program A. Then, the same question was put to another group of students, using the same scenario, but the wording was now as follows:

If Program C is adopted, 400 people will die.
If Program D is adopted, there is a one-third probability that nobody will die, and a two-thirds probability that 600 people will die.

Given this new choice, 78% of the students chose Program D, whereas only 22% chose Program C. The wording of the alternatives changed the choices made, yet the two versions are identical (Tversky & Kahneman, 1974).

From this and similar studies, we find that when people are presented with a problem phrased in terms of gaining, whether money or lives, they tend to choose the "sure thing," that is, to avoid risk. On the other hand, when the problem is presented in terms of losses, people tend to avoid certain loss by choosing risk. This principle became known as prospect theory (Kahneman & Tversky, 1979) and simply says that people are more likely to avoid risk when a message is framed positively than when it is framed negatively. In a positive frame we are told what we will gain, whereas in a negative frame we are told what we will avoid losing. In other words, to choose to save 200 seems better than choosing to allow 400 to die. That is, saving 200 seems better than losing 400, even though with a base of 600 they are identical.

This principle may be the reason that a statement of price (price being a form of loss) does not work as well as a statement of the saving (saving being a gain), and bargains seem so much more valuable than they really are. For example, phrases such as "save 20%," or "save $3" are so common that "save" must be the word most often used in marketing. It is more important to us to know what the saving is than to know the price because we tend to focus on gains, not loss. This is why "97% fat free" is likely to sell more cold cuts than the equivalent, "3% fat."

You may have noticed that when we respond to "save 20%," we are focusing on gain, and we are also ignoring the base rate. We seem to assume that a markdown is from a standard price, and we often do not check to see. In a recent example, a local mattress company was found guilty of raising their prices just before a sale, so that what appeared to be a sale was really regular price. Such a scheme is illegal, but the reason it must be made illegal is that it works so well.

Another application of framing is suggested by Dawes (1988) in the case of seat belts that people are often reluctant to use. Perhaps they are seeing it as a case of a very small chance of either gain or loss. More people might see use of seat belts as a desirable option, if it were presented to them rather as a case in which all of the things you enjoy now, such as mobility and even life itself, are sure to be saved if you use seat belts, versus the way it is more often presented as a chance you could lose them if you do not. Then, a sure gain should be chosen over a possible loss. The problem, in other words, is that we are not seeing it as a sure gain but as an unlikely gain. Similarly, life insurance is better presented as a means to a sure saving of all you have, rather than as an avoidance of a possible loss.

Endowment Effect.   When a person already owns an object, (that is, it is part of their "endowment") it apparently has more value to them than if they were bargaining to acquire it. They require more money to part with it than they would pay to acquire it (Thaler, 1980) because losses are felt more strongly than equivalent gains (Kahneman, Knetsch, & Thaler, 1990).

Hirsch (1996), writing about a conference on behavioral economics and typical attitudes toward investing, has given additional support to this finding and measured the amount of this discrepancy in a simple example. He says that

> People ... feel the pain of financial loss more acutely than the pleasure of financial gain. In studies, people are given $10 and asked to bet on a coin toss. If it's tails, they lose all $10. If it's heads they win. The question is, How much money do they have to win before they agree to the bet? Answer: About $25. Thus, people feel pain about 2.5 times more severely than pleasure, according to these studies. That hurts investment by breeding excessive caution (p. C1).

We certainly do seem to have an overstrong avoidance of the risk of loss. In chapter 10 we consider the notion that this may be a reasonable result of viewing our possessions as extensions of self.

Cognitive Consistency Theory

Sometimes it happens that the inferences drawn from a situation, whether from perception or memory, conflict with each other. Cognitive consistency theory, based on considerable empirical evidence, claims that when this happens, unpleasant psychological tension is created which leads to a cognitive reorganization to relieve or eliminate that tension by bringing the inferences into harmony. The human mind clearly demonstrates a strong cognitive need for consistency, but we often maintain our consistency at a cost of distortion. In other words, to classify things as similar they must contain similar characteristics, but because things—objects, products, people, companies—always contain many other characteristics, they usually contain some quite different characteristics along with those similar. Cognitive consistency theory predicts that we often tend to overlook or disregard those parts which do not fit our classification.

Halo Effect. As Heider noted, cognitive consistency means that we tend to see that good people do good things, good companies make good products, bad people do bad things, and so on, but this often leads to distortions. More specifically, a positive rating in one area often produces overgeneralization, also resulting in more positive ratings in other areas. The positive transfer is called the **halo effect**. For examples, Dion, Berscheid, and Walster (1972) found that the personalities of attractive people were judged to have more favorable qualities than unattractive people. Essays were judged to be better if the male judges thought they were written by attractive rather than unattractive females (Landy & Sigall, 1974). Job applicants are more likely to get the job, if they are physically attractive (Dipboye, Fromkin, & Wiback, 1975).

The converse effect, when someone who is labeled as bad is seen as having all bad qualities, has no common name, but both "negative halo effect" or "forked-tail effect" have been suggested (Sears, Freedman, & Peplau, 1985, p. 54). These companion tendencies mean that we are probably more generous in rating the products of a company that has a good reputation or that we respect over one we dislike. Our likes and dislikes of the company color our judgment of its products.

Well-established information, such as that on which a halo effect is based, is given more weight than new information, particularly weak or ambiguous information. Thus the halo effect has maximal effect when the established attitude is strong and the new information is somewhat ambiguous. When the established attitude is not particularly strong or the new information is more strongly positive or negative, the halo effect is not as strong.

These expressions of the need for cognitive consistency lie behind the whole field of public relations. We are far more likely to discount a mistake by a company that has a good reputation than one by a company with a bad one. Thus it is to a company's advantage to spend considerable sums polishing its image by advertising and other ways.

Other than public relations, the marketing area most relevant is probably that of brand name extension. When a brand name is known in relation to a single product, it develops a considerable force as it becomes familiar and respected. The argument for doing this is, of course, that having already established a reputation for quality, this reputation transfers easily to the new product and gives it a rapid start over the competition: the halo effect. A problem exists in the technique, however, because averaged attitudes tend toward mediocrity, and eventually overextended brands may become perceived as mediocre. More on this when we consider the topic of attitudes.

Memory Distortions. We have seen how we organize material in memory, and unconsciously form categories of similar things, but memory goes further than this. When we remember things, we also tend to distort our memory of them in the direction of the category in which they were placed, just as we do in perception because much of memory is actually reconstructed at the time of recall, not simply pulled out of storage. Osgood, Suci, and Tannenbaum (1957) did some of the classic work in this field. They showed that people would distort their memories of ambiguous figures in the direction of the label that was attached, that is, we often remember what things meant, not what they were. This means that, other factors being equal, we tend to see all members of a remembered group as approximately the same as we have said previously. It also means we will remember what we perceived that an ad means rather than what it actually said. We turn to this now.

False Inferences in Advertising

Some types of inferential errors may be made because words were misinterpreted when they were heard. For example, terms are used in advertising to suggest properties that are not really a necessary characteristic of the class. "Genuine" is one of these. We have seen it used with so many valuable things, like diamonds or gold, that we forget there is a much larger category of genuine trash. "Genuine" by itself means very little. Antique dealers, of course, know this and have been known to refer with a wink to "genuine simulated antiques."

Another example is found in the word "pure." On my shelf I have a bottle of Banana Boat Aloe Vera Gel, an excellent product, but it proclaims on the label "100% pure." On the back it says, "Ingredients: Aloe Vera Gel, SD Alcohol 40, Glycerin, Polysorbate-20, Carbomer, Triethanolamine, Methylparaben, Imidazolidinyl Urea, Benzophenone-4, FD&C Blue 1, FD&C Yellow 5, Natural Fragrance." Perhaps it means that pure aloe is added to the other ingredients, because it also says on the back, "Aloe Vera Gel-100% Pure plus stabilizers and required preservatives." By this reasoning anything might be 100% pure even though mixed with a host of contaminants. Does the word have any meaning used this way? It does make the product seem better.

Procter and Gamble's advertising of Ivory soap as "99 and 44/100ths % pure" carries the misleading inference one step further. It came from an early attempt to find out what all the elements in their soap were. Their lab tests were able to account for 99 and 44/100ths % of all the ingredients, but had nothing to do with quality, good or bad, nor did it refer to a single ingredient. However, the term "pure" seems to represent goodness, although there are equally large classes that are pure trash, pure evil, pure junk, or whatever. The slogan has been very effective and is still used, though the company never says pure what.

Another variant of mistaken inference occurs when people remember information as having been present, when they really add it at the time of recall (Matlin, 1989). This is really an extension of the perceptual tendency to construct what is not there. Much of the recent research has focused on the notion of schemata, scripts, and personas as sources of the inferred material. People are likely to infer details which are consistent with the other aspects of their memory of an event, even though the details never actually occurred.

Sometimes we remember the meaning without the specific sentences that contained the meaning (Flagg, Potts, & Reynolds, 1975). In the same way we tend to perceive meaning rather than the pieces which produced the meaning. In fact it may not be possible to determine whether the false inference took place at the perception or the memory level. It matters little, however, because the end is the same. When we draw inferences from an ad, perhaps about some characteristic that the product has, we simply remember that the ad itself said so, or we may remember even less and remember only that somebody said so.

The design of ads to capitalize on this trait and allow false inferences is an old game. The Federal Trade Commission explicitly forbids advertisers from making false claims, but the question of false inferences is quite vague. For instance, what inference do you find yourself making from this commercial?

> "Wouldn't it be great," asks the mother, "if you could make him coldproof? Well you can't. Nothing can do that. (Boy sneezes). But there is something you can do that may help. Have him gargle with Listerine Antiseptic. Listerine can't promise to keep him cold-free, but it may help him fight off colds. During the cold-catching season, have him gargle twice a day with full-strength Listerine. Watch his diet, see he gets plenty of sleep, and there's a good chance he'll have fewer colds, milder colds this year" (Harris, 1977).

Does Warner-Lambert claim that Listerine helps prevent colds?

Harris (1977) used this commercial in a research study, only changing the product name to "Gargoil." All 15 of his subjects checked on their response sheets that "gargling with Gargoil Antiseptic helps prevent colds," even though this claim was not actually made in the commercial. The false inference hinges on how you interpret the phrases "help him fight off" and "there's a good chance he'll have fewer colds, milder colds this year." One can perhaps "fight off" and not be successful, or one might argue that to "fight off" indicates one already has the cold. The fewer colds could be from the diet and sleep, also recommended. However, the courts apparently agreed that Warner-Lambert was implying a false claim because they decided against the company in this case.

Harris also reports research in which people heard some tape-recorded mock commercials. Some commercials directly made false claims about the product. Other commercials implied false claims but never directly stated them. For many commercials, including some based on actual television advertising, people did not distinguish between what they had actually heard and what they had inferred (Harris & Monaco, 1978).

Food and nutrition claims are particularly prone to deception. The Center for Science in the Public Interest wrote recently:

> Deceptive ads for foods or supplements are a dime a dozen. The Federal Trade Commission (FTC), which regulates ads, has a tough time keeping up. Here are a few of its recent actions. Several started with complaints by the Center for Science in the Public Interest (CSPI):
>
> - **Pizzeria Uno.** In January, the Boston-based restaurant chain agreed to stop advertising its line of "Thinzettas" as low-fat thin crust pizzas. Six of the eight "Thinzettas" were not low fat. Some had 36 grams of fat per serving.
> - **Ensure.** In January, the FTC ordered Abbott Labs to stop making unsubstantiated claims like "#1 Doctor Recommended" in ads for its liquid meal replacement. However, in March, CSPI complained that ads still imply that Ensure has everything in food that promotes health. The "Doctor Recommended" ads remain on TV.
> - **Gerber.** In March, Gerber agreed to stop claiming that four out of five pediatricians recommend its baby food. In fact, only 12% of pediatricians recommended Gerber. (Gerber left out doctors who did not recommend baby food at all and those who do not recommend specific brands.)
> - **Chromium Picolinate.** Nutrition 21 (the sole supplier of chromium picolinate), Body Gold (maker of Super Fat Burner Formula and other chromium supplements), and Universal Merchants (distributor of Chroma-trim chewing gum) agreed to stop claiming that chromium causes long-term weight loss, burns fat and builds muscle, raises metabolic rate, controls appetite, lowers blood cholesterol or blood sugar levels, or treats or prevents diabetes. Unfortunately, other companies can still make the same claims (Ad Nausea, 1997).

A good review of how claims can and cannot be worded can be found in Liebman (1997, September).

False Inference in the Media

Television programming and Hollywood movies reflect the same natural process of inferring a whole from a part. It is understandable that advertisers want to surround their product with popular, upbeat advertising images and that they want to associate their products with similar programming. Upbeat shows are more popular, and they also avoid the risk of a depressed or angry carryover from program to product. Thus, advertisers tend to prefer to sponsor popular shows, those that allow people to escape their dreary everyday worlds, and they are often reluctant to sponsor shows that are at all risky or downbeat. The networks, in turn, to find sponsors, reflect the advertisers bias in the programming they offer, even, it has been suggested, extending to the evening news. Hollywood too, though to a lesser extent today, has traditionally reflected a bias toward impossibly well-adjusted families and the happy ending. The distortion appears only in the aggregate. Taken all together these shows reflect a distorted picture of life in the United States.

Of course, television or movies are not legally required to reflect a balanced picture of life, but the distortion has social consequences all the same. Typical television homes are homes of the wealthy, and soap operas generally depict the very rich. The endless sitcoms, with a few exceptions such as "Roseanne," generally take place in large, spotlessly tidy houses, very well furnished and peopled by beautiful upper middle class families, whose clothes never become mussed or soiled. The unintended false inference from these shows is that we are viewing average people in average surroundings, and we can come to believe these houses represent the norm of our culture. Even more so, foreigners, whose only idea of the United States often comes from our movies and television, sometimes have a very strange concept of our country.

Action television is similar. The tremendously popular shows of action and violence, particularly those featuring car chases, explosions, fistfights, and gunplay, in which the good guys seldom get hit and seldom get hurt, are no more real than the sitcoms. For example, in Miami Vice the police detective drove a Ferrari. Even the evening news, whether it is coming via newspaper or television, is a selection of the day's most dramatic and violent events. Commenting on this, one sociologist writes:

Study after study shows Americans trust the authenticity of the images they see on the tube. In the process, however, heavy viewers often develop a distorted view of social reality. They tend to exaggerate, for example, the amount of violence they are likely to encounter in everyday life, the proportion of criminal cases that end in a jury trial, and the likelihood that physicians will perform miracle cures. For these viewers, the fantasy world on television becomes the reality.... Whenever a *Days of Our Lives* star either gives birth (it's only a pillow), gets married (a rhinestone wedding ring), or dies (usually a failure to re-negotiate the actor's contract), cards and gifts appear at the studio. (Levin, 1990)

As we have seen previously, the white coat of Marcus Welby along with the erudite dialogue have led viewers to infer falsely that the actor had the expertise of the physician. Now, the industry requires actors wearing characteristic white coats in commercials to say they are not doctors, but it is doubtful whether such a statement overcomes the power of the white coat. The number of letters, at the rate of 1000 a week, documents the strength of the illusion and the power of perceptual inference.

Disclaimers and Children

Because it works so well, false inference with children often takes the form of a picture that is disclaimed somewhere else. For instance, one case came to my attention in *Consumer Reports* expressed lightly in this way:

See Ken. Ken is a doll. He is made by Mattel Inc. See the box Ken came in. It has a picture of Ken. See Ken strutting down the beach. He has a frisbee in one hand. He has a soda can in his other hand. Why is Ken laughing? Read the itsy-bitsy print near the bottom of the box. It says, "Doll cannot hold accessories as shown." (A child's primer, 1989, October)

Raju and Lonial (1990) reviewed the topic of advertising to children and found that young children tend not to process the disclaimers that are added to their commercials to prevent false inferences. This means, of course, that young children can be expected to draw false inferences from much of their advertising. For example, they report a study that found the phrase "some assembly required" was not understood by six to eight year olds, whereas the same thing said in a different way, "you have to put it together," was. They point out that one study found 41% of children's advertising had visual or audio disclaimers, and another found that 33% had disclaimers. Breakfast cereals and toys were the biggest categories for disclaimer usage. They conclude:

> Most disclaimers used the audio format and used adult terminology such as "part of a nutritious breakfast," "fortified with vitamins and minerals," and "sold separately." Such terminology has a tendency to make disclaimers ineffective with children.... Stern and Resnik (1978) found that the visual impression created by a commercial on young children is so strong that an audio disclaimer is often not sufficient to correct for this misperception (p. 244).

Because the commercials continue to use phrases like "some assembly required," one can only speculate about their intentions.

MAKING CHOICES: COGNITIVE ELEMENTS

Major Decision Variables

Marketers used to speak as though typical consumers always gather factual information and reason out the best decision before all of their purchases. Thus, late nineteenth century ads were mostly verbal appeals to the virtues of a particular product, but the cognition-dominant view probably represents an ideal of human behavior that was seldom realized. In our approach to decision making, we have separated the two types of elements, cognitive and affective, but in fact it is probably not possible with real world decisions to determine when each type takes place, nor how important to the whole they were. In this chapter we consider the cognitive side of decision making, which certainly takes place sometimes, and in the next chapter we pick up the affective side, which is probably more common.

Decision making has been defined as "generating, evaluating, and selecting among a set of relevant choices, where the choices involve some uncertainty or risk." (Medin & Ross, 1992, p. 395) The topic is of considerable interest to marketers because most purchases are the result of two decisions: whether to buy or not and which brand to buy. What determines just how much deliberation (i.e., cognition) we put into a decision? A huge number of variables could be cited here, but we will limit ourselves to a few of the most important.

Elaboration Likelihood Model. One approach to the amount of cognition required is found in the **elaboration likelihood model** of Petty and Cacioppo (1981). They argue persuasively that involvement determines whether one elaborates about a product. Involvement is, of course, produced by affect, and as such, is a factor in attention and, as we shall see, in forming attitudes. Thus, the model suggests that involvement is an important factor in determining whether one applies an essentially cognitive mode (central) or low affective mode (peripheral) to a purchase decision. Rising affect tends to shift us to cognition. More on this in the next chapter.

For now, we can say that we are more cognitively involved when the risks are higher, for example, when spending a large sum of money and when there is personal relevance. Thus, high ticket items, such as homes, cars, and major appliances, are likely to produce more information gathering and longer deliberation. So are products publicly used, especially by people who are particularly sensitive to their image, like adolescents. On the other end of the scale, we do less cognitive deliberation on inexpensive items we buy frequently and use privately, such as detergents or deodorants, or daily foods like bread and milk. These are particularly susceptible to the forces of habit and affect and generate relatively little cognitive effort. Many times items will cost so little and brands may be so similar that we operate in a state that Langer (1989) calls mindlessness. This is essentially habit, that is, conditioning, at work.

Stages Theory.   The decision process changes as we become familiar with products and product classes. Howard (1977) has distinguished three stages of consumer decision making, but they are probably simply three places on a continuum rather than discrete stages. Position on the continuum is determined by degree of familiarity with the product.

He calls the first stage extensive problem solving, in which consumers need a great deal of information, because the whole class of products is new to them. He uses the example of instant coffee. When instant coffee was a new item, consumers needed more information to decide whether to buy it or not. They were not familiar with the characteristics which were going to be important to them. Consequently, they sought out information and made up their minds slowly.

Once consumers were familiar with the product class "instant coffee," they entered a limited problem solving stage. They have the criteria for decisions in mind and less information is needed. Now, they particularly need information about brands and how they differ. Finally, as instant coffee becomes commonly used, consumers settle on a favorite brand, and their behavior becomes routinized response behavior. In the third stage very little information is required, and consumers tend to buy the same brand each time, perhaps only checking price occasionally. Howard's stage theory means that cognitive effort varies with product familiarity and usage. Newer products require more cognition, and familiar ones require less.

Search Versus Experience Attributes.   Comparing attributes is basic to decision making, but it does not always proceed cognitively. Lutz

(1986) distinguishes between search attributes and experience attributes in a product. Search attributes are those that a consumer can assess before the purchase, and experience attributes are those assessed only during consumption. He claims that the greater the proportion of search attributes over experience attributes, the more likely that the appraisal of quality will be a cognitive judgment. On the other hand, as the proportion of experience attributes rises, judgment of quality is likely to be affective. Thus, he says, experience may be minimal for industrial products and consumer durables, and their quality is likely to be judged cognitively. On the other hand, experience is most important for services and nondurables, and their quality is likely to be judged affectively.

Noncompensatory Strategies in Choosing

Various strategies are apparently used by people faced with deciding which brand to buy. Noncompensatory strategies require that a product have certain attributes or be rejected. Compensatory strategies, on the other hand, allow having one attribute to compensate for the absence of another. Let us look at some of the approaches used.

Elimination by Aspects.   This is the strategy most commonly employed by consumers, probably because it is the easiest to do in your head. You choose the feature (aspect) that is most important to you, and you check across products, eliminating any which are unsatisfactory in this feature. Then, you go on to the next most important feature, compare all those left from the first round, and eliminate some more. You continue this process until only one product remains (Tversky, 1972).

The approach is also called the **lexicographic strategy**, so-called because of the similarity with alphabetizing in a dictionary. You sort words by the first letter, then within the resulting group by the second letter, and so forth. Some make minor differentiations between the two methods (Engel, Blackwell, & Miniard, 1986), but we will treat them as equivalent.

The procedure is easy because all you have to remember is the list of products still under consideration as you go along. You do not have to remember why products were rejected, nor why they were retained. Also, the strategy usually leads to a single choice, if pursued far enough. Furthermore, if the features are considered in the order of their desirability, the choice will be a reasonably good one, but if considered simply as they "come to mind," the procedure is "decidedly flawed." (Dawes, 1988)

Conjunctive Strategy.   In this approach, you work through the products one by one, considering all the features of each one. A product which is unsatisfactory in any feature is eliminated. In other words, evaluations of all of the features are combined, or cojoined. Note that the products are not rated or compared, but simply judged satisfactory or not. You may end up with more than one product, in which case you have to raise the criterion for elimination, add some new features, or change the method. Unfortunately, you may also end up with no satisfactory products, if none passes all tests. In this case the criterion for eliminating one of the features must be lowered, and the whole process repeated.

This strategy may take much longer than elimination by aspects because you have to start over each time you change the criterion. Moreover, you may have to change the criterion more than once. You must also repeat the test with all the products or remember which items failed on which feature when retesting. All of this makes it hard to do in your head. Its effectiveness also depends on choosing the right number of features to compare. Too few mean you cannot eliminate enough, and too many mean you eliminate them all. Adding or subtracting features is cumbersome, as opposed to elimination by aspects which simply adds them as needed. Sometimes the conjunctive strategy is used to eliminate a few choices before shifting to the elimination by aspects strategy for the final decision. This might be the case where a small number of features are all equally important.

Compensatory Strategies

These approaches may require pencil and paper. Here no one feature is critical. A product weak in one feature may still remain in contention by being strong in another feature, that is, strength in one feature may compensate for weakness in another, hence the name.

Simple Compensatory Strategy.   In this approach, the final decision is determined by an average of all of the features. Products may be simply noted as 1 or 0, that is, satisfactory in a feature or not, and a total, or perhaps an average, taken. On the other hand, they may all be rated as to how good each feature is on a scale of, say, 1 to 10. Because all products must be rated on all features and averages calculated, this strategy clearly takes more time and effort than the others. It has the additional problem that all features are treated as equally important, when in fact they seldom are in real-world decisions. To deal with this problem of relative values of features, we have yet another method.

Weighted Compensatory Strategy. This approach, although the most time-consuming of all, would probably give the best selection. Here each feature is evaluated and rated from 1 to 10 on the basis of how important it is in the final choice. Then each product is rated for each feature, just as in the compensatory model. This method adds a final step, however, in which each product's rating for each feature is multiplied by that feature's rated importance to get a final score. This means that more important features have a bigger impact on the final score. The weighted compensatory model is a linear model, and Plous (1993) reports that "even though people do not normally use linear equations to arrive at their decisions, linear decision rules often yield choices that agree closely with the choices people make." (p.102)

Additive Difference Strategy. Plous (1993) provides a concise explanation of the additive difference strategy:

> This model is similar to the linear model, except that in the linear model, each alternative is evaluated on all the dimensions and then compared with other alternatives, whereas in the additive difference model, each dimension is first evaluated across alternatives, and only the *differences* among alternatives are weighted and summed together. Focusing on differences has at least two advantages—it greatly simplifies the choice between two alternatives, and as a model of decision making, it seems closer to how people actually make decisions. For example, a car buyer would be much more likely to focus on the difference between two cars than to examine every dimension of each car and sum the weighted values (as in the case of a linear model) (p. 102).

CHAPTER 5

Aspects of the Unconscious

The question of unconscious influences on behavior is as old as psychology itself. Freud gave new meaning and excitement to the word unconscious and caused it to be often associated with the psychoanalytic approach. It has surfaced as an important consideration in perception, conditioning, and in motivation, but it is seldom dealt with completely and often retains a murky character of mystery. The unconscious probably involves a number of separate systems, any of which operate simultaneously with the higher level. Some of these systems may be called "monitors" that perhaps keep track of sensory inputs about which we are unaware. We introduced these in the chapter on attention. They do not act except routinely on the results of their monitoring but may store to some extent, while generally functioning simply to interrupt and shift the higher level. We refer to this interruption as "getting our attention." It is not yet at all clear how many subattentional systems or monitors exist, nor how they interact. There may be other processors that also make connections between memories, but these are even less clear. In this chapter we try to illustrate some of the ways the unconscious operates in memory and perception and some of the applications to advertising.

When we enter the world of perceiving without being aware we have perceived, we find a close connection to a similar area, that of learning without being aware of having learned. The reason for the close connection is that we tend to measure perception and memory in the same way. We ask the subjects to tell us what they saw. If immediate, it is considered perception, if a while ago, it is considered memory. Other more sensitive methods, developed to measure less directly what the subject saw, are used in both perception and memory. One of the early studies to point out the confusion and begin to pull these effects apart was that of Sperling (1960). He was investigating the span of perception, how many items could be perceived at once. Using a tachistoscope, he would present a matrix of letters to subjects, and, after the flashed matrix was gone, ask them, for example, to report the first row. He found that they could, on the average, report about 4.5 items. But then he discovered an interesting thing. No matter which row he asked them for (remember the request came after the flash was gone), they could correctly report about 4.5 of them. In other words, his evidence showed that they had perceived many more than 4.5, but while they were reporting, the memory of the others faded away. Thus, the problem was not perception, but memory.

Though we know that there are differences, the problem still remains that it is often impossible to distinguish between perceptual and memory phenomena. This close interaction of memory and perception makes understanding this field very difficult. It is likely that some effects which pass as subliminal effects, are in fact memory phenomena, so that rather than not having seen the stimulus, the subject does not remember having seen it. To illustrate just how this can happen, we review several areas of memory which are of this type, as explained in an excellent recent review by Schwartz and Reisberg (1991).

UNCONSCIOUS MEMORY INFLUENCES

It has long been known that our memory system works on several levels. For example, Freud spoke of the preconscious, which contains material of which we are not actually aware, but which can be called up at any time. This includes names and phone numbers, and also most accessible memories. Below this, containing inaccessible memories, is the unconscious. Freud felt that things were pushed into the unconscious when the recall would produce pain or anxiety, and he identified the process as one of our ego defenses.

Encoding Specificity

Empirical evidence has shown that recall of memories is highly related to their meanings and the number of associations they have with other memories. Back in the nineteenth century, William James called associations the "handles of memory," and research has supported his notion, that is, we cannot remember randomly. We reach memories through associated ideas, so that our thoughts are strung together like a string of pearls. If an association is not drawn either when the memory was filed, or added at a later time, then it cannot be used as a retrieval handle. This is the reason that rote memory is so inefficient. You must have the right starting place, or the memory cannot be reached. This means that some memories may be inaccessible (i.e., unconscious) because we are looking with the wrong handle, rather than because of their painful connections, as Freud maintained. Tulving (1983) called this effect **encoding specificity**. A typical study to illustrate it has been well summarized by Schwartz and Reisberg:

> We bring a group of subjects into the laboratory and ask them to memorize a list of words. Midway down the list is the word JAM, and, by manipulating the context, we arrange things so that subjects are likely to understand the word as indicating the kind of jam one makes from strawberries or grapes. (This can be done in various ways; at the simplest, we can precede the word JAM with a word like JELLY or FRUIT. In this situation, the context "primes" subjects to understand JAM as we intend....) Some time later, we test memory by presenting various items and asking whether or not these appeared on the previous list. JAM is presented, but now we arrange the context so that JAM is understood as in "traffic jam." Under these circumstances, subjects will typically say that the word was not on the previous list, even though their memory for the list seems to be quite good. That is, subjects are quite likely to remember accurately most of the other words on the list (Schwartz & Reisberg, 1991, p. 290).

In this situation, this means that learning could take place, but not be recalled unless the appropriate association is present to trigger it.

Implicit Memory

Implicit memories are distinguished from explicit ones by the method used to measure them. Rather than the direct memory testing used with explicit memories, implicit memory is revealed by indirect methods. A direct method might involve giving subjects a list of words to study, and then at some later time testing them with another list and measuring how many they could identify as having been in the earlier list. In the indirect method, we do not ask them directly, but rather see if some behavior has been affected. For example, a tachistoscope might be used. This is a device that flashes words at such a very brief duration that subjects are not sure what any of the words are. Again we let subjects study a list of words, and find that they cannot remember words from the list any better than the other group. Then we use the tachistoscope to flash new, ordinarily unrecognizable, words on a screen. It turns out that they are more likely to recognize words that were on the previous list, yet they cannot tell you they have ever seen that word before. This technique, called **repetition priming**, is known to last for several days (Jacoby & Dallas, 1981, as reported in Schwartz & Reisberg, 1991). In other words, subjects were unaware of having seen the words before, but the words were influencing their behavior by improving recognition.

State-Dependent Learning

Encoding of memories takes place in very subtle ways. This is what is happening in another group of studies which illustrate state-dependency. In these studies the finding is that recall of learned material is improved if the recall conditions are the same as those under which the learning took place. For example, studies have been done in which subjects have learned and have been tested under a wide variety of conditions: after using marijuana, alcohol, amphetamines, and caffeine, underwater and above, in one room and another, in one mood and another. There is no question that subjects did better if they were not under the influence of the drugs, but putting this factor aside there is a consistent state-dependency effect, in which subjects always did better if test and learning took place under the same conditions (see Gardner, 1985; Schwartz & Reisberg, 1991).

The implication from these studies is that one might not remember something, but at another time more closely matched to the learning conditions, the memory might be accessible. The learning would have been there all along, but the person does not recall it unless the conditions are right.

Conditioning Without Awareness

Ever since Freud, we have been aware of the power of unconscious associations. Pavlov provided the procedure whereby stimuli might trigger the unconscious, as we discussed in an earlier chapter. There are "countless experiments" which show that indeed it is possible to condition someone classically without their awareness of it (Malone, 1990, p. 86).

There is little doubt that operant conditioning can also be unconsciously done, just as classical conditioning can. Most of the early studies of both operant and classical conditioning were done with animals that have low levels of consciousness to begin with. If consciousness were necessary, one would expect to find the principles of operant conditioning becoming weaker and even disappearing as the subjects involved are drawn from lower on the phylogenetic scale, but this is not the case. Although more trials may indeed be necessary, the principles apply down to the lowly flatworm. The fact that we learn unconsciously means that we pick up many habits of which we are unaware. A more appropriate approach is the question of just when unconscious conditioning takes place and when it will not. We return to the question later.

SUBLIMINAL PERCEPTION

The Threshold Concept

To begin our discussion of subliminals, we need to consider what the term "subliminal" means because it has become particularly imbued with an air of magic. Frequently subliminal is used as if it were a synonym for unconscious. Although this usage is common, it is essentially incorrect. For example, one popular author says "subliminal" is "merely another word for the unconscious, subconscious, deep mind, third brain—there are a dozen labels which have attempted to describe the portion of the human brain which retains information and operates without our conscious awareness."(Key, 1976, p. 2) Such a definition could include stimuli that we did not notice, but which were plainly visible, and these are not really subliminal at all. These stimuli are really **subattentional**, rather than **subliminal**, because we do in fact detect them if we turn our attention to looking for them. In other words, they are detectable, but unnoticed. The reason that it matters which term one uses is that the underlying processes are completely different. Calling subattentionals subliminal suggests the possibility of undetectable mind control, whereas the term subattentional does not.

The derivation of the word **subliminal** indicates its meaning. The word comes from the two Latin words: "sub," meaning below, and "limen," meaning threshold. In this case threshold refers to detection, the lowest level of stimulus intensity that we can detect. Subliminals are stimuli below that threshold. Because subattentionals are clearly above the threshold, they do not really belong under this heading. However, the meaning of subliminal sets up an apparent paradox because if we are perceiving something below the level of detection, then there must be some unknown sense operating or some strange way of knowing that does not involve our usual senses, and it all becomes very spooky. But the interpretation is wrong for at least four reasons.

The Center of a Zone.   First, thresholds are not really points, but transition zones. There is no sharp point where we suddenly stop detecting, below which we never detect, and above which we always detect. Rather, our detection gradually gets worse and worse until we no longer detect. Because humans are not very consistent, at a given stimulus intensity, a person sometimes will detect and sometimes not. Similarly, at a given level, some people will detect and others will not. Because a zone is hard to work with like all big groups of numbers, we let the midpoint (the mean or average) represent the whole, just as an average might represent some other group. That midpoint, the point where detection occurs exactly 50% of the time, is called the threshold. Above the sensory threshold, detection is possible more often than 50% of the time, and below the threshold, detection is still possible, but less than 50% of the time.

A threshold of detection, in other words, is a point only for convenience, a statistically derived point, and, as odd as it sounds, stimuli can still be detectable a good proportion of the time when they are below threshold, and no additional sense system is called for. Such below threshold stimuli would perhaps be better understood if they were sorted out as either "occasionally detectable" or "never detectable." Such labels, at least, would not suggest mysticism and magic, but at the moment they are all simply called "subliminal."

The Subject's Role.   The second reason that confusion appears is that subjects are not consistent in what they mean by detection. For example, the question of just how much one can rely on the subject's verbal report has been a particularly difficult point. What the subject says is called the subjective threshold. Other more indirect measures, such as GSR, are called objective thresholds (Cheesman & Merikle, 1984). GSR is the galvanic skin resistance, a physiological measure that is totally undetectable by the subject. In other words, subjects may say they see nothing, but indicators other than verbal reports may indicate that some level of perception was taking place. Furthermore, other physiological indexes, such as blood pressure or heart rate, may not all yield equivalent objective thresholds.

Even the subjective threshold has further problems. One problem arises from the personalities of the subjects. Flamboyant subjects may be willing to guess when they in fact see nothing at all. Conversely, people who are reluctant to be wrong, may not guess unless they are quite sure their answers are correct. Guesses will be right sometimes, so that these two subjects produce very different thresholds based on their reports, yet they may actually be seeing the same thing.

The forced choice technique was developed to handle this problem. In this method subjects are asked to tell which one of maybe four presentations contained the stimulus. In other words, the technique does not allow "no stimulus" answers and requires all of the subjects to guess, so that it does not matter how sure they are of their responses. In a forced-choice task involving four possible choices, 25% correct is the predicted chance level that indicates no perception and pure guessing. When Cheesman and Merikle measured detection thresholds of color-naming prime words (primes and masks to be explained shortly) using the forced-choice technique, they found that

> As expected, all subjects claimed to have absolutely no awareness of the primes in the 25% detection condition and to have complete awareness of the primes in the no-mask condition. Surprisingly, all subjects also reported that they rarely, if ever, noticed the primes in either the 55% or 90% detection conditions. In those conditions, subjects simply did not have any confidence that a prime may have preceded the presentation of a color target, even though the objective detection measure, administered immediately prior to these trials, had indicated that the subjects could perform a forced-choice discrimination task with a relatively high level of accuracy (Cheesman & Merikle, 1984, p. 391).

In other words, what sometimes appears to be nondetection may rather be nonconfidence. Cheesman and Merikle further maintain that when true detection thresholds derived by the forced-choice method are used, their "results provide no support whatsoever for the perception-without-awareness hypothesis." (Cheesman & Merikle, 1984, p. 390) Clearly the controversy hinges on what we mean by "awareness."

Method of Measurement. A third reason for confusion is that threshold determinations vary with the method used to measure them. In the 1860, G. T. Fechner described three ways to measure sensory thresholds. Other better methods have been added since then. However, thresholds measured even by Fechner's three ways are not exactly the same. In experimentation one gets around this problem by using the same method for all conditions one wishes to compare, but it means that studies done by different methods may not be directly comparable.

Ways of measuring unconscious effects vary even beyond the subtleties of Fechner's methods. Verbal reports of what was seen (or not seen) are the most common index, but verbal reports have a number of research problems associated with them as we shall see in a moment. Other more sensitive measures of unconscious influence have sometimes been used besides verbal reports, such as the GSR, introduced above. This is a measure of the resistance between two points on the skin surface, which drops with emotionality. It can be used in lie detection, as long as the lying produces emotionality of even a very low nature in the individual, and has been frequently used in lie detector tests. It is a response of the autonomic nervous system, but exactly how it is produced is still not clear. Sometimes verbal reports produce a lower (that is, more sensitive) threshold than the GSR (Dulany & Eriksen, 1959), and sometimes the opposite holds. In the latter case, when the GSR detects the presence of stimuli unreported verbally, the effect has sometimes been called "subception" (Lazarus & McCleary, 1951), but the term seems to have the same meaning as subliminal perception. Bowers calls these stimuli as "perceived, but not noticed," and points out a number of other types of nonverbal responses, including "reaction times (Posner & Snyder, 1975), word associations (Spence, 1964), dreams (Poetzl, 1960), affective responses (Zajonc, 1980), [and] physiological measures (Corteen & Wood, 1972; Shevrin & Fritzler, 1968)." (Bowers, 1984, p. 230) It appears that these stimuli cannot be "noticed" and therefore are truly subliminal.

Type of Material. The fourth source of confusion is the problem of type of material because thresholds for words, images, and sounds, to mention only the most common varieties, are not necessarily comparable. Sometimes, it is assumed that suggestive verbal materials act just as pictures of suggestive scenes, but in actuality this is clearly not the case. Verbal materials take longer to process, and the time necessary varies from very quick for single letters, a bit longer for familiar or common syllables, longer yet for nonsense syllables, and much longer for whole sentences. Figures, on the other hand, vary from simple outline drawings to complex ones, from nonsense figures to familiar pictures, and from black and white images to color. Thus, a finding from a study done with figures does not automatically mean that a similar arrangement using sentences, or even other figures, will necessarily work at all.

Additional major factors are familiarity of the subject with the material and the complexity of its meaning. Familiar and simpler stimuli, whether words or figures, take less time to be perceived and thus can be perceived at lower thresholds. Finally, the affective content of the material is a major consideration. As pointed out in an earlier chapter, the affect detection system is separate from and faster acting than the cognitive system.

Subliminal Methods in Advertising and Marketing

We focus here on four methods of presentation because they apparently have been used more than others. We must say apparently because most of this information is considered proprietary on the part of the ad agencies and companies involved, so that a clear picture is not possible. Two of these methods are visual, and two are auditory. First the visuals.

Two techniques have been used primarily to produce subliminal visual stimuli, and they are by no means equivalent in their action. One method is to present visual stimuli in such brief exposures that they cannot be reported. Such exposures, in the range of 4 to 10 ms can produce images that may be seen clearly but are not present long enough for complete processing. Questions of depth of processing, of speed of affective processing, and of time necessary for transfer to working memory all become relevant. A quite different approach involves presenting fuzzy images, such as from an out of focus projector, for exposure times of 15 s or so. However, with this technique the images are never seen clearly, regardless of the duration of exposure.

To label both of these techniques, brief exposures and fuzzy images, simply "subliminal" is to confuse the process by which they work. Brief exposures are probably putting the information into sensory memory where some processing can be done. Time is too short for it to move into short term storage, so it cannot be recalled later, but it may still be able to trigger associations, particularly affective ones. Fuzzy images, on the other hand, cannot be processed no matter how much time is allowed. The associations they trigger are quite different in nature, often involve inferences from general shape outlines, and they will be particularly sensitive to suggestion, priming, and set. We shall look at these in more detail.

Brief Visual Exposures. The key variable in briefly presented stimuli is the duration of the informational flash. Durations of 1 millisecond, one-thousandth of a second, are sufficient for subjects to report letters and short syllables accurately, if no other images interfere. This happens partly because a negative afterimage occurs, particularly with images of sharp contrast, which briefly changes the chemistry of the retina so that the image persists for some time after the flash is gone. An extreme case of this is what happens when someone sets off a flashbulb in your face, and you see a black spot everywhere you look for some time after. What became the most famous of all attempts to subliminally influence behavior claimed to use the brief flash technique.

Concern over unconscious behavioral control has sporadically surfaced ever since a study reported in 1956, which sensitized people to the term "subliminal," stirred up considerable discussion of the ethics involved and even led to demands for corrective legislation. According to the report, messages that exhorted patrons to "EAT POPCORN" and

"DRINK COCA-COLA," flashing too fast to be detected (1/3000th of a second), were projected on a movie screen every five seconds for six weeks. Huge jumps in sales for both products were reported (Brean, 1958; Wilhelm, 1956).

Runyon and Stewart commented as follows after pointing out that the firm that conducted the test also was seeking to sell subliminal projectors:

> These findings are notable for several reasons: (a) the exposure rate of 1/3000 of a second is far briefer than any previously reported stimulation; (b) there were no reports of even the most rudimentary scientific controls that would lend credibility to the study; (c) in a demonstration set up for the press, "technical difficulties" permitted viewers to become aware that they were being stimulated. Further attempts to gather specific information on the details of the study were ignored. In short, the entire report appears to have all the characteristics of a fabrication (Runyon & Stewart, 1987, p. 448).

In his book on advertising Ogilvy (1985) says that the whole event was really just a hypothesis of James Vicary's that he never tested. Ogilvy goes on to say that no advertiser has ever used subliminal advertising, though it is not clear that he would necessarily be aware of it if they did.

A major variable in work of this type is the presence or absence of masking stimuli. Because the presence of a gradually fading afterimage makes the effective duration of the flash hard to measure, researchers began following the informational flash with a second flash, called a masking pattern, to interfere with the afterimage. The procedure has come to be known as **backward masking**, or metacontrast. The masking pattern may consist of lines, dots, figures, or random letters and typically follows the information exposure by only about 50 to 100 ms. The presence of the masking pattern disrupts the afterimage from the first exposure and limits the time available for its use. It seems to erase the memory of the first exposure effectively. Subjects sometimes report that they have seen a syllable clearly, recognized it as familiar, but still cannot report what it was (Webb, 1962). There is considerable evidence that the unreportable material still influences perceptions and/or memories. A variation of backward masking, called repetition priming, has already been considered previously under memory phenomena.

Subliminal psychodynamic activation is the name given to the most surprising and controversial use of the brief exposure technique. Studies in this category of subliminals are difficult to interpret, but because they may be motivating advertisers to try the technique, some comment may be in order. The chief experimenter has been Lloyd Silverman who described the technique as follows:

> The method involves the observation of behaviors before and after 4-milli-
> second tachistoscopic exposures of experimental and control stimuli under
> conditions in which both subject and experimenter are blind to stimulus
> *content. The experimental stimuli consist of verbal messages and/or pic-
> tures, with content designed to stimulate the unconscious wishes, anxieties,
> and fantasies that psychoanalysis views as central motivators of behavior.
> The control stimuli consist of neutral verbal and pictorial content (Silver-
> man, 1983, p. 70).

Most of the studies reported by Silverman were done using clinical populations, but a few were done on nonclinical populations. Interpretation is made difficult by the fact that the hypothetical psychoanalytic explanations are so intertwined with the results of the experiments. Silverman typically uses short sentences for stimuli. For example, the sentence he uses most frequently is, "Mommy and I are one." These are sometimes accompanied with pictures, and sometimes not, and he seems to find the distinction unimportant. However, visual images are processed much faster than sentences because they are perceived all at once, as gestalts, whereas sentences must be processed sequentially. Visual images also deliver affect quickly and efficiently compared to words. In the one case where he addresses this question, he reports (in a footnote only) that Shifren (1981) failed to replicate the findings of Florek (1978) when he changed the picture but not the words. This suggests strongly that at least in these cases the picture is more important than the words, yet his interpretation focuses almost completely on the psychodynamics of the words. Affect assessment too would be faster from an image than from a sentence, but pictorial affect levels are not measured or even mentioned.

Several important aspects of these studies come to light on examination. Of the 111 total references cited by Silverman (1983), 65 are unpublished. The importance of this is that editors of most journals put submitted manuscripts through rigorous peer review to catch faulty design or interpretation before publication. Therefore, unpublished studies have not been subjected to peer review. Of the 46 published studies, 24 are by Silverman himself, and a number by his students. In fact, only 11 studies are done on nonclinical populations in laboratories other than Silverman's and by other than his students. Of these, Silverman reports that five were clearly supportive, two were mixed or reversed, and four were clearly nonsupportive. Considering further that many negative findings never get published, one would have to conclude that the effect, if it happens at all with nonclinical populations is not very strong. In addition, the interpretation is open to considerable question, and a psychoanalytic explanation, particularly with nonclinical populations, is far from convincing. Moreover, the effectiveness of the technique when used in advertising has yet to be demonstrated.

Obscured Visual Images. A number of studies have been done under the title of perceptual defense, but again, it is very hard to say whether they are perceptual or memory phenomena. Generally, the element which produces them is prior meaning that the stimuli have, clearly a memory influence, but the task is identifying present stimuli rather than recalling past ones, clearly a perceptual task. Because the task is perceptual, in this case we will consider the findings under perception.

A number of advertisers in recent years are reported to have obscured sexual figures and/or words and inserted them into their advertisements, claiming that they sell better that way (Key, 1976). Key found that one of the techniques was to write the word "sex" all over an advertising picture, particularly of clothes. Then, this is reduced to illegibility by airbrushing or other means, and most viewers would have no idea it was there. In some current ads occasionally it appears to be there, when detected by a magnifying glass. So it seems that some advertisers are still using it. More often than not, however, even with a magnifying glass, one is left wondering whether these lines and scratches are words or not. Key argues that because these ads are so expensive that it must have been found effective, but this is a weak argument and far from empirical evidence. We would have to conclude that words that you cannot detect, even when you are searching for them, have very doubtful effectiveness. Good controlled studies that document the process are lacking, and at the same time researchers who have tried to produce an effect could not do so (DeFleur & Petranoff, 1959).

Auditory Messages. Two auditory techniques have received some attention in recent years, self-help tapes and backward messages. We look at both of these. Self-help audiotapes are produced by several manufacturers to subliminally suggest alterations to our psychological state in some way. Greenwald, Spangenberg, Pratkanis, and Eskenazi (1991) put tapes from three manufacturers to a well-controlled test. For a month they had subjects use either a tape marketed to improve self-esteem or a tape to improve memory. Other subjects used the same tapes, but with the labels switched. At the end of the month those who thought they were listening to a memory tape, whether they were or not, tended to report memory improvement. The same was found for the self-esteem tapes. Whatever effects there were, in other words, were there because of the labels, not because of the content of the tapes, a classic placebo effect. The tapes, in short, have no effect at all. Whether this applies to all such tapes is not demonstrated, but supportive evidence is lacking.

Auditory messages can be taped and played backward, while some other message or song is in progress. Parents are concerned that their children are getting satanic messages in this fashion, some going so far as to sue (they lost) because of it (Neely, 1990). Matlin summarizes one study done by Vokey and Read (1985) to test this technique:

> Vokey and Read specifically examined the claims about the effectiveness of the messages played backward. In one of their studies, for example, they played short messages such as "Jesus loves me, this I know" backward to a group of listeners. These people were asked to sort the statements into one of five content categories: nursery rhymes, Christian, satanic, pornographic, and advertising. If the meaning of backward messages can be obtained at a subliminal level, then people should be more accurate than the expected 20% chance level in sorting the messages. Of the 10 sentences (two from each content category), the average accuracy rate was 19.4%—clearly no better than chance (reported in Matlin, 1989, p. 64).

Subliminal auditory effects, frontward or backward, continue to be unconvincing.

To summarize subliminal effects, we have seen that the transmittal of affect at levels too rapid for cognition have been repeatedly demonstrated. These are legitimate subliminal effects. Embedded figures, claimed by Key (1976) to be rampant in American advertising, involved obscured images and words made too fuzzy to read. These too would be subliminal but their effectiveness has yet to be demonstrated. Other images are not "subliminal," but rather "subattentional," because one can see them if attention is turned to them. Subattentionals may work on an affective level, but because they are detected readily if one tries, they are not a threat. Finally distorted auditory messages are yet to be shown effective in any way, in spite of considerable effort to produce an effect. In sum, affect is raised a small amount by subliminals and thus may alter preferences. However, any direct subliminal influences on behavior, short of outright hypnotism, have never been convincingly shown.

SUBATTENTIONAL PERCEPTION

We can be influenced by stimuli in a number of ways and yet not be aware that it is happening. If we could become aware of stimuli by just turning our attention to them, then they are really not subliminals, but subattentionals. Advertising is filled with images of this type, and they are sometimes incorrectly referred to as subliminal effects. This use of the term clouds the process. They do have some effectiveness in creating positive affect that should aid the advertising goal. Specific results are hard to come by because advertising agencies are unwilling to help their competition when it works and reluctant to admit it if it does not. The use of subattentional sexuality, however, is not hard to find. True, such symbolisms are in the mind of the beholder, but I have pursued the point enough to know they are in the minds of many beholders. Unfortunately, I was unable to find a company that would let me reproduce their ad when I suggested that it had a sexual interpretation. One company representative, whose ads are repeatedly run this way, became quite indignant that any one would suggest such a thing.

BACKGROUND MUSIC

The Complex Nature of Music

One aspect of subattentional stimuli, so widespread that it needs a section all to itself, is background music. As Lanza (1994) notes,

> Background music is almost everywhere: avant-garde "sound installations" permeate malls and automobile showrooms, quaint piano recitals comfort us as we wait in bank lines, telephone techotunes keep us complacently on hold, brunch Baroque refines our dining pleasure, and even synthesized "nature" sounds further blur the boundary between our high tech Platonic caves and "real life." (p. 2)

The first and most daunting problem in discussing the effects of music is the question of just what is meant by "music." The term is complex and includes almost endless variations in many dimensions. The following are the most important dimensions:

1. genre or style, e.g., classical, country, rock, heavy metal, rap, jazz, elevator
2. tempo, e.g., slow, romantic, upbeat, lively, rock, driving; usually measurable in beats per minute
3. form, e.g., major or minor mode, tonal or atonal, melodic, harmonic, consonant or dissonant
4. pitch, including rising and falling effects of pitch
5. texture, simple or complex, particularly in the type of instrument(s) or voice(s) involved and their combination
6. volume or loudness, anywhere from soft to painfully loud, steady, or variable

7. lyrics, with, without, or with understood but not verbalized lyrics
8. meaning, has associations from the nature of the music itself, as in the sound of water in a brook, or from past events that have previously occurred with the music, as in a remembered video, movie, or even a particular date
9. familiarity to the listener, e.g., is able to whisper the words, or hum the tune; is familiar with the style, but not this piece; is only vaguely familiar with the style
10. degree liked by the listener or not, e.g., buys the CD; seeks it on the radio; listens if it comes on; changes the station

These complexities mean that it is not always exactly clear which characteristic in the music causes it have a particular effect, but, on the other hand, what the studies have so far indicated is not that surprising. The dominant characteristics are tempo, pitch, and texture. Relationships found include the following. Fast music is happier than slow, and 70 to 110 beats per minute is the preferred tempo. Firm rhythms are more serious, smooth rhythms more playful or dreamy, and uneven rhythms more dignified. The major mode is more happy, whereas the minor mode is plaintive or mysterious. Consonant harmonies are more serene, dissonant ones more agitating, ominous or sad. Loud is more exciting, soft more tranquil. Finally, the type of instrument determines texture and has a number of predictable effects on mood. Much more detail on each of these factors is provided in an excellent review by Bruner (1990). Moreover, Bruner also cautions that one has to be concerned with the main effects and also the interactions, which have seldom been explored.

Because of these endless complexities, interpretation of the "effects of music" is extremely difficult. What all this means to those who would like to use music as a background in a store or to an exhibit is that evaluation is a must. Fortunately, there is enough agreement among people that subjective interpretations of the potential effect are probably pretty close, but wide differences sometimes exist across ages, cultures and situations, so that actual testing is essential. Because of the complexity, I bypass the research on the specific characteristics of music as such and deal with more general aspects. For recent discussions of specific literature, only recently beginning to appear, see Alpert and Alpert (1990) Kellaris and Kent (1991, 1993), and Bruner (1990).

The more general effects of music have been studied by retailers and marketers to find out its effect on service delivery, and also by advertisers and educators interested in its effects on learning and retention.

Creating Mood

There is little disagreement that music creates moods. Gardner (1985) defines "moods" as "feeling states that are subjectively perceived by individuals." (p. 282) She notes they are general and pervasive, not directed at any particular object, transient, and less intense than emotions. Hers is a good review of the effects of mood.

There are various reasons for wanting to change the mood of the listener. Actually, "hearer" would be a better term, for hearers are not always listeners, because listening implies a directed attention that is generally not there. In fact, viewers may be so absorbed by what they are seeing that they do not consciously notice the music at all, yet their mood is influenced. Let us consider the main reasons for creating mood.

Relaxing to Increase Likelihood of Buying.   Malls and many stores play background music to relax shoppers, and put them in a frame of mind to shop. If they are tense or in a hurry, they are not likely to take time to examine the merchandise. Christmas music is particularly effective because it has been associated so often in the past with extra spending, gift giving and getting, and a holiday atmosphere. More on the relaxation factor in a moment.

Increasing the Pleasure of the Moment.   The purpose may be to simply increase the pleasure of the moment for the hearer. Properly applied in a museum setting, just as in a store or restaurant, this might be to make the visit experience more pleasurable, and the consequence is repeat visits or favorable reports to friends. This use would clearly have importance to exhibit and to nonexhibit spaces, such as the museum shop, the cafeteria, restrooms, or the admissions desk. Note, however, that the term "background music" should not be construed as equivalent to "easy listening" music, such as Muzak per se, because there are hundreds of other forms. A particular music's ability to increase pleasure is a matter for testing.

Of course, music does not always increase the pleasure of the moment, but the negative side apparently also has its uses. For example, the management of 7-11 stores has used loudspeakers playing Mozart, Mantovani, and 60s folk songs to clear their parking lots of young people who liked to hang out there. According to reports, "They hated it," and went looking for an alternative site (Glamser, 1990). The lesson is to be acutely aware of age differences.

Temporarily Enhancing the Perception of Objects. Mood creation may also have the purpose of bringing a particular affect (or feeling) to the moment, thereby enhancing the objects being seen. Music can do this in a number of ways by increasing drama, tension, and affect, so that we become more involved. This clearly applies to exhibits and to marketing. Ken Burns, the producer of the Public Television documentaries on the Civil War and Baseball, works to a large extent with still photographs. He is a master of using music and sound tracks, as he says, "to jump start the pictures." (Burns, 1994) When he does this, we become emotionally involved and begin to care about the subjects, but he spends an enormous amount of time choosing music with just the right nuance. Advertisers regularly use the same technique to make us care about their products.

Music increases and also directs affect, so that it can determine how we feel about what we are seeing. This is, of course, the aspect that is so powerfully used in movies and television. The music in movies often precedes the action, so that we anticipate the action and feel suspense. At the same time it is a capability that some may specifically not want, say, in an art museum. The argument here is that the work of art should be allowed to create its own affect, not have to overcome or compete with some else's idea of what is appropriate. Thus a quiet atmosphere is seen as most favorable to interaction with art. Some products require the same consideration. The type of music needs to be carefully matched to both product and target audience.

Advertisers and marketers use mood to create affect as part of the general application of **atmospherics**, a term that originated with Kotler (1973), and refers to the multiplicity of sensory experiences that accompany shopping and influence purchase probabilities. For example, commercials and stores use classical music to create a sense of luxury. Acura uses Prokofiev, Federal Express uses Bizet, and Victoria's Secret uses Mozart (Queenan, 1993). To see whether classical music actually enhances objects in its environment, Areni and Kim (1993) selected a small wine cellar, located in a restaurant, where patrons could purchase wine. In a carefully controlled study, they compared a number of behaviors when "Top 40" music was playing as compared to "classical." They found that customers did not purchase more items, but they did spend more money, buying more expensive wines when classical music was playing. One could say the value of the wine had clearly been enhanced, but another factor may also be operating, as we shall see in a moment.

Applications are not simple. One problem is that as more and more commercials and stores use music, its effectiveness declines. John Trivers, said to be a supplier of sophisticated background music for high visibility ads, was quoted in Forbes Magazine as saying that "Classical music has been so overused that it's starting to lose its impact." (Queenan, 1993)

Attaching Permanent Affect to Objects Via Mood. The purpose of creating mood may be to make us feel differently about objects, during the present exposure and also in the future. This is, of course, the process of classical conditioning, and it underlies nearly all advertising. The principle predicts that the mood we are in when we encounter an object partially returns, triggered quickly and automatically when we next meet that object. Thus if you encounter in a store a product to which positive affect has been attached, you will feel better about it than its competitors and be more likely to select it. Whether this is technically classical conditioning is still debated, but there is little argument that it often works.

Attaching Affect Without Mood

Recently Groenland and Schoormans (1994) made the point that two mechanisms may be working in these situations. First is the creation of a mood and its attachment to a stimulus presented, but a second factor may be affective conditioning, whereby affect is associated directly with a stimulus without having to induce a mood. It is thought that affect attached to a stimulus through the mood mechanism is short-lasting compared to affect transferred directly through conditioning.

The conditioning of affect has been amply demonstrated over the years, particularly with pictures and words, but very few studies have used music to create the affect. One of the most influential demonstrations of this process was a study by Gorn (1982). He sought to show that mood induced by music could be attached to actual products and to words or images. Chance (1988) provides an excellent synopsis:

> American college students listened either to a tune from the film Grease or to classical Indian music. (It was expected that the students would enjoy the popular American music more than the unfamiliar Eastern variety.) While listening to the music, the students viewed a slide showing either a beige or blue pen. Later, the students were allowed to have one of the pens. Of those students who had listened to the popular music, 79 percent chose a pen of the same color they had seen while listening to that music, while 70 percent of those who had listened to the Indian music chose a pen of a color different from the one they had seen on the slide. Evidently, ad agencies are correct in

believing that they can induce people to feel good about, and want, a product by pairing that product with stimuli (pleasant music, attractive people, and the like) that make them feel good (Chance, 1988, p. 67).

Kellaris and Cox (1989) tried to replicate Gorn's study but were unable to do so. From their research they concluded that his results were partially due to demand artifacts and that classical conditioning of music from one exposure has yet to be demonstrated in the case of actual product (that is, three-dimensional object) preferences. More recently, however, Tom (1995) replicated the Gorn study with some success. In this case, about 60% of those listening to music they liked chose the pen that was exposed at the same time for the whole 60 seconds, whereas in the negative condition, hearing music they found irritating, only about 54% chose the unexposed pen. The negative group did not differ statistically from a chance 50%, however, so that the negative affect, although in the right direction, could not be said to have been attached.

A study that does not purport to be conditioning, but which did look at effects on product, with only two exposures, is one by Gorn, Goldberg, Chattopadhyay, and Litvack (1991). In this study commercials for apple juice were prepared in which four conditions were tested: information only (I), information plus music (MI), music only (M), and neither information nor music (N). The commercials were embedded in a program. After the program, participants were offered a choice of four coupons worth $1.00 toward either Seven-Up, Libby's Tomato Juice, Salada Tea, or the advertised apple juice. The likelihood of choosing the apple juice coupon for the N group was 14.6%. When music alone was added to the commercial (M), the percentage that chose the juice coupon rose to 26.8%, but the difference was not significant. The percentage that chose it rose significantly in both information (specific claims) conditions, 41.7% for I, and 48.7% for MI. Again, these were not significantly different from each other, but were significantly higher than the other conditions. If music has a small effect, the results are in the right direction, but another study is needed to be sure. One should note that their subjects ranged in age from 60 to 84. This group may prefer informational sources more than a younger sample and may not be representative of younger adults.

Attaching the affect of music to nonproduct (nonthree-dimensional) stimuli has been demonstrated a number of times, which leads to the assumption that three-dimensional conditioning should be equally possible. For example, Bierley, McSweeney, and Vannieuwkerk (1985) set out to try Gorn's procedure with better controls to find out whether it was really classical conditioning or not. They presented slides of red, blue, or yellow circles, squares, triangles, or rectangles to subjects. These became conditioned stimuli for some subjects and were followed by music from Star Wars, which, they had determined previously, the subjects liked. The study utilized elaborate controls, and the results supported the findings of Gorn. Initial color preferences were altered for the two groups who received the conditioning procedure of color followed by music but were not altered for the control groups. Stimuli that were followed by music were more highly preferred than those that were not, but note that the stimuli were two-dimensional images.

More recently, Blair and Shimp (1992) showed the conditioning of negative affect using music. They chose music that their subjects originally liked, but came to dislike because of its use as theme music that introduced every session of extra class work involving video tapes. After it came to be disliked and when it was then paired with a fictitious brand name, the rating of the brand dropped. This underscores the necessity of choosing music carefully and the likelihood that because of prior associations, not all visitors will react to it in the same way. On the other hand, if it were completely idiosyncratic, advertisers could not use it so effectively.

Behavioral Effects

Supplying Cues to Behavior. Following the suggestion of Markin, Lillis, and Narayana (1976), Areni and Kim (1993) found another interpretation of their data from the wine cellar that we introduced previously. Rather than enhancing the value of the wine, the music may be providing cues to guide behavior. In the unfamiliar setting of the wine cellar, the music may have been particularly effective as a cue, indicating that "more expensive purchases are appropriate here."

Lending support to this interpretation are studies showing that people are more likely to look for external cues to guide their behavior in places with which they are unfamiliar. For example, Clark and Isen (1982) reported that mood states are more influential in ambiguous than in clear-cut situations. For example, because museums are generally unfamiliar places, music there might possibly have greater effects as a cue to behavior. One might also predict that the impact of music would be less for regular visitors, who are more familiar with the place, than for first-time visitors.

Moreover, if people look to the music for behavioral cues, it might be important to avoid general background music, such as "elevator music," in exhibit spaces or any space where attention is desired, because such music has usually been present in situations requiring little or no attention to surrounds. Thus, it may provide a cue that turns off attention, suggesting that "nothing of importance is going on here."

Greene (1986) hypothesizes why such music tends to drive us inward. He says our world is so fragmented with endless "disconnected, decontextualized commodities" that the familiar music serves to unify our world, just as a soundtrack unifies a film montage. As we get used to it, Muzak softens the impersonality by establishing a familiar setting. But the price, he feels, is that it "privatizes meaning, discouraging one from perceiving a physical environment in terms of the shared meaning behind culture and encouraging a perception based on intimate, half-realized memories. It internalizes symbolism in which not a few but only one can participate." (p. 289) One could conclude from this interpretation that the use of Muzak or other "elevator music" in such spaces might be counterproductive.

Speeding Up or Slowing Down. It has been well documented that background music changes people's pace. Fast music speeds them up, and slow music slows them down. In these cases the creation of mood does not happen, and the effect is clearly direct. For instance, McElrea and Standing (1992) found that subjects, who were asked to rate the flavor of a soda, drank significantly faster in the fast music condition compared to the slow music condition.

Milliman (1982) tested this notion in a store, defining "slow" as less than 72 beats per minute and "fast" as more than 94 beats per minute. Not only was in-store traffic 17% slower in the slow condition, sales volumes were startlingly 38% higher. The same researcher tried out music differentials in a restaurant (Milliman, 1986) and found that with slow music as compared to fast, customers stayed longer (56 min compared to 45 min), but in this case they did not spend more for food. Apparently, they filled the extra time with conversation. However, because tables turned over more slowly in the slow condition, customers did spend more in the bar ($30 as opposed to $21) as they waited for their tables.

In yet another study, Milliman (1988) reported that one restaurant increased profits at lunch, when turnover is crucial, by using bare tables and faster music. On the other hand, profits at dinner were increased by using linen tablecloths and slow tempo music. In this case, as opposed to his earlier one, the slower tempo at dinner did increase beverage and dessert sales.

Smith and Curnow (1966) reported in their study of music volume that shoppers spent less time in a store when loud music was played as opposed to soft, but they did not spend less money. Apparently, they simply shopped faster. Surprisingly, there was no difference in customer satisfaction in their two conditions.

Milliman (1988) differentiates between "foreground" and "background" music in his study. As he uses the terms, foreground music is popular music with lyrics and a faster tempo, whereas background music is instrumental, slower, and less differentiated. In the study of shoppers in a wine cellar noted previously, Areni and Kim (1993) used Top 40 as one condition and classical as the other. As you will recall, their study, one of the few differing from Milliman, did not find that shoppers spent more time in the store under the slow condition but they did buy more expensive items. In this case the tempo of the music changed and its character also. Replication of this type of study in other settings is warranted. The dependent variable of dollars spent could be replaced by perceived satisfaction or a learning index to measure its applicability to a museum or exhibit setting.

Perception of Time

Would the presence of unpleasant music make time seem slower, as we think when we say, "Time flies when you are having fun?" The evidence on this point is not at all clear, but pleasantness does not seem to be the crucial dimension. One of the earliest studies of time perception did not involve music, but was done by Gulliksen (1927) who found that "an interval of 200 seconds was estimated at 242 seconds, on the average, when filled with mere waiting, but as only 169 seconds when devoted to work on problems in long division (as reported in Woodrow, 1951)." In other words, Gulliksen found that time slows when waiting, but speeds up when doing problems. This agrees with the popular view that time drags when you are bored. It indicates that it is not "having fun" that makes time speed up but being absorbed in a task.

Recent research, however, has made the waters very murky. Ornstein (1969) proposed a storage size model, according to which remembered events "seem longer" when more information is stored in memory. If events seem longer than they really are, time is dragging. By this reasoning, more cognitive involvement would cause time to drag. This is directly opposite to Gulliksen's findings. The difficulty in evaluating these two opposing views has been assumptions made as to what constitutes cognitive involvement, but there are few measurements of it.

For example, Kellaris and Kent (1992) reviewed the literature on this point and tested the idea by using modality of music to alter its appeal. In their study the mode liked least was atonal, as you might expect, whereas the reported preference of the major and minor modes did not differ. They found that time was overestimated (i.e., time was dragging) by 38% in the major mode, 23% in the minor mode, and 18% in the atonal mode. Their finding, reversed from what they expected, showed that time moves fastest during the least-liked mode. They explain their finding with a cognitive capacity model that assumes that familiar music causes "the allocation of greater cognitive resources." (p. 373) This aligns it with Ornstein, but other evidence suggests instead that the atonal music uses more resources and that increased cognitive activity makes time fly, as Gullicksen said.

Yalch and Spangenberg (1990) compared Milliman's foreground and background conditions for shoppers in a store department. In their study, foreground music was "popular Top 40 with lyrics," whereas background music was "easy listening" without lyrics. Unfortunately, they did not measure actual time spent in the store, but they did measure perceived time spent. As in the Kellaris and Kent (1992) study, the effect does not result from subjects' liking or disliking the music more, because there was no difference in their reported preferences. Although not entirely clear in the paper, it appears that "spending more time than one intended" is equivalent to having time fly, and they found that this happens when the music is unfamiliar. Younger shoppers (age 24 and under) reported that they spent more time than they planned to when exposed to the "easy listening" background music, but older shoppers (age 25 and up) in the "Top 40" condition reported just the opposite, feeling they had spent more time than they intended. Thus, both groups reported that they spent more time than intended when the music was of a kind they would not normally select, regardless of what the music actually was. Thus, time flies when the music is unfamiliar. Because a number of studies (e.g., Hilliard & Tolin, 1979) have shown that comprehension tasks suffer when background music is unfamiliar, there is strong argument that the unfamiliar music uses more cognitive resources and the use of these resources makes time fly.

The implications of these studies are interesting. Playing familiar music for those waiting in a line may actually make the wait seem longer rather than shorter. Pleasant, but unfamiliar, music is probably best. Clearly, evaluation and additional studies would be helpful here.

Getting and Holding Attention

The Music–Message Congruence Factor. One of the properties that music has is its ability to attract attention. The distant sound of a brass band brings people out to see the parade. Sometimes, however, music can attract so much attention to itself that the message, whether advertising or educational, is ignored (Macklin, 1988). Wakshlag, Reitz, and Zillman (1982), for example, found that fast-tempo music is best at attracting attention but is also the most distracting in interfering with the message. A key point is that the music and the message must match in their basic meaning or the music will distract from the message as it gets stronger. This is called **music–message congruency**. Recent literature has begun to clarify the nature of the music–message relationship.

It is well known that music conveys images and meanings and that listeners generally agree as to what these are. Building on this, Kellaris, Cox, and Cox (1993), following Macklin (1988), proposed that music has two properties, attention-getting and message enhancement. When the music gets attention and also delivers a theme similar to the message, then increasing audience awareness of the music increases the impact of the message. On the other hand, if they are incongruent, that is, the meaning of the music is different from the meaning of the message, then increasing audience awareness of the music distracts from the message. They explain what they mean by congruent as follows: "Music–message congruency refers to the congruency of meanings communicated non-verbally by music and verbally by ad copy." (p. 115) Alpert and Alpert (1990) add that the congruence is "between associated feelings and behaviors consistent with that advocated in the message." (p.129) Music–message congruency is essential to avoid competition between them.

To understand a bit better what is meant by music–message congruency we can look at how Kellaris, Cox, and Cox (1993) produced it in their study. They had students rate 12 pieces of instrumental music for attention-getting value and also list their thoughts as they listened to them. They reported that the images evoked by the music were "remarkably similar" across subjects. Then, the images were matched to appropriate products (for example, music that suggested action was paired with an ad for an action movie), and copy was written to agree. Using these materials, tests were then run on new subjects in congruent and incongruent conditions. Results generally supported their proposal of congruency. (The names of the specific musical pieces they used are provided in their reference.) As Kellaris says, "You can't show Grandma reading a Hallmark with a bouncy tempo. You've got to run slow to elicit emotion." (quoted in Kanner, 1992)

The Involvement Level Factor.   Park and Young (1986) introduced another major variable and reported that music affects people differently depending on whether they are of high or low involvement. High involvement consumers are those who are more likely to use a cognitive mode and to pay attention to the message. Low involvement consumers, on the other hand, are those who do not pay particular attention and drift more or less mindlessly. Low involvement people are more vulnerable than the high involvement group to affective appeals and are thus more strongly affected by music, particularly toward a change in attitude. [For a further discussion of involvement see Webb (1993) and Petty, Cacioppo, and Schumann (1983)].

MacInnis and Park (1991) continued to explore the differences of the high and low involved. Referring to music–message congruency as the music's "fit" with the message, they found that poor fit between music and message registered with the low involvement person as an unpleasant attitude toward the ad, which as has been shown elsewhere, carries over to the product. The finding translates that poor music–message fit in the case of low involvement viewers may lead to negative emotions toward an ad or exhibit without the viewer attempting to understand it. It suggests that the negative emotions may also carry over to brands and stores.

High involvement people, on the other hand, who are more cognitively engaged, use some of their energy trying to resolve the incongruity of the music–message mismatch, reducing their attention to the message. They are not as likely, however, to generate as much negative emotion in the process. A surprising finding from this study was that the good fit condition generates strong positive emotional responses toward the ad in both high and low involvement subjects. MacInnis and Park (1991) conclude that "[a good] fit has a powerful role in creating favorable ad and brand attitudes." (p.171) Attitude toward the ad, of course, is the equivalent in an exhibit setting of attitude toward the exhibit and is of major importance in attitude toward any message it contains. Thus, particularly because of their low involvement visitors, exhibitors should pay close attention to music–message congruency, if they plan to use music.

Comprehension Effects

Of some concern to the museum field is the literature on the use of background music to aid retention of material. For example, can students learn better with the radio on? Do visitors learn less from an exhibit if there is background music? The answers are not all in, but studies have uncovered several important factors.

The Music Information-Load Factor.   Kiger (1989) showed that it is useful to distinguish between high and low **music information load**.

Generally, the more that music demands attention, the more information load it has, and the more distracting it is when competing with verbal material. In the language of the cognitive capacity model, high information load requires more cognitive resources. Then, it is not surprising that Kiger's subjects showed the best comprehension when the background music was of low load compared to high load. What was a bit surprising was that subjects did better with low information-load music than they did with silence. The explanation is that the low-load condition masked distracting sounds, allowing for greater concentration, yet did not have sufficient information itself to be distracting. The principle probably has wide utility. For example, low-level "white noise" generators are sold as concentration enhancers because of their ability to mask sounds that contain information.

Miller and Schyb (1989) referred to the information-load factor as "attentional effort required" (p. 50), and found general agreement with Kiger, but there is not precise agreement on just what constitutes "information load," so it is not easily measured. The presence of lyrics or vocals certainly increases it, but beyond this it comes down to an ill-defined complexity within the music. Familiarity probably also reduces information load, because what one has already processed can simply be recognized and does not need to be processed again. Hilliard and Tolin (1979) found that familiarity of the background music increased comprehension test scores, even when familiarity involved only hearing a piece and then taking a test while hearing it again. Usually atonal music would be considered complex and of high information load, but Pearsall (1989), studying music students, found no difference in effect on comprehension between tonal and atonal background music when both were familiar, suggesting that familiarity is more important than tonality. This supports the idea that music has less information load when it becomes familiar.

The Task Factor.   Another factor in background music's effect on comprehension is the type of task one is doing. Miller and Schyb (1989) investigated this variable and found, though there was some conflicting evidence, that interference is strongest for verbal reading tasks and verbal learning tasks. Math tasks, on the other hand, and figural and pictorial tasks may not be as negatively affected and may even be facilitated. Wolf and Weiner (1972) actually found math scores improved by rock and roll. Miller and Schyb suggest that hemispheric differences in processing preferences may be the key here.

On reading comprehension tasks, the task most like the museum environment of reading labels, Etaugh and Ptasnik (1982), Fogelson

(1973), and others have found that silence produced even better scores than preferred music. Their findings agree with what I have found in my laboratory, whenever I have tested it. Nearly all students consistently do worse on comprehension tests with music of any kind, though they often claim music helps them study. The exceptions may be when music screens distracting noises or helps anxious students relax.

In the case of oral messages, when music is also present with any intensity, it is clearly harder to separate message from distractor because they are both within the same sense modality. For example, Pearsall (1989) found interference from familiar tonal or atonal background music on a listening comprehension task, though as noted above neither affected reading comprehension. The volume of the background music is important here. Any strong sound simultaneous with a spoken message is likely to lead to interference, particularly if it has high information load. In these cases it probably is a matter of increased information confusion and also a matter of hearing clearly.

Miller and Schyb (1989) found that nonverbal tasks are enhanced by background music. On the other hand, Sogin (1988) used an eye/hand performance task and three types of music background, classical, jazz, and popular, and found no differences. Subjects reported interferences from rhythm and loudness, but the number of problems completed did not indicate any differences in performance under any condition. It is clear that subject reports must be checked against actual score comparisons.

Task variables are important to museums because their "tasks" include reading and comprehending labels, and perhaps nonverbal interactives. But what about the low involvement viewers, who are not really engaging in any task? We need to reach them and change their attitude without much cognitive effort on their part, and the evidence suggests that involving music helps. Affect reaches low involvement people, and music is quite efficient at communicating affect. Hence, Sullivan (1990) found that the more involving "adult contemporary" music was much more effective at generating a favorable attitude toward the ad than "easy listening." This was so for low involvement ads on radio. Favorable attitude toward the ad (exhibit) is an essential ingredient in attitude toward message. Thus, the formula is to use involving music to draw low involvement viewers into involving exhibits, but to keep music–message congruity so as not to distract the highly involved viewers from their reading comprehension.

The Relaxation Factor. Several studies have shown significant effects of music on comprehension. The intervening variable is relaxation. Low-level background music in discussions is beneficial, and probably music's relaxation property is the factor here. Davidson and Powell (1986) looked at the effect of "easy listening" background music on the ability of fifth-graders to stay in engaged in discussions. They found a significant increase for boys, but because girls were already highly engaged, there was little room for improvement, and the effect was not significant, though it was in the right direction. Here, because the situation involves auditory comprehension, the music is better if it is uninvolving. It is not being used to draw people in but to relax.

The dominant effect of "elevator music" may be to relax people, but this too may not always be a good idea. The amount of attention as a function of relaxation is an inverted U-shape, so that some relaxation increases attention, but too much reduces it again. Again, a matter for testing. For cognitive participation, a science museum that is an exciting place may want more relaxation, whereas a history museum may want less.

It is not always clear whether relaxation works through the mechanism of creating mood or whether it acts directly. For example, Stratton and Zalanowski (1984) looked at the influence of music on the ability of focus groups to reach consensus. They report that the groups who worked in the presence of soothing music verbalized more and took longer than those in stimulating music or no-music conditions. Their accuracy of judgment, on the other hand, was not affected. Another study found that conversations of focus groups taking place in the presence of background music were rated as more satisfying, especially when the music was in the major mode rather than the minor (Blood & Ferriss, 1993), but the authors never tell us exactly what music they used. Clearly, research in the museum setting would be useful here because visitors often arrive in small social groups and discuss as they move along.

However, as we have seen, although relaxing music may interfere with exhibits. Is there a way to use it for relaxation without the interference? Perhaps so. A few studies have shown that music used for relaxation before a comprehension task increased scores. For example, Thaut and de l'Etoile (1993) induced a relaxed mood before a learning session and found that comprehension is better than any combination of music presented during the learning or during the recall stages.

Stanton (1975) compared subjects who had high and low anxiety on a verbal comprehension task under three conditions, no music, music before the test while subjects were entering the room, and music throughout the test. The music in this case was a slow movement from a Mozart symphony. For the students of low anxiety there were no differences, but the highly anxious did better with music than with silence.

For some subjects even the few minutes of Mozart had a important beneficial effect because there was no difference whether they heard music only while entering or for the whole test time.

Individual Differences. Individual differences are doubtless also important, though marketers cannot usually act on them. For example, (Daoussis & McKelvie, 1986) showed differences in the effect of background music depending on whether subjects were extroverts or introverts. Extroverts showed equal retention scores when their comprehension was tested in music versus no-music conditions. Introverts, on the other hand, did significantly worse in the presence of music compared to no-music. The reason is not clear.

Another variable in the effect of music on comprehension is the frequency with which the subjects normally study with music, that is, a practice effect. Etaugh and Michals (1975) found that the more frequently college students reported studying with music, the less music impaired their performance on a reading comprehension task. This suggests there may be generational differences to consider, because younger people are more used to constant music. Gender differences have also been reported (Miller & Schyb, 1989). To get at some of these effects, one might hand out cassettes with different types of music to accompany an exhibit and evaluate various variables afterward.

FREUDIAN SYMBOLISM

For much of the twentieth century marketers have flirted with Freudian symbols, but to understand how we must digress to introduce a bit of Freudian theory. In the early twentieth century few individuals had a greater impact than Sigmund Freud. He began his writing about 1890 but remained in obscurity until the turn of the century. By 1910 his psychoanalytic theory had become discussed in academic circles in the United States, and by 1920 it was part of everyday discussion (Gay, 1989). His concepts of id, ego, and superego, and his description of ego defense mechanisms have become so widely utilized that it is hard to imagine a time when such ideas were missing. His greatest contribution was probably to make the potential role of the unconscious generally understood. Today, there is little argument about the reality of the unconscious, but considerable disagreement remains about its nature and dynamics.

In Freudian theory, the id is the source of strong instinctual urges, wishes, and desires, particularly of a sexual nature. The superego arises from one's culture and represents all the do's and don'ts of society. Thus, the id and superego are brought into conflict with resulting psychological feelings of guilt and anxiety. Faced with resolving the conflict, the ego turns the wishes of the id toward socially acceptable outcomes (sublimation), or, if they are just too evil to find expression, buries them in the unconscious (repression). There, Freud argued, even though they are no longer accessible to the conscious mind, they continue to exert pressure for satisfaction. Freud saw his method of free association and dream analysis as the only mechanisms available to observe the conflict, and these would provide enlightenment only if one understood the role that symbols played.

Freud attempted to determine the meaning of dream symbols by studying ancient legends and myths, by looking carefully at word origins, by analyzing clinical cases, but it seems clear now that he was biased in looking almost exclusively for meanings which supported his theory of sexuality. To get an idea of the way Freud interpreted symbols, we can go to the translation of Freud himself. In 1915–1917 he delivered a series of lectures at the University of Vienna in which he laid out the essentials of psychoanalysis. The tenth lecture on the symbolism in dreams probably his most concise statement on the topic is still available in bookstores in paperback form (Freud, 1960). For Freud, "an overwhelming majority of symbols in dreams are sexual symbols." (p.161) He writes:

> The number of things which are represented symbolically in dreams is not great. The human body as a whole, parents, children, brothers and sisters, birth, death, nakedness—and one thing more [sexuality]. The only typical, that is to say, regularly occurring, representation of the human form as a whole is that of a house,... When the walls are quite smooth, the house means a man; when there are ledges and balconies which can be caught hold of, a woman. Parents appear in dreams as emperor and empress, king and queen or other exalted personages;... Children and brothers and sisters are less tenderly treated, being symbolized by little animals or vermin. Birth is almost invariably represented by some reference to water:... For dying we have setting out upon a journey or travelling by train,... clothes and uniforms stand for nakedness (Freud, 1960, p. 160).

In Freud's analysis nearly all objects represent sexuality. For example, he believed that the dream occurrence of any of the following represented symbolically the male sexual organ: any long object, like umbrellas, trees, pencils, hammers, and particularly guns, because they also shoot; sharp pointed objects or weapons; objects from which water flows, like taps, or water cans; long reptiles or fishes, particularly snakes or serpents; the number three; objects related to rhythmic movement, like machinery; and various other things of less clear origin, like hats, cloaks, mountains, and rocks. The female sexual organ also appeared symbolically for Freud in objects which enclose a space or act as receptacles, like caves, boxes, ships, cupboards, and particularly rooms; less clearly, materials of many kinds, like wood, paper, and objects made of these, such as tables and books; also, churches, chapels, landscapes, gardens, blossoms and flowers. The breasts are symbolized by fruits, particularly apples and peaches.

Freud felt that id forces exist in the unconscious as wishful impulses sometimes of a repellent kind. The wishes are satisfied in the dream state, but they are transformed into symbols by the ego to make the forbidden meaning unrecognizable to consciousness. In other words, "dreams are the disguised fulfillment of a repressed wish." (Gay, 1989, p. 28) Freud believed that these same symbols might also appear in the waking state, where they might form the basis for "symptomatic actions," for example, the now famous "Freudian slip." Thus, the Freudian approach is that many behaviors have unconscious sexual significance but represent a socially acceptable expression of an unacceptable wish. It is this connection that some claim appears in the guise of consumption.

Another aspect of Freud's psychoanalytic theory is the concept of psychosexual stages of development. Disturbances in any of these stages leads to adult behavior which particularly focused on, and showed need for, activities of that stage. For example, in the first, or oral, stage the mouth is the prominent source of tension reduction (e.g., eating) and pleasure (e.g., sucking). Frustration or overindulgence at this stage, Freud maintained, led to an adult who was likely to show fixation, that is, a particularly strong need for oral expression. Thus, eating, drinking, and smoking, and increased needs to incorporate or identify with objects (i.e., consume in general) are symbolic expressions of an unresolved oral stage need. Similarly, fixation originating in the second, or anal, stage reveals itself by compulsivity, overneatness, hoarding, collecting, and in general acquiring and holding on to things (more consumption).

Clothing Applications

By the 1920s, Freud's ideas were being widely accepted, in spite of the fact that they had little empirical support. Indeed, the ideas of psychoanalysis were so popular that they were applied to all kinds of situations. Their application to marketing and advertising was no exception. Freud's impact broadened the concept of need to include unconscious psychological needs, and the appeal to consumers became an appeal to their unconscious sexual wishes. Sproles and Burns (1994) summarized a number of psychoanalytic approaches to the sexual symbolism of clothing. They point out that Flugel felt that clothes might symbolize sexual organs. They furnish an apt quote:

> a great many articles of dress, such as the shoe, the tie, the hat, the collar, and even larger and voluminous garments, such as the coat, the trousers, and the mantle may be phallic symbols, while the shoe, the girdle, and the garter (as well as most jewels) may be corresponding female symbols (Flugel, 1930, p. 27, as cited in Sproles & Burns, 1994).

You will note that the shoe appears as both a phallic symbol and as a female one. Just when it is one or the other is not clear.

As late as 1981, writers still invoked Freudian symbolism in clothes. For example, Lurie maintains that hats, umbrellas, walking sticks, excess jewelry, neckties, and breast pocket handkerchiefs have served as phallic symbols throughout history, and a purse conveys erotic information. She wrote:

> a tightly snapped, zipped and buckled purse suggests a woman who guards her physical and emotional privacy closely, one whom it will be difficult to get to know in either the common or the Biblical sense. An open-topped tote bag suggests an open, trusting nature: someone who is emotionally and sexually more accessible (Lurie, 1981, p. 243, as cited in Sproles & Burns, 1994).

Apparently, it was sufficient for Freud simply to say so, and it became fact.

Dichter's Applications

The approach reached its zenith in the 1950s particularly with the work of Ernest Dichter, who was catapulted into national prominence when he was featured by Vance Packard in his best selling book, *The Hidden Persuaders*. Dichter was the president of the Institute for Motivational Research, Inc. and as early as the mid-thirties pioneered the use of "depth interviews" to uncover the real reasons consumers were buying (or not buying) clients' products.

Packard reported how Dichter and other "motivation researchers" were using Freudian concepts to sell products:

> A classical example of the way motivation analysts found merchandising possibilities in our deeper sexual yearnings was a study by Dr. Dichter made for Chrysler Corporation in the early days of M.R. [motivation research]. His study is now known as "Mistress versus Wife." Dr. Dichter was called upon to explain a fact puzzling marketers of the auto. While most men bought sedans and rarely bought convertibles, they evidently were more attracted to

convertibles. Dealers had found that they could draw more males into their showrooms by putting convertibles in the window. After exploring the situation Dr. Dichter concluded that men saw the convertible as a possible symbolic mistress. It set them daydreaming of youth, romance, adventure just as they may dream of a mistress. The man knows he is not going to gratify his wish for a mistress, but it is pleasant to daydream. This daydreaming drew the man into the auto salesroom. Once there, he finally chose a four-door sedan just as he once married a plain girl who, he knew, would make a fine wife and mother. "Symbolically, he marries the sedan," a spokesman for Dr. Dichter explained.... The spokesman went on to explain Dr. Dichter's line of thinking: "If we get a union between the wife and mistress—all we sought in a wife plus the romance, youth, and adventure we want in a mistress—we would have ... lo and behold, the hardtop!" The hardtop was soon to become the most successful new auto style introduced in the American market for several years, and Dr. Dichter's organization takes full credit for inspiring it by its "Mistress versus Wife" study (Packard, 1957, pp. 73–74).

To emphasize the Freudian connection here, remember that to Freud the car is a female symbol because, like a ship, it is basically a container. The common male desire to drive and control with more horsepower, speed, and acceleration to thrust forward were interpreted as symbols of the unconscious wish for sexual mastery and domination over women.

A Freudian interpretation could be applied to almost anything. For example, the roundness of design that became popular in the late thirties and forties was generally considered to have originated with streamlining and the desire to represent speed visually, as we discussed in an earlier chapter. Dichter, however, maintained that it represented the roundness of the female body and was particularly symbolized in the automobile. Is this a correct interpretation? There were no empirical tests of this Freudian interpretation, and the unreliability of such speculating appears when, on another occasion, the automobile was not claimed to be a female symbol, but a phallic symbol, and hence, obviously masculine.

Other claims made by Dichter and his organization included the following: large amounts of life insurance enhance feelings of male sexual potency; women bake cakes out of a symbolic desire to give birth; vegetable shortening is preferred over animal fats because the latter stimulate a sense of sin; men who wear suspenders do so because of an unresolved castration complex (cited in Engel, Blackwell, & Miniard, 1986, p. 48).

The problem with Dichter's analyses may be illustrated by the following case. Dichter recommended that ice cream in advertisements should be shown as overflowing the cone or plate to encourage viewers to sink their mouths in it and indulge their voluptuous oral needs. He predicted that such pictures would be more effective than neatly presented ones because "ice cream symbolizes to many of us uninhibited overindulgence or voluptuousness, via the mouth." (Packard, 1957, p. 86) Until recently, ads for Bailey's Ice Cream Parlors were all done that way. In this case Dichter may be right, and pictures of overflowing ice cream plates may indeed suggest more sensuous channels and increase attraction, but such elements do not require any reference to oral stages of psychosexual development to be understood. Pleasure and sensual delight does not need a Freudian explanation. The example illustrates the general problem with Freudian theory, in advertising and also in clinical use. It can be made to fit a tremendous variety of situations, but this does not mean it is correct.

Evaluation of Freudian Application

It has proven nearly impossible to confirm Freudian theory empirically. For example, good unbiased studies on the effectiveness of Freudian symbols used in advertising are almost impossible to obtain. Rosser Reeves, the CEO of a large and successful advertising agency, spent more than 20 years in the advertising business and wrote a book hailed by his colleagues as "the definitive book on advertising." He was known as a careful researcher of advertising effectiveness, and writing only a year or two after *The Hidden Persuaders* appeared, Reeves comments on measuring the effectiveness of Freudian symbols:

> On our staff are specialists whose only job is to follow all the developments in the Freudian field. We work with, and retain, many distinguished academicians who are pioneers in originating new measurement of this kind; but it is a plain, simple, and very unvarnished fact that we have not yet reached the day when such research techniques can be applied to population masses.... There are one or two practitioners in advertising who claim to be in touch with the Freudian infinite. Like the Delphic oracle, they stay in business, we suspect, because people want to believe that they know the answers. We have tried them, and we find their reports vague, subjective, and as confusing as a hall of distorting mirrors. Their findings, certainly, are not duplicable. Detroit, at one point in its history, paid an enormous fee for "research" of this kind. It revealed that motor cars were actually phallic symbols, and that people wanted them bigger than ever—rolling juke boxes, flashing and glittering with chrome. The public, unaware of so hidden a motivation, proceeded to buy small cars by hundreds of thousands, costing Detroit tens of millions of dollars. If you find this story extreme, we could give you many others (Reeves, 1961, pp. 71–72).

In the Freudians' defense, however, it should be pointed out that they never said it was the only factor. In the case of Reeves' last cited example, it could be argued that fuel economy simply became the over-

Figure 5 The tripartite symbol was seen by Freud as an expression of masculine sexuality. Whether this meaning was intended by the ad designer is, of course, not known. (Reproduced by courtesy of The Gillette Company.)

whelming consideration. At any rate, some applications of Freudian symbolism thus fell out of favor with some advertising people because it could not be shown that it is effective. On the other hand, other advertisers have retained the Freudian idea that sexual interest can be unconsciously aroused by suggestive images. Ads continue to appear that could certainly be interpreted as Freudian symbolism. An example is shown in Figure 5 (and I thank The Gillette Company for their unusual cooperation). The ad for *Dry Idea* employs the classic Freudian tripartite symbol of masculinity, but whether it was intentionally chosen for its Freudian significance is not known. Another example, contributed by my students, is an ad for Parliament cigarettes that shows a pack of cigarettes with several cigarettes protruding upward through a wooden dock. On the surface it simply seems to dramatize the slogan, "The taste breaks through," but it is an odd choice. Cigarettes themselves, being cylinders, are quite Freudian, and a cylinder bursting through a barrier could certainly be interpreted as a Freudian extension. Again, whether this is consciously or unconsciously done is not known.

CHAPTER 6

Affect, Emotion, and Involvement

DEFINITIONS AND DISTINCTIONS

Affect as Different from Cognition

In the way of thinking we are following here, emotion and affect differ from cognition because they are feeling states. They are processes of liking or disliking, wanting to have, or wanting to avoid. They are pleasure, anger, fear, pain, or desire. Following Zajonc (Zajonc, 1980, 1984), it is argued that the neural circuits involved in emotion and affect differ from the cognitive circuits, and thus they are separate functions.

This view was first expressed in the late 60s, when Robert Zajonc (pronounced like "science") made the claim that affect and cognition are independent systems, basing his claim on his own research (Zajonc, 1968). His findings were surprising and turned the common sense notions upside down. He flashed stimuli that subjects had seen before on a screen at very rapid rates. He was able to show that subjects could report the affect of the stimuli at consistently better than chance levels, when they still could not tell what the stimuli were, or even whether something had been there at all. He was not believed at first, but the finding has been replicated (e.g., Anand, Holbrook, & Stephens, 1988) and appears to be solid.

The opposing view is represented by Richard Lazarus (1981, 1984) who argues that whether the stimulus is consciously noted or not, it is still the stimulus that triggers the emotion. Thus, because perceived stimuli are elements of cognition, cognition must always come first. The resolution of the controversy hinges mainly on one's definitions of cognition, emotion, and affect. Lazarus (1991) distinguishes two modes of appraisal, both cognitive in his view, "one automatic, unreflective, and unconscious or preconscious; the other deliberate and conscious." (p. 128) The automatic mode clearly triggers affective response, yet the cognitions involved are of a decidedly low level, even unconscious. The deliberate mode has more commonly been regarded as cognition. Yet Lazarus himself says that "I think it is wise to exclude reflexlike processes from what we are calling cognition." (p. 129) These "reflexlike processes" include what others call affect and are the source of argument with Lazarus. Although some sort of cognitive appraisal is sometimes necessary on the first encounter with a stimulus, the stimulus appears to be affectively tagged at that point, so that in subsequent encounters no appraisal is required, but rather the affective tag is "read" and action taken automatically on the basis of the reading. This reading of the affective value is no longer cognitively based, but affectively based, and can be considered a separate system.

Support for this view of separate systems is growing because neurological evidence indicates two distinct levels of operation in the brain, and they act more independently than we had previously thought (e.g., LeDoux, 1992). Thus, for our purposes here we will follow Zajonc and regard cognition and affect as two distinctly different processes and leave for others the question of where the boundaries of cognition lie.

Cognition certainly comprises an important side of consumer behavior, particularly with products that have greater importance, but our actions often result from feeling states instead of cognition, and we may not know it at the time. For example, when we ignore logic in favor of a position we have already taken or because of an authority we already trust, we are really putting affect above cognition. Much of the controversy in consumer psychology has concerned the question of how much we buy from reason (cognition) and how much from feelings (affect).

In the 1980s cognitive psychologists and consumer behavior researchers renewed interest in affect and emotions, whereas previously they had focused almost exclusively on intellect (Holman, 1986). Various labels have been used, such as "affect," "affective response," "feelings," "emotional response," and "emotional feelings." (Machleit and Wilson, 1988)

Affect, Emotion, Evaluation, and Mood

In the last decade, the term "affect" is gradually being preferred to "emotion" in consumer research because of the developments discussed above, but the argument is by no means settled. Considerable debate has focused on whether affect and emotion are really the same, or whether they are distinguishable, and whether there are other terms equally appropriate. Some treat them as equivalent, and others as different in some way. For reviews of the distinctions drawn among affect, emotions, moods, feelings, and drives, see Batson, Shaw, and Oleson (1992) and Batra and Ray (1986).

Rather than getting bogged down in the controversy, we have followed Russell (1979) and consider affect as referring essentially to the pleasure-pain dimension, a form of feeling, but not necessarily an aroused form. On the other hand, we consider that emotion implies some level of arousal and also feeling. Emotion also includes levels of meaning, so that all of the particular emotions have their distinctive meanings. When we speak of behavior which is emotional, we are referring to affect plus some particular meaning and some level of arousal, the more emotional, the more aroused. Emotion is usually accompanied by physical indexes of arousal, such as increases in heart rate, blood pressure, and breathing rate, and is typified by terms, such as anger or love. "Emotion" refers to the high end of the arousal scale and includes affect. "Affect" can refer to feelings at the low end of the arousal scale, such as mild liking or disliking (usually considered preferences), levels not normally considered emotional. Whether either end of the affective-emotional spectrum actually leads to behavior is yet another matter.

Recently, Zanna and Rampel (1988) have argued for the separation of the terms "evaluation" and "affect." They see a possible state characterized as simply a cognitive determination, for or against, with no feeling involved, whereas affect, they argue, requires an experienced feeling state. They argue that, by definition, one cannot have affect without being aware of it, for does not the word "feeling" imply conscious awareness?

However, the weight of the evidence suggests that one can indeed feel without being aware of it and also that one can be aware of feeling without being aware of the source. In fact, this often makes us think we are being rational, when in fact we are responding affectively. To be "for" something is, I would argue, to feel a certain way, but we may be aware only of the cognitive component, not the affective one. The problem is essentially the same as that encountered in the field of attention, when we say some level of ourselves attends, but we are not aware of it in our highest level. Many studies have shown that information, particularly of the affective type, is processed while we were unaware of it at the time. We can no longer think of our minds in the unified way we once did, but rather we must see ourselves as multiple processors operating in parallel. Hence, here we will use the single term affect and include within it unconscious and conscious feelings, paradoxical as that may sound to some.

"Mood" is yet another related term, but is quite different. Morris (1992) argues that emotion and affect are cued by properties of the environment, whereas mood is produced by cues about the state of the self. Mood, he says, tells us about the internal resources we have available to meet the environmental demands. Mood's biggest impact is on the process of attention, and we considered it primarily in that chapter. Mood also influences and is influenced by memory (See Kuiken, 1991).

Emotion: Affect Plus Meaning and Arousal

Debate as to just what emotion is goes back centuries, but we will start with the twentieth century when different theories have emphasized one or the other aspect of emotion. For example, the behaviorists felt that feeling states are too subjective and not measurable and so avoided the question of feelings by defining emotion as aroused behavior. To William James at the turn of the century it meant something quite different, the sensing of our aroused internal physiological states. With the studies of Schachter and Singer (1962) that view was no longer tenable. Instead, emotion came to mean a directive state that accompanies arousal. All of these theoretical approaches contain aspects of truth and together point up the three important elements of emotion: affect (or feeling), direction (or meaning), and degree of arousal (or intensity). More on these in a moment.

An Approach-Avoid Cue.   We tend to think of emotion as a bad thing, but emotion is vital to us, because it is a signal that something we are perceiving has importance, and it tells us how to respond appropriately. Consider, for example, a young gosling. Tinbergen (1951) found that when the silhouette of a hawk, cut out of black paper, is moved above a gosling, the gosling becomes extremely agitated and shows fear responses. The fear motivates it to run and hide. In other words, the emotion of fear is vital for its survival. Katz (1960) pointed out the utility of affect in providing structure to a chaotic world by enabling us to distinguish and categorize objects, persons, and ideas on the basis of attractiveness. Such structure has survival value because it allows rapid direction of the behaviors of approach or avoidance when these objects are encountered again in the future.

From all of the evidence, one could argue that the cueing of approach-avoidance behavior is the main purpose of emotion and affect. Pleasant things cue approach, whereas painful or unpleasant ones cue avoidance. Thus, our behavior is directed quickly on the next encounter with a stimulus. However, although the dimension of approach-avoid is dominant, other dimensions have also evolved so that emotion comes in many flavors.

The Qualities of Emotion. Feeling, direction, and degree of arousal, the three elements of emotion, combine in an astonishingly large variety of ways with unique meanings, so that they vary in quality. A number of researchers, using several methods, have attempted to catalog these emotional qualities. Plutchik (1984), after extensive rating by subjects and sophisticated mathematical analysis, concluded that there are eight fundamental emotions which he arranged in a circle, and eight others on the borders between the first eight. The emotions he identified in order (the main eight underlined) are: joy, love, acceptance, submission, fear, awe, surprise, disappointment, sadness, remorse, disgust, contempt, anger, aggressiveness, anticipation, and optimism. These sixteen nouns provide a manageable number of emotions for working purposes, yet reveal the wide range possible.

Izard (1977) proposed a similar list and found ten primary emotions, including shame and guilt, which Plutchik omitted. Both Plutchik's and Izard's systems have been tested and their validity has been essentially borne out by research. For example, Allen, Machleit, and Marine (1988) tried out Izard's list on people viewing ads. They reported that the differential emotions scale which Izard developed from his work allows the researcher to detect diverse and sophisticated emotional experience during ad processing, but they suggested that these experiences may not take place in the real world of advertising exposure. This criticism is common with laboratory research, but simply means that whatever is found needs to be further tested in the field. A stronger criticism was that both Izard's and Plutchik's formulations are too unwieldy to be useful because of their potential complexity.

Simpler formulations have been proposed which are easier to use. For example, three dimensions were worked out as basic to emotion by Schlosberg (1954), based on Wundt (1902): pleasant-unpleasant, relaxed-tense, and accepted-rejected. Osgood, Suci, and Tannenbaum (1957) also found that three dimensions are adequate, but labeled them good-bad, strong-weak, and fast-slow.

PAD Paradigm. More recently, Russell and Mehrabian (1977), using extensive statistical analysis, also distinguished three basic dimensions of emotion: pleasure-displeasure, arousal-unarousal, and dominance-submissiveness, sometimes called the PAD paradigm (Holbrook, 1986), after the first three letters of the dimensions. Their formulation is not unlike that of Schlosberg (1954) but differs a bit in the last category. Russell and Mehrabian characterize this category, dominance, as the extent to which a person feels in control and has freedom to act in a number of ways. They mean control over one's environment, rather than necessarily over other people. This dimension is an important aspect of environmental psychology and has considerable relevance for designers of retail spaces and exhibits, as their explanation makes clearer:

> An individual's feeling of dominance in a situation is based on the extent to which he feels unrestricted or free to act in a variety of ways. This feeling can be hampered by settings that limit the forms of behavior and enhanced by settings that facilitate a greater variety of behaviors. For instance, an individual has greater freedom, and therefore a feeling of dominance, in his own territory (e.g., listening to music at home relative to doing so in a concert hall or reading the same book in his office rather than in a library). A kitchen or an office that is well stocked with a variety of tools facilitates more behaviors (and enhances feelings of dominance) than one that is only sparsely equipped. Flexible interior decorations, such as movable room partitions, adjustable levels of lighting, or movable furniture allow many arrangements suited to a greater variety of activities. Thus, relative to others that are fixed and difficult to change, such flexible arrangements are conducive to a feeling of dominance (Mehrabian & Russell, 1974, pp. 19–20).

In commenting on changing intensities of the other two dimensions, Mehrabian and Russell find that, although the pleasure dimension usually becomes more effective when there is more of it, the arousal dimension has the most behavioral payoff when it is moderate, neither too high nor too low. In this they support the findings of Yerkes and Dodson (1908) and subsequent researchers (e.g., Duffy, 1962) who found an inverted U-shaped curve of behavior as a function of arousal, such that too little arousal fails to produce behavior because of lack of motivation, whereas too much blocks behavior because of anxiety and indecision.

Havlena and Holbrook (1986) compared the Plutchik and the Russell-Mehrabian analyses for use in marketing applications and concluded that "In general, the three dimensions of pleasure, arousal, and dominance captured more information about the emotional character of consumption experiences than did their measurement via the eight basic emotional categories recommended by Plutchik." (p. 402) They confirmed that the marketer would lose little by focusing on these three qualities.

Pleasure and Arousal. Finally, Russell (1979) changed his mind on the quality of dominance and writes that dominance is not a separate dimension after all, but rather a subcategory of pleasure-displeasure. He feels that although it is a major determinant of whether an event is experienced as pleasant or not, it should not be considered a separate dimension. As we have mentioned, however, it has particular relevance in some areas, where it is an important aspect to bear in mind.

Thus, the dimensions particularly important for the marketer come down to two: pleasure-displeasure (essentially the basic information of approach-avoid) and arousal-unarousal (essentially the information of intensity or importance). Because some consider that emotion requires arousal and preferences are often unaroused, it is better to use the term affect rather than emotion for the quality in question. In other words, what one has to worry about in the affective content of advertising is simply whether people associate pleasure with the product or not and how much.

It is not as simple as it sounds, however, because even pleasure comes in many forms, for example, dominance, which we have just discussed in the work of Russell and Mehrabian (1977). Although many sources of pleasure are fairly common and universal, it may be that certain target groups have unique tastes, so that ultimately the task of determining just which ads are perceived as pleasurable and just how intense they are perceived to be may be a question for empirical measurement and will make actual application more difficult than it appears at first.

Buying Versus Consuming.   We have seen that simplifying the emotional qualities is a legitimate way to simplify the marketer's task. On the other hand, we should not be misled into thinking that the consumptive experience itself is reducible in this way. Holbrook (1986) makes this point quite strongly and offers some anecdotal examples of Plutchik's primary emotions as they might be experienced in a consumptive situation:

> Acceptance: deep personal liking for your favorite talk-show host
> Disgust: discovering that you have just swallowed a large mouthful of sour milk
> Fear: eating your first mouthful of canned tuna that was recently recalled because of a botulism scare
> Anger: realizing that the auto salesman sold you a car that gets eight miles per gallon in highway driving
> Joy: listening to the finale of Beethoven's Ninth Symphony
> Sadness: being seven years old on Christmas morning and finding out that your new video game does not work
> Expectancy (Anticipation): beginning to read the last chapter of an Agatha Christie novel ...
>
> one expects that emotions such as those just listed will feed back upon subsequent purchase decisions in a manner that might build repeat buying (Beethoven recordings, murder mysteries), enlarge audience share (talk-

show ratings), and boost attendance (basketball games) or, conversely, that might discourage future buying behavior (milk, automobiles, tuna, and video games) (Holbrook, 1986, pp. 40–41).

Holbrook feels that if the consumption experience involves emotion, and it clearly does, then understanding this factor is important to marketing, and he notes that advertisers have begun to use the full range of emotions in their appeals. On the other hand, after researching and discussing the full range of emotional experience in consumption, he finally concedes that the simplified PAD approach (Russell & Mehrabian, 1977) is probably more useful in investigating emotional responses to consumption (Holbrook, 1986).

This long discussion of affect and emotion is more than academic because when you trigger affect in someone, it has important influences on behavior. In general, it is the triggering of affect that gets people to pay attention, think more, and remember better; all important advertising goals. It turns out that most of affect is personally relevant, and when it is, it is called involvement. As we have seen in chapter 2, involvement increases attention. Here we also consider some of the other effects affect has on cognition.

COGNITIVE IMPACT OF AFFECT

Increased Cognitive Effort

The evidence has accumulated that affect and cognition may drive each other at various times. Cognition is driving affect when we read a story about a tragedy and we find tears coming to our eyes. On the other hand, affect drives cognition when a picture of a twisted wreck draws us to read about the circumstances. The use of affect to drive cognition is much more common in advertising because affect can be delivered so much faster. Reading takes time, and readers must be engaged before they will spend that time. Because advertising is often a matter of a few seconds, time counts. I was showing some ads to a class to illustrate some point in consumer psychology, when one of them remarked that they were old. They were in fact from magazines of eight years before. To me that does not seem "old" in any way, but to them it clearly did. The point here is that they lost interest because the ads were old. Their cognitions were turned off by their feelings of negative affect. Note that the age of the ads is cognitive, but the meaning that age has for the students is a negative one of irrelevance, and the meaning shuts down the cognitive process. Ads, of course, use positive affect to turn on cognition. We consider next some of the common sources of positive affect in ads.

Involvement: A Special Case of Affect. We introduced the concept of involvement in chapter 2 under attention. It might be well to review that discussion here. It is clear that personal relevance is a dominating characteristic of attention-getting stimuli. Not surprising, it turns out that involvement is also relevant to the topic of decision making, and indeed to most other topics in psychology. The key is that it arouses affect. This moves our decision making away from a cognitive mode toward a more affective mode, and we may even ignore logic completely. If involvement becomes high enough, as in a life-threatening situation, emotional panic may set in accompanied by a total loss of decision making ability. For marketers, there is probably an optimum level of involvement, enough to get attention and provoke elaboration, but not enough to block cognition completely.

Now we will look more closely at just what involvement is. Since research on the topic began, a number of papers have shed light on the major aspects of involvement. The social psychologists Sherif and Hovland (1961), probably the first to use the term, meant by it the degree of linkage to strong beliefs and ego-involving attitudes. This link to attitudes set the direction of most of the subsequent psychological research until a shift away from attitudes to simply personal connections occurred in 1965 when Krugman applied the term to advertising. He concluded that the reason that some material never makes the transfer from short-term to long-term memory is that it is essentially meaningless or unimportant to the viewer. He argued that for material to be retained it must be personally involving. By personal involvement, he says, we do not mean attention, interest, or excitement but the number of conscious "bridging experiences," connections, or personal references per minute that viewers make between their own lives and the stimulus. This may vary from none to many (Krugman, 1965, p. 355). The connections may be cognitive or affective.

Krugman went on to distinguish two levels of involvement, one low and the other high, and claimed that the impact of communications is different in these two states. He also noted that involvement is a continuum, not really a two-state condition. Krugman implies that many of the traditional rules of learning were developed in the high involvement condition and may not be applicable in low-level involvement conditions. Some types of persuasion seem to work well with low involvement, whereas more cognitive elements, such as verbal learning and argument, require high involvement.

In general, Krugman's early analysis has been borne out by the empirical evidence. His modest beginning inspired three decades of research to understand involvement. For example, an influential model of persuasion that extend Krugman's theory was proposed by Petty and Cacioppo (1981) and called the **elaboration likelihood model**. They proposed two routes to attitude change: the central route, in which the message is actively thought about (elaborated), and a peripheral route, in which the message is not thought about much at all. The peripheral route includes the mere exposure effect and affective reactions that are low in cognitive content. It turns out that the difference in using these cognitive routes is produced by involvement. The model predicts that when we are highly involved, we use the central route, pay attention to the message, and are sensitive to the credibility of the source. On the other hand, when we have low involvement, we pay more attention to the communicators, and respond to their perceived expertise and attractiveness rather than to the credibility of the source (Fiske & Taylor, 1991). We will return to Petty and Cacioppo and the concept of involvement in the chapter on attitudes because most of the research has been from that point of view.

After summarizing a number of the approaches, Greenwald and Leavitt (1984) write, "There is consensus that high involvement means (approximately) personal relevance or importance." (p. 583) Antil (1984) also reviewed the literature and points out that there is general agreement that involvement arises from personal importance, but that there is less agreement on what actually causes personal importance. Ego defensiveness and connections to one's past are certainly primary causes. Laurent and Kapferer (1985) analyzed the major components of product involvement and found that they are:

1. the personal meaning of the product;
2. the symbolic value attributed to the product's use;
3. the ability of the product to provide positive affect;
4. the perceived importance of negative consequences in the case of poor choice; and
5. the perceived probability of making such a mistake.

Thus, product involvement comes down to the three things that make a product important to us, personal meaning, symbolic value, and affective appeal, and the risk involved in deciding to buy it or not. In other words, these are the factors that make consumers remember a message about a product. The central role of affect in the process is clear.

Information-Processing Intensity. Cognitive information processing is nearly always accompanied by affect, simply because the human experience, life itself, is seldom without affect or emotion. But what exactly does this affect do? Mitchell (1979, 1981) drew our attention to the arousal aspect of involvement and argued that involvement resulted from arousal. It is confusing that they argue that involvement results from arousal, when most writers argue it produces arousal. It is likely that involvement results from affect, not arousal, and affect produces arousal. In attempting to sort it out, Burnkrant and Sawyer (1983) continued on Mitchell's theme but expanded the notion a bit. For them involvement stems from arousal, but a specific kind of arousal which gets us to look for information, and they call it "information-processing intensity." Again, it is likely that ultimately affect is signaling our cognitive need for information.

Levels of Processing Theory.   Some clarification of these viewpoints came with a model proposed by Greenwald and Leavitt (1984) in which they reviewed the involvement literature since Krugman's paper and put it together with the cognitive literature. Their theory was briefly introduced in chapter 2, and you may recall that they proposed four levels of involvement. rather than two. Their contribution was to associate each level of involvement with a successively more complex type of cognitive processing. They write that they "... associate the idea of increases in involvement with qualitatively distinct forms (levels) of cognitive activity that (1) require increasing amounts of attentional capacity and (2) produce increasingly durable effects on memory." (p. 584) The levels of processing theory concerns the interaction in involvement of two components, affect and cognition. In their model, affect usually moves involvement through the four levels, adding cognitive elements at each stage, but other attention-getting mechanisms also do this. Each of the lower levels of involvement in their model activates the next higher level if the content is determined to be important enough, that is, if the affect, or stimulation, is intense enough. Lower levels also produce the representations that the next higher level use for additional processing. The increasing levels of involvement are called preattention, focal attention, comprehension, and elaboration.

Preattention.   They term the lowest level preattention. This is the monitor level that we discussed in chapter 2. It monitors sensory input for those features we know as attention-getting, but material at this level is not retained. A person at this level is attracted by motion, bright color, novel sounds and the like, but not by meaning. Because they considered affect a type of meaning, Greenwald and Leavitt maintained that affective connections (that is, gut level reactions, such as "Wow, neat!" or "Ugh, gross.") do not occur until the second level of processing. However, considerable research suggests that Zajonc was right and that affect is indeed detected at the preattentional level, but only if it has previously been associated with the stimulus, that is, a stimulus must have been affectively tagged by a previous encounter. A kitten, for example, triggers a strong positive attraction because we have cuddled kittens before. The common sense view would dictate that one must register "that is a kitten" before the affect could be elicited, but the research surprisingly shows otherwise, as we explained above. For more on this, one should start with Zajonc and Marcus (1982).

The affective component constitutes involvement at the lowest level. It can be argued that even intense stimuli that are not yet affectively tagged produce affect because of the possible threat they present. Affect signals personal relevance and directs attention, but by itself does not permit retention. However, being usually detected earliest, it is likely to be the force that moves the cognitive processing to a higher level.

Focal Attention. The second level of cognitive functioning, focal attention, involves forming an image. This is probably when we distinguish figure and ground that the Gestaltists found was the earliest step of perception. Here a viewer may be pointing and, looking carefully, identifies something. Images may be retained at this level, but viewers will retain little else, because they are still in a low involvement condition. Meaning is not introduced until the next level.

Comprehension. The third level, comprehension, introduces "propositional content" (i.e., what things are). We would recognize familiar things, but identification of new things would not be complete because the stimulus is not yet connected to other ideas or retrieval cues. This level is characterized by, "Look at the bear!," but memory is limited to familiar things.

Elaboration. Full retention of cognitive information can come about only at the highest or fourth level, elaboration, where integration of the material with existing memory takes place. At this level we think *about* things. It is the multiple connections with our personal past that occur at this level which constitutes the highest level of involvement and leads to maximum retention. When these personal connections occur, there is usually a search for more information and a tendency to remember because the process of learning is one of drawing associations between new material and material already stored. Generally this involves thinking about the material in any one of a number of ways, such as, inventing a story, creating an image of some sort, or noticing connections to things we already know. We might notice that "this is the same as ...," "this explains why ...," "or this must be what happens when ...." The more connections we make, the better the new material relates to what we know. This is what we mean by understanding. Thus, the more elaboration that takes place, the better is the memory.

Studies have confirmed that our ability to remember is a function of how much of this elaboration we do with the new material, not a function of whether one intends to learn or not. As long as the person engages in the same mental activities when intending to learn as when not, the memory performance is identical (Anderson, 1990). The reason that intentions matter is that people who intend to learn do more elaboration.

The importance for the marketer here is that only ads or brand names that provoke more elaboration are better remembered. Take brand names, for example. Nouns are more likely than verbs to call up an image. Verbs need an actor, and if the actor is different on each recall, memory can become fragmented. Meaningless names or acronyms are hard to remember because they do not hook into anything else and are not elaborated. Thus, brand names that are associated with strong images produce the best recall.

Support for the Theory.   Let us look again at the study by Rogers, Kuiper, and Kirker (1977) that we introduced in the last chapter to illustrate the importance of increased elaboration in processing information. The same study also supplies strong support for the role that involvement plays in processing. Recall that self-referenced words are recalled best. In fact, the number of self-reference words recalled is more than double the highest purely semantic category. By definition self-reference is almost involvement, and this study illustrates its powerful effect.

A study by Mittal (1988) supports this analysis, as does one by Celsi and Olson (1988) in the realm of advertising. The latter authors found that if an advertising stimulus is personally relevant, it triggers a search for more information. Confirming the affective nature of this relevance, they use the term "felt involvement" and write:

> ... the consumers' felt involvement is a motivational state that influences (1) the amount and direction of their attention, (2) the cognitive and physical effort they expend during comprehension, (3) the focus of their attention and comprehension processes, and (4) the depth and breadth of semantic elaboration during comprehension (p. 223).

Thus, involvement works in two ways. First, affective links to our personal past get and hold our attention and motivate us to move our processing up to the level of elaboration. At the lowest level, personal relevance is detected through images or sounds that have previously established a strong affect. At this level affective connections and images may be retained, but little cognitive retention occurs. However, the presence of personal relevance moves material up to the level of elaboration.

Second, cognitive links to personal experience at the level of elaboration allow us to store new information by connecting the new with the already stored, resulting in better retention. The literature on consumer behavior establishes that increasing the viewers' perceptions of personal relevance leads to greater involvement at this level, thus producing more cognitive transfer and better memory. It is also clear that viewers may shift among levels of involvement moment to moment.

Mittal (1988) showed that products he calls "expressive" are more likely to be appraised by the affective mode than mainly utilitarian or functional products. By "expressive" he means those purchased for "psychosocial goals [that] include sensory enjoyment, mood-states attainment, social goals (e.g., impression management), and self-concept fulfillment." (p. 505) However, he does not imply that products must be of one type or the other, but that many products have aspects of both types.

Prioritized Cognitions

As we discussed in the attention chapter, cognitions that have strong affect get priority, absorb our attention, and dominate our thinking (Klinger, Barta, & Maxeiner, 1980). Now that we have introduced levels of processing theory, we can reconsider the study of Bitgood, S., Patterson, D., & Benefield, A. (1986), introduced in chapter 2. You will recall that their study found that dangerous species in a zoo attract attention more strongly than nondangerous ones. These authors also found that although attracting power increases, holding power does not, and now we are in a position to speculate why. One might speculate that the attention-getting is working first on the level of preattention and then on the level of focal attention. Finally the comprehension level is reached, and the realization arises that the stimulus is in a cage and not actually harmful. At this point the personal threat is gone, so focal attention decreases, and the viewer turns away. In other words, the personally relevant factor (personal threat, in this case) that controls holding power is lost once comprehension occurs.

What this means, in other words, is that affect often, if not usually, selects cognition. The process is unconscious, but what it means for the marketer is very important. For example, we gather information about a new car, and this is cognitive. But why are we interested in that particular car? It is likely that we have narrowed the search because of affective elements. For example, the car may be beautiful, maybe it has high status value, or maybe it is the brand my father always used to buy and was a part of my childhood. So although we may cognitively select the best among several, much of the sorting out may already been done on the basis of affect. How many people buy a car that they think is ugly? For other examples of affective control, think of how often we buy something we just want, cannot afford, do not really need, or may never use. Cognitively, such purchases do not make sense, but affectively they do.

Competition with Cognition

Mild affect is generally a motivator, but strong affect may be a distractor. Izard, Nagler, Randall, and Fox (1965) did a series of studies in which pictures were paired with nonsense syllables, which the subjects were to learn. The pictures differed in affective ratings, in which affect was rated on a simple bipolar scale of pleasant-unpleasant. The researchers expected that the stronger the affect, the better the learning. The unexpected findings were that mildly positive affective pictures produce faster learning than strongly affective pictures, whether positive or negative. In explaining this, the authors noted that some of the pictures were of girls' faces, and because the subjects were all male, the sexual interest in the faces was felt to be a competing factor. To test this, even more positively affective pictures of young women (in lingerie) were used, and the learning was, as predicted, worst of all. This study confirms the finding that the use of sexy stimuli in ads does get attention but may interfere with getting the message across, that is, stronger affect helps only when it is part of the message or far enough away not to interfere.

The study was repeated, but by using the same pictures only as background, while three-letter syllables to be associated appeared at the bottom of the screen. This arrangement reduced the competition between affect and cognition by making the affective material less noticeable and more easily separated. In this case positive affective rating of the pictures produced faster learning, rather than slower. When female subjects were tried, the results were surprising in that they were even more pronounced for females than males. The difference in the two studies seems to be that the second creates "free-floating" affect, whereas the first makes the affect a competing property of the stimulus to be learned. Then, the important general conclusion is that increases in affect increase learning, as long as competition with the message does not develop.

Kennedy (1971) found that advertising set within a situation comedy produced recall greater than when the same messages were set within a suspense thriller. Presumably the suspense thriller created more competing affect. This finding has been replicated several times since (see Anand & Sternthal, 1992). Unfortunately I fear this finding may become an excuse for endless production of low involvement sitcoms.

Blocked Cognition

A recent study by DeBono, Kerin, Shaker, and Shapiro (1992) is particularly interesting, because the affective stimulus in this study is gone before the cognitive stimulus appears, and yet it blocks the cognition. Two groups of subjects observed a perfume ad. One group was given the opportunity to sample the perfume beforehand, whereas the other was not. The authors report: "Those subjects who sampled the perfume were more influenced by the model's attractiveness than by argument strength. Subjects not exposed to the perfume were more influenced by argument strength than by the model's attractiveness." In other words, sampling the perfume created affect so strong that it shifted their attention away from the intended cognition, effectively blocking it.

Other Affective Influences

Affect may be playing several roles in information processing, as a recent study illustrates. Peracchio and Meyers-Levy (1994) studied the effect of ambiguity in ad pictures that is caused by cropping out an important part of the picture. We introduced this study in chapter 3 as an example of the perceptual process of conceptually constructing the missing part. Other ambiguities involve a verbal component (say the brand Pepsi, that we associate strongly with a dark cola drink) that disagrees with the picture (a clear colorless drink). They found that viewers feel a push or tension to resolve the ambiguity (by finding out that Pepsi has a new, clear form of the old drink, called Crystal Pepsi). Thus, they agree with the considerable literature that affect, the feeling that impels the attention, increases the likelihood of cognitive processing.

However, a second aspect of affect also appears in this study. They found that the resolution of the ambiguity produces positive affect. In other words, we get a feeling of relief, or pleasure, from getting the information we need. This is, of course, positive reinforcement, to which we will return in chapter 9.

A third role for affect occurs as a result of the information itself, that is, whether the picture we are looking at is happy or sad. A fourth level could be said to be represented by what it triggers in the way of connections to happy or sad events in our past. These last two levels represent affect that is supposed to transfer to a product or brand.

MAKING CHOICES: AFFECTIVE ELEMENTS

Predispositions

We are all familiar with the phrase, "Don't confuse me with the facts, my mind is made up." Zajonc gives us a particularly good anecdotal example of this behavior:

> Phoebe Ellsworth once wrote me about a decision process in which she was engaged. She was at Yale University at that time and had received a very attractive offer from Stanford University. Being at Yale, she of course followed the Irving Janis (1982) procedure for decision making in which one takes a large sheet of paper and on the left side lists all the positive points and on the right side all the negative points. All of the points are then weighed very carefully. At the end of this process, the decision maker should know exactly what to do.
>
> Phoebe wrote me that she and her husband tried to follow the procedure. They looked at the sheet for a long time and finally Phoebe exclaimed, "Oh hell, this is not working. I have to get some more pluses on the right side or else I will make the wrong decision." In other words there was an underlying prior predisposition that preempted what would be, in normative terms, a rational choice (Zajonc, 1986, pp. 2–3).

The "prior predisposition" of which Zajonc speaks is the affective component in the decision, whereas the technique of listing pluses and minuses gets only at the cognitive component.

Responding to Felt Need.   In the early years of the twentieth century there was a tendency to regard purchase decisions as generally reasoned and logical. Because of this, advertisements were mostly words and were directed at convincing by reasoned argument why the product in question was the best one to buy. Gradually, the effectiveness of pictures began to be understood, fueled in part by the rapidly improving technology of photography and printing. By the forties and fifties there was a shift to creating needs, rather than simply filling them. It was not until the eighties, however, that full realization of the role of affect began to dawn. In the last decade we have seen a big jump in the research on the topic. Now the research is focusing more on when cognition is used and when we fall back on affect. To complete the picture, we require a whole chapter on psychological needs.

Value. Although we may like a product, when we get to the store, we may not buy it. For one thing, the price may be too high. For another, there may be a competitor who offers better value. Let us look at what is meant by "value." First a formal definition: perceived value is the consumer's overall assessment of the utility of a product based on perceptions of what is received and what is given (Zeithamel, 1987). "While what is received varies across consumers (i.e., some may want volume, others high quality, still others convenience) and what is given varies (i.e., some are concerned only with money expended, others with time and effort), value represents a trade-off of the salient give and get components." (Zeithamel, 1987, p. 20) We focus specifically on the "give and get components" under the label of reinforcement.

Forming Preferences

The question of how we come to have our likes and dislikes is a complex one, called generally forming preferences. The topic is central, however. For example, one could argue that making decisions as to what to buy comes down to preferences. So too, one could argue, does the forming of attitudes. And, again, what is reinforcement but the application of preferences? Although these positions are generally true, each type of process has particular variables that influence it. So we study them from different viewpoints in subsequent chapters.

There are two kinds of preferences which are close to each other but differ slightly. The term "preference" is used to mean simply "liking" something, but the term also implies comparison between at least two things, so that we "like this one better than that one," a choice process. We are concerned mostly with the first meaning here. But the two uses are intertwined, and in the real world one cannot always say whether they are simply coming to like something, or coming to like it relative to available others.

Biological or Learned? Some preferences have biological origins and are unlearned. For example, infants prefer sugar to quinine without prior experience with either (Zajonc, 1986). The quinine taste is essentially bitter, and the taste for bitter things is one we must acquire. Both coffee and beer, which are bitter in taste, are not generally liked by children. Sugar certainly is, as is attested by the huge number of sweet products for children.

Other preferences are harder to categorize. For example, where does visual attractiveness come from? Cunningham (1986) found that when the features of the very young were found in women, they made the women more attractive to men in many countries. Indeed they make the young of most species seem cute and attractive. Attention to faces is so important to us that a special center in the brain has evolved whose sole function is recognizing faces. We also read faces and determine a great deal of information about people from their facial expressions. By far the most important thing we read there is in the evaluative dimension, that is, liking and disliking, that are forms of affect. The process is very rapid, and physical attractiveness plays a major role in this assessment (see Hatfield & Sprecher, 1986).

Attractive people are much more likely to be liked, and this evaluation spills over into most other judgments. Attractive children are judged less harshly by adults than unattractive children (Dion, 1972). Unattractive defendants are likely to get longer sentences than attractive ones, and crimes against attractive victims are likely to bring sentences longer than those against unattractive victims (Landy & Aronson, 1969). In one study, pictures of people who were previously rated attractive and unattractive were given to subjects to rate on a list of characteristics having nothing to do with physical attractiveness. Attractive people were rated highest on nearly all characteristics. (Dion, Berscheid, & Walster, 1972). It certainly is one reason that pretty faces are used to sell products.

There is a gradual lessening of attractiveness with age, in that "research studies have consistently found a negative linear relationship between model age and model attractiveness; older models are viewed as less attractive." (Mazis, Ringold, Perry, & Denman, 1992, p. 22) They confirmed this with their own study and found that it applies to both genders and to 50-year-olds and to 13-year-olds. This suggests innate mechanisms.

On the other hand, Sabini (1992) points out that facial scarring in some cultures is considered beautiful. Within our own culture many find tatooing beautiful. The ideal weight that men seek in women also appears to be cultural because it has changed markedly over the years. The women considered beautiful by the artists of the eighteenth and nineteenth centuries were considerably heavier than the anorexic ideals of our culture today. Thus, it is partly innate and partly cultural. Whatever the source, it is clear that attractive people have a halo effect, and this is why they are used to sell all manner of products.

Most preferences are probably learned from experience and cultural bias. Conditioning is clearly the main mechanism, as we shall discuss in upcoming chapters. Briefly, it involves closely associating an object that has no meaning or a mildly aversive meaning with a strongly desired object. The neutral object takes on the meaning of the desired object. Having said this, however, many loose ends are still unexplained. For example, it is hard to tell if we learn to like things or simply learn to tolerate them to reach a desired goal. Thus, one might say that as we grow up we learn to tolerate better, for example, to appear mature, sophisticated, or simply to be accepted in a social group that we value. The psychological sensation, however, is not always that of tolerance but becomes one of actually enjoying the new taste. Is there an actual change in the taste system, or is it still tolerance, but on an unconscious level? Or is it sometimes one, and sometimes the other? At the moment we cannot say, because we still do not know much about these basic processes (Zajonc, 1986).

Mere Exposure Effect.   Much, if not most, of the formation of preferences is at a subconscious, or unconscious, level. This is the level we introduced as the lowest level of the analysis of Greenwald and Leavitt (1984), which they called the preattentive level. Material encountered at this level may never be moved higher for more processing, and consequently it may not be retained in the cognitive sense of being able to recall it later. However, it may still acquire an affective tag. The documentation of this remarkable state of affairs goes back to the late sixties.

Zajonc (1968) carried out a series of experiments which he claimed showed that affect could be connected to things even before they could be recognized. Extending these studies, he showed unfamiliar figures to subjects, for example, Chinese ideographs, nonsense syllables, or faces. Later subjects were asked to rate the probability that figures had been in the earlier group and also to rate them on an attitude scale of liking. Figures which had more exposures were rated higher on the attitude scale (indicating they were liked more) than those with low exposure. This happened even when the figures were rated as not having been seen before. Here a feeling of familiarity seems to be interpreted as preference, but the subjects do not know that they are doing it. The effect has come to be called **the mere exposure effect**.

In another study using the same procedure, subjects were asked to rate the names of people according to how famous they are. They had previously seen some of the names on a different task. They could not remember which they had seen and which were new, but subjects rated as more famous the names they had seen before, apparently because they had an unexplained familiar feel to them. It was found that subjects tested immediately after exposure were likely to credit the increased familiarity they felt toward the made-up names to having probably seen them on the other list. After 24 hours, however, the names still seemed familiar, but now there was no connection to the source, and the subjects rated the names as being those of famous people (Jacoby, Kelley, Brown, & Jasechko, 1989).

The implications of this study for advertising are considerable. It demonstrates that we tend to look for reasons for feelings of familiarity and may ascribe them to the wrong source. Here a feeling of familiarity was interpreted to mean fame. Notice that the feelings came from simple repetition and not from anything more.

A number of studies have supported Zajonc's findings. Janiszewski (1988) lists ten such studies and specifically relates the mere exposure effect to the preattentional level. The principle is important for marketing because it means that repetition alone unconsciously produces preference for a product. Bornstein (1989) showed that the effect continues up to ten exposures, but not beyond. Zajonc cites Harrison (1977) and recounts an interesting experiment in which it was shown that the mere exposure effect also occurs in rats:

> Some ingenious experimenters at Wittenburg College in Ohio exposed rats to a twelve-hour-per-day diet of music by either Mozart or Schoenberg (Cross, Halcomb, & Matter, 1967). The rats lived with the music for two months and afterward were given a test of musical preference. They were placed in a cage in which the floor was hinged in the middle and suspended over microswitches. If the rat were on one side of this floor, Channel I of a tape recorder would be heard. If the rat crossed to the other side, the microswitches would activate Channel II, and the rat would hear Schoenberg. The tests were performed over a period of fifteen days. A control group also was given this test without prior musical experience.... For the group exposed to Mozart, there was a considerable preference for Mozart over Schoenberg. The group exposed to Schoenberg preferred Schoenberg to Mozart. The control group elicited a slight preference for Mozart over Schoenberg.... This may mean that rats are similar to people, or vice versa (Zajonc, 1986, p. 6).

Why should repetition alone increase our preference for something? We saw that repetition increases availability, but this does not explain why preference increases. With consumer products there may be an influence from the perception of popularity, but it is hard to see how this would apply to simple stimuli. Two alternative explanations are currently still viable: association of mood and uncertainty reduction. The first of these, the active processing explanation, regards the mere exposure effect as one of cognitive associating, though at an unconscious level. The increase in positive affect comes about, in this view, by simply associating in a classical conditioning model. Our mood at the time becomes associated with a stimulus, and because our moods are generally positive, the stimulus is tagged with this positive affect. Then, repetition simply increases the opportunities for affective associating with the stimulus.

The second explanation, uncertainty reduction, maintains that repetition reduces uncertainty about the stimulus. Uncertainty is disturbing because it may represent a potential threat. The more familiar a stimulus becomes, the more we like it (Obermiller, 1985). Uncertainty creates anxiety reflected in the phrase "fear of the unknown." In other words, the more familiar something is, the more sure we are that it does not constitute a threat, and thus the stronger the positive affective tag. It may be that each time we encounter it, we tag it nonthreatening, and positive affective tagging accumulates over time.

There is little disagreement that repetition increases preference, but the reason is still obscure. Moreover, additional research is required before we can determine how large the effect actually is and how important the mere exposure effect is for preference formation in the consumer world.

Hemispheric Differences.   Preference formation is influenced by page position in advertising, but the reason is a bit roundabout. It has long been known that the left hemisphere of the cerebral cortex is the site of language processing, and the right hemisphere processes images. In recent years it has been shown that this situation has implications for advertising. Remember that the right hemisphere receives impulses from the *left* visual field, and the left hemisphere receives impulses from the *right* side. Recall that the lower brain stem centers process affect, but they pass responses up to the cortical hemispheres, particularly the right hemisphere, for interpretation. Neurological evidence has found a major role for the right hemisphere in perceiving, experiencing, and expressing emotions (Geschwind & Galaburda, 1987). Perhaps it is not surprising then that a study by Mittal (1987) concluded that high *affective* involvement is a function of the right hemisphere, whereas high *cognitive* involvement is a function primarily of the left. But remember now, that the *right* hemisphere processes material seen to the *left* of the fixation point, whereas the *left* hemisphere processes material from the *right*. Then, one might suppose that verbal material to the right and images to the left might be more readily absorbed by the preattentional system that is looking for affect than the same material placed on the opposite side. Putting this hypothesis to the test, Janiszewski (1988) found that this is the case. More surprisingly, he also confirmed that image ads were better *liked* when placed to the left of an attended article, whereas verbal material was better *liked* on the right. He concludes that when a hemisphere is a more efficient processor of a particular kind of information, it provides a stronger trace to the higher level of processing, and this is read as preference.

Two years later, Janiszewski (1990) demonstrated this principle and carried the idea a bit further. He presented subjects with simulated advertising pages in which the placement of a model's face, a verbal passage, and a brand name were systematically varied. Brand names by themselves are so simple that they are readily processed at the preattentive level on either side. He found that measured affect toward the brand name increases when the brand name is placed to the right of an image task, that is, over on the side being monitored by the other hemisphere which was not as busy. Similarly, brand names placed to the left of a verbal task show increased affect.

In other words, he supports the notion that an ad that activates one hemisphere at the conscious level also enhances the subconscious processing of information by the other hemisphere. At the same time it competes with and reduces the subconscious peripheral processing by its own side. The differences become more noticeable as the material to be processed becomes more complex. Thus, a brand name, being very simple, gets little advantage from right field placement, but relatively larger effects are found as words become phrases and images become scenes (Beaumont, 1982). Ads based on this principle have begun to appear, so that the left side of the page contains an image and the right side contains the text. An example is the Glaxo Wellcome Company ad for Flovent (Figure 6).

Preference formation is also influenced by a products' relative position. In a study by Nisbett and Wilson (1977), subjects were asked to select the best quality nightgown from several arranged in a row. Subjects were four times more likely to pick the nightgown on the right, though, of course, the nightgowns were identical. As we have come to expect, these subjects strongly denied that position influenced their decision.

Preference for turning to the right, at least in our culture, has been demonstrated. Museum exhibit designers discovered early that people tend to turn to the right when they enter exhibit halls (Melton, 1933). It is thought that this occurs because we read from left to right. We scan from left to right and tend to move off in the direction we are facing when done scanning. In another early study, Melton found that 80% of the

Figure 6 Research shows that images placed to the left and verbal material placed to the right reach the opposite hemisphere more readily and are also liked better. This ad for *Flovent* utilizes this principle to advantage. (Reproduced with permission of Glaxo Wellcome Inc.)

visitors to an art museum turned to the right and started viewing on the right-hand wall. Over 60% of them never viewed the left-hand wall at all (Melton, 1935). It would be interesting to see if the Japanese, whose language reads from right to left, favor the left side instead. Bitgood (1995) makes the point that the right turning bias only occurs when other forces, such as goal-directed behavior, open doors, strong attractors, or inertia, are absent.

CHAPTER 7

Attitudes and Persuasion

The whole field of advertising is directed at creating good attitudes in us toward products. Attitudes can be defined as favorable or unfavorable dispositions toward a particular person or object, and the favorable side is what marketers are after. In this chapter we look at how attitudes are formed and how they are changed.

OVERVIEW AND DEFINITIONS

Affect Versus Cognition Again

We discussed cognition and affect in earlier chapters, and now we can turn to a discussion of how they have been studied together under the label of attitudes. The study of attitudes goes back to Plato, who identified three components of attitudes: cognition, affection, and conation (literally striving, making an effort, and so, behavioral intentions). In today's language they are perhaps cognition, affect, and behavior. It is an amazing testament to Plato's insight that disagreement with him, even 2400 years later, has not been on the components themselves but on how they interact. The traditional approach puts cognition first, directing affects, which in turn direct behavior. It was understood that cognition must come first, because one could not have a feeling about something unless one first knew what that thing was, but as we saw in the last chapter, Zajonc turned the order around.

Gordon Allport (1935), who became a major figure in the study of attitudes, agreed with the dominant behaviorism of his day, and felt that we could not measure either affect or cognitions, but only behavior. Thus, it is not surprising that he defined attitudes as "a predisposition to respond in a certain way." Nothing here about feelings toward things or cognitions either for that matter. In Allport's view, when we measure attitudes, we measure a state which assumes that affect and beliefs have interacted and combined, but he does not specify how these previous combinations may have occurred. This approach is still used by some marketers, because, they argue, marketers are ultimately interested in the behavior of buying. The difficulty with this view, however, is that, though we measure attitudes, we still relatively poorly predict buying behavior.

Fishbein and Ajzen (1972) picked up on this point and argued that Allport's formulation requires congruence between attitudes and intention to act because for Allport they are the same thing. But research shows there is no such congruence, that is, although I may like something, still I may have no intention of buying it. Thus, although they agree with Allport that behavior is influenced by a combination of affect and cognitions, they argue that we must be clear about what the attitude is toward the product or buying it.

They formulated the **theory of reasoned action**. For them, the term "attitude" applies only to the affect part, not cognitions, that is, in their view, affect is attitude, and cognition remains separate. In addition, whether we act on our attitudes also depends on situational factors. In their model attitude toward product, that is, the value placed on it (affect), interacts with belief, expressed as the likelihood of occurrence (cognition), and situational factors to produce attitude toward behavior (behavioral intention). Their view reflects a newer approach to attitudes in which affect has become the dominant element. [The waters are muddied, however, because some still refer to behavioral intentions as the person's attitude with no object specified (e.g., Milburn, 1991)].

This newer approach originated with the research of Zajonc. Although the traditional approach made very good sense, Zajonc (1968, 1980) showed as we have seen that surprisingly one can have a feeling about something before the thing itself can be identified. More research confirmed this (Zajonc & Markus, 1985), and he reversed the traditional sequence, putting affect first, directing cognition and also behavior.

Zajonc was not without his critics, however. An alternative argument was made by Lazarus (1981) that though affect appears early in the process, it is still attached to cognition, though the cognition at this stage is unconscious (Lazarus, 1984). In this view, cognition, sometimes unconscious, always accompanies affect, so the best model would be one of parallel operation of affect and cognition. Consistent with such a view, Mitchell (1986) found that "it is possible to create different brand attitudes toward products with the same product attribute beliefs." (p. 21) It means that affect must be considered as important as beliefs in the process of persuasion, yet there are still writers who consider that attitudes are solely a matter of beliefs. For example, D'Souza and Rao (1995) write, "Brand preferences (or attitudes) can be regarded as a consumer's predisposition toward a brand that varies depending on the salient beliefs that are activated at a given point in time." (p. 33)

The dominant view today favors the parallel model, though the controversy is by no means resolved because disagreement remains over what affect is. According to Sabini (1992), attitudes today are generally considered "evaluations," made up of beliefs, feelings, and behavior. This approach, a surprising return to Plato, like Fishbein and Ajzen's, allows for attitudes in the absence of any intention to behave, but considers that attitudes consist of both affect and beliefs. Note that we are not back to Allport, for attitudes are considered possible with no intention to behave.

Although agreeing essentially with the notion that attitudes are made up of cognition and affect (they call them facts and feelings), Olney, Holbrook, and Batra (1991) feel that it is useful to try to get at the components of affect and cognition. They write, "attitude involves more than just an overall, unidimensional evaluative measure of global affect." (p. 442) They refer to studies that have used a four-item index (good-bad, like-dislike, irritating-not irritating, and uninteresting-interesting) that together have still not accounted for nearly one-third of the evaluative variance. The first three items sound like forms of affect, whereas the last sounds like cognition. We cannot resolve all the disagreements here.

For the marketer measuring the attitudes of potential consumers, this means that other variables (discussed later) need to be factored in before those attitudes can be used to predict sales.

The Function of Attitudes: Directing Behavior

Valencing Stimuli and Objects. There is little disagreement among theorists that the first and main function of attitudes is to direct our thinking, feeling, and behaving. Affect simplifies life, because, having placed affective tags on things, we do not have to devote any more brain power to that task again, yet we know how to behave appropriately. This is, of course, the origin of most of our biases. This means we tend to stick with tried and true brands, a phenomenon called brand loyalty. Thus, because attitudes are the central director of all human behavior, the activities of buying, selling, and consumption can be approached as problems in the manipulation of attitudes primarily about products.

Attitudes have a second and a third function that are not so obvious: the second, to help define individual identities, and the third, to help establish and define our social groups (Pratkanis & Greenwald, 1989; Schlenker, 1982). These two aspects are what give attitudes so much of their social power.

Defining Individuals.   The second function of attitudes is to define for us who we are and determine how we are known. They are what makes us distinctive in other people's perceptions. Vince Lombardi, coach of the Green Bay Packers when they were a football powerhouse, was known for his attitude toward winning: "Winning isn't everything, it's the only thing!" Who would he have been without that attitude? President Lyndon Johnson had a similar attitude, revealed when he said he refused to be the first president to lose a war and escalated the Vietnam war with tragic consequences. To give up our attitudes is often seen as having to give up a part of ourselves. Our egos get involved, our cognitions may completely give way to affect, and we become stubborn and even "pig headed." Attitudes markedly different from our own may be perceived as personal attacks and be met with defensiveness or anger, as the war protesters and "nervous nellies" were by LBJ. Thus, attitudes may have much more power than they logically should have. It means that ads that appeal to attitudes may carry more weight than expected.

Defining Social Groups.   The third function of attitudes is to define social groups, and provides the commonality that holds social groups together. The shared attitude the members have toward something specific is what they all have in common. For example, in religion shared beliefs and feelings define a particular sect. In sports, shared attitudes toward a particular team define the fan. In politics, shared attitudes define a party. Thus, we put positive affective tags on the members of our group and often put negative tags on outsiders. The power comes because abandoning an attitude may mean running afoul of our social group or even abandoning a social group as well, and that is hard to do.

Thus, a large part of selling becomes a matter of determining the key attitudes of the individual or group and appealing to them. When the individuals in a group hear their own attitudes being expressed, the speaker tends to be listened to, accepted and trusted as "one of us." Cognitive consistency in turn makes whatever product the speaker is selling more acceptable also. Conversely, differing attitudes may be perceived as negative ideas, and also as an attack on the group.

Selling on a national level is particularly difficult because one is trying to sell to many different groups at once, all of which have different attitudes. What might ingratiate us with one group may very likely alienate us from another. This is the dilemma of national politicians who are really selling a viewpoint to consumers, their constituents. Political campaigns are very like marketing anything else. Politicians have learned to appeal to the most widely-held attitudes and otherwise to remain vague as long as possible. The minute they become specific on an issue, they lose votes. This is the reason that they generally do not deal with the issues we would like them to. Rather, they deal with big issues about which there is little controversy, for example, being against raising taxes. Few people would not share that attitude, but to be for a specific action to avoid raising taxes, say, the closing of Homestead Air Force Base in South Florida, that is a different matter. Being specific in this way might cost presidential candidates the South Florida vote, so they remain indefinite as long as possible.

Advertisers of national brands are in a similar position. They must be careful about the specific attitudes they express in their ads, or they will lose potential customers. They must also be careful about which television shows they sponsor. Such is the power of consistency that attitudes toward a show spill over into attitude toward the advertised product, even though there is no logical connection. As a result, there is pressure to sponsor only bland, noncontroversial shows and also those that contain positive affect. Game shows and situation comedies are again the preferred vehicles.

Attitude Toward the Ad

Mitchell and Olson (1981) argued that the attitude toward the ad could have effects on evaluating a product that are independent of their product attribute beliefs. Because attitudes have long been considered to be composed of both affect and beliefs, this is not surprising. What was new, however, was the suggestion that measurement of attitude toward the ad could reveal attitude toward the brand. Since then, because of a demonstrated positive relationship between attitude toward the ad and attitude toward the brand, a considerable number of studies has evolved directed at assessing viewers' attitudes toward ads (Machleit and Wilson, 1988). For example, Burton and Lichtenstein (1988) found that when an ad contained cognitive information (like a price deal), combining cognitive evaluations of the ad with affective reactions to the ad gave a better predictor of attitude toward the ad than affect alone.

More recently, Celuch and Slama (1995) showed that the best measure of attitude toward the product depends on the involvement of the viewer. In the low involvement condition, brand attribute information did not influence the overall brand attitude but predictably affect did. In informational ads, where higher involvement occurs, cognitive attitude toward the ad was the best predictor of attitude toward the brand.

Attitude Toward the Purchase

You will recall that at one time, specifically with Gordon Allport in the 30s, it was considered that attitudes reflect a predisposition to act. It was found, however, that attitudes do not always predict behavior. In fact, attitudes account for less than half of the variance. Part of the confusion was that there are at least two objects of attitudes, the attitude toward the product and a more complex attitude toward the actual purchase. So far we have been discussing attitude toward product, but now we turn to the attitude toward the purchase which is in the nature of a decision.

The topic of decision making comes down to the formation of an attitude toward the purchase, which may differ from that toward product. For example, we may find a new car very attractive but not have the money to buy it. Attitude toward the car itself, the product, is strongly positive, but attitude toward the purchase is not, because of the shortage of resources. In other words, evaluation of the consequences of the act of buying, in this case debt and associated problems, leads to the conclusion that they are aversive, and the intention to purchase does not occur. If one does not think of the consequences, the strongly positive attitude toward the product may be unchecked, and an unwise purchase may result. This is exactly why impulsive people so often end up in trouble.

Consideration of Consequences.   As we noted previously, the distinction between the two attitudes was aided by Fishbein and Ajzen (1975) who formulated the theory of reasoned action, in an attempt to achieve better prediction of behavior. The essence of the theory is that if instead of measuring attitude toward the product, one measures attitude toward the purchase, prediction will be improved. Attitude toward the purchase, they maintained, includes the subject's evaluation of the consequences of the behavior and their perception of how likely those consequences are to occur. In other words, according to Fishbein and Ajzen, one's evaluation of the consequences of a behavior and their probability make up one's intentions, that is attitude toward the behavior.

This is essentially the concept of reinforcement, which originated as Thorndike's law of effect at the turn of the century and which is unquestioned today after thousands of confirming studies. Reinforcement is the topic of chapter 9. In brief, evaluating the consequences of a behavior as positive is the same as saying we perceive that it will lead to positive reinforcement. We tend to go ahead with things that lead to positive consequences and to avoid things that lead to aversive consequences. The effect of the behavior is the key, just as Thorndike said. The question of just how a consumer will combine all the factors in their evaluation of consequences, however, remains a difficult prediction. There is no mechanical formula that can be applied here because of the sheer number of variables and their complex interactions. Fishbein and Ajzen argue that by measuring attitude toward the purchase, we come into the process after the complex combining has taken place, and so the prediction of actual purchase will be fairly good. Indeed, subsequent research has shown that this is a "highly predictive" relationship (Milburn, 1991, p. 11).

Fishbein and Ajzen argue that another factor adds to the attitude toward the behavior and should be considered, and they report fairly good prediction when it is considered. This factor is the perception of subjective norms (the opinions of significant people), which we will consider later. The studies subsequently used to support including it in the theory, however, are those in which the opinions and reactions of others are particularly important, for example, the study by Smetana and Adler (1980) of women deciding whether to have an abortion. Except for these special kinds of cases, however, there is no real reason for singling out this variable from all of the others because it acts on the evaluation consequences just like the others do. For this reason we will treat it as simply another important factor in evaluating of consequences and come back to it in a moment.

Although there are some reports of good prediction using the theory of reasoned action, it is really too general to be very useful as an explanatory instrument. One of its contributions is that it has been convincing in making the point that behaviors are rational because ultimately they are undertaken to produce positive outcomes.

It is a matter of ongoing debate as to how much cognitive deliberation goes on in some of these decisions. If you have more than one alternative and you eventually act on one of them, by definition you have made a choice. But the choice can involve almost no cognition and be essentially a random response, or it can involve years of research and lengthy deliberation. Most choices fall somewhere between these extremes. The task becomes one of identifying when deliberation is extended and how it is done when it is extended.

Combining Attitudes

Most products have a number of attributes, and we may have attitudes toward each. What happens when inconsistent attitudes must be combined in a single object? For example, a soup may have good taste, but high fat content and moderate sodium content. A watch may be beautiful, but too expensive, and made by an unknown company. Several models have been proposed to describe how a number of characteristics, sometimes inconsistent with each other, are cognitively combined to result in a single attitude. The process serves to eliminate cognitive inconsistencies, much as group disagreements are eliminated when a single spokesperson represents the group. Do we add them or average them?

Some sort of averaging takes place. First-formed impressions, more salient characteristics, and negative traits get more weight (Anderson, 1965; Fiske, 1980). Support for an averaging process is found in a surprising study by Troutman, Michael, and Shanteau (1976). Two groups heard a product described. One group heard only one very positive characteristic of the product described. The second group heard the same very positive characteristic and also heard an additional mildly positive one. Later, both groups were asked to rate the product. Now you might think that the more good things you heard about a product, the higher you would rate it, but that is not the way it turned out. These researchers found that products were rated higher by the group who heard only one strongly positive characteristic than by the group who also heard a mildly positive characteristic. The product was disposable diapers, and they were simply described to one group as having high absorbency. They were described to another group as having both high absorbency and above average durability. When the groups were asked to rate them on the basis of what they had heard, the group which had heard only one characteristic rated them higher than the group which heard two.

The study strongly supports the authors contention that consumers average characteristics as they get them, rather than simply adding on to them. Let us clarify the difference here. Adding attributes would mean that a mild attribute attitude added to a strong one would raise the total somewhat. If we average attribute attitudes, on the other hand, the overall rating will be pulled down when a strong attribute is averaged with anything other than an equally high rating of another attribute.

In the case of brand name extension, each new product is thought to add to the meaning of the brand in the same way. This principle means that, unless each new product is equal to or better than the last, the brand name's reputation will inevitably decline toward an average. In other words, it will be almost impossible to prevent the brand name from gradually becoming perceived as mediocre. Eventually the halo effect for new products will also be lessened because it will become a halo based on mediocrity. Not only will the gain for new products be lost, but existing products are also likely to lose. It may be this process at work that caused Ries and Trout (1986) to argue, using numerous examples, that brand extension seldom works well any more.

There are still some unanswered questions here. Do affective experiences average together in the same way as cognitive ones? Are cognitions and affects combined in the weighted mean that Fishbein and Ajzen propose? Such questions are research opportunities.

ATTITUDE FORMATION:
THE COGNITIVE COMPONENT

Traditionally, the cognitive component of attitudes has been called beliefs. In this view attitude formation becomes a matter of convincing through factual argument. A hundred years ago this was often the only way advertisers sought to persuade consumers. Ads would relate the virtues of their product, ticking off how it was superior to the competition. We still have ads that are predominantly cognitive of this type, because some products lend themselves better to cognition. For example, insurance, investments, and machines all require considerable information for a wise choice, as apparently do mattresses and financial services. Figure 7 by Tempur-pedic and Figure 8 by GMAC show recent ads that are nearly all cognitive.

Cognitive Consistency Theory

Cognitive consistency theory itself has a extensive history, originating mainly with Heider's balance theory (Heider, 1946). According to this formulation, objects, people, and events have positive or negative associations with the observer and with each other. Our beliefs sort themselves out so that balance is maintained. For example, we expect two people who like each other to like the same things. Similarly we expect two people whom we like to like each other and two whom we dislike also to like each other. When a discrepancy occurs, as when someone whom we like turns out to like someone we dislike, Heider said the cognitions will be out of balance, and there will be an attempt at cognitive restructuring to restore the balance, that is, we are likely to change our attitude, either liking our friend less or liking the disliked person more.

Test of the theory has proven difficult. Part of the difficulty arises when we try to measure the degree of similarity or difference among

Figure 7 Some products are better sold by presenting information about them. This ad is an example of such a case and thus is mostly cognitive. (Reproduced by permission of Tempur-Pedic, Inc.)

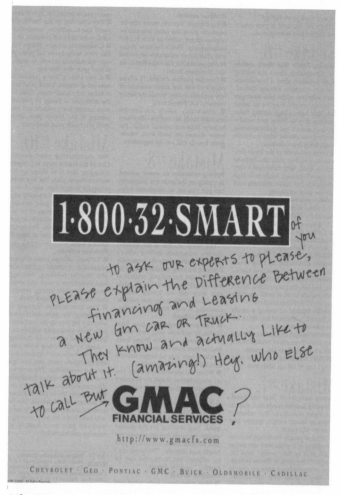

Figure 8 Like Figure 7, this ad is primarily cognitive in composition because of the nature of the product being sold. (Reproduced by permission of General Motors Corporation.)

things. Similarity is a matter of perception, rather than objective reality alone, and therefore variables, such as attention, come into play. Another part of the complicating circumstance is that people evaluate new information on the basis of their existing attitudes, so that, without knowing all of their relevant attitudes, it is hard to predict whether they will see a new situation as balanced or unbalanced. In other words, the reality of the world is not as important as how it is perceived, and this is not always possible to know.

Although Heider's original theory was tremendously important and certainly often true, it was too simple to be easily applied. As reviewers have noted, "... its predictions are far from firm because imbalanced states can lead people to change in a number of different ways. More damaging is the fact that the evidence for the theory is at best equivocal." (Tedeschi, Lindskold, & Rosenfeld, 1985, p. 172) Heider's theory was transformed by Festinger and as **cognitive dissonance theory** became the most influential theory of attitudinal change.

Cognitive Dissonance Theory

As Heider (1946) first proposed it, a cognitive tension state occurs whenever two cognitions were in conflict but the evidence failed to show that this always developed. Festinger added the concept of action, and it became much more predictive. Although Heider focused on discrepant attitudes toward things, Festinger focused on discrepant realities revealed by action. In other words, Festinger maintained that cognitive imbalance would not cause conflict and attitudinal change in people, until they actually acted counter to some of those attitudes. When we do act this way, it was proposed that it causes "cognitive dissonance," a state of internal tension. His point was that action has a reality to it that is hard to deny. Until we actually act, there is no dissonance because essentially we can put off the decisions and avoid making up our minds. It is all theoretical—I would act, I would not act. Once we have acted, however, the hypothetical has become real.

Having acted counter to our attitudes, now we must see ourselves either as hypocritical, professing one thing, but acting another, or as a person who does not know his own attitudes. Because both of these options threaten our valued idea of ourselves, we tend to reduce or eliminate the cognitive inconsistency (and thereby eliminate the threat) by altering our attitudes.

Festinger saw cognitive dissonance as the reason that we rationalize. Remember that rationalization is one of Freud's defense mechanisms, so that it would not be surprising to find that ego defense is involved. Indeed we find that dissonance is particularly strong when our actions imply that our favorable self-image may not be really true. When our action creates a threat to our sense of worth (our ego), then dissonance is likely to result. When we rationalize our way out of the dissonance, we are saying to ourselves, "OK, I did it, but ...". We seem compelled to come up with a reason that the action was justified. We qualify our beliefs so that they become consistent once again. The ultimate need is to see ourselves in an acceptable light and restore our favorable self-image. The theory has value as a guide to changing people's attitudes, if it works.

Tests of Cognitive Dissonance Theory

Festinger's theory produced many studies to test it and gathered considerable support. Tedeschi, Lindskold, and Rosenfeld (1985) listed four types of research used to study cognitive dissonance: forced compliance, effort justification, postdecision evaluations, and the forbidden toy paradigm. Let us consider some examples of each of these.

Forced Compliance Studies. Festinger and Carlsmith (1959) carried out an experiment in forced compliance to see whether people who act contrary to their beliefs change their beliefs to bring them into agreement with their actions. Subjects were enlisted to participate in an experiment and were given a task to do which was designed to be incredibly boring. Afterward, they were asked to rate the task, and all agreed that it was dull. When leaving the experiment, however, they were asked to tell others waiting that it would be an exciting and enjoyable task. In other words, they were asked to lie, a behavior that was counter to their beliefs about who they were. Two groups were offered something for doing this, $20 or $1, and the other group was offered nothing. Thus, the amount they were offered became the independent variable.

For the most part, the subjects did as they were asked and lied. According to the researchers, this action of lying became the trigger for cognitive dissonance because it was a real fact and public, not just a suppositional one, and it contradicted the view they wanted to hold of themselves. The supportive evidence for this interpretation came when the subjects were asked to rate the task again, and it was found that the $20 group and the group offered nothing both rated the task as before, but the $1 group rated the task this time as more interesting and enjoyable than they had rated it before.

The researchers explained the finding by maintaining that neither the $20 group nor the group who lied for nothing saw the lie as a personal statement, and therefore their action did not threaten their self-worth. In the case of the $20 group, they perceived that anyone lies if you offer them enough (and $20 was a lot more money in those days), so they were no different from everyone else. Because the group offered nothing got nothing out of it, the action was not personally motivated, and the blame fell instead on the scientists. In other words, it was perceived as a minor thing done for science. Both of these actions are fairly easy to justify and require no further cognitive adjustment.

On the other hand, the $1 group has to grapple with the reality that they lied for a very small incentive. Because our culture makes it clear, as we grow up, that lying is unacceptable and that people of personal integrity do not lie, the realization that they had lied produced considerable dissonance. Their action had threatened their sense of personal worth, but by changing their perception of the task, the lie became more of a modest exaggeration, rather than a lie, and the threat to self-image was removed. Note that the group with ego involvement is the one which changed its cognitions.

Effort Justification Studies.   A similar perceptual change in a positive direction occurs when we work hard to get something. The phenomenon is known as effort justification. According to cognitive dissonance theory, we tend to see the object of our effort as valuable, because to see it as otherwise is to label us fools. The application of this principle is what occurs in fraternity and sorority initiations. It can be predicted that people who undergo humiliation and even pain to get into an organization perceive that organization as more worthwhile than, for example, someone who gets in easily.

Likewise, in the consumer realm, the farther we have to go to get a bargain, the bigger the bargain will appear to be. Do we not feel more clever when we have clipped a coupon, saved the sales receipt, filled out a form, found an envelope, addressed it, and paid for a stamp, all for a $1 rebate? Would a dollar off in the store have the same impact? Probably not. If Festinger is right, and it appears he is, then we should also value the product itself more because of the process.

Postdecision Evaluation Studies.   The postdecision type of study is similar to the effort justification ones, except that the precipitating action involves cost, rather than effort. The more you pay for something, the more you tend to value it. For example, Knox and Inkster (1968) asked bettors at the $2 racetrack window about their confidence in their chosen horses. Those who had already placed their bets expressed considerably more confidence in their choices than those who had not yet done so. Rosenfeld, Giacalone, and Tedeschi (1983) found a similar situation when they questioned undergraduate junior and senior students at preregistration about how good they expected their courses to be the next semester. Students who had already completed their registration rated their courses as significantly more attractive than did those who had not yet registered.

On the other hand, some postdecision studies show minimal cost and yet cognitive change. Brehm (1956) asked college students to rate how much they would like to have each of eight different products, such as a toaster or a radio. Then, the students were allowed to choose between two of the products and were told they would be given the one they chose. When later asked to rate all the products again, the subjects increased the rating given to the one they had chosen and decreased the rating of the other. The cost here seems to be psychological, publicly changing your mind.

The Forbidden Toy Paradigm Studies. The final type of research on dissonance theory is the forbidden toy paradigm. It illustrates the concept that to choose not to do something because of threats may also produce dissonance. In one of these studies (Aronson & Carlsmith, 1963), children rated their toys for desirability and then were left alone with them. Before leaving, however, the adult told them they could play with any except their second highest rated one. One group was simply told that the experimenter would be annoyed if they played with the toy while she was gone. The other group was given a stronger admonishment not to play with the toy, involving an angry experimenter threatening to take the toys away and send the child home. As expected, most children avoided playing with the toy, but later when asked to rate the toy again, the forbidden toy was rated more negatively by those in the mild threat group. The severe threat group apparently saw more justification for not playing with the toy and hence experienced less dissonance. Just what causes the dissonance is not clear, but the rating of the toy as less desirable would decrease the perception of being under constraints. The finding documents an effect that has been known for hundreds of years as the "sour grapes" phenomenon, after Aesop's story of the fox who could not reach a bunch of grapes. After considerable effort the fox decided that the grapes were probably sour anyway. The process of rationalization in these cases seems to reduce our sense of our own limitations and lack of control over our environment.

Conditions Necessary for Cognitive Change

The conditions necessary to bring cognitive change about by creating dissonance can be summarized this way:

Subjects must have choice to perform the counterattitudinal behavior, which must have negative consequences for either the self or others, and they must publically commit themselves to it. If any of these conditions are not fulfilled, subjects will not change their attitudes following counterattitudinal behavior" (Tedeschi et al., 1985, p. 177).

In addition, studies show that when the decision is difficult there will be more dissonance. We will consider each of these factors in more detail.

Choice.   It has been shown that choice on the part of the subject is necessary for dissonance to occur. The reason that choice works this way is probably that it carries a sense of responsibility for the consequences (Sears, Freedman, & Peplau, 1985). Thus, my ego is involved only when I freely choose. If I have no other choice or if I perceive myself as coerced, no dissonance results. Brehm (1956), who asked students to choose among products in the study reported above, also included a group which was simply given a product with no choice on their part. When they later rated the products for the second time, this group made no rating changes at all, indicating that they felt no dissonance.

Similarly, forced compliance changes attitudes only when it is perceived as not forced. In one study students were asked to write an essay that disagreed with their opinions. Some felt they had a choice to write the essay, and others felt they had no choice. Those who had choice changed their attitudes more than those without (Linder, Cooper, & Jones, 1967).

Ego Involvement.   Studies in cognitive dissonance have shown that ego involvement is necessary for cognitive changes to occur. For example, a study by Rosenberg (1965) found that cognitive tension is greater when the cognitions are personal in some way. He concludes that whether a cognition carries gain or loss is determined to a large extent by people's perception of goal attainment or goal frustration for themselves. Similarly, involvement was an important variable in Heider's balance theory (Hovland, Harvey, & Sherif, 1957). Just what constitutes ego involvement is not always easily predictable, but personal gain or loss and threats to perceived self-worth and public reputation are its essential components.

Public and Irrevocable Commitment.   When Festinger first proposed his cognitive dissonance theory, he stressed that there must be an action to produce dissonance. Now, we can add that the more public and irrevocable the action, the stronger the dissonance (Sears et al., 1985). Thus, decisions about publicly used products, particularly expensive ones, are likely to produce more dissonance than privately used, low cost items. Automobiles, houses, and to some extent our clothes fall into the former category. Clearly, the more people who know about our behavior, the more impact it has on our image.

Difficulty of Decision. The closer the alternative behaviors are in terms of incentives, the harder the decision, and the more dissonance is likely to be created. Maximum dissonance results when the incentives for the precipitating action are "barely sufficient." (Sears et al., 1985) Brehm (1956), who asked students to choose among products, as we saw previously, also found information about this other dimension. When the products between which the subjects had to choose were close in rating, the later rating changes by the subjects were greater. Similarly, with the forbidden toy study of Aronson and Carlsmith (1963), it was the mild threat group that experienced more dissonance. When the threats were stronger, the decision to play or not play was an easier one. And again, as we saw previously in the early study of Festinger and Carlsmith (1959), when subjects lied about the boring task, it was the $1 group that changed their ratings. In other words, close decisions are likely to cause greater dissonance. The reason is probably that when the incentives for other actions are about equal, we can no longer use the excuse of larger incentive as an escape from our behavior, and the behavior seems more personally motivated.

Applications

Postdecision Behavior. In applying cognitive dissonance theory to the consumer realm, we can predict that people who make purchases, particularly those made publicly at considerable cost, will subsequently look for strong points in the product, ignore weak ones, and generally justify their purchases. If the purchases were expensive, and they have doubts about whether they should have spent all that money, they may read articles and ads about the products, looking for supportive evidence, to convince themselves that it was a good decision. Surveys which ask consumers whether they are satisfied with their purchases may not be accurate if they do not take this phenomenon into account.

Cognitive adjustment sometimes fails. Sometimes the product is just too bad to allow us to rationalize it away because the change in cognition would be too great. We may feel taken, and we shift from rationalizing to seeing ourselves as victims, and we get angry. Because our self-worth is threatened, the intensity may be raised to extreme levels. This situation can be made much worse, if friends say (after we have bought it, of course), "I could have told you that," or "I told you so." (They say such things, incidentally, to reduce their own ego threats, which they feel from the suggestion that they would have been similarly taken.)

For example, if our brand new car spends a lot of time in the shop instead of on the road, we can no longer reduce our anxiety about buying it by claiming it is a better than average car, and we cannot claim it was a smart move to buy it. In such a case we feel that others think us foolish, and the anxiety goes up, not down. When the avenues of rationalization are closed to us, we must reduce our anxiety in another way, sometimes by directing anger at the company for having deceived us. We loudly proclaim, in fact, that it was not a fault on our part. We move the locus external and label it uncontrollable in attribution theory terms. This may explain why a man drove around with his car labeled "lemon" in big letters until the courts made him stop. The faults of the car are just too much for him to overlook by rationalization. His feeling of being deceived has intensified into an unusual level of anger. He is still reducing his anxiety, but this time by acting out against the company.

In this example, we, as outside observers, do not know whether the car was really unusually defective or whether he is falsely perceiving it that way, because he feels he acted foolishly and is trying to justify himself. His behavior will look the same to us in either case. Which way we perceive it depends on our prior experience with the company or the individual, and it could go either way. The company had better have good public relations.

Foot-in-the-Door Technique. Cognitive dissonance theory may help explain another type of behavior that demands to be understood. The technique that has come to be known as "foot-in-the-door." Although apparently it has been used by salespeople for a long time, it did not capture the attention of psychologists until it was tried out experimentally. The idea involves asking for a small request, that anyone would be likely to grant, and then following up with a much larger one some time later. People are much more likely to grant the large request if they have already granted the small one. Freedman and Fraser (1966) asked householders whether a team of six people could come into their houses for two hours and inventory all the household products they used. Only about 22% agreed to this request. A second effort was made, however, in which the householders were asked a few questions about two days before the larger request. When this was done, about 50% agreed to the inventory request, an increase of 28% in cooperation.

Intrigued by this result, the researchers conducted a second more elaborate study. There were three groups in this study. One group simply received the large request: Would they be willing to let the group install a huge sign in the front lawn, a sign so big it hid the house and was poorly written, and said, "Drive Carefully." About 20%, interestingly enough, agreed to this request. A second group received a smaller request first: Would they be willing to place a very small sign in one of their windows that said, "Be a safe driver." This sign was only about three inches square. The experimenters returned about two weeks later with the large request, worded just like the other group, and this time 76% agreed to it. In the third condition, the small request was for a sign saying, "Keep California Beautiful," which was made by someone other than the person who returned with the larger request. Yet 47% agreed to the larger request.

Freedman and Fraser suggested that self-perception theory might provide the reason for this unusual finding. Having agreed to the smaller request, we perceive ourselves as "the sort of person who does this sort of thing." Subsequent research supports the theory (Sabini, 1992). Note that a cognitive dissonance theory could also fit. In other words, having acted counter to my belief that I do not allow signs on my house, I change my attitude toward ads on houses to see them as not so bad. Or, consistent with self-perception theory, I change my view of myself for the same reason, or perhaps change both attitudes. Then the later request would reflect this earlier accommodation. Whichever the reason, the technique remains useful in sales.

SCHEMA CONGRUITY THEORY

Festinger's cognitive dissonance theory involved the perceiving a discrepancy between beliefs and actions. Mandler (1982) focused also on a perceptual mismatch, but between expectations and actuality. His theory, known as schema congruity theory, focused on a type of cognitive inconsistency that arises when our expectation for a product or a product category (our schema) is not borne out by a new product or by a change in the old one. For example, when Coca-Cola changed its formula, many people objected because it had become incongruous with their expectation. The new drink was not what they had come to expect Coca-Cola would be. Mandler hypothesizes that a change in attitude will arise from these inconsistencies. Let us see how this works.

According to the theory, the attributes of the existing products in a category define the category and create the expected schema. For example, in our experience soft drinks are expected to be carbonated, cold, slightly sweet, and often containing cola and preservatives. When a changed or new product appears, it may differ somewhat from its category. In fact most new products are purposely labeled as such by using the labels "new," "improved," "now containing X." This difference between the new product and its old category is what Mandler calls "incongruity" (essentially similar to Festinger's dissonance), and he says that we change our evaluation of the product because of this incongruity.

Mandler hypothesized that schema incongruity produces attention and arousal and requires cognitive energy to resolve. He went on to hypothesize that we tend to like a moderate amount of incongruity, because it adds interest and prevents boredom, but we do not like too much incongruity. Specifically he says that the amount of change in evaluation is a function of the amount of incongruity experienced and an inverted-U shaped curve describes the relationship. At the zero incongruity level, a product which has not changed is still perceived as mildly positive because people like predictability in their world, and thus, nonchange is good. Recall that Zajonc (1968) reported a similar result when he found that mere exposure of a stimulus was sufficient to increase subjects' preference for it.

As incongruity increases, Mandler says, up to a point evaluations become more positive. Remember from our discussion of attention mechanisms that change is information and that we are built to notice changes, here called incongruities, in seeking information. Thus we notice them and attempt to restructure to accommodate them because we need cognitive consistency. Moderate incongruities are those which are easily and successfully resolved. Mandler argues that because the resolution of incongruities is reinforcing to us, moderate incongruities generally produce an increased positive evaluation.

When incongruities become too great, however, there is an increase in negative evaluation which counteracts the positive and brings evaluations down again. This happens when incongruities are so great that they force major changes in cognitive structure. It is as if we cannot simply adjust our categories with large changes, but the categories themselves are called into question. Thus, a product may be so different that it loses the positive affect of familiarity and the reward value that resolution of the discrepancy would bring. In addition, it gets negative affect from the uncertainty of where to categorize it. Thus, Mandler's schema congruency theory predicts maximum evaluative improvement from products which change somewhat, but not too much.

The theory was considered very relevant to marketing, for it meant that products would be favorably received when they were moderately changed. But if they were changed too much, it is likely that they would be negatively evaluated. Although the theory has appeal, it suffers from a lack of good definition as to what constitutes moderate and extreme incongruity.

Meyers-Levy and Tybout (1989) attempted to address this problem by using an approach based on cognitive structure found in semantic, or knowledge-based, memory. They hypothesized that product attributes are arranged hierarchically, so that some attributes are essential to a category, whereas others are optional. Using a beverage model, they tested and confirmed the principle that a change which moves more than one level is seen as extreme and leads to unfavorable evaluation. In other words, adding an attribute from the next level is seen as a moderate change, and an attribute from more than one level away is seen as an extreme change. This probably occurs because some attributes define a product more than others. They caution, however, that these results have been shown only for beverages, which are a category of product that people are not likely to feel strongly about. Intense affect, from whatever source, is a variable that is likely to alter the relationship. Their research supported Mandler's theory and offered a way for applying it. The cognitive hierarchy of each product would have to be worked out but once done would furnish guidelines as to how much a product could be changed without risking negative reception.

Before we leave this topic, let me emphasize one point. It is not the actual differences that matter, but rather the perceived differences and discrepancies that cause dissonance. Because perceptions are not always predictable, work in this area is difficult.

ATTITUDE FORMATION:
THE AFFECTIVE COMPONENT

The 1980s have seen a marked increase in emotion-based advertising appeals (Holbrook, 1986). Ogilvy, advising young advertisers, writes, "Emotion can be just as effective as any rational appeal, particularly when there is nothing unique to say about your product." And then he reveals that he found just what psychological researchers find, when he goes on, " I hasten to add that consumers also need a rational excuse to justify their emotional decisions. So always include one." (Ogilvy, 1985, p. 109) We like to think of ourselves as rational, even though we often are not. For example, Mason and Bearden (1978a,b) reported that 84% of their elderly respondents believed that they were rational and purchased after comparisons. Whether they really did or not was not measured, but we rarely recognize our affective biases. Today it is not uncommon to see ads that are almost pure affect and contain only the brand name and a picture. Products of this type include perfumes, food, beverages, clothes, and other items of fashion. Fashion itself is largely an affective response. For representative ads of nearly pure affect consider Figure 9 from the Guess company and Figure 10 from Nike. The ad for Guess watches illustrates the type of ad that uses the model's sensuousness and beauty and also presents the affect of the product itself. Just in case you were baffled as to the Guess product, the single word "watches" is put in the upper right corner. Nike relies on the product alone to convey affect.

Cigarette ads tend to be mostly affect because it is hard to verbalize taste convincingly. Philip Morris' Parliament brand is consistently effective in their use of affect. One ad that shows a couple on a beach uses bright blue and white colors, splashing water, the sexuality of the couple, and their smiling, happy faces all associated with the brand name. The scene is often a gorgeous corner of the Greek isles that carries the additional implication of foreign travel and associates the brand with an upscale lifestyle. It does not matter that these qualities really have no connection to cigarettes. They give the product an image, and it is their image that separates one cigarette from another and comprises most of the attitudes about them.

Endorsers and Situations

Actors are used to sell products because they convey affect better than others, not because they convey facts better than others. Our culture often trains us to hide our emotions, particularly in the case of males. Thus, often we cannot tell from someone's face how he or she is feeling. The essence of good acting, on the other hand, is the ability to show clearly how you are feeling, so that viewers empathize or react. Thus, actors are ideal for advertising.

Another manipulation of affect occurs when actors play the same role repeatedly, as happens in TV serials or the "soaps." They are so convincing that we often forget that they are only actors and respond to them as if they were the character they play. In this way, actors and celebrities trigger the affect associated with their character.

Advertisements often play on affect. They associate products with affective situations so that the affect from the past or the present transfers to the product. (We will consider more detail on this process under classical conditioning.)

Figure 9 This ad for *Guess* watches is an example of the type that is nearly all affect. Notice that there is no copy except for the brand name and one word in the upper right corner to tell us the category of the product. It draws affect from both the model and the product. (Reproduced by permission of Guess? Inc. All rights reserved.)

Figure 10 This ad has no copy except the brand name. It is an example of an ad that is nearly all affect, and it draws its affect from the product alone. (Reproduced by permission of Nike, Inc.)

Negative and positive affect can be transferred to products, but it is clearly advantageous only to do this with positive affect because you do not want to make people dislike your product. As a result it is easier to find sponsors for comedies than for serious documentaries. It is also the reason that humor is so widely used in advertising. Humor, of course, is a strong positive affect, but it is a tricky one, for what is humorous to one person may not be at all funny to another.

Implying Future Affect

Ads can also suggest that usage of the product will trigger affect from at least two sources: first, how the product itself makes us feel as we use it and second, how it makes us feel when people see us using it. Let us look first at implications of how the product will make us feel as we use it. Consider how these examples suggest that using a product alters our affect:

> Coca-Cola, "Have a Coke and smile"
> Pepsi-Cola, "Get that Pepsi feeling"
> Maxwell House, "Get that good-to-the-last-drop feeling"
> General Motors, "Get that great GM feeling"
> Belmont Park, "It's an unbeatable feeling"
> Sealy Posturpedic, "Feeling so good it shows"
> Remy Martin, "Arouse your sense of Remy"
> AT&T, "Reach out and touch someone"
> Burlington Mills, "Never go to bed with a sheet you don't love"
> Kenwood, "This system is ... pure ecstasy"
> Dim pantyhose, "For the sheer pleasure of it"
> Nieman–Marcus, "Live with a sense of pleasure" (from Holbrook, 1986, p. 42).

Similarly, ads may emphasize the second source of affect, how we feel when others see us using the product. Consider these examples:

> Jaguar, "If you could drive one car to your high school reunion, this would be it."
> Diamonds (no brand), "Tomorrow, she'll be on the phone to all her friends."
> Cadillac, "Nowadays, my kids aren't the only ones making a statement. I make one every day in the car I drive.... My DeVille says it all."
> French Company luggage, "Even before you appear they know who you are."
> Toyota trucks, "It gets me more places than my sports car ever did. And a lot more attention."
> Mazda MPV Luxury Edition, "It not only says you've arrived. It says you've brought the whole family."

Proctor and Gamble detergent, "You'll be more appreciated if you use Dash."

Suma+ moisturizing cream, "You will notice the difference and everyone else will notice you."

These affective reasons are probably more important to us than all the cognitive information about how well the product is made. We return to this aspect in the next chapter.

Image Making

Both direct and indirect sources of affect make the concept of image important. An image is good when the brand or logo is a tag to create positive affect from either source, using it or being seen. Consider, for instance, that beer is bought for image more than for taste because studies show that consumers usually cannot distinguish between most beers on the basis of taste. For this reason beer commercials are designed to convey primarily affective information, rather than factual information, and to associate the brand name with positive affect. All products which differ very little from each other (perfume, cigarettes, and jeans) rely heavily on affective associations to distinguish them from the others. You should note, however, that rationalization is alive and well, and few people will tell you they buy beer for anything but taste. They are not necessarily being deceitful. They probably don't know. Real motivations are hard to assess.

Schema-Triggered Affect

Affect and cognition interact in a continuous spiral, each affecting the other, so that although affect directs cognition, the converse is also true that cognitions can trigger affect. This is the reason that the source of attitudes is so hard to pin down. Memories, for example, do this. Maybe you remember an evening date at the beach last summer or being hassled by police because they mistook you for a felon. Memories are clearly not stimuli because they are not outside energy sources, but they can act very similarly and arouse us. Fiske (1982) has called this "schema-triggered affect." It means that when we encounter a situation similar to an older one, we are likely to experience some of the affect that accompanied the older one. Schemas can be complex collections of people, places, and events, and their affect is correspondingly hard to characterize. Individual brands share some of their affect with others in their category. Some schemas recall more personal memories than others and are consequently more powerful because they are more involving.

Schema-triggered affect is widely used in advertising. For example, a product is placed in a particular scene. For example, ads for Salem cigarettes place their brand name in a beach scene. The beach scene is meant to recall memories of the beach (the schema), which, it can generally be assumed is remembered as pleasant and relaxed (affective tag). The affective tag should cause our present mood to become pleasant and relaxed, which should then attach to the brand name. If it works, it should make us prefer Salem over other brands. The process is classical conditioning to which we return in chapter 9.

Halo Effects

We introduced the halo effect in chapter 3, but we bring it back for an encore because it applies to attitudes particularly. It may in fact be a special case of a schema-triggered affect. For example, in one of the early studies of this tendency, Asch (1946) measured the attitudes of two groups toward a fictitious person. One group received a description of the person that contained six adjectives including "warm." The other group received the same adjectives, except that the word "warm" was replaced with "cold." The first group saw the person as sociable, generous, good-natured and humane, whereas the second group perceived the person as unsociable, ungenerous, and ruthless. As you might expect, the effect is strongest with the adjectives which are the most salient in the list.

Seeking to take the Asch study out of the lab, Kelley (1950) used the same two words in the same way with two groups when introducing a visiting lecturer. Then, both groups heard the same speaker. The group which had heard the word "warm" in the introduction rated the speaker as less self-centered, less formal, less irritable, more sociable, and more interesting than the other group. This means that in forming new preferences, we are guided to a large extent by our existing attitudes. We tend to maintain consistency. Thus, well-liked speakers are more likely to be believed than disliked ones (Abelson & Miller, 1967).

We have mentioned that brand extension is one place where the halo effect is used. Another is public relations generally. We tend to hear things as consistent with the attitude we already have. Thus we may distort new information to fit where we want it to fit. For example, just talk to strong party members after a presidential debate. Thus, bias clouds our judgment. It also means that ads encountered early will have less impact than those seen later and that positive affect introduced in early ads allow more favorable acceptance of messages in later ads.

VARIABLES OF ATTITUDINAL CHANGE

Cognitive dissonance theory deals with attitudinal changes that result from action counter to beliefs. Schema incongruity theory deals with discrepancies in expectations. These theories do not mean, however, that attitudinal change is simple. A number of variables have been identified that interact to keep the picture cloudy. We consider some of them. Note that they vary in their affect/cognition content, and some are important in both dimensions.

Audience Variables

Subjective Norms. As we noted, the theory of reasoned action gives the particular variable of subjective norms a prominent place. Subjective norms are essentially the collective opinions of significant others in our lives and depend on our perception of how others view the behavior in question. The reaction of these others is surely a significant part of the behavior's consequences, not some unrelated factor that comes later. Subjective norms are socially and culturally determined. Their influence is increased or decreased by one's level of motivation to get approval from those others, as we discuss at some length in the chapter on psychological needs. In other words, just how this one factor is perceived turns out to be very complex.

Mood. Affect, as we have been using it, refers to feeling about something. It is directed toward a specific object. Mood, on the other hand, is affect that is not directed at any particular thing (Fiske & Taylor, 1991). It is global and modifies everything one is doing. Morris (1992) argues that emotion and affect are cued by properties of the environment, whereas mood is produced by cues about the state of the self. Mood, he says, is telling us about the internal resources we have available to meet the environmental demands. If this is so, then cheerful people are those who feel more able to cope with their world. Consistent with this interpretation, Fiske and Taylor comment that "cheerful people are more compliant with persuasive communications, while angry people are generally less compliant," and they give no less than 14 references to back it up (Fiske & Taylor, 1991, p. 449). They go on to speculate that "The positive mood results may explain the effectiveness of free samples, soothing music, and friendly banter in marketing efforts." (p. 450) It may also bear on the reason that advertisers want to advertise in happy, upbeat shows and not in heavy, controversial shows.

Involvement. We introduced involvement in an earlier chapter. You will remember that it means personal relevance and refers to a message that affects us personally in some way or concerns something about which we care strongly. Involvement gets our attention, and it also effects attitudinal change. You will recall from chapter 5 that Petty and Cacioppo (1981) proposed two routes to attitudinal change in their elaboration likelihood model: the central route, in which the message is actively thought about (elaborated), and a peripheral route, in which the message is not thought about much at all. To change attitudes in the high involvement condition involves cognitive arguments, but in the low involvement condition they go unheeded, and affective appeals that reach the person through the peripheral route will be more effective (Petty, Cacioppo, & Schumann, 1983).

Considerable research supports the elaboration likelihood model. For example, the study by Celuch and Slama (1995) mentioned previously found that in the low involvement condition (the peripheral route) brand attribute information (that is, cognitions) did not affect the overall brand attitude, but affect did. In informational ads, on the other hand, involvement must be higher or they will not get attention at all. Thus, if they are read, the central route is involved and cognitions dominate. Hence, the theory explains why they found, in the informational condition, that the cognitive attitude toward the ad was the best predictor of attitude toward the brand.

Another use of the term "involvement" may cause confusion here. In an early study testing social judgment theory, Hovland et al. (1957) showed that involved people are less likely to change their attitudes, but this is a second use of the term. This use of "involvement" means that people feel strongly about an issue, not that they are in any particular state at the moment. The theory maintains that statements are perceived on a continuum that runs from accept to reject. The closer to the poles a statement is perceived to be, the more likely it is to meet with acceptance or rejection. There is also a zone in the middle of the continuum that is one of noncommitment, where statements are neither accepted nor rejected. The theory says that when people are involved (i.e, feel stronger about an issue), they take more extreme views, their zone of noncommitment is reduced, and their zone of rejection is increased (Tedeschi et al., 1985).

We can put it all another way and avoid the confusing second meaning of the term, involvement. How easy it is to change people's attitudes depends to some extent on how strongly their current attitudes are held. Incidentally, attitudinal strength is often as much a function of personality as it is of information. Thus, if people with extreme views do change their minds, they are likely to become just as extreme in their new views. They also tend to be extreme on many issues.

Age.   Opposite acting factors come to bear in the case of the elderly. On the one hand, they are "more set in their ways" and self reliant. For example, Phillips and Sternthal (1977) write: "Although persuasion studies have sampled only individuals ranging in age from 14 to 32, they are univocal in reporting a consistent decline in persuasibility as a function of increasing age." (p. 448) They attribute this to increasing cognitive skills, but one might also attribute it to an increasing sense of identity and increasing ego strength, which continues until age 30. This increase in independence is probably reflected in Rotter's I-E scale which records the gradual internalization of a sense of control. Phillips and Sternthal report several studies using this scale which all show that older adults have as good or better sense of control than younger adults, leading to the conclusion that persuasibility levels off after age 30.

On the other hand, cognitive slowdown and failing abilities work against resistance to persuasion. For example, Phillips and Sternthal identify the cognitive slowdown discussed in chapter 5 as a contributor here. They write,

> Because elderly people show a slowness in processing information, they may have difficulty generating counterarguments as the basis for rejecting an appeal. This is likely to be the reason why elderly are susceptible to influence in contexts unfamiliar to them. (p. 452)

So, persuasibility reaches a middle-aged plateau of maximum resistance and then starts down again at some point.

Context is an increasing factor that often works against the elderly. When subjects felt they were more competent, they were less conforming, but with increasing frequency they find themselves in contexts in which they do not feel complete competence. This is a function of gradual loss of physical capacity but also an increasing unfamiliarity with their world. Changes in technology with its continually new products and the changing social relationships that accompany the technological changes combine to make the task of staying *au courant* increasingly difficult. Phillips and Sternthal write:

When elderly individuals perceive themselves to be competent they are no more susceptible to social influence than younger adults. However, when elderly perceive themselves to lack the competence to make a decision they manifest greater influenceability than younger people. Furthermore, the lack of resistance to influence attempts is likely to be most acute for those elderly who are isolated from contact with others (Nahemow, 1963); in such situations there may be a lack of exposure to the social reinforcement necessary to enhance individuals' perception of their own self-competence (Philipps & Sternthal, 1977, pp. 449–450).

Even with social reinforcement, at some point a growing sense of incapacity is likely to weaken their perception of self-competence, and the elderly will become more vulnerable to persuasive pressure. Thus, we are likely to see real differences in the elderly, and those who are incapacitated in some way, or in nursing homes, will be more vulnerable. Self-competence is a major component of the self-worth that we expand on in chapter 10.

Product Variables

Brand Familiarity. Machleit and Wilson (1988) compared the effectiveness of ads for familiar and nonfamiliar brands. They found that affect transfers to nonfamiliar brands, but not to familiar brands, most likely because the familiar brands already have affective tags, and any new inputs will have to average out with what is there, as we have discussed previously. Thus, forming an attitude toward a new product is much easier than changing an attitude toward an old product.

Source Variables

Credibility of the Source. Baum, Fisher, and Singer (1985) summarized a number of variables taken from a number of studies that increase the acceptance of a message. We will consider some of these. Attitudes change more when the message is heard from someone who we feel is not trying to persuade us (Walster & Festinger, 1962). When someone is coming at us, we naturally put our guard up. This means that commercials may work better when they show two people in a conversation we appear to be overhearing. In addition, we may want that conversation to appear casually undertaken, so that the participants are not apparently trying to convince each other, but simply discussing. This is standard fare for commercials.

Attitudes are more likely to change when the communicator is perceived as similar to the hearer (Berscheid, 1966). This is the element of identification that increases involvement. Here we add that identification gets attention and also adds to the convincing power of the message. Thus, older models are perceived as less credible than younger models by the youth market (Jordan, 1983). This is one reason that advertisers are reluctant to use older models in ads. They are afraid of losing the younger market in the process. On the other hand, younger models had a lower credibility score than middle-aged or older models among a representative group over age 65 (Milliman & Erffmeyer, 1990). This suggests that as the over-65 segment grows, we should see more "dual promotional mixes" that use different models for different segments, and more use of older, but not too old, models.

Identification may also be behind the finding that persuaders who have powerful positions are more effective in changing the attitudes of others than those less powerful (Rosenbaum & Rosenbaum, (1975). Similarly, we tend to believe authority figures, as we mentioned under perception. Perhaps we want to identify with power, or maybe powerful people are perceived as having expertise.

Expertise is the dominant factor in ascribing credibility (Oscamp, 1977), that is, we believe the speaker really knows. Perhaps the perception of increased expertise is the reason that we are more persuaded by people who talk fast, and they are seen as more credible (Miller, Maruyama, Beaber, & Valone, 1976). Expertise is certainly the reason that the white laboratory coat is so powerful in selling items related to health. It symbolizes people who are in the business of knowing about health: doctors, nurses, and laboratory technicians. Similarly the phrases, "Doctors recommend ..." or "More doctors use ..." carry the weight of expertise. Much of Crest toothpaste's popularity is traceable to its early endorsement by the American Dental Association. When the ADA said you got fewer cavities, we believed they had studied the issue and knew. Midas Mufflers films their ads under the lift in the shop, using an older spokesperson in shop dress, which gives the impression, never stated, that this person has worked on mufflers a long time and really knows what he is talking about.

Credibility is greatest when the speaker's expertise is relevant to the topic under discussion (Oscamp, 1977), but sometimes high status increases persuasiveness even when the expertise is totally irrelevant (Aronson & Golden, 1962). Thus, Michael Jordan does best selling products related to sports and fitness, but his charisma is so high that he could probably sell anything. In general, advertisers seek to match the image of the celebrity to the desired image of the product (Kamins, 1990).

Perceived Objectivity of Source.   Objectivity, also important in judging credibility, is essentially how much you trust the speaker. It can be established by reputation, but it is necessary that the spokesperson not have a personal stake in the message. For example, suppose that a local business person argues in town meeting for approval of a new shopping mall on the grounds that it would benefit the town. Then suppose it is revealed that he owns the land on which the mall would be built. His arguments about town benefits would lose credibility at once. In fact, such an occurrence might lead to a hardening of old attitudes, rather than a change to new ones. Being paid for making the ad itself, however, often seems to be an exception. It is a form of personal gain that we seem to overlook. If we did not, celebrities would not be very good sales-people. Do we really forget they are paid well to make these statements?

The Sleeper Effect.   We have just discussed that highly credible sources produce more attitude change than sources of low credibility. Hovland, Lumsdaine, and Sheffield (1949), however, found that after some three weeks the picture may have changed considerably, and the credibility influence is likely to have disappeared. Arguments dismissed originally, because of the source, are likely to be more acceptable three weeks later. This delayed impact of a persuasive message is called the "sleeper effect," and the discoverers hypothesized that the source becomes disassociated from the message over time and thus loses its effectiveness. In support of this interpretation, Kelman and Hovland (1953) found that when subjects were reminded of the original source at the three week test, the credibility difference reappeared. The finding stimulated considerable research and evidence was presented both for and against the phenomenon. Oscamp (1977) wrote after reviewing the literature, that the sleeper effect happens only in highly unusual cases and is not considered any longer a real phenomenon. He was apparently premature, however, for Pratkanis, Greenwald, Leippe, and Baumgardner (1988) reported that after a series of sixteen studies they had determined that, though a weak effect, it occurs because the message and the lack of credibility of the source are forgotten at different rates. Factors that make the message stronger and direct less attention to the source increase the effect. Conversely, things that draw more attention to the source and less to the message decrease it, so that it is often not present.

Sabini (1992) suggests that the sleeper effect is probably the reason that, usually after an environmental disaster, a "company spokesperson" dismisses the event with an explanation that is highly unlikely, given the vested interest of the source. Although we dismiss the claim immediately, it may have some impact later because of the sleeper effect.

Message Variables

Discrepancy of Message.   The schema congruity theory gathered evidence that the change of attitudes occurs when the discrepancy of the new perception differs moderately from the old, but not when the discrepancy is too large, as we discussed previously. When the discrepancy becomes too large, it becomes easier to discredit the source to reduce the incongruity. Similarly, people who hold extreme views are less likely than moderates to change their attitudes (Hovland et al., 1957) in part because they perceive that even moderate messages are very discrepant from their own views.

Additional support for the need for moderation in attitudinal change is found in a study by Wilson, Lisle, Kraft, and Wetzel (1989) who propose that if people's experience fits their expectation (a type of schema), they have a faster affective reaction. When the experience differs markedly from the expectation, people will have more trouble forming preferences. This might have significance in television where successive ads come so quickly and there is no time for lengthy deliberation. If the attitude is not changed quickly, it is possible that the discrepancy will simply be pushed aside by the next ad and forgotten, so that the change never occurs. This possibility suggests that lengthy treatment is necessary for large discrepancies. The significance for political advertising would be considerable. Such a possibility has not been tested, however.

Presentation Variables

Repetition.   As we noted previously relative to the formation of preferences, repetition generally produces more positive than negative changes. Obermiller comments:

> Few people would question the existence of exposure effects in the broad sense of the phrase. Most of us have experienced the changing evaluations that result from repeated exposures. For example, a poem that struck one as senseless after one reading became rich in meaning and was much appreciated after several thoughtful readings. An initially horrid hairstyle grew acceptable and was even enjoyed in time. The taste of beer (coffee, scotch), bitter and repugnant at first, became not only tolerable, but increasingly pleasant after sufficient trials.... A difficult choice among unknown brands was simplified by choosing the one with the familiar name. In each of these examples, something that was initially unfamiliar and disliked came to be liked or preferred after repeated exposures (Obermiller, 1985, p. 18).

The timing of the repetitions and the amount of attention paid to them are considerations that make repetitions vary in their effectiveness. Moreover, several studies have shown the inverted-U shaped curve produced when some repetition leads to increases in positive evaluation of the stimulus, but higher levels lead to a decrease again (Obermiller, 1985). This suggests we can become "sick" of an ad, and it could become counterproductive, but evidence here is lacking.

Order Effects. Two effects have been noted in learning studies. One, a primacy effect, occurs when the information first heard (e.g., first words in a list) is retained better than the rest of the information. A second effect, a recency effect, occurs when the last information (e.g., last words in the list) is retained better than the rest. Which effect pertains to a given situation involves a number of variables. Although early research favored primacy, considerable later research contradicted this to favor recency. Oscamp (1977) concludes that there are sufficient variables involved that prediction follows no universal law. For example, we have seen that saliency is aided by recency, but a sufficiently strong or unusual early argument might achieve even greater saliency in a primacy effect. Recently, Haugtvedt and Wegener (1994) investigated these effects in a persuasion context in conditions of high and low involvement. They found that there is a greater influence of the initial message on final judgments in conditions that foster high levels of message elaboration (high involvement), a primacy effect. In conditions that foster low message elaboration (low involvement), on the other hand, a second message had the greater influence, a recency effect.

Direct Versus Indirect. Festinger found that action triggered cognitive dissonance because action has a sense of reality that is far stronger than fantasy. Similarly, attitudes which are based on direct, personal experience are stronger than those based on indirect, second-hand information. Fazio and Zanna (1981) attribute the greater strength of direct experience to three things: that we tend to have more information; that experiences have greater salience; and that experiences have increased availability from memory. Sabini (1992) adds the element of inference, pointing out that attitudes not based on direct experience are likely to be based on inferences, and as such can be wrong. On the other hand, attitudes based on direct experience are less inferential and thus are less likely to be wrong.

CHAPTER 8

Psychological Needs

The study of personality development has been an extensive area in psychology, and scores of theories have been advanced. You will be relieved to know that it is not our intent to summarize all of them here. Many, if not most, of these theories have suffered from a lack of empirical validation, so that their application to marketing is questionable. We have seen Freud, for example, applied vigorously to advertising in the 40s and 50s, but with doubtful results and eventual contradictions, so that advertisers in general abandoned the approach. Still, there are one or two themes that occur universally and consistently in many theories and are particularly useful. The most useful of these is the concept of the need to feel self-worth. First we look at just what it is, and then we consider its wide applications.

NEED TO FEEL WORTH

To understand the **concept of self-worth**, we turn to the work of Carl Rogers who reached the height of his popularity in the early 60s, but whose ideas have continued to influence psychology. Rogers' theory provided one of the first major alternatives to Freud's psychoanalysis (Liebert & Spiegler, 1987). The first of his two major assumptions, "the actualizing tendency," was that people tend to act in positive rather than negative ways, so that:

> Experiences perceived as maintaining or enhancing the individual are evaluated positively and are sought. Such positive experiences result in feelings of satisfaction. In contrast, experiences perceived as opposing maintenance or enhancement are evaluated negatively and are avoided (Liebert & Spiegler, 1987, p. 287).

Reinforcers in operant conditioning are things we work to get, as we will explore in Chapter 10. Perhaps you will recognize that, without labeling it as such, what Rogers does expands the idea of reinforcement into the arena of ego forces. In other words, in terms of operant conditioning, Rogers means that people find those things reinforcing that enhance their sense of self-worth but avoid those things which threaten or reduce their sense of self-worth.

Rogers goes on to clarify the source of self-worth:

> ... all people have a need for positive regard. This is a basic need for acceptance, respect, sympathy, warmth, and love. At first these feelings of worthiness come from other people ... [but ultimately] the individual relies on the self rather than others for overall feelings of worth and esteem (Liebert & Spiegler, 1987, pp. 292–293).

In other words, many of our human needs, such as the needs for acceptance, respect, sympathy, warmth, and love, get much of their power from the way they enhance our more basic need for a sense of personal worth. Thus, our understanding of human motivation can be simplified a bit by realizing that many seemingly different behaviors all may have the common purpose of enhancing the sense of self-worth.

SOURCES OF SELF-WORTH

Cultural Definition

Although we all have a need to feel worth, we do not all experience it in the same way. Each of us is told by our culture what the conditions of worth are, what it is that makes a person have worth. The chief vehicles of culture for preschoolers are their parents, but other adults, siblings, and peers play increasing roles, as development progresses. We internalize the dos and don'ts of these cultural agents and society in general (Freud called it superego development), and almost as a by-product we form a sense of our own value. We learn what about ourselves is valued and what is not. Rogers says that it comes about "when the positive regard of a significant other is conditional, when the individual feels ... in some respects ... prized and in others not." (Rogers, 1959, p. 209) Learning theorists would point to differential reinforcement operating here. How we find our worth occurs through reinforcement, but why we seek worth in the first place is not so clear.

The need to feel self-worth may go back to security needs and is really a sensing of security. For the young child, survival itself depends on acceptance by and being valued by key, all-powerful adults. Thus, it is likely that self-worth needs spring from security and survival needs because those who have it survive and those who do not perish. But whatever the origins, the major reinforcers for human beings derive from feelings relating to self-worth.

To clarify this point, we can consider the action of cultural reinforcers. Culture gets its power over individuals from their need to feel self-worth. If we did not want to feel valued, we would not care how other people felt about us. But we do care, and so we pay attention to the things that get us social approval in our culture. For example, if one culture says that when you are angry the appropriate behavior is to strike out and not be pushed around, then that culture is saying that the way to be valued by those with whom you live is to be aggressive. Thereby, aggression becomes reinforcing because it enhances feelings of self-worth, and one could predict that that culture will be characterized by aggressive people. On the other hand, another culture may say that the appropriate course of action when angry is rather to withdraw, cool down, and avoid conflict. In this case, people are likely to be less aggressive because the reinforcement of social approval, sought because of the need to feel self-worth, is obtained by avoiding aggression. We return to the concept of culture in the next chapter. The important point here is that although the behavior of members of these two groups will be quite different because their cultures set different conditions of worth, yet underlying both will be the same motivational need to feel valued. Here we want to consider the consequences of this continual search for self-worth.

The need for self-worth is the power behind a host of other needs and affects what we perceive, what we find to be reinforcing, and, of course, what we buy. In other words, to understand human motivation, it is essential to realize that psychological needs and in particular the need to feel self-worth are just as real and operative as physical needs. Indeed, psychological needs are often stronger and lead to decisions which seem to defy logic.

At this point, it would probably be well to reiterate the principle that the impact of psychological need is largely unconscious. We are often not aware of our needs, but they control and direct us all the same. Modern therapists seem to believe, more than Freud did, that we can bring some of our needs to awareness with support and effort, but some of our needs will stay hidden beneath the surface.

To make it all more complicated, psychological needs change with many factors. For these reasons, marketers seem to have assumed that psychological needs are so individualistic that they cannot be addressed by anyone who must deal with a group. But although it is true that no two people are quite the same, it is also true that we all share many psychological needs. Underlying most of them is the strongest need of all, the need to feel self-worth. Moreover, because of the commonalities of culture, large groups of people experience worth in the same way.

Threats Require Reconfirmation

The need for self-worth has been widely applied in advertising, sales, and consumption. The reason that it has such utility lies in the fact that self-worth is not something with which one deals once and then is done. To the contrary, the need to confirm that we have worth turns out to be in the nature of a ravenous beast, forever with us, constantly demanding to be fed. The more doubt we have about our worth, the more the beast demands to be fed. We confirm our worth, only to feel the need to do it all over again. In other words, confirmation of worth is something we keep on doing throughout our lifetimes, but the way we do it gradually changes. In addition, our need to reaffirm our self-worth can be made more urgent by our culture and by changes in our personal condition.

The ways by which we reaffirm self-worth change with age, as do our psychological priorities in general, in response to continuing changes in our environment. Some threats to our self-worth appear earlier in our development than others, but none of them ever go away completely. To understand the full range of threats in the adult, we will follow their development in the child, adolescent, and adult, pointing out how they are used in marketing at each of these levels.

To make clear how this proceeds we will start with Erik Erikson. His well-known analysis (Erikson, 1956) distinguishes eight stages of psychological development from birth to old age. He theorized that a new concern comes to the fore at each level and becomes the focus of psychological energy. Each level represents a major psychological issue which must be accomplished or resolved before moving on. If left unresolved, it continues to absorb psychological energy, holds the individual back, and prevents appropriate development at the next level. In other words, Erikson's stages indicate the focus of psychological energy, the motivational core, at each level of life. However, it is important to realize that, though we resolve an issue for the moment, we may go back to these same issues, sometimes again and again, when our life circumstances change and even mild threats to our self-worth appear. Here we are putting Rogers and Erikson together.

Preschoolers

Parental Identification.   Erikson's first three stages are particularly concerned with the development of the psychological individual and take place before the age of six. In these stages we see the development of trust, autonomy, and initiative. At this age, children get their sense of self-worth mainly from the way they are treated by their parents. Being perceptually limited and self-centered (not the same as selfish), children credit or blame themselves for whatever their parents do to them. Thus, children who are treated lovingly by their parents grow up with confidence and a sense of having worth. On the other hand, a rejected or abused child instead wonders, "What is wrong with me that my parents treat me this way?" Such mistreated children grow into adults who feel there is something wrong with them, that they are inferior, and they will show a correspondingly stronger need to confirm their self-worth repeatedly.

Along the way, children attempt to reduce the anxiety of potential parent rejection by becoming as similar to their parents as possible, the process called identification. Thus children imitate their parents not only to be "grown up," but to illustrate their alignment and to reaffirm that they are accepted and have worth. Similarly, nearly any authority figure is believed and trusted by children. In fact, all adults and even older children are usually trusted. This is the reason that we tell them to avoid strangers. Clearly, marketers have used this tendency to their advantage. Children take at face value whatever they see on television, unless they are educated to be more skeptical.

Identification is a continuing process for adults, some much more than others. One sees much more variability in adults. As a lifetime of learning begins to accentuate differences, their behaviors pull further apart. Many adults are surprisingly influenced by authority figures and celebrities with whom they can identify, particularly the "rich and famous." Children identify in large part with their parents to feel self-worth, and a similar process is probably at work here for adults. In chapter 2, we introduced the power of identification as an attention-getter, because it taps into the basic, personally relevant level and is thus involving. In other words, although the process of identification appears early, it also remains a powerful adult force, one of which advertisers are aware.

Elementary Schoolers

Industry and Competence.   The elementary school stage, between the age of 6 and puberty, begins school life and involves developing social, physical, and school skills relative to others and an ability to face one's own limitations. Erickson stresses that at this age children must learn "industry" or carry the consequence of feeling inferior. School success or failure begins to add to or detract from the sense of self-worth.

Papalia and Olds (1986) write, "These are important years for the development of self-esteem. As children compare their own abilities to those of their peers, they construct a sense of who they are." (p. 275) As White and Watt (1981) put it, "A sense of competence is a vital root of self-esteem." (p. 21)

In our culture particularly, competence and success mean achievement as one gets older. The evidence collected by McClelland (1976), who studied achievement needs for many years, supports Erikson by indicating that adult achievers are people who were rewarded for small achievements as children. In other words, we learn early that we can achieve, and our later behavior reflects it. Moreover, our culture values achievers, so that those who do not feel able to achieve do not feel valued by society and experience diminished self-worth.

Once again, although the need to feel achievement begins in the early years, it does not leave us. An ad which is a particularly good illustration of the universal appeal of achievement and competence in our culture is one for the Dow Chemical Company. It depicts a middle-aged man sitting on his desk at Dow, while above him a scene from his past shows him as a young man receiving an Olympic medal. The copy reads in part,

> As a young boy, I dreamed of doing great things. My name is Pusko Jezic. And, in my youth, I dreamed of bringing home a medal to my country. The dream came true, both in Helsinki in 1952 and in Melbourne in 1956. Today, I'm an American citizen, holding a doctoral degree in organic technology. And I'm part of another team ... at Dow.

The good feeling toward this man because of his achievement is attached to the name Dow, and the appeal is clearly not to children, indicating the advertisers experience that the positive value of achievement continues throughout adulthood.

Adolescents

Peer Orientation.   The onset of puberty ushers in the next stage. It signals the beginning of the transition from childhood to adulthood. Ideally, we have increased confidence in our selves as others see us and choose a career or occupation. However, it is often a time of anxiety about self-worth. Puberty changes the way we see others, the way they react to us, and often puts us out of developmental synchrony with our friends because some develop early and some late. The changes are physical, sexual, and emotionally powerful. As if this were not enough, usually responsibility makes new demands, as we are children one day and yet we are expected to be adult in the next. Questions of our ability to fulfill our new roles abound. Thus adolescents are particularly threatened by issues of self-worth.

By this time, however, adolescents are looking to their peer group for this reassurance, rather than to their parents, because parental attachment represents childhood, which they are attempting to leave behind. This is the reason that the peer group holds such power over the adolescent, for it has become the source of the feeling of self-worth. The unconscious reasoning seems to be: if the group accepts me, then clearly I have worth, but if the group rejects me, I am worthless. Then, one must do what the group does or risk rejection. One must look just like the rest of the group to prove membership and acceptance and also to reduce the risk of rejection. Identification has shifted from parents to peers but is stronger than ever. Here is the basis of both teen fads and gangs.

Some writers feel that our society delays adulthood more than other societies, and we are more adolescent than European countries, that is, our citizens are more susceptible to group pressure than they should be. Americans tend to be friendly because they want to be liked by the group, but at the same time they are potentially vulnerable to group pressure. They may also experience conflict between the traditionally strong American ideal of individualism and the lingering adolescent need to conform closely to the group. Adolescents tend to be high conformers to their peer group, but not to society in general. Moreover, they want to appear to be just the opposite, independent and self-sufficient. Then, Americans would be predicted to conform but to want to be seen as acting independently, which is, of course, just what happens with the Marlboro ad. Similarly, when the Audi ads say of its sports sedan, "The only thing it conforms to is the road," it makes nonconformity a part of its image, but clearly the market is not adolescents.

High Self-Monitors.   Because much of the adolescent remains in all of us, these ads have much wider impact than just the adolescent market. Many adults do not move much beyond the adolescent level, particularly in our society. Moreover, finally we may be fulfilling a wish from childhood or adolescence now that we can afford the price. Adolescence is a term of psychological development, not age. Ideally, adults eventually internalize their standards and then begin to compare their behavior to that standard, rather than relying on the opinions of their peer group. This gives freedom from the group and maximum independence, but we are also seldom free of our past. That final step, internalization of standards, requires a level of self-confidence and self-esteem that many adults never achieve. Thus, the dominant adolescent themes continue to have importance for many adults.

Supporting this contention are the studies by Mark Snyder, who has focused on individuals he calls self-monitors. He developed a test for adult consumers called the Self-Monitoring Scale (Snyder, 1974). He uses his test to distinguish between two types of people, which he calls "high self-monitors" and "low self-monitors." The high self-monitors are psychologically similar to the adolescent group we have been discussing here, and his test identifies people in whom the adolescent concerns are still strong. Of these he says, "high self-monitors strive to be the type of person called for by each situation in which they find themselves ... their behavior often displays marked shifts in the images they convey to other people." (Snyder, 1989) Zanna (1989) too finds that high self-monitors are less likely than the low self-monitors to stick with their own attitudes. Low self-monitors, on the other hand, are those who have internalized their values and would be expected to be more numerous among older adults. "Low self-monitors are more consistent because they are guiding their behavior from relevant inner sources, such as attitudes, feelings, and dispositions. Their private attitudes and their actual behavior in social contexts are in substantial correspondence." (Snyder, 1989)

In an empirical study with college students, Snyder found that high self-monitors assigned more favorable evaluations to those ads that convey information about the *images* to be gained by using the product (image oriented ads), whereas low self-monitors assigned their most favorable evaluations to those ads that convey *information* about the product itself (product-oriented ads) (Snyder, 1989). Some ads (e.g., cigarettes, beer, and perfumes) clearly depend almost exclusively on image rather than information and would appeal particularly to high self-monitors. But even on expensive items that are supposed to involve maximum cognitive decision making, image was more important to high self-monitors.

> [When] people rated automobiles, high self-monitors responded favorably to the car with the more attractive appearance, judging it to be of higher quality; by contrast, low self-monitors assigned higher quality ratings to the less attractive car, perhaps reflecting an implicit theory that one should be wary of the quality of attractive products, since an attractive exterior may be hiding deficiencies (DeBono & Snyder, 1989).

In other words, adolescents, and adults especially concerned about their self-worth, monitor self more, are more concerned about their image, and thus, are more susceptible to image advertising.

Independence and Identity. One reason that image is so important to adolescents is that it is a time of searching for an acceptable identity, an identity valued by their peer culture, and one that separates them clearly from their parents. While actually quite conforming to peer group, it is their identity that asserts their independence for them. Erikson (1956) concludes that identity is the most important task of adolescence. It is a matter of choosing who you will be and also becoming comfortable with who you are. Adolescents listen to peers, rather than parents or any adults, are superconscious of what the peer group is wearing, saying, and doing, and direct their image to the peer group. Unfortunately, the fragile nature of their perception of self-worth and their strong need to establish an identity make them excellent targets for sales pressure based on their anxieties in these areas. They pay particular attention to and are involved by products seen as a means of reducing anxiety about identity issues, particularly those concerning sexuality, popularity, personal qualities, or adult status.

The internalization of the standards of self-worth is more complex than simply maturing, however, for one can break from the group in some spheres and not in others. One can be secure in some aspects of identity, but not in others. We feel our worth threatened in some situations and not in others. For this reason, the concept of self-worth has application throughout the life span, not just adolescence. In other words, all of us are susceptible to anxieties of self-worth in some areas at some times and playing on these anxieties sells products.

Masculinity/Femininity. One of the dominant aspects of our identity is worry over sexuality, being and appearing to be sexually competent. In fulfilling our cultural gender roles are we masculine or feminine enough? Because this is a particularly strong anxiety, it has been exploited extensively. The ad for Marlboro cigarettes, to cite perhaps the most famous example, pictures a tough, masculine cowboy with whom we have all become familiar. He is supremely independent, masculine, and clearly in control in a rough, challenging occupation. At the time it was introduced, Marlboros were widely regarded as women's cigarettes, and the company wanted to change the image because men buy more cigarettes than women. The Marlboro man ad became one of the most successful ad series of all time. The ad has run with little change for more than 30 years and moved Marlboro to the position of the best-selling cigarette in the world (Ogilvy, 1985).

Coincidentally, winning over an adolescent is far more cost effective than winning over an adult because smoking generally starts in adolescence and preference habits are established that may persist for a lifetime. The company denies that the ad was meant for adolescents, as indeed all tobacco companies until very recently have denied advertising to adolescents (see Mazis, Ringold, Perry, & Denman, 1992), but the new appeal happens to be clearly focused on those values with which adolescents are particularly concerned. As we have noted, smoking generally begins as a symbolic way for adolescents to show maturity and independence because smoking is something our parents typically tell us not to do and children cannot do openly. The Marlboro man is the personification of these qualities.

This ad clearly had the right appeal for its particular audience. In fairness, however, we should point out that concern for identity and independence does not end with adolescence, so the ad continues to have appeal, even for older males, particularly those who continue to have self doubts on those issues. Thus, adolescent and adult males are attaching to themselves a symbol of the values they want for their identity by adopting this brand. Younger males may identify more with Joe Camel, who stresses being cool over being masculine. The Marlboro man, after all, has been around a long time, and younger adolescents may see him as a symbol of an older generation.

Males, of course, are not alone in being concerned about sexuality in adolescence, and advertising reflects this. Virginia Slims appeals to young women as a counterpoint to the Marlboro appeal to men. Now, independence has become a female ideal, and in their ads attractive women specifically reject the outdated values of the older generation: "You've come a long way baby." Femininity is touted by endless products, some very directly, as when the Oscar de la Renta ad asks the reader to "experience the power of femininity," or when another perfume, Ciara, is touted as "devastatingly female."

The irony, of course, is that it is all illusion. The individualism is illusory, for how unique is smoking the best-selling brand in the world? The masculinity or femininity is illusory, for what does smoking have to do with these values? Or why is one cigarette more masculine or feminine than another? It is really just another cigarette. Incidentally, my students pointed out to me that a man with a cigarette always has it in his mouth (a gesture they consider masculine), whereas women are always holding theirs (a more feminine gesture).

Social Acceptance and Popularity. Let us consider some other examples. As we noted above, cigarettes have a natural appeal to adolescents who seek to demonstrate adulthood, an appeal that is easy to exploit. Beer drinking falls into a very similar category because it is generally something forbidden until the age of 21. Beer drinking in ads always takes place in jovial groups and trades on the anxieties of being accepted by the group and having close friends, both particularly strong needs of adolescents and younger adults because of their orientation to peers. Because most beer is consumed by males, the models are chosen to be extra masculine, football players with bulging biceps, and the implication is that large size and physical strength are characteristics of beer drinkers. The connection is effective because of identification. As with cigarette ads, it is vastly more efficient to beam ads at adolescents who are just choosing brands and who have years of consumer buying ahead, but the companies deny they do this. A lot of young adults and adolescents attend sports events, and in fairness it may not be possible to separate these two groups.

When Miller first introduced its Lite beer, it was seen as weak beer for women, but the market for beer is predominantly male, a problem very similar to that of cigarettes. As with the Marlboro man, by picturing brawny athletes drinking Lite, Miller made it acceptable as a masculine drink and sales climbed. By sponsoring sports events, manufacturers of beer and cigarettes reach the adolescent/young adult market, even though cigarettes are banned from television advertising. For example, one study reported in the *New England Journal of Medicine* and cited in the *Boston Globe* found "5933 'verbal and visual' references to Marlboro cigarettes during a single 90-minute broadcast of a Grand Prix auto race." (Zuckoff, 1995) Zuckoff goes on to report growing concerns about the connections continually being drawn between sports and cigarettes and alcohol.

Although they are among the most common examples, beer and cigarette ads certainly are not unique in appealing to masculinity. Wheaties, for example, has for years claimed to be "the breakfast of champions" and advertises with masculine sports figures, like Michael Jordan. Ads targeted to men for antiperspirants often use brawny sports figures to sell the product. Dry Idea by Gillette screams in huge print, "It's man enough" (Figure 5, p. 143). What begins in adolescence continues on into adulthood.

Beauty is the female counterpart to masculine strength. What is the implication, for example, in the statement, "The most beautiful women in the world wear Lejaby?" Does not the ad imply that unless you wear it, you are not in this group? Other examples are not hard to find.

Self-Conciousness and Embarrassment. Sexuality is new to adolescents and is often a cause of self-consciousness. Avoidance of embarrassment is very important in adolescence because of new bodies and new roles. Embarrassment and self-consciousness reduce a bit as adolescents become more confident in their identity. Meanwhile, personal hygiene products are particularly suitable for adolescent sales pitches based on anxiety over embarrassment. Being personal, the appeal to self-worth is very direct and particularly powerful: if you do not use the product, you are likely to be offensive in some way, or perhaps just look stupid and be rejected by your peers. Buy the product and reduce your anxiety. Thus, starting in adolescence, Americans buy soaps, skin and hair care items, deodorants, antiperspirants, toothpastes, mouthwashes, and on and on, in huge quantities and endless numbers of brands. Adolescents represent a huge market because they have few responsibilities to absorb their money, and thus it is largely discretionary income. However, embarrassment is also an adult theme.

For marketers to apply these motivational forces, such as embarrassment, the technique is to add social significance to an everyday situation. For example, dandruff on one's shoulders is presented in terms of how others react to it, usually considerably exaggerated for emphasis. Note that the appeal has nothing to do with the truth or falsity of the claim that these situations cause embarrassment. In many cases one could argue that the anxiety is well placed. On the other hand, such a steady barrage of messages, some of them from absurd situations, probably makes us superconscious of these stimuli and creates anxieties we could do without. Be that as it may, the aroused anxiety certainly makes us good consumers.

Early Adulthood

Sophistication. The peer group is often a fickle tyrant. As adolescents move into adulthood, as we have said, the ideal developmental path is for the standards of self-worth to be internalized, so that, relying on themselves, individuals can judge their behavior against a relatively constant criterion, not one that fluctuates with the whim of the moment. When this happens, they should be able to break away from their peer group, even as they earlier broke away from their parents, and become more resistant to conformity. Quite often, as adults, we actually return to the standards of our parents, sometimes without being aware we are doing it. True independence comes only when our behavior no longer depends on an external force but on an internalized standard we carry with us.

However, a partial vacuum comes with the decline of the power of the peer group. If before, we showed our worth by being accepted by a particular peer group, how will we demonstrate our worth now? The function of possessions shifts a bit, no longer as important for simply signaling membership in a group, but now showing personal qualities as well. In fact subgroups are forming. We become more susceptible to appeals based on sophistication, success, and economic advancement. Now, the adolescent appeals require more sophisticated satisfactions, and sophistication has been added to our identity. This will be stronger in urban environments. As we get a job, we are encouraged to "upgrade" nearly all our possessions. Appeals to popularity, masculinity/femininity, and independence remain strong but are expressed more sophisticatedly. Fred Hayman Beverly Hills perfume bills its perfume, called simply "273," as "Wealthy, elegant, wildly seductive," a phrase that captures three elements of sophistication, money, taste, and sexuality. Saks Fifth Avenue markets a watch which "tells its timely story with classic precision." The word "classic" implies sophistication and the wrists which wear these watches in the picture are placed against a picnic basket containing grapes and French bread, symbols of sophistication more than wealth. Nor is the appeal only for expensive items. Habitant soups advertises with huge print that its soup is for "Adults Only ... When your taste for soup grows up." Clearly we are being asked to be a bit more sophisticated in our soup choices. Sylvan Pools ran this copy: "Back when you were little, it didn't take much to keep you cool. But you're all grown up now, with more sophisticated tastes. So if you're thinking about a swimming pool, better think about a real pool—a Sylvan pool.... If you're not swimming in a Sylvan, you're not swimming in a real pool." This ad could also work to have adolescents pressure mom and dad for a "real" pool.

The blue collar/white collar differential also begins to appear with the transition to adulthood. Hard liquor ads focus on the white collar and professional market, rather than on the blue collar worker, who is more of a beer drinker. The white collar appeals stress sophistication more. The dynamics of appeal to masculinity are still there but have added elements of success. For example, Johnnie Walker Scotch ran an ad in which two attractive, muscular, sweaty racquetball players appear to be relaxing after a strenuous game. The message is, "He works as hard as he plays. And he drinks Johnnie Walker." Because racquetball is associated with both fitness and wealth, these are seen as successful professionals. The implication is that this scotch is what fit, hard driving, masculine, successful professionals drink and that, incidentally, if you want to demonstrate your membership in this group (your identity), then you will drink Johnnie Walker too. To widen the appeal (and the market), one player is black, the other white. The adolescent need to belong to a group is still there but played down, made more subtle, and directed at a more adult group.

Consider, however, another ad for hard liquor. In 1976 Calvert proclaimed that its whiskey was "Soft drinks for adults," and raised the interesting question of whether their ads were aimed at adolescents or adults. On the one hand, were they trying to get adolescents to give up soft drinks, a strong adolescent symbol, and to prove they were no longer adolescent? The curious thing about these ads is the question of why adults would need to prove they are adult? The age group most into proving adultness is the adolescent. Thus, an argument could be supported that these ads are oriented to adolescents for whom this is a characteristic issue. On the other hand, one could argue that the marketers of hard liquor are simply trying to shift the habits of young adults into a "more adult" pattern from one left over from adolescence. In this case no one is being asked to prove anything, they are simply being educated. Of course, the two possibilities are not mutually exclusive, and they could be trying to do both. Dewars provides an 1997 example showing that the ambiguity of target still exists. Its ad shows an attractive young woman bringing a tray with two drinks on it to the viewer. The copy simply says, "This drink has been rated for mature audiences only. Dewar's."

Target ambiguity can also be used with cigarettes. A recent ad for Capri cigarettes says simply, "A taste for the sophisticated." It shows a young model, nicely dressed, holding a cigarette, and looking decidedly sophisticated. What is the age of this "sophisticated" model? Certainly a very young-looking twenty-one, but her age is not clear. Is it meant to appeal to a younger market? Doubtless, we shall never know. For a less ominous example of target ambiguity, refer to Figure 4 (p. 61), a recent ad from Woman's Day magazine. The headline says, "You'll be the talk of the 4th grade," but it is not clear whether the ad is directed at mothers or their children, or perhaps at both. The recipe is simple enough for a nine-year-old to follow, so it may be a suggestion of something mother and child could do together. Probably a nine-year-old who starts making these could be expected to make them occasionally for a good many years, incidentally buying the product to do so. There is no question that the young market is profitable. The ad seems to be a clever use of ambiguity.

Relationships. In the stage of early adulthood our social needs also become more sophisticated, and we begin to feel the need for deeper, intimate, and cooperative social and occupational relationships. An example of ads that are based on this recurring need is that for AT&T whose theme is "Reach out and touch someone." A similar appeal is found in the Chivas Regal ad that shows a young man laughing with his father and says, "You used to hate it when he told you what to do. Now sometimes you wish he would." The ad attempts to associate the neutral brand with the strong appeal of the father–son connection. We saw the mother–daughter relationship used in the same way in Figure 2 (p. 47).

Many people have a fear of intimacy, stemming usually from earlier experience, and they feel conflict at his stage. They want intimacy, yet they fear it. Without it, however, Erikson says that they are likely to feel isolated, lonely, and rejected, so that their self-worth is severely threatened. As in the other stages, people may pass this stage successfully, only to find themselves back here again later, when, for example, they have lost a mate through divorce or death. The possibility of that happening at any time is an ongoing source of anxiety for all of us.

The use of couples in ads, particularly those clearly in love, capitalizes on the strong concern of this age bracket. Personal embarrassment concerns remain a strong fear for this age group, but now we can add other sources of embarrassment, anxieties as we get homes and families of our own. We become susceptible to even more needs. Detergents, cleansers, disinfectants, air fresheners, and polishes of every possible description are marketed with the admonishment that they will avoid an embarrassing situation. Such potential social disasters as "ring around the collar" or "spots on the glasses" have been enormously successful in selling products. Just as adolescents are vulnerable in relation to their new status, so just marrieds, new home owners, and new parents are vulnerable until they become comfortable with their new roles.

Middle and Late Adulthood

Career Respect. For males particularly and now for increasing numbers of women, their careers are a major determinant of their sense of self-worth. A career often shapes our identity during our middle years, and challenges to our career competence can quickly threaten our sense of worth. For example, the arrival of an expert in our supposed area of competence or movement to an arena in which we are less well trained may make us feel threatened. Technology is changing our world so fast that now we can seldom simply learn an occupation and relax. If we do not continue working to stay current, we may find ourselves falling behind or being replaced. If that happens, the issues of achievement, competence, and identity become central to us again. Few people are totally immune to these recurring threats, and thus issues of competence remain powerful attention-getters and motivators.

As we move into middle life we become more conscious of our relative place in our careers. When you are young, entry level is appropriate, and one has plenty of time to advance, but as middle life becomes a reality, we begin to realize that time has passed, and we begin to be concerned about reaching our life goals. As we get older still, we focus less on where we are going and more on what we have become. Thus we become vulnerable to issues of success. If we feel successful, we may want to be sure others know it. If in doubt, we may be looking for signs to confirm that we still have worth. Thus status symbols are sought because they "make a statement" to others and also because they reassure ourselves. Thus, a luggage manufacturer's ad says, "Some luggage says you're traveling, Diane Von Furstenberg travelware says you've arrived." This ad implicitly asks, "Will you buy new luggage to demonstrate that you are successful and therefore have worth in the culture? Or will you continue to use that cheap old stuff you have, with all we are aware it is saying about you?" If you were not worried about your luggage before, you may be now.

The Oxford, a tower of condos in New York, advertised with this message : "Entering and arriving. There are still some New Yorkers who understand the difference." The appeal to elitism in this case comes quite close to "snob appeal." The ad clearly implies that if you are not concerned about "arriving", then you do not know the difference, and you are not a person who matters at all. All you have to do to be one of us and to prove you do know the difference (and that you have worth) is to buy the condo.

Staying Young.   Although success in one's job is still more of a masculine issue and beauty is still more of a feminine issue, loss of youth clearly makes both genders anxious. Fitness apparatus, vitamins and oat bran, weight loss programs, cosmetics of all kinds, hair dyeing preparations, skin creams and moisturizers, and even cola drinks all trade effectively on our anxiety over the passing of youth, the loss of attractiveness, and our diminishing sense of worth. For example, in Pepsi commercials we see young, beautiful, popular models, who are clearly members of the "Pepsi generation," drinking Pepsi and being terribly popular. The message is that drinking Pepsi shows you are aware of the modern drink, guarantees your popularity, and thus reduces your anxiety and proves you are still a part of the younger generation. With all this going for it, who cares how it tastes.

An ad for Suma+, a moisturizing creme, reminds us that, "Stress, emotional or physical, can leave its mark on your complexion." As if a person under stress did not have enough to worry about. Another ad, this time for SilkSkin, over a picture of a gray-haired woman being caressed by a dark-haired, considerably younger man, says, "Because looking younger can eliminate the difference ...." Older men with younger women have been a staple for sometime, but only recently have we begun to see older women and younger men in ads. Now women are asked to worry about not being among those women found attractive by younger men.

On the masculine side, an ad for Rogaine, a hair loss treatment, carries the message, "Success is more than knowing how. It's knowing when." There is considerable information exchange in the verbal content, but the picture shows a professional football quarterback handing off the ball, and the large print says "if you're losing your hair, don't lose time." Creation of anxiety over the threatened loss of youth and masculinity is a major dynamic working here. Football is a young man's game. Quick response shows you understand the football metaphor, still have your timing, and are still young. Failure to respond means you have lost it, you are practically in your rocking chair. Advertising and television generally reflect the high value placed on youth in the American culture, so that anxiety about the passing of youth is fairly universal and quite powerful. We feel our self-worth slipping away with our youth.

Generativity. The key concept in the middle years is productivity, and in later years it becomes feeling needed. Erikson says that much of our sense of productivity and feeling needed comes from guiding the next generation, what he calls **generativity**. It often counteracts the two things older people worry about most, which according to Beck (1990) are loneliness and dependence on others. In other words, by helping others we feel needed. Consequently, we feel we still have worth, and this enables us to tolerate our condition. The theme is often used in advertising to older consumers. For example, the cover of Sporty's Preferred Living Catalog for Christmas of 1990 featured a white-haired man (one infers a grandfather) helping a young boy (one infers a grandson) find a geographical place on a two-foot globe. Intergenerational concerns make the company and its products appealing to an older market, as, for example, the idea of buying a globe for a grandchild for Christmas.

COHORT VERSUS AGE DIFFERENCES

One of the factors that makes comparing psychological differences across ages difficult is the fact of the changing world in which we grow up. Is a difference really a matter of age, or is it that individuals grew up in such different times and thus have widely different backgrounds? Generational differences, caused by the changes in the world and not a function of age per se, are called **cohort differences**. For example, Levinson (1978, 1990) proposed a now well-known theory of adult stages that focuses on the midlife crisis. Rossi (1984) noted that most of the individuals studied by Levinson were born about the time of the Great Depression. All of these individuals, in other words, have a common historical influence. If you had seen one of these men driving down the street in a red convertible, would you have attributed his behavior to a sudden renewed passion for youth or to a severe deprivation in his childhood? It would be hard to know, though attribution theory says you would likely ascribe it to the individual characteristic. The reason it matters is that if ascribed to the individual, you would look for the effect in other people as they reached forty, but if ascribed to the times, you would not.

The effects of the Great Depression on the older generation were often severe. They often hoarded things, believing that another depression could come at any time. They often did without to save for that day. They distrusted banks because they had failed in large numbers. They were reluctant to invest in stocks because they were very likely in their eyes to fall. I grew up with the dictum, "Waste not, want not," and it was not all Yankee miserliness. Much of it was the fear of another depression. It made for very conservative consumers. Some of the reason for the soaring popularity of mutual funds today may result from the dying off of this more cautious generation.

Another era of severe deprivation occurred during World War II, right on the heels of the depression. Many products, like sugar, nylons, and gasoline, were strictly rationed. Housing shortages became acute. But this period ended with a period of prosperity, a time to make up for the decade-long restraint, and for many it became a time of high spending. Product design took a huge jump forward, and appliances particularly were designed for beauty even more than function. People just entering their maximum consumptive years, such as many returning servicemen and women, were oriented to credit buying in a way that brought anguish to their parents. They in turn are appalled by their children's even greater dependence on credit cards. As each generation reaches old age, they will not look like the generation that has preceded them. For example, older people today are living longer, in better health, and more actively than their parents.

Other changes in the eras of their lives also contribute to the picture. Most people today in their sixties grew up with the automobile. Their family may not have had one, but there were plenty in town as early as they can remember. They grew up with radio, but not television, whereas their children have never known a world without television.

Today's young have never known a world without computers. The fact that they take to them easily is more related to cohort than to age.

OTHER APPROACHES
TO PSYCHOLOGICAL NEEDS

As we have seen, the need to feel self-worth has been heavily utilized. However, although dominant, this is not our only psychological need. Over the years a number of psychologists have struggled to list the major concerns that typify human behavior.

Henry Murray's List

One of the more successful attempts was that of Henry Murray. He condensed hundreds of statements into twenty categories of social needs, but even then sometimes one finds psychological appeals which are not included. Murray will do as a starting point, however.

To understand his formulation, however, we must discuss just how it is that Murray uses the term "need." "Need" for Murray does not represent something one must have to survive in a physical sense, which would be a more commonly held meaning, nor does he mean a requirement for psychological well-being, as Erikson uses it. Rather, by "need" he means "the latent attribute of an organism ... or readiness to respond in a certain way under given conditions." (Murray, 1938) A later formulation indicates that one will be more responsive to certain forces.

Having defined need in this way, Murray goes on to list 27 psychogenic needs (see Table 2). As you scan down Murray's list, notice how many of them serve the function of enhancing our value or worth.

Murray's definition of need as readiness to respond explains why there are some negative needs in his list. Aggression, for example, is not in common usage considered a need. However, one has only to look for a few minutes at television or the latest movies to see that our culture certainly has a strong appetite for violence and that producers are eager to feed the need. Murray's list reflects this and should not be interpreted as a moralistic value judgement in any way. In other words, he is not saying that this is what our needs ought to be but what they are.

Murray's needs do not work in isolation from each other, but are often combined to produce behaviors which satisfy several needs at once. Some are opposites and will not normally be seen together. Also, not all of these needs are equally strong for everyone, nor are they fixed

Table 2 Henry Murray's List of Psychogenic Needs[a]

Actions toward inanimate objects	**Actions toward power**
Acquisition—to gain possessions	Dominance—to control or influence
Conservance—to collect or preserve	Deference—to admire and cooperate
Order—to organize or be clean	Similance—to identify or empathize
Retention—to be frugal, economical	Autonomy—to strive for independence
Construction—to build	Contrariance—to be unique, different
Actions relative to ambition and prestige	**Actions in response to others' power**
Achievement—to overcome obstacles	Aggression—to assault, harm, pay back
Recognition—to get praise and respect	Abasement—to surrender or atone
Actions to defend status or avoid humiliation	**Actions relative to affection between people**
Infavoidance—to avoid failure or ridicule	Affiliation—to love or form friendships
Defendance—to justify one's actions	Rejection—to exclude, discriminate
Counteraction—to act to defend honor	Nurturance—to help or protect others
Blamavoidance—to obey the law	Succorance—to seek aid or sympathy
Actions relative to knowledge	**Actions relative to entertainment**
Cognizance—to explore, be curious	Play—to relax, amuse oneself, laugh
Exposition—to explain, interpret	

[a]Source: Henry Murray (1938), *Explorations in Personality*, New York: Oxford.

over time. Thus, as individuals mature or as environmental conditions change, some needs rise in importance, and others fall.

Elsewhere you may see Murray's list in the original form, where each need is preceded by an "n." If this is the case, do not let this shorthand confuse you. His "nAchievement," sometimes shortened to simply "nAch," simply means the "need for achievement," which is interpreted as "the tendency to act in a way which will produce achievement."

Murray's list turns out to be, in effect, a useful catalog of the most common human reinforcers, that is, major sources of positive affect. Seeing his needs in this way brings them together with the powerful conditioning concepts. Physical requirements are listed by Murray in another list of twelve needs, and they too are reinforcers. But here we are concerned with his psychological needs because these are the more important and complex for human beings. To illustrate the connection, let us take the most researched of all of Murray's needs, the need for achievement. Murray defines in more detail the need to achieve as the desire

> To accomplish something difficult. To master, manipulate, or organize physical objects, human beings, or ideas. To do this as rapidly and as independently as possible. To overcome obstacles and attain a high standard. To excel

one's self. To rival and surpass others. To increase self-regard by the successful exercise of talent (Murray, 1938, p. 164).

Notice how self-regard, or self-worth, is the power behind the scenes. We
can see the need for achievement in the marketing world, as in the cases
cited in the operant conditioning chapter in which it was found that
much of the motivation for using coupons comes from the feeling of
being a thrifty and smart shopper (Babakus, Tat, & Cunningham, 1988;
Price, Feick, & Guskey-Federouch, 1988; Shimp & Kavas, 1984). Thus, a
form of achievement acts as a reinforcement. The feeling of being thrifty
and smart fits Murray's need to achieve and also the broader concept of
the need for competency formulated by White (1959) and considered at
the center of the feeling of self-worth. In a similar way, all of the needs
that Murray lists would be found as motivators in the marketing process.

Conspicuous Consumption and Status

One category of psychological need plays such a large part in consumer behavior, we should expand on it a bit. The process was first
termed "conspicuous consumption" by Thorstein Veblen in his 1899
book, *The Theory of the Leisure Class*. The leisure class in Europe was
comprised of the wealthy and titled people who did not need to work. To
signify their inclusion in this class, the nobility developed new meanings for ownership. Veblen says it appears to have originated with the
successful hunter bringing home game and the successful warrior bringing home booty. Both game and booty had meaning beyond their physical value, for both were indicators of the prowess of the men involved.
Eventually, in this way ownership, whether of slaves, women, or objects,
came to have meaning as a symbol of the success of the owner and
became a measure of social status. The phenomenon was clearly incorporated into the culture and became a cultural characteristic, and in this
regard we shall continue discussion of it in chapter 11. Here we are
emphasizing that though agreed to by the culture as a whole, the force
was still personally felt. Thus, Veblen writes:

> The motive that lies at the root of ownership is emulation.... The possession
> of wealth confers honor.... The need of subsistence and of an increase of
> physical comfort may for a time be the dominant motive of acquisition for
> those classes who are habitually employed at manual labor, whose subsis-
> tence is on a precarious footing, who possess little and ordinarily accumulate
> little; but ... even in the case of these impecunious classes the predominance
> of the motive of physical want is not so decided as has sometimes been
> assumed.... Ownership began and grew into a human institution on grounds
> unrelated to the subsistence minimum (Veblen, 1967, pp. 25–26).

From this base, Veblen goes on to say, developed the need to publicly display one's property, so that the benefits of status could be realized. He used the term "conspicuous leisure" for the practice of demonstrating that one does not need to work and the term "conspicuous consumption" for the practice of showing how unimportant money is, and, of course, how much wealth one has. Note that in either case the process enhances the users' self-esteem and ultimately their self-worth. Even in 1899 Veblen recognized this when he wrote:

> A certain standard of wealth ... is a necessary condition of reputability, and anything in excess of this normal amount is meritorious. Those members of the community who fall short of this, somewhat indefinite, normal degree of ... property suffer in the esteem of their fellow men; and consequently they suffer also in their own esteem (Veblen, 1967, p. 30).

Veblen uses the term self-esteem here much as we have used the term self-worth. Mason (1981) reports that John Rae, a Canadian, was one of the first to cut through the rationalizations and as early as 1834 ascribed luxury to vanity and the need to feel superior to others. (My own guess would be that Plato also said it 2000 years ago, but I lack the evidence.) Vanity, is of course, the need to confirm self-worth. It follows from all of this that one would see more need for conspicuous consumption in those whose sense of self-worth is threatened.

Recently, Braun and Wicklund (1989) reported a series of six studies which sought to gather empirical evidence for this conclusion. They questioned why, contrary to traditional economic theory, some products become more attractive as their price gets higher. The authors found that their subjects, who came from the field of law, athletics, and business, respond to a sense of "incompleteness," which translates to the need to be accepted by the chosen group. In all cases they found that the more important a chosen identity area was to their subjects and the less experience, expertise, or security the subjects had in that area, the more likely they were to acquire symbols associated with that identity area. Their findings provide strong support for our central theme, that our possessions give us identity, which in turn provides us with the basic security of a sense of self-worth. Thus, we look to possessions to bolster a momentarily threatened sense of worth.

For a good example of conspicuous consumption, we need look no further than designer jeans. Why are we willing to pay a lot more for the conspicuously placed labels on our fannies? Sports clothing and equipment are particularly loaded with brand names. Clearly, we want everyone to know that we paid top dollar for these items. We are considerably less happy displaying pedestrian or cheap names. Would we pay extra to wear "Kmart, Sears or J.C. Penney" on our hips? These companies are aware of this, invent brand names to use instead, and then spend considerable money enhancing the image of those names. The process of this enhancement is classical conditioning, the topic of our next chapter. As we shall see, many products, particularly perfumes and jewelry, are simply placed in advertisements in scenes symbolic of opulence with very little verbal message. The names take on the affect of the scene around them and then serve in the role of conspicuous consumption.

Self-Expression and Identity

Clearly, conspicuous consumption has elements of vanity and social class consciousness in it, but it is not just luxury items which reflect self. Indeed a case can be made that nearly all consumer goods reflect the personalities of the owners, whether or not they intend it. This is particularly true in the United States, where we put a great deal of emphasis on the individual. Our very constitution specifically guarantees individual rights of speech, religion, and action. We like to see ourselves as a nation that takes pride in ethnic diversity and individual differences (though unfortunately we often act the opposite and show suspicion and hostility toward those who are different). Nevertheless, there is unusual diversity, and with it comes increased pressure on individuals to express their individual identities. But identity is more complex than that.

Sirgy (1982) reviews a considerable literature that deals with attempts to classify and measure the many varieties of the self concept. From this he identifies four aspects of the self concept that recur frequently: The "**actual self** refers to how a person perceives herself; [the] **ideal self** refers to how a person would like to perceive herself;... [the] **social self** refers to how a person presents herself to others," (p. 287) and the **ideal social self** refers to the image one would like others to hold. Sirgy has developed a self-congruity theory, in which consumers are seen to conceptualize an image of themselves using the product to see if it is appropriate for them and to purchase positively valued products to maintain a positive self-image. As Claiborne and Sirgy (1990) point out, "the consumer who is evaluating a product is not evaluating the product *per se*, but s/he is evaluating herself/himself using the product." (p. 3) Thus, Johar and Sirgy (1991) maintain that a self-congruity process between the image of a user of the product and any one of the four self-images of the consumer is an important intervening step in value-expressive products and appeals. The greater the congruence between the product image and the audience's relevant self-image, the greater the likelihood of persuasion, because this is the situation that most enhances self-esteem.

In other words, affective appeals depend on four different kinds of self-images that in turn derive from the mechanisms of self-esteem, social approval, self-consistency, and social consistency. We can go one step further back and note that each of these variations ultimately springs from the individual's need for the feeling of worth. Thus, we are generally consistent in choosing things that enhance our worth, but the problem of applying this concept is that who we are or want to be seen as changes with the situation, that is, my identity may change with the social role I play at the moment.

Alternative Selves. In fact, I have multiple selves, depending on the particular social situation in which I am engaged (Markus & Nurius, 1986). For example, my self is somewhat different when I am acting as a professor, or father, or friend, or lover, to mention just a few of my selves. Which self I focus on depends on context (what social role I play at the moment) and on time (who was I in the past, and ideally who do I want to be in the future), and, of course, I need different possessions to signal the self I am acting at the moment. Thus, possessions in a complex society become essential to social communication.

Almost any role we play defines a self, which may change as rapidly as the situation. Thus, when the male urban professional wears a dark suit and necktie, he responds to the need to identify himself as a member of the successful professional group, and he also creates an image that he wants for himself in this setting. Molloy (1988) maintains that every item of clothing makes a statement and argues that one must "dress for success." Women, too, have found that they must wear similar clothes in the professional setting or run the risk of not being considered serious and competent, parts of the desired business self. But the business power suit does not not fit the other selves, such as the home self, the leisure self, or the parent self. Thus, we change our clothes when we come home, and we need a wardrobe more extensive than a single self would demand.

Products are given meanings that allow them to fit with the different selves. As we saw in an earlier chapter, even as utilitarian an item as toothpaste has been given a particular emphasis in meaning for each brand, allowing or requiring separate images. One is the one that dentists recommend most; another has the zippiest taste; another whitens best; another fights gum disease; another has cool stripes; and so forth. Thus, when we use even so mundane a product as toothpaste, we are encouraged to believe we are making a statement about who we are. To whom we are making this statement is not always clear. How many people really know what toothpaste you use? Apparently, we are making a statement to ourselves, and in doing so we are consistent with our momentary role. For each self, some products are better image builders than others. Even utilitarian products (such as hardware items) retain elements of image because some are of better quality and higher price, and some would be rarely used by beginners. Clearly, more expensive and more publicly used products "make statements" in the loudest voice.

The Extended Self. Russell Belk (1988) collected together the literature on the relationship between possessions and the concept of the self and coined the term **extended self** to refer to the identity we create through our possessions. He maintains that possessions are used to show who we are and actually become a part of us:

> We cannot hope to understand consumer behavior without first gaining some understanding of the meanings that consumers attach to possessions. A key to understanding what possessions mean is recognizing that, knowingly or unknowingly, intentionally or unintentionally, we regard our possessions as part of ourselves. As Tuan argues, "Our fragile sense of self needs support, and this we get by having and possessing things because, to a large degree, we are what we have and possess." (Tuan, 1980, p. 472) That we are what we have ... is perhaps the most basic and powerful fact of consumer behavior (Belk, 1988, p. 139).

Belk marshals an impressive array of evidence (over 280 references) to support his position. On the other hand, Cohen (1989), although generally supportive of Belk's article, feels that he overstates the importance of the concept of extended self in consumer behavior. Cohen particularly takes him to task because he feels that the concept is too vague, lacks the preciseness of meaning necessary to test it, and also that it covers too much too easily to be useful.

The criticism is somewhat reminiscent of arguments directed some years ago at both the concepts of reinforcement and Freud's ego defense mechanisms. It was argued that almost any behavior can be explained by using such concepts, but there is no way to know whether the explanation is correct or totally wrong. Both reinforcement and ego defense were considered untestable theory and guilty of circularity of argument. For example, does it add to our understanding to say we know things are reinforcing because people work for them and then say they work for them because they are reinforcing. Similarly, in the case of the extended-self, we only know what things are extensions of self, rather than merely possessions, by observing how strongly people feel about their preservation or loss. Then, can we say that they feel strongly about their loss because they are extensions of self?

The only way out of this critical dilemma occurs when we apply the concept to others than those on whom it was developed. For instance, the fact that a group of rats works for pellets allows us to predict that other rats will do the same. The prediction turns out to be excellent, and we label the process reinforcement, though we are still not sure just why it works. However, at this point, circular or not, the concept of reinforcement has high utility. Similarly, the notion of the extended-self seems to have utility.

Belk's excellent anecdotal accounts suggest that one feels strongly possessive of objects because they represent some aspect of self. For example, supporting his position with several research references, he points out the case of the relationship between many young American males and their automobiles:

> The process of creating and nurturing extended self through an automobile may be seen in customizing (personalizing) the car and in lavishing great care on its maintenance. When such a car is damaged, the owners react as if their own bodies have been injured (Belk, 1988, pp. 143–144).

Maybe the endowment theory we introduced in chapter 4 exists because we feel all our possessions are part of us. In other words, being part of us, we value things we own more highly than the same things when we are acquiring them, and losses are felt more strongly than gains.

General Motors advertisers seem to have found reason to agree with Belk that certain possessions are perceived as a part of us and are basing their ads on the same principle, as we can see in a few examples. From GMC Trucks, "It's not just a truck anymore. It's part of your life," or from Buick, "It's not just a car. It's your freedom." GM makes perhaps the ultimate extension of self by billing Chevrolet as "the heartbeat of America."

Drawing on the work of McClelland (1951), Prelinger (1959), and Ellis (1985), Belk summarizes the categories of things which are likely to become a part of our extended selves: "body, internal processes, ideas [particularly the morals and laws of society], experiences, and those persons, places, and things to which one feels attached." (1988, p. 141) The latter includes home and much of its contents, collections (particularly of art), mementos of the past (particularly of people who are gone and experiences we have had), pets, and things chosen for personal expression (like clothes or automobiles). Belk reports the findings of Dixon and Street (1975) and Prelinger (1959) who found a widening of the scope of self as children developed, sixteen-year-olds being more likely than younger children to categorize other persons and possessions as part of self. The important point of all this is that purchases in any of these areas cannot be understood simply as economic decisions.

The implication of this list for the marketer, as with Murray's list, is that these categories represent particular sensitivity and concern to many people. Advertisements based on these themes are more involving and get extra attention, and implied threats to these areas are likely to cause extra anxiety. Moreover, affective appeals in these areas are likely to be more powerful than cognitive, informational ones.

The concept of the extended self may be debated for some time, but it will remain a useful concept, for it provides an explanation of why some groups feel more strongly about some products: the products are regarded as if they were extensions of self. As McCracken (1988) puts it,

> The consumer [is] someone engaged in a "cultural project" ... the purpose of which is to complete the self. The consumer system supplies individuals with the cultural materials to realize their various and changing ideas of what it is to be a man or a woman, middle-aged or elderly, a parent, a citizen, or a professional. All of these cultural notions are concretized in goods, and it is through their possession and use that the individual realizes the notions in his own life (p. 88).

The Empty Self.   The notion of the extended self has been carried one step further. Cushman (1990) speaks of the "present self" of the United States. He means a self typical of many of us, much as we speak of typical American values. Though the criticisms of vagueness and untestability are equally relevant here to other notions of self we discussed previously, Cushman has made a somewhat convincing argument that the present self of the United States is an "empty self." The idea is not a new one. It is a recurring theme of the twentieth century. T. S. Eliot, for example, referred to modern man as a "hollow man" living in a "wasteland." (Baumer, 1952, p. 579) As we noted previously, Braun and Wicklund (1989) found their professionally competent subjects suffering from "incompleteness." Today, people often face feelings of alienation, loneliness, and loss of purpose because the world is continually changing, a process which began to accelerate with industrialization. The forces of change include the increased stresses of population growth, urbanization, personal anonymity because of the tremendous mobility allowed by the automobile, the breakup of the nuclear family, losses in environmental quality and the destruction of nature, endless wars and violence around the globe, and the proximity and reality of it all because of television.

Cushman feels that consumption is one of the ways we respond to these empty feelings. He starts from the position that what we regard as our self has not always been as it is today, but rather has changed because it is culturally determined. For example, the nineteenth century self was the "deep, secret, instinct-driven, potentially dangerous self" of the Victorians. During the twentieth century the concept of self has gradually changed. As Cushman writes,

> It has become apparent to cultural historians such as Susman (1973) and Lears (1983) that Americans have slowly changed from a Victorian people who had a deeply felt need to save money and restrict their sexual and aggressive impulses. Americans in the post-World War II era seem to have become a people who have a deeply felt need to spend money and indulge their impulses.... the current self is constructed as empty.... It is a self that seeks the experience of being continually filled up by consuming goods, calories, experiences, politicians, romantic partners, and empathic therapists in an attempt to combat the growing alienation and fragmentation of its era (Cushman, 1990, pp. 600–601).

Lears (1983), to whom Cushman refers, drew a parallel in a similar vein between the perceived role of therapy and that of advertising in the early twentieth century. He feels both offered a means of curing the ills felt by the consumer. As the ills increased, the influence of both these media also did, so that advertising began to portray "an imaginary state of being" (p. 19) and implied that the use of its products would transform individuals and their lives. Cushman's point is that this shift in advertising was made possible by the new empty self which had developed in the country:

> Americans in the post-World War II era came to need self-improvement in a form and to a degree unknown before. As the individual's growth, enjoyment, and fulfillment became the single most valued aspect of life (Baumeister, 1987), several industries grew up to minister to this newly created need. The cosmetics industry, the diet business, the electronic entertainment industry, preventive medical care, and the self-improvement industry (containing mainstream psychology, pop psychology, and pop religion) all came into prominence.... Again, I am speculating that it is the formation of the empty self that has made this situation possible; a sense of meaninglessness and absence feeds these businesses (Cushman, 1990, p. 604).

One could argue, however, that the opposite is also true, that rather than resulting from the emptiness, advertising actually helped produce the emptiness of self. Continual bombardment, for example, of images of the affluence of others, and the intentional creation of anxiety over our own shortcomings is bound to produce a sense of despair in the hardiest consumer. But whether the empty self is the cause or consequence of the consumer culture (or perhaps, both) is hard to determine empirically. The concept is similar to a chronic feeling of low self-worth, and this is the connection to our main chapter theme. Unfortunately, although advertising offers the illusion of a way out of the empty self through the purchase of ego-enhancing products, at the same time, as we have pointed out, the need for self-worth is a ravenous beast, and the self is likely never to feel full.

Implications of Psychological Appeals

As we have seen, psychological needs, particularly the need for self-worth, make a fertile field in which to find themes that will involve people. However, whether to sell products we raise anxiety by simply calling attention to psychological needs or whether we go further and attempt to increase the anxiety, we cannot help but make people more anxious over self-worth issues. There is a downside implied by all of this anxiety raising, a price to be paid, that should be mentioned. In a world of advertisements and commercials, everyone is successful, everyone is beautiful, everyone lives at a high level of economic security. By comparison, even the average person must feel left behind, a second-class citizen. The assault on self-worth is severe. Although this fuels the consumer-based economy, it does so at considerable personal cost, worsening our alienation by calling attention to our emptiness. For example, by implying that most people are thin, beautiful, popular, and successful, or that the lifestyle of the rich is the norm, ads tend to make viewers feel inadequate, failures, because they are not as good as what they perceive to be the norm. In other words, "What is wrong with me that I don't have what everyone else has?" Of course, everyone else does not really have all these things. The picture we get is heavily biased.

The technique works on nearly everyone to some extent, but unfortunately, it hits particularly hard on the vulnerable: adolescents already anxious about identity, the poor, who already have low self-esteem and consequent doubts of self-worth, and the elderly, anxious for their safety and their future and increasingly doubtful of their continuing value. We need to be aware that an increasingly anxious and thus an unhappy society may be the by-product of heavy use of these psychological appeals.

Advertising is certainly not alone in this assault. Television is fueled by the same engine because advertisers create pressure for acceptable vehicles for their ads, and television producers respond with endless sitcoms. These will , of course, be upbeat and happy, so that products are not associated with negative affect. In both movies and television the famous Hollywood ending has always been, of course, that virtue wins, followed by happiness ever after. Today, we also have a relentless picture of a violent society. Few major movies are without gun battles, car chase/crashes, and explosions bigger and better than the last blockbuster. The impact of this distortion has been very difficult to document, but it would be surprising if a rise in a sense of alienation did not result. People who see a continually distorted picture of their culture, come to believe that they are different from others, that they are no longer a part of the mainstream, even that the mainstream is no longer worth being part of, and their lives can come to feel lonely, empty, and meaningless.

Whether all these forces are good for society is debatable, but there is no question it is good for consumption. In class discussions of why we shop, invariably there is consensus that we often shop to make ourselves feel better. It may be a chocolate ice cream sundae, a new item of clothing, or something to add to our collection. Or we may go out to dinner, go to a movie, or seek out some other form of entertainment. The reinforcement value is probably working on several levels at once, including the level of physical pleasure, the escape from a depressing mental state, the opportunity to associate with others, perhaps an addition to our extended selves, and even a temporary filling of our empty selves. Thus, how much of our consumption is entirely for psychological reasons has yet to be determined.

CHAPTER 9

Classical Conditioning in Marketing

In the earlier chapters we examined the process of perception and demonstrated a number of ways in which learning plays a crucial role in interpreting what we are seeing. Now, we need to take a closer look at this mechanism that we call learning. Without getting bogged down in the differences between the many definitions of learning, let us simply consider learning to be the process of storage and retrieval of experiences. Sometimes retrieval is spoken of as a separate process called memory because storage and retrieval clearly operate separately. For example, our conscious minds remember only a tiny fraction of the experiences we have had in our lives, but under the right circumstances, for instance, with prompting, we are able to recall much more. Indeed, some evidence suggests that everything we ever knew is still there, and recall is hampered, not by storage, but by retrieval.

Part of the problem, I believe, is similar to that we discussed in attention, that we have traditionally put too much emphasis on our conscious mind and not enough on the unconscious. Freud drew our attention to the role of the unconscious, but he so limited his theory to sexuality that we failed to see the broader picture. Much of our learning is not at all consciously processed. We make many associations of which our conscious mind is not aware, and these associations later contribute to the retrieval and interpretative process. The cognitive process links all ideas together and groups them by similarity, proximity, and meaning, exactly as we have seen in perception. We store them as we perceived them, and we retrieve them as we stored them.

One of our guides in the retrieval of memories is affect or emotionality. It is the indicator of both pleasure-pain (that is, reward-danger, approach-avoid) and priority (intensity, importance). Affective tags give reencountered stimuli their most important meanings and guide their retrieval. Just as in perception, we usually do not think about why we are attending to what we are, so in learning we do not think about why one idea leads to another.

Philosophers argued for many years that learning is a process of building associations, but the precise nature of the association building was not known until Pavlov stumbled on to it at the turn of the century. His work became the catalyst for a whole new approach to psychology, known as behaviorism.

CLASSICAL CONDITIONING BASICS

Ivan Pavlov

Though Pavlov's work has become so central to psychology, he himself was not a psychologist at all, but rather a physiologist. Physiologists are interested, of course, in the way that biological systems function, and Pavlov, a Russian, was working on a typical physiological problem, how the salivary mechanism is triggered. Two main theories existed, both beginning with the absorption of food chemistry in the mouth. One theory argued that the secretion is locally produced. The other theory argued for a neural link that runs up to the brain and back, and the secretion is produced by this neural message. To test these theories using a dog, by a simple surgical procedure Pavlov brought a salivary gland to the outside where its activity could be monitored and its drops of saliva could be collected and measured.

Work had been proceeding for some time when a strange thing was observed. The dog was in his harness up on the table, and the assistant was bringing the meat powder down the hall, but before the assistant even entered the room, the dog began to salivate. Such evidence demolished both theories, but did not supply a more credible alternative. Mysticism was suggested and considered dangerous to investigate by some, but Pavlov refused to abandon the project. Gradually, by eliminating unnecessary factors, he worked out just what the essential elements were. The technique came to be called **classical conditioning**.

Terms

Stimulus and Response. We will run over that again, but first let us introduce Pavlov's terms. A **stimulus** is an external energy source that the organism can detect. Pavlov used a metronome at first, and later a bell, but nearly any external energy source will work. Sounds are particularly effective, because you do not have to be facing them to sense them. (In recent years it has been shown that a few stimuli do not work, but they are unusual exceptions.) A **response** is a physiological reaction, here a glandular secretion, elsewhere, in operant work, large muscle contractions, but its essential nature is that it is observable. The other term needed is "conditioned." Pavlov probably intended the word "conditional," but translation difficulties resulted in the use of the English word "conditioned," and it has remained that ever since in the American literature. The problem is that in English, the "-ed" on the end implies past tense, and you expect that something has been done to it. Eventually something is done and past tense becomes appropriate, but when you start, the term simply designates a particular stimulus, one whose properties are conditional on a certain procedure, and it becomes a conditioned stimulus simply by your designating it as such. At any rate, the **conditioned stimulus** (CS) is the neutral stimulus. An essential characteristic is that it does not produce the response when you start. The **unconditioned stimulus** (UCS), on the other hand, has its effect without any procedures. The UCS always produces the **unconditioned response** (UCR) and without it having to be learned. The sequence looks like this: CS : UCS–UCR at the beginning, and when the CS has become effective it looks like this: CS : CR(UCR). Now the CS produces a response, called the **conditioned response** (CR).

The demonstration of classical conditioning starts with an already existing link, an unconditioned stimulus which always leads to an unconditioned response. In Pavlov's experiment these were meat powder (UCS) and salivation (UCR). In other words, when you put meat powder in the mouth of a hungry dog, it salivates. It does not have to be taught to do that. It occurs naturally. Then, separately, we ring a bell (CS), and we show that the dog does not salivate to this stimulus. Why should he? It has no meaning for him. Now comes the conditioning. We ring the bell (CS) and follow it immediately with the meat powder (UCS).

Extinction.   When the CR occurs following the presentation of the CS alone, conditioning has been demonstrated, but if the UCS continues to be absent following the CS, the CR weakens and dies out. This phenomenon is called **extinction**. It is important to realize that the conditioning has not been erased or removed but is only temporarily replaced by another learning, namely, that now the CS does *not* lead to UCS–UCR. If the UCS is reinstituted, the CR reappears very quickly. Originally it may take more an a hundred pairings to get the CR, whereas to bring it back after extinction usually takes only one or two. Clearly, the learning is still there.

Specification of Stimuli. A note is in order about the CS. The labeling of the CS by Pavlov turns out to be deceptively simple, because, in fact, the bell was really only one stimulus in a large array of stimuli presented to the dog at that time, but unnoted by the researchers. For example, think of all the stimuli present around the dog when the bell was being conditioned to the meat powder: people gathered together, the feel of the harness, being up on a table, distinctive lights, sounds, and odors. At least some of these stimuli were being conditioned at the same time as the bell, even though it was unintentional. All of these stimuli were usually present just before the UCS was presented. If Pavlov's dog was anything like others, he probably anticipated the day's events and began to wag his tail as his keeper came to get him out of his cage. That tail wagging would have indicated that considerable conditioning had taken place outside the experimental situation, although no one intended it at all. Thus, the recorded CS will always be only the most salient stimulus of an indefinitely large set of stimuli, most of which are not recorded.

All of this means that the specific stimuli that may produce a given affect/emotion response is very hard to distinguish. Some level of affect is nearly always present in any situation, even though the stimuli that produce it may be nearly impossible to identify. In other words, any scene is probably affectively "flavored" toward pleasure-displeasure, maybe giving it a vague attractiveness or perhaps producing a mild uneasiness or dislike. This affective component, or tag, colors the memory and attaches to many things present at the time.

Major Variables of Classical Conditioning

Timing. Pavlov discovered that the key to the process is the temporal relationship between the CS (the neutral stimulus) and the UCS (the meaningful stimulus). When the neutral stimulus repeatedly preceded the meaningful stimulus by just half second, the neutral stimulus took on the properties of the meaningful stimulus (that is, took on its meaning). The CS functions as more than just a predictor of the UCS because the response to it begins to happen instead of to the UCS. We can tell that this invisible cognitive event occurred, only because a visible response is tied to the meaningful stimulus, which occurs every time the meaningful stimulus occurs. This indicator response begins to occur following the neutral stimulus and the meaningful stimulus, which show that they have come to have equivalent meanings.

About a half second between CS and UCS seems optimal for nearly all animals, but delays of more than a few seconds usually result in no conditioning. Also, the CS must always come first. Backward conditioning, where the UCS comes before the CS, almost never occurs. After all, the CS is a signal that the UCS is about to happen, and if the UCS has already occurred, the CS is hardly a signal for it.

After pairing CS and UCS many times, we can test for conditioning by ringing the bell and this time leaving out the meat powder, that is, we present the CS alone. Conditioning is demonstrated when salivation follows this formerly neutral stimulus in the absence of the meat powder. This type of salivation is called the conditioned response (CR), or in Pavlov's terms, the conditioned reflex. "Reflex" implies it is automatic and uncontrollable, which it seems to be, so the term is appropriate.

Predictiveness. Rescorla (1967) showed that simply pairing in classical conditioning was not enough to produce conditioning. Because what the subject learns is the relationship between the stimuli, the CS and the UCS must have a contingent relationship. The CS must reliably predict the occurrence of the UCS. In other words, for optimum conditioning, the CS should not have occurred without the UCS following, nor should the UCS have occurred without the CS having preceded it. Either of these events weaken the conditioning. Thus, unfamiliar CS's condition better, as do unfamiliar UCS's.

Awareness. Allen and Janiszewski (1989) conducted several studies which support the conclusion that subjects must be aware of the contingency relationship or conditioning does not occur. They mean conscious awareness and claim that their research supports a cognitively mediated model of conditioning. They are concerned mostly with the conditioning of attitudes and go on to say:

> ... We do not suggest that conditioning entails careful or deliberative thought processes: to the contrary, though conditioning procedures may begin to affect individuals' attitudes only after they have learned the CS/US contingency, this fact need not imply that they are aware of the effect (Allen & Janiszewski, 1989, p. 38).

In other words, subjects must be aware of the contingency but not necessarily of how it changes their attitudes. But before you lock this away in your elaborated storage, read on.

Not all researchers agree with them. In fact, this is one of the hotter research issues of the day. The opposing view was expressed by Zajonc (1980) who demonstrated that detecting affect occurs without a cognitive step. This is consistent with the studies on conditioning in lower animals, who certainly have limited conscious awareness. These studies have nearly always involved stimuli that are affectively significant for them, rather than cognitive stimuli (which they would be unable to process). Bierley, McSweeney, and Vannieuwkerk (1985), who were conditioning human preferences, arguably a level of affect, found that awareness produces stronger conditioning but was not necessary for conditioning to occur. More recently Janiszewski & Warlop (1993) reversed Janiszewski's earlier stance and showed that both increased attention to the CS and semantic associating take place without contingency awareness.

Thus, now it is possible that subjects need conscious awareness of the contingencies to condition *cognitions* under some conditions, whereas to condition *affect*, conscious awareness of contingencies is probably not needed. Supporting such a conclusion is a recent study (Tom,1995) in which Chinese characters were subliminally conditioned with music that was liked. Although the effect was modest, it shows that awareness is not necessary for at least affective conditioning.

Repetition. The CS-UCS pairing must sometimes be repeated many times for the conditioning to occur. On the other hand, one-trial learning happens even with animals and learning in five or six trials is common (Rescorla, 1988). The exact number of necessary pairings depends particularly on two factors. The first is the intelligence of the organism. The higher in the phylogenetic scale the animal is, the fewer pairings are generally required. However, conditioning will apparently work eventually with every living creature and has been tried on a wide variety, even including flatworms. The second factor is the intensity of the stimuli. Generally, more intense stimuli require fewer pairings. More on this in a moment.

If the pairings are continued after the CR has been produced, the literature on classical conditioning generally holds that the strength of the CR continues to become stronger, an effect called overlearning. This does not hold for other types of learning, nor does it hold when classical conditioning is applied to advertising. For example, Batra and Ray (1986b), among others, found that when repetition is applied to advertising, it produces an inverted U-shaped function, so that the effectiveness increases for a few exposures (two or three), but then begins to decline, perhaps because of tedium and negative affect. Grass (1968) argued that viewers lose interest when maximum learning has occurred, their attention drops, and learning declines.

Stephens and Warren (1984) looked for differences among older adults, expecting to find that more repetition would be necessary than with younger adults, because other studies, e.g., Arenberg (1967), had shown that older adults have difficulty learning rapidly presented material. They placed commercials in movies, but did not find the inverted

U-shaped function. They found no differences in recall or recognition as a function of age, either at one day or seven days later. However, the study was done in a theater-like setting, and the authors suggest this may have forced attention to the commercials. This lends support to the argument that the U-shaped function and other reported age differences are likely to be the result of attention mechanisms, not learning or memory per se.

Intensity. It remains the subject of debate just how much all learning and memory fit the conditioning paradigm. When an event happens just once, for example, why is it that it may sometimes be remembered and other times not? Some memories are so vivid that they have been termed "flash bulb" memories and are equivalent to one-trial conditioning. For example, many people remember where they were when they heard of the death of President John F. Kennedy. One explanation would be that the things going on at the moment were conditioned in one occurrence by the very powerful and emotionally charged event. This may be in the nature of double conditioning because the conditioning of the stimulus is of its cognitive meaning and also of its emotional intensity. In support of this idea, there is some evidence that emotionally charged things are more likely to be remembered. For instance, subjects in one study were questioned six to eight weeks after a single viewing of emotional and neutral advertising messages. They found that the emotional messages were consistently more strongly remembered than the neutral messages in both recall and recognition methods (Friestad & Thorson, 1986).

Higher Order Conditioning

Once a CS (we will call it CS_1) has been conditioned, it exhibits all of the properties of the UCS and now can be used as if it were a UCS to condition another CS (call it CS_2). This process came to be called higher order conditioning, and it has an important proviso. If the UCS does not continue to follow the CS_1, this constitutes extinction, and the CS_1 begins to lose its power. Subsequently, the CS_2 also begins to lose its power because of the same extinction relationship; its "UCS" is the diminishing CS_1. Then, the proviso is that the UCS-UCR unit must remain in place after the CS_1. Long chains can be conditioned, if this proviso is followed, because the CS_2 can become a "UCS" for a CS_3, and so forth. Each CS is a bit weaker than the one before, however. Then, a chain might look like this: $CS_4 : CS_3 : CS_2 : CS_1 : UCS : UCR$. The intelligence of the animal probably limits the length of chains. Humans are capable of forming almost indefinitely long chains.

So far we have been referring to classical conditioning through the example of Pavlov and his dog. Although his was the first and definitive demonstration, the process would have little importance to us if it was limited to salivation alone. One could perhaps refer to the golden arches of McDonald's and suggest that they become a CS, producing salivation on sight. However, such a suggestion is so far untested and doubtful at best. Moreover, to stay within such a literal and narrow interpretation is to miss the whole significance of the process. Rather, we need to look at the two ways in which classical conditioning has been extended. The first is in the area of affective conditioning, and the second is cognitive conditioning.

AFFECTIVE CONDITIONING

Conditioning Emotional Behavior

In a previous chapter we introduced the term "affect" as meaning essentially feeling states without the arousal component which turns it into emotion. Now we turn to the question of whether affect can be conditioned. The question is still the focus of controversy, but we shall attempt to sort it out. What evidence is there?

Watson's Demonstration.   We go back to the early days of classical conditioning when the century was but two decades old. At Johns Hopkins University in his now infamous "Little Albert" study, John Watson and his graduate student Rosalie Rayner showed that emotional responses could be conditioned in human subjects. A young boy, Albert, was conditioned to fear white furry things by presenting him with a white rat and immediately clanging a steel bar behind his head. After only two or three trials, the child cried in the presence not only of the white rat, but white fur in general (Watson & Rayner, 1920). The study clearly demonstrated the conditioning of emotional behavior and was taken as an example of how all phobias are established.

Watson, a flamboyant and dynamic speaker, soon became the dominiant voice of behaviorism and gave lectures to standing-room-only crowds at colleges all over the East. He advocated that only observable behaviors were the legitimate content of psychology. Feeling states could not be scientifically established because they give no observable physical index except the subject's own report. Therefore, they were outside the realm of science and also outside of psychology. In the enthusiasm for the new approach, however, people went beyond the evidence and accepted the idea that the feelings of emotion were purely illusory because they could not be measured and thus did not matter. Psychology could ignore them. Thus, the kind of emotion that psychology studied became defined, not as feeling states, but as a group of behaviors, often physiological. (Unfortunately, behaviorists themselves became somewhat devoid of feelings probably because no one wanted to be seen as the dupe of an illusion.)

Feelings Return with Humanism. When the computer appeared in about 1950, the process of thinking emerged from the banished realm of magic and mysticism and became seen as something physical after all. Computers seemed to be thinking, though not very high level thoughts. Arguments were often intense, but the research emphasis in psychology shifted from conditioning to cognition, and once again closely related topics, such as feelings, began to be of general concern. Because computers did not feel and still do not, the question of feeling states has lagged a bit after thinking. But the physical nature of feeling states seems less impossible because thinking has been accepted as such.

About the same time as the computer made its appearance, a group of psychologists reacting to World War II also appeared and began the process of putting feelings back into psychology. They became know as humanistic psychologists, and they created the climate in which the experimental investigation of feeling states could grow again. Many of the old conditioning topics began to be reexamined.

Conditioning Feelings Themselves

Watson's demonstrations of the conditioning of emotional *behavior*, which we discussed previously, became widely accepted, and many studies followed using animals and demonstrating the conditioning of emotional behavior. On the other hand, demonstrating of the conditioning of emotional or affective *feeling states* has been much more elusive. Seventy years after Watson's study, we are still debating whether affect can be conditioned.

The problem of demonstrating affect itself is formidable and is as old as psychology itself. The solution was developed by behaviorists, devising behaviors which indicate affect, so that the subject behaves one way with one feeling and another way with a different feeling. This is not the old behaviorism that would have regarded the behavior itself as the emotion but a newer approach that regards the observable behavior only as an imperfect indicator of an affective/emotional component within. The method is less direct than simply asking the subjects how they feel, but it is necessarily so because, as the history of experimental psychology indicates beyond doubt, people cannot always be counted on to communicate or even to know their feelings directly. However, even though a behavior is appropriate to the conclusion that the subject felt this way or that, we have not demonstrated the affect directly, and this continues to be the focal point of controversy. Meanwhile, advertisers are clearly acting as if it works, but it has not been unequivocally shown that the effectiveness of their ads is a function of the conditioning of affect. Let us see what supportive evidence there is.

Supportive Studies.   In the late fifties, Carolyn and Arthur Staats conducted a series of experiments which demonstrate the classical conditioning of affective feeling states. As summarized by Paul Chance:

> In one experiment (C. K. Staats & A. W. Staats, 1957) the researchers had college students look at nonsense syllables, such as YOF, LAJ, and QUG, as they were flashed on a screen. At the same time, the students repeated words spoken by the experimenters. For some students, the syllable YOF was always paired with positive words such as *beauty, gift,* and *win,* whereas the syllable XEH was always paired with negative words, such as *thief, sad,* and *enemy.* For other students, the associations were reversed. XEH was paired with positive words, YOF with negative ones. (Notice that no UCS was ever presented.) After this, the students rated each nonsense syllable on a seven-point scale ranging from unpleasant to pleasant. The results indicated that the nonsense syllables had acquired emotional meanings similar to the emotional value of the words to which they had been paired. When a nonsense syllable was regularly associated with pleasant words, it became pleasant; when it was paired with unpleasant words, it became unpleasant. In other words, YOF came to elicit good feelings in some students and bad feelings in others, depending upon the words associated with it (Chance, 1988, p. 64).

In two other experiments in the same report, the authors showed that words sorted into "active" versus "passive" meanings or "strong" versus "weak" meanings could also be used to condition the common meaning. In the following year, the same researchers also showed that affect can be conditioned to people's names or to ethnic adjectives like "German," "Italian," or "French." Ratings on a scale of pleasant-unpleasant for these types of stimulus words showed changes in the appropriate direction following pairing with emotionally charged pleasant or unpleasant words (A. W. Staats & C. K. Staats, 1958).

Influencing Behavior.   The behavior used as an index in these studies indicates that ads can induce us to like an advertised item by associating it with pleasant stimuli. But would it translate into behavior? It would be more relevant to marketing if somehow we could have subjects actually choose between products. Of the few studies in which this has been attempted is one done by Gorn, and we shall again use Chance's excellent synopsis:

> Gerald Gorn (1982) conducted an experiment in which American college students listened either to a tune from the film *Grease* or to classical Indian music. (It was expected that the students would enjoy the popular American music more than the unfamiliar Eastern variety.) While listening to the music, the students viewed a slide showing either a beige or blue pen. Later, the students were allowed to have one of the pens. Of those students who had listened to the popular music, 79 percent chose a pen of the *same* color they had seen while listening to that music, while 70 percent of those who had listened to the Indian music chose a pen of a color *different* from the one they had seen on the slide. Evidently, ad agencies are correct in believing that they can induce people to feel good about, and want, a product by pairing that product with stimuli (pleasant music, attractive people, and the like) that make them feel good (Chance, 1988, p. 67).

Although Gorn's study was a promising beginning, some researchers questioned whether what he found was really classical conditioning. Allen and Madden (1985) tried to replicate Gorn's study, but using humor instead of music, they were unable to show any effects.

Bierley et al. (1985) set out to try Gorn's procedure using better controls to find out whether or not it was really classical conditioning. They presented slides of red, blue, or yellow circles, squares, triangles, or rectangles to subjects. For some subjects these became CS's and were followed by music from *Star Wars* which they had determined previously that the subjects liked. The study utilized elaborate controls, and the results supported Gorn's findings. Initial color preferences were altered for the two groups who received a conditioning procedure of color followed by music but were not altered for the control groups. Stimuli that were followed by music were more highly preferred than those that were not. It appears that classical conditioning indeed occurs in this fashion.

COGNITIVE CONDITIONING

S–S Associating Versus S–R Learning

S–R Learning. The learning process which Pavlov described had a feature never seen before in studies of learning: the elements were completely external and measurable. There were no assumptions about the internal state of the dog's mind and no appeal to unseen forces, such as will power. Because of this, it was received enthusiastically by the psychological community as a chance for a total break from philosophy, an opportunity to establish psychology as a science at last, and it became the cornerstone of the new behaviorism.

The behaviorists, who came to be known as S–R psychologists, focused on the fact that neutral stimuli produce certain responses whenever they appear. It was known as response learning. Eventually, the process would be seen as tremendously significant for psychosomatic medicine, but for some years their narrow focus on autonomic responses almost caused the behaviorists to miss totally a major significance of the Pavlovian model, the S–S component. Janiszewski and Warlop (1993) pointed out the difficulty:

> To appreciate how conditioning might encourage attention, approach behavior, and an affective response simultaneously, one must view conditioning as a procedure, not a process. When viewed as a process, conditioning is theoretically constrained to explaining all learning as a response transfer between the unconditioned stimulus and the conditioned stimulus (Pavlov 1927). Thus, when multiple responses result from conditioning there must be multiple transfers, a prediction that is at odds with Pavlovian explanations of conditioning processes." (p. 171)

S–S Associating.   Janiszewski and Warlop (1993) showed that attention to the CS increased following classical conditioning procedure. Increase in attention was not the main purpose, but rather the associating of semantic connections. Yet both occurred in the same procedure. This is hard to explain in the conditioned response model but makes sense in an information processing model. Let us look at this now.

There was a second way of looking at Pavlov's classical conditioning, that he himself recognized, but which was swept aside by the eagerness for behaviorism. Starting back with the increase of cognitive interests in the 50s, this approach has gradually become more widely accepted. Instead of regarding the conditioned reflex as the purpose, that is, the end product of the procedure, one can see it instead as an index, a flag, that something more important has taken place. That other effect is the relationship between the two stimuli. What has happened in this view is that the CS signals that the UCS is about to happen. This is why the CS must come first and predict the UCS. In other words, the important effect is the association that takes place between CS and UCS.

In this way of thinking, the CR is important only because it shows that a cognitive association has indeed occurred. There would be no other way to know that a cognitive connection had happened because, of course, there is nothing to see, particularly in the case of animals. In the information processing model, the importance of the CR is simply to indicate the cognitive connection. In other words, the interest is shifted from the S–R relationship to the S–S, and the new approach became known as associative learning.

This allows for the possibility of a variety of responses, depending on what the occurrence of the UCS means in the particular context. For example, it predicts that in situations of uncertainty (where the CS is not always identical, yet is followed by the same UCS), more attention will be paid to the CS to find the information necessary to resolve the ambiguity and predict the relationship. This is what Janiszewski and Warlop (1993) found. They used alternative forms of the CS in each of six conditioning trials, found increased attention paid to the CS, and no significant difference with the constant CS condition. A response learning model would have predicted that the constant CS would produce faster learning and that attention would be increased to the UCS, rather than the CS.

The behaviorists argued that we still do not know anything about cognition. All we know is that a stimulus leads to a response, but a number of avenues of research eventually pointed to the inescapable conclusion that something cognitive connects the stimuli, even though it is tricky to demonstrate.

Sensory Preconditioning

Pavlov himself demonstrated this cognitive association in the absence of any responses at all, and he called it **sensory preconditioning**. In this procedure, two stimuli, both neutral relative to the UCR, are paired in the same temporal relationship as in the better known CS–UCS condition. It might be referred to as a S_2–S_1 pairing, but this is not the same as higher order conditioning because the two S's are paired *before* either one is conditioned, whereas higher order conditioning would come *after* one of them had been conditioned. In other words, neither one has any relationship to the UCS–UCR pair when they are associated with each other. When the two stimuli have been paired many times, the second, S_1, is conditioned in the normal way to a UCS–UCR combination and now becomes CS_1. This CS_1, of course, eventually produces a CR. Now here is the interesting part. After this procedure is done, presentation of the S_2, all by itself, produces the CR. The sequence looks like this:

Step 1. Pairing stimuli $S_2 : S_1$
Step 2. Conditioning second stimulus (C)S_1 :UCS–UCR
Step 3. Testing other stimulus S_2–(U)CR

Sensory preconditioning demonstrates that an association between S_2 and S_1 occurred when they were paired in the absence of any responses at all, but the finding would have upset the behavioristic applecart, and it was buried. The significance of S–S learning was fully as important as the touted S–R connection. In fact, Pavlov had demonstrated that cognitive connections are formed similarly to stimulus–response connections. The S–S process had a few vocal adherents, such as Tolman and Guthrie, but mainstream psychology ignored it until the rise of cognition in the late fifties.

Verbal Associating

The essence of S–S associating had actually been studied for some years under the banner of verbal learning, but it was not called conditioning. Ebbinghaus in the nineteenth century was the most famous of all these researchers. Using nonsense syllables to reduce the effects of previous learning, he extensively investigated the situation called serial anticipation, in which lists are learned without changing their order. When you hear the first item in the list, you try to anticipate what the second item is going to be. With each item you anticipate the next, and your errors are recorded. You keep going over and over the list until you make no errors and learning is accomplished.

Ebbinghaus described a procedure that could in fact be called a long chain of S–S connections but without the autonomic response at the end that conditioning would have had. Because the behaviorists were focused on responses, they resisted the assertion that this was the same process as the S–S part of Pavlovian conditioning. Rather, they considered the verbalized responses as putting the whole procedure into the operant conditioning realm. The behaviorists also tended to ignore verbal learning anyway because they worked largely with animals, and verbal learning clearly does not occur in animals lower than humans.

Countless examples after Ebbinghaus could be drawn from the verbal learning literature, but we need only reiterate the point that verbal learning works in the same way as the S–S part of classical conditioning. For example, the adult says "ball" as she holds one up for the child to see. In this way the image of a ball is connected to the sound of the word "ball." If sometimes the word is said first and other times it is said after the ball is held up, the learning proceeds both ways, which is, of course, desirable. The child does not have to say anything, though its response generally improves the learning. To summarize, then, the essential mechanism of associating two ideas is for one to follow the other predictably and closely in time.

Vicarious Conditioning

Another form of classical conditioning has also been widely demonstrated. In this form the conditioning occurs, not because of direct stimulation, but from watching others being conditioned (Bandura, 1969; Bandura & Rosenthal, 1966). For example, Bernal and Berger (1976) reported a study in which videotapes were shown to subjects. The tapes showed other subjects being classically conditioned to blink their eye to a puff of air. The conditioned stimulus that preceded the puff was a tone. The subjects watching also began to blink their eyes in response to the tone. The specific conditions that sometimes cause this to happen, but sometimes not, have not been worked out.

Application to Advertising

Conditioning examples of both affective and cognitive varieties can be found in advertising, but the most common is the conditioning of affect. Support for the fact it works can be seen in the close positive relationship we mentioned in chapter 7 between attitude toward the ad and attitude toward the brand. In other words, attitude (being largely affect) has been transferred to the brand, and this has been demonstrated a number of times (see Machleit & Wilson, 1988).

First we will run over the specifics and label the parts. In the advertising application, the CS is usually the product in some form, whether brand name, picture, or the item itself. When a new brand is introduced, for example, the consumer is probably neutral toward it, perhaps not having much feeling one way or the other. In other words, the product is like the bell to Pavlov's dog. It has very little meaning at first. Our task is to give it meaning, and obviously we want it to be a desirable one. Recall that the CS must come before the UCS, that is, when the CS appears it triggers the affective response associated with the UCS. (Whether an intervening thought of the UCS always occurs or is necessary is one of the controversial points, but not important for our purposes.)

We need to pair the CS with a UCS that evokes the desired feeling state. Among the most frequently used stimuli are those associated with sex, because the pleasure of sex seems to be remarkably universal. (Because not everyone wants the same kind of sex, you reach a wider audience if the suggestion of sex remains a bit vague, letting the viewers interpret the stimulus in their own way, which, as you recall from the perception chapter, they will do.) Sexual stimuli are particularly resistant to habituation effects and continue to work well year after year. But sexual stimuli are by no means the only effective UCSs. If you want to create the feeling of relaxation and calm, then a picture of a quiet country valley, or perhaps soft classical music may be appropriate. On the other hand, if excitement is what you want, bright colors, action, and crowd noise may be appropriate. The supply of UCSs is endless, but must be carefully chosen to produce the desired mood or feeling state.

A technical point. The meaning of many of these stimuli, of course, has really been previously conditioned, and thus they are not technically UCS's, but higher order CS's. Fortunately, we do not have to know which they are because, as we have seen, they act as UCS's in either case. If naturally occurring circumstances have conditioned them, they can probably be counted on to remain effective by the same natural means.

Let us look at some real world examples of classical conditioning put to use. The prime concern of advertisers and designers of stores, merchandise displays, and promotional exhibits is making a consumer feel good about their products. The task becomes that of attaching an affective feeling state, such as joy, love, or social acceptance to the product, and the procedure is classical conditioning. All of the ads in the figures in earlier chapters contain the element of classical conditioning. Some condition the brand name primarily, whereas others are focused on the logo. One would guess from the way the principles are used that all ads are equally effective applications, but the evidence is not available. There is, of course, the recurring problem of getting and holding attention. It appears that sometimes the principles of conditioning have been put aside in the interest of attention-getting, but we have no way of knowing whether this is always an effective trade-off. Published research in this area is one of the glaring gaps in the literature.

Other examples of classical conditioning can be found in any magazine that includes advertising. Certs mints pairs the product with a couple kissing. Folgers coffee pairs their brand name with people smiling. In addition, the stimulus of steam rising is meant to trigger our memories of the smell of coffee, which then is also associated with the brand name. ADAP spark plugs are shown under the music of James Brown's song "I Feel Good." They appeal to a group for whom the song would have good associations to attach to the brand. Fruity Pebbles cereal pairs the product with Fred Flintstone, who is expected to be a good association. Because it is much more likely to be a good association for the child rather than mother, it seems clear that they are not advertising to mother, but to the child directly. MTV pairs artists and songs with exciting, often sexual, situations. TV ads run during football games are automatically paired with the mood of excitement. Malls play Christmas music to create a mood of happiness and generosity. This happens because of previous associations of the music with good times and the giving and receiving of gifts. Examples are endless.

It is important to tie our chapters together to show that the forces we are discussing seldom work in isolation. For example, in the last chapter we introduced the notion of the need to feel self-worth. Here we can see that dynamic used in classical conditioning. For example, Safari (one must assume it is a perfume, since it does not even say what it is) was promoted by Ralph Lauren in a two-page spread in *The New York Times Magazine* by accentuating the bottle on the left page (cut glass and sterling silver of clearly high quality) with a right page collage of a beautiful woman, sexily reclining with fine fabrics and gold accessories, a closeup of her dressing table with more cut glass and silver, roses, a scrap of a handwritten letter with the word "London" underlined and other words suggesting world travel, and two scraps of luxurious wallpaper or fabric. The only message says "A personal adventure." We do not know whether or not this ad worked, but it is almost pure classical conditioning, pairing the neutral perfume bottle and brand on the left with the affect evoked by the symbols of luxury and opulence on the right.

Other examples of classical conditioning of images of luxury are not hard to find. The Lincoln town car is parked in front of what appears to be a French chateau, and the couple in evening dress emerges. The perceptual principle of the part standing for the whole is employed here to expand the meaning of these symbols of luxury to include the whole luxurious lifestyle. It implies that this is the normal lifestyle of the successful, and a Lincoln car is the most salient ingredient.

Notice, however, that these conditioned connections would still not actually sell perfume or cars unless people wanted to share in that image and associate it with themselves. Why do they want it? Especially in the case of perfumes, jewelry and indeed all expensive designer products, self-worth enhancement is clearly the main component. Ralph Lauren is selling image more than odor. We do not even know how much the perfume actually costs, but the image is luxury. Acquiring these luxurious items clearly enhances one's sense of worth.

Another interchapter tie. We introduced the concept of affectly powerful ads in chapter 6. Here we add the process that allows them to work, that is, when it is understood that conditioning of affect is generally behind the ad, then it becomes clear why we are seeing ads with simply a picture and a brand name. Often the product is not mentioned though the brand is, because these are directed at people who are already familiar with the product–brand connection. The picture may or may not have anything to do with the product. Sometimes the affect is carried by an image of the product itself, as is happening with the running shoe in Figure 10 (p. 194), and often happens with clothes. But at other times the picture is simply a strongly affective one, and the product is not shown, as often happens with products like perfume that are not primarily visual. There may or may not be a model, but when there is one, the model usually carries strong affect as well (as in Figure 9, p. 193) and communicates it in posture, facial expression, and figure that add other dimensions to the attractiveness. By inferring the type of person who would use this product and by connecting it to the brand, the ad is creating image through classical conditioning.

Implications. McSweeney and Bierley (1984) have worked out a number of implications for advertising which follow from Rescola's principle introduced earlier, that predictiveness is important. First, brand names or product pictures should be more effective when presented before the UCS, compared to those which present the UCS first or present the UCS occasionally. In many ads we see the tendency to place the brand in the lower right-hand corner (see, for example, Figures 2 (p. 47), 4 (p. 61), and 8 (p. 181)), or at the bottom (Figures 1 (p. 40), 3 (p. 49), and 9 (p. 193)). This placement would be backward if indeed the reader started at the top and scanned down. Sometimes the brand occurs in the upper left and also at the bottom. Many times, however, we tend to look at the strong source of affect first, in this case the picture. Then, we shift to the written material, perhaps up or down. Only because then we go back to the picture again is the order right. Theoretically, having the brand both above and below the picture should produce better conditioning by allowing for attention directed either way. In television commercials the order is controlled because they occur in a sequence. Theoretically they may lose effectiveness here too if the brand name occurs last, not first, though this is the way in which they are commonly done. Arranged backward, it means that the picture is being conditioned to remind you of the brand, and this is not very useful because the picture is not likely to be seen again, let alone seen in a marketing situation. Unfortunately, research to test these theoretical predictions is not available.

McSweeney and Bierley's second point is that products that are seen frequently in everyday life may be less effective as CS's than products that are seldom seen because they become in the nature of CS's which are not predictive of the UCS. Third, using several types of UCS's with a single product may weaken the effect of all of them. Thus, using music as a UCS on one occasion and a beautiful scene as a UCS on another may detract from their effectiveness. Fourth, the exposures to the UCS without the preceding CS should be minimized (adapted from McSweeney & Bierley, 1984).

The question of which advertising medium is involved becomes important here too, for not all media are equivalent. For example, in a television commercial the creator has the possibility of sequence control, but in a magazine ad all of the stimuli are there at once. Perceptual studies show, however, that we tend to look at the middle of a page first, so that is the best place to put the CS. On the other hand, we do need to get the reader's attention, so we may want an attention-getter there instead. In general, English-speaking people read from left to right and from top down, so CS's probably should be generally toward the top and to the left. In fact, however, in print ads the reader's eye is likely to go back and forth several times among the parts, so that different pairings are probably taking place in a single exposure. Readers can also go back to an image as often as they like or dwell on a single image if they wish, so that magazine ads have considerable power.

On the other hand, TV can increase the power of ads with motion and sound, but the sequence becomes crucial because one cannot go back. The point is that the particular characteristics of the medium should be considered and utilized.

In all likelihood the process will remain unconscious, so that consumers, if asked, may not be able to tell you why they selected those they did. Nevertheless, if you ask, they will nearly always feel compelled to provide you with a reason, and therein lies the bane of the market surveyor. The reason they supply is nearly always cognitive, that is to say, reasonable, rather than affective. All of us, but particularly males, are conditioned early to value reason more than emotion, so we learn to rationalize. But we cannot escape our feeling states. In other words, even when we use our reason, it is because it makes us feel good to do so. For example, even when the reasons are completely legitimate, as perhaps when you investigated to find the car with the best repair record before you bought it, it was probably a feeling state that directed you to make this kind of information top priority. You were conditioned to feel more comfortable choosing on the basis of consumer reports as opposed to acting on impulse. This is not to say cognition is unimportant, but rather to point out that both elements are typically intertwined. Yet we are more aware of the cognitive elements.

If successful, what ultimately happens from the advertisement's pairing is that our product, seen later on the store shelf, is regarded more warmly than the competition's product, so that the consumer chooses ours. Classical conditioning is not intended to make the consumer go out and buy the product. All it does is make the consumer feel better about the product. If the consumer feels better about it than the competition's product, then it may eventuate in a sale, but we are not conditioning people directly to buy. If that were at all possible, it would be operant conditioning, not classical. We come to it in the next chapter.

CHAPTER 10

Operant Conditioning in Marketing

Next we turn to operant conditioning. Experiments in this type of conditioning started within a year or two of Pavlov's work, just at the turn of the century. The source in this case was an American, Edward Thorndike, who was studying the way animals solve problems. From watching a number of animals learn to solve mazes and to get out of puzzle boxes, he concluded that when an action is followed by a "satisfying state of affairs," it tends to be repeated, and when it is followed by an "aversive state of affairs," it tends not to be repeated. He called this principle the Law of Effect, because the factor which controls behavior is the effect it has on the environment. Later researchers, most notably B. F. Skinner, expanded the work of Thorndike, and worked out the conditions under which it takes place.

SIMPLE CONDITIONING

The process of operant conditioning is very similar to classical conditioning, but the element of choice has been added to operant. In classical conditioning, the two stimuli are paired by the experimenter or by nature, but in operant conditioning they are paired only if the subject makes the appropriate response. If the response is not made, the stimuli are not paired. In other words, the subject controls the pairing.

The essential difference between the two types of conditioning can be seen in the following sequence: CS : CR–UCS–UCR. In operant conditioning the CS is not followed by the UCS immediately but rather is followed by the CR. The CR in turn is followed immediately by the UCS–UCR. If this CR does not occur, then UCS does not follow. The second half of the process, the UCS–UCR bond, is very similar to classical conditioning. Where the UCS was meat powder for Pavlov, here it might be a food pellet. Whereas the animal salivated to the meat powder, here he eats the pellet. Eating would have been seen in classical conditioning, if the amount were sufficient, and salivation would be seen in operant, if the gland were visible. In both cases, however, it is a linkage which does not have to be taught but rather occurs naturally. Operant conditioning is not simply a matter of two stimuli being connected but includes the control of a behavior. Habits are clearly formed this way, but, incredibly, all behaviors probably operate this way for every living creature.

The Law of Effect appears in operant conditioning because the element of choice is introduced. If the animal wants the UCS, it responds, but if the UCS is something it does not want, then it does not respond. Skinner argued that the animal really has no choice, but the point appears to be impossible to test. The question is somewhat moot, for animals and humans act as if they had a choice. Thus, we can note that either a desired or an undesired UCS makes the CR stronger in classical conditioning, but in operant conditioning only a desired UCS does so.

We need some examples here. Your dog learns to sit when you tell it to. "Sit" is the CS, the dog's response is the CR, a biscuit is the UCS, and eating is the UCR. This is an interesting case, incidentally, because praise works well as a UCS for training most dogs. But what is the UCR for praise? A wagging tail, perhaps. Behaviorists might simply say "joy responses" because invoking a feeling state in the dog would go beyond any evidence. Experience tells us that praise works for dogs, but it does not work for cats. Probably it is related to the social nature of dogs, but we really do not know why. In fact, however, we do not really have to know what the UCR is, if there actually is one, or why. All we need to know is that the UCS must be desired by the responder.

Operant conditioning is not something that applies only to animals, however. You learn which is your front door key because using that key leads to turning and opening, whereas the others do not. You chose your cereal because it tastes good to you. You chose your friends because they are nice to you or perhaps you chose them because they gain you entrance to the right social group. Some people learn to feel guilty when people treat them well, and they learn to chose friends who are *not* nice to them. They feel better without the guilt, which acts as a punishment. We generally learn our sex roles and all our values because of cultural approval or disapproval. In short, the principle is as basic as any in psychology.

Reinforcement and Punishment

When a UCS makes a CR become stronger, it is called a **reinforcement**. This means that in classical conditioning the term reinforcement can refer either to a desired or to an undesired UCS. Either one increases the strength of the CR because the subject has no choice. In operant conditioning, however, reinforcement can refer only to a desired UCS. The term reinforcement is often misused and generally reveals a lack of understanding of this difference between the two types of conditioning. An undesired UCS in operant conditioning is called **punishment**.

In operant conditioning, reinforcement means generally the same as reward, but the terms "reward" and "punishment" both carry an unnecessary implication of "ought." Rewards result when you do what you are "supposed to," and punishments when you "disobey." Both imply a judge, often a parent, handing out judgments. In operant conditioning, however, the terms are meant to carry no such connotation. No judge is involved. When the consequences of a response are desirable, that response has been reinforced, whether or not it is socially acceptable. For example, successfully robbing a bank may be reinforcing, or speeding at one hundred miles an hour may be reinforcing, but these behaviors are hardly condoned by society. That is the reason that the term "reinforcement" is preferred over "reward." Likewise, putting your hand on a hot stove is punishing but by the pain, not by a parent lurking around the corner. In the case of punishment, there is not a better word, so that "punishment," so strongly associated with parents, is often misunderstood. In other words, in operant conditioning, regardless of how it came into being, the nature of the consequence, as it is perceived by the responder, determines whether it is reward or punishment. This is the reason that perception is such an important ingredient in understanding psychology.

The essential rules of operant conditioning are simple: (1) any behavior that is reinforced tends to be repeated; and similarly, (2) any behavior that is repeated must have had a reinforcer somewhere. In other words, we do only things that we think will lead us to what we want. Having said this, however, we must be add that determining what is reinforcing under what circumstances is not as easy as it sounds. Reinforcement of human beings gets far beyond food pellets, and most human reinforcers are psychological. More on this in a moment.

Applications of simple operant conditioning to marketing abound. The most obvious example of reinforcement is a product that works well. If we find that a product is good, then we buy it again. If it does not work, or if it breaks easily, that is punishment, and we look for another brand. Similarly, if we get good service at a store, we go back there, but if we feel ignored or unimportant, then we go elsewhere. For a time there was interest in the possibility that confirming or disconfirming expectations was a basis for consumer satisfaction and reinforcement. However, Churchill and Suprenant (1982) found that neither consumers' initial expectations nor their disconfirmation experience affected their satisfaction with the product. Rather the satisfaction came directly from the performance of the product.

Although the way the product works is the major reinforcer, when a number of products all work equally well, other factors tip the scale among the competitors. In such cases reinforcement involves other dimensions. Often reinforcement involves ego functions, like pride, status, and self-image, and we will see how in a moment.

Negative Reinforcement. One more term that deserves mention here is **negative reinforcement**. It is a term often confused with punishment because of the differences between classical and operant conditioning. The key to avoiding misusage is to remember that it is indeed reinforcement and in operant conditioning must, therefore, be a desired state of affairs. It is really a double negative for it refers to the situation when a response is followed by the ending of an undesired stimulus, that is, something bad stops. It is particularly important in escape and avoidance.

In escape behavior one casts about for ways to escape from a bad situation. When a response works, it is reinforcing because the bad situation stops. Often it is hard to say whether a bad thing has stopped or a good one started, but the distinction is not important. They both have the same consequence, and they are both reinforcing because the situation improves. Ads built on this principle remind consumers of a problem they have and offer products to remove it. They are sometimes called problem identification ads. For example, "Drains stopped up? Try brand X." "Shoes uncomfortable? Ours are made to be comfortable." In these cases the ads allow the reader to visualize ahead and anticipate that the product use will be reinforcing.

Avoidance behavior occurs when we respond to avoid a bad situation that would otherwise develop, potential problems, in other words. Because we are not aware that we have the problem now, we must be made to feel anxious that perhaps we have it without knowing. We see this principle at work with surprising frequency in marketing. The standard formula involves creating anxiety about a potential social error or bad situation and then offering the product that will avoid the disaster. The more anxiety created, the more a product that reduces it is seen as reinforcing. This is not only negative reinforcement but also avoidance because of the factor of avoiding a bad situation. For example, personal hygiene product advertising makes us anxious about dandruff, bad breath, yellow teeth, body odor, perspiration stains, and on and on. "Aren't you glad you use Dial? Don't you wish everyone did?" The most often used motivators in this category focus on social status, popularity, youth, masculinity or femininity, and embarrassment. We are cautioned about everything from static cling to spots on glassware. In each case, following a reminder of the dire social consequences of these conditions, we are offered a product which will prevent them. To avoid them, we respond because the threat creates anxiety, and by reducing that, the product is negatively reinforcing.

Not all products carry such dire warnings. For examples, the *Oldsmobile* ad (Figure 3, p. 49) offers a way to open the van door when your hands are full, and the *Certs* ad in Figure 11 offers a way to avoid sugar and incidentally tooth decay, though only the tiny line on the package reminds us, "Expressly for not promoting tooth decay." Avoiding even mild displeasures is a form of operant conditioning.

Punishment also produces avoidance if it is strong enough, because we learn how to avoid it. This is what happens when a product breaks or we get hassled by a salesclerk. The bad event following a consumer behavior, like entering a store or purchasing a product, is the definition of punishment. We avoid repeating the behavior unless there is more to be gained than lost by doing it.

Stimulus Generalization and Discrimination

When we are reinforced for responding to one stimulus, it turns out that we show an increased tendency to respond to stimuli that are similar to it. This is called stimulus generalization. Then, if we are reinforced for responding to that similar stimulus, we treat all similar stimuli the same. In other words, we have been reinforced for ignoring any differences.

The other side of the same coin is called stimulus discrimination. This occurs when stimuli are similar, but one of them leads to reinforcement, and the other leads to no reinforcement or actual punishment. Our response becomes very selective under these circumstances, and we search for differences, so that we can treat the stimuli differently. Here we have been reinforced for paying attention to differences.

Let us apply this to marketing. Suppose that a supermarket chain produces a dishwashing detergent and markets it under its own house

There's more sugar in this grape
than in all these Certs combined.

All that's in it for you is great taste.

Figure 11 This ad for *Certs* is an example of an ad that identifies a problem, in this case sugar, and offers a product to avoid it. The ad also illustrates the effective use of contrast to get attention. It was even more powerful in color because the only color was the grape and the package. (Reproduced by permission of the Warner-Lambert Company.)

brand. Because they make it, they stand to make a larger profit on it than on the sale of a nationally advertised brand. On the other hand, the nationally advertised brand is the best seller and formidable competition. They can undersell the national brand, but for the price differential to be effective, the products must be perceived as of equal quality. The supermarket achieves this by making its product the same color and packaging it so that it looks very like the competition with a label that is barely distinguishable. Customers generalize, "This is probably made for the store by the same national company and just packaged differently." Generalization is probably an extension of the gestalt law of similarity introduced in chapter 3. The consumer buys the cheaper brand.

Now, however, differential reinforcement comes into play. Consumers try the house brand. If they find it works just as well, they probably continue to buy it because of the lower price. On the other hand, if they try it and find that it is watery and does not work well, they probably abandon it and return to their former brand. In this second case, the house brand purchase has been punished because the product does not work well, and making the national brand seem even better. The tendency to generalize has been countered through differential reinforcement, the consumer has learned to pay attention to the minor differences in the packaging, and no longer groups them together.

Extinction

The process of extinction works just as it does in classical conditioning. When the UCS no longer occurs, the CR weakens and dies out. The learning is not erased because just as in classical conditioning, it needs only the return of the UCS to reappear quickly. This principle is the evidence that led to the rule that any behavior you see must have a reinforcement somewhere because responses extinguish without reinforcement. It also means that when a behavior stops, producing it again is a matter of applying the right reinforcer, though this may be harder to do than it seems. The trick, it turns out, is to know what is reinforcing to a given person at a given time and then to deliver it.

Major Variables

Timing. In animal research it became clear that timing was a crucial element in operant conditioning, as in classical conditioning. With animals, the UCS must follow the CR immediately within a half a second or less, or the required association does not occur. With human subjects the timing is often not so critical. The effect is stronger if the UCS follows immediately, but humans tolerate long intervals because of our ability to symbolize. For example, we often take dishwashing detergent home and put it on the shelf, not using it perhaps for several weeks. The package itself still reminds us where we bought it and that it was the house brand. Note, however, that if it were not for the package, we might easily forget where we bought it, and thus not be in a position to learn to avoid it in the future or to buy it again if it works especially well. I find T-shirts particularly frustrating in this way. By the time I find out whether they wear well or not, the label, if there was one, is obscured or gone. I suspect that manufacturers lose considerable repeat purchases because of impermanent labels.

Young children are much more like animals, no slur intended. Reinforcements for them must be immediate, or they generally lose their effectiveness. Moreover, because the UCS furnishes information about which responses are necessary for reinforcement, if it is delayed a bit, the correct connection may be lost, and also some other response may be reinforced instead.

Repetition. Just as in classical conditioning, repetition is usually necessary to establish the CR. Exactly how many times is hard to predict. Clark Hull spent a lifetime of research trying to predict the course of behavior. Though he had some success with simple organisms in simple situations (rats pressing levers), his theory did not prove very useful when it came to human behavior. He did, however, uncover a number of factors that are important in determining how many repetitions are necessary. Among the most important are the complexity of the task, the intelligence and attention of the organism, the intensity of the stimuli, the desirability of the reinforcer or the painfulness of the punisher, and the effort involved in responding. As in classical conditioning, repetitions beyond the minimum necessary to produce the CR continue to strengthen the response. Brand loyalty develops from just such repeated instances of satisfying purchases.

COMPLEX CONDITIONING

Shaping

By now it may have occurred to you that the operant procedure we have outlined might be very lengthy indeed for some behavior. The process requires reinforcing behavior we wish to continue. But what if the animal never does what we want it to? How can we reinforce a behavior that never happens? Fortunately, Skinner worked out the answer to this. The procedure has been called "successive approximations" or simply "shaping." It involves starting with a behavior that is in the right direction but not what we ultimately want. Perhaps an example is the best way to show how it works.

Suppose that you want the animal to put its nose in the corner. You start by reinforcing it when it is facing the general direction of the corner. The sound of the food delivery system causes it to break off what it was doing, get its reinforcement, and then return almost exactly to the position it was in when it was reinforced. This time you withhold the reinforcement until it is looking toward the corner. Next time it must be moving slightly toward the corner. In this way, it can be brought to the corner quite quickly.

You may have done this already as a child, if you played the game we called "Warmer, warmer." Someone goes out of the room, and the group chooses an object for the child to touch. When the child comes back, the only instructions are "warmer" if the child moves toward it, and "colder" if it moves away. In a very short time the child is brought to the object and touches it. In this case, the verbal message fulfills the same function as the food pellet does for animals.

A marketing example of the application of shaping is a practice often found in opening a new store. When you come to the store there is an opportunity to enter a giveaway of some sort, "no purchase necessary." Perhaps the "First 100 customers will get a free case of soda." These giveaways are in the nature of reinforcements for coming to the store. The idea is to show you where the store is and help get you used to going there. A "loss leader," an item sold at little or no profit, is another example. Any inducement to come to the store, rather than to buy something there, is a form of **shaping**, reinforcement for a move in the right direction. The owner hopes that once you are there, you will buy something, find it reinforcing, and come back to repeat it another day. Is this not the same motivation found in a recent Pepsi ad? (See Figure 12.) The inducement of getting "stuff" (reinforcers) for drinking Pepsi will, if it works, lead the responder to find a bigger reinforcement in the taste and become a regular customer.

A 1991 promotion of Tylenol came with a free sample that pointed out the reinforcers its use would produce, "… will relieve your aches and pains without causing stomach irritation." Then it provided a coupon that would lead to another reinforcer, "… save money on your next bottle …" Repeated use should lead to the purchase of this product by habit. Shaping is really establishing a small chain, which eventually becomes a unified, fluid movement. We turn to chaining next.

Figure 12 This ad employs reinforcers to motivate the use of the product. Shaping is being used to draw the consumer to the larger reinforcement (taste) that, it is hoped, will lead to repeated usage. (Reproduced by permission of the Pepsi-Cola Company.)

Chaining

A complex form of conditioning that involves combining many simple units is called **chaining**. It is essentially the same as higher order conditioning in classical conditioning. In other words, when a CS (we will call it CS_1) comes to be understood as an opportunity for reinforcement, it has become reinforcing in its own right and can be used from then on as if it were a UCS. Thus, a response (CS_2) may lead only to the opportunity to make another response (CS_1), which in turn leads to a reinforcer (UCS). With humans these chains can be indefinitely long. For example, CS_4 leads to CS_3, leads to CS_2, leads to CS_1, leads to UCS. The proviso discussed previously still stands, however. There must always be a reinforcer at the end of the chain, or extinction sets in.

Let us consider a real world example of chaining. Suppose that you want to go downstairs in your office building. You head for the elevator. Why? Because this behavior has usually been reinforced, that is, you have found a ride down there many times. You get to the doors with two unlighted buttons (CS_6). You know that pushing one usually leads to the elevator stopping to take you down, whereas the other does not. In other words, one button has been reinforced in this situation, and the other has not. (It is because you want to go down that the down button is reinforcing. When you no longer want to go down, it is no longer be reinforcing, and you no longer push it.) You push the down button (CR_6). It lights up and becomes a CS (CS_5) meaning "stop pushing and wait (CR_5), elevator coming." Next, a bell rings (CS_4), signalling the response "move toward the doors (CR_4); they are about to open." The opening of the doors (CS_3) signals the response of stepping into the elevator (CR_3). (If the elevator were not there, you would probably begin to step into the open shaft, because you act reflexively and are not processing consciously.) Once inside the elevator, the sight of the button panel (CS_2) is a signal to push the button (CR_2) of the floor you want. (Have you ever forgotten to push a button and stood there going nowhere? This a weak part of the chain, because sometimes you do not have to do it, that is, when someone else has already done it, and sometimes you do not see it because someone is standing in front of it or you are looking elsewhere.) Finally, the (CS_1) occurs as the doors open, and you respond by stepping out (CR_1) where you wanted to be (UCS). This is the reinforcement at the end of the whole chain, that is, reaching the goal.

The whole sequence becomes a reflexive chain. One CS leads to the next and little conscious thought is required. Suppose that someday the elevator is out of order. If you remember that it is, you might very well head for the stairs. If you forget, on the other hand, the early part of the chain might still occur until the extended delay reminds you that the reinforcement can no longer be reached this way. Then you abandon the chain and choose what would ordinarily be a less desirable route (probably not without a bit of muttering and grumbling).

Publishers Clearing House uses a sort of chain when each entry you submit turns out only to "qualify" you for the next round and presents more opportunities to pressure you into buying magazines at each step. Note that each successive entry is powered by the same potentially grand reinforcement at the end. Without that, all entries would stop. Pausing for soda and popcorn on the way into the movie is a short chain in the nature of a habit for some, reinforced ultimately by eating in the theater. Clearly, if you can get your product into a chain of behavior it is likely to be purchased regularly.

Schedules of Reinforcement

When one is conditioning a new behavior, the most efficient procedure requires reinforcing every instance of the new response. This is called **continuous reinforcement**, or CRF for short. But what happens after the response has been learned, and we want the animal to keep on responding? The question becomes more one of motivation than learning, but fortunately the rules still apply. As long as the reinforcement remains desirable, the response will continue. In the 1930s Skinner began investigating what would happen if, instead of reinforcing every response, we reinforce only some of them. There are probably an infinite number of ways this can be done, but most of the findings can be summarized under only four types of **schedules**: fixed ratio, variable ratio, fixed interval, and variable interval.

In general, Skinner found that all animals, including humans, work to maximize reinforcements and minimize effort. In retrospect, the changes that occur in behavior under the different schedules are predictable from that principle, but it took years of research to prove it.

Fixed Ratio. The easiest schedule to conceptualize is the fixed ratio, or FR. In animal research under this schedule, instead of reinforcing every response, we reinforce say every fifth one, or every third one. That is, we pick a ratio of reinforcements to responses (like one-fifth or one-third) and use it consistently. If the initial ratio is too high, the animal simply extinguishes. But if one starts with a low ratio, and gradually increases it, very high ratios are possible. The main characteristic of responding under FR reinforcement is the high rate.

Fixed ratios work for people and animals. For example, salespersons have been placed on a FR schedule when they work for a bonus for every five sales or a vacation in Hawaii for the top salesperson. The purpose, of course, is the higher rate of output it produces. Another example is the collection of Betty Crocker coupons which are found on nearly all General Mills products. When you have enough, you can turn them in for silverware. The more General Mills products you buy, the faster you get your reinforcer, so it can be predicted that it increases sales. A local bookstore used small cards that were punched every time you bought a certain amount. After 10 punches you could get a free book.

Variable Ratio.   The variable ratio schedule, or VR, is similar to the fixed ratio, but rather than using one consistent ratio, the subject never knows how many responses are necessary. The ratio changes after each response. In a study in which a VR schedule was tried in a consumer setting, Deslauriers and Everett (1977) compared a VR schedule to a CRF schedule in a study of bus ridership. They knew that if you give riders a token worth the price of the ride every time they board the bus (equivalent to free ridership), that ridership would increase about 50%. They found that giving out tokens to every third rider on the average (a VR3 schedule) was about as effective, and was clearly one-third of the cost. The net loss for the continuous condition was 75% (because not all tokens were redeemed) but was only 5% for the schedule. A number of special conditions prevent application directly to a municipal system, but they suggest that a higher VR schedule might balance the cost and still increase ridership. The increase must be motivated by a desire to reduce cars on the roads, rather than the desire for increased profits, because profits do not necessarily increase. The technique certainly warrants additional study. Stores might come out ahead if they offered big bargains to occasional shoppers chosen on a random basis.

Notice that under both *ratio* schedules, the more often the subjects respond, the more reinforcements they get. Both ratio schedules give a high rate of output. VR rates are a bit higher than FR, but why this is so, even when both schedules earn the same reinforcement for the same work output, is still not known (Chance, 1988). Perhaps subjects are more eager to work, if they know there is a possibility that the reward could happen any time. With fixed ratios they know when it will occur, and immediately following a reinforcement the subject knows another reinforcement will not be along for awhile. On the other hand, with VR there is, at the same time, the opposite possibility that the reward will be longer in coming this time. Why don't the two possibilities cancel out? It may be an example of the "good old days" phenomenon, which suggests that we remember good things more vividly than bad things. Gamblers certainly remember their wins much more clearly than their losses, or they would extinguish.

We can go to Publisher's Clearing House again, this time for a good example of a VR schedule. Our mail brings letters with increasing frequency from a seemingly endless number of companies offering million dollar giveaways, apparently copying the success of Publisher's Clearing House. These are usually announced with the possibility that "you may have already won," a wording that has much more appeal than one suggesting possible good fortune in the future. The variable ratio of reinforcement to response here is extraordinarily high, 1 to many millions, but the reinforcement is also correspondingly high. So we even pay the post office 32¢ to send it back, and sometimes we even buy a magazine subscription. All gambling is on a VR schedule, and until you come to believe that winning in the long run is not possible, you may engage in it at a high rate. Once you feel you cannot win, the reinforcement is gone, and the behavior ceases.

Fixed Interval. Both types of ratio schedules are governed by work output. The more work, the more reinforcements. In interval schedules, on the other hand, a reinforcement is governed by the clock, not by the number of responses. Making a response starts the clock, and there will not be another reinforcement until some preset interval has expired. The first response after the expiration of the interval results in a reinforcement. In this case, more work does not lead to more reinforcements, and so the response changes accordingly. Just as in the ratio schedules, there are two types, fixed and variable.

The fixed interval schedule, or FI, involves an interval that is always the same length, which allows the subject to learn what it is. One must start with short intervals and work up to long ones, or the animal extinguishes before a reinforcement arrives. Experienced animals are amazingly accurate in judging fixed intervals. How they accomplish it without wrist watches is still not known. Response rates clearly reflect the reinforcement contingencies, for early in the interval, where they have never been reinforced, animals stop completely. Somewhere about the middle they begin occasional responding and gradually transit to a very high rate at the end of the interval where they have always been reinforced. On a typical record which plots number of responses on the Y-axis and time on the X-axis, the response records are characteristically a scalloped shape.

By now it should not be surprising to discover that interval schedules work with humans and other animals, but humans can conceptualize intervals marked on calendars, not just clocks. For example, student papers assigned to be due at the end of the term draw no work at all for several weeks. Then occasional reading begins, writing eventually starts, and the night before the papers are due frenzied activity goes on. As another example, consider how many people are still working on their IRS tax forms on April 14th. In spite of the fact that the IRS spends a lot of money exhorting taxpayers to file early, procrastinating is so common that the post office often keeps a special window open for last minute filers.

Variable Interval. Finally we consider the variable interval schedule, or VI. Under this schedule, the individual never knows how long it will be until the next reinforcement. They must believe it will arrive eventually, or they will extinguish. Unlike the VR schedule, it does no good to work faster because the reinforcements are controlled by the clock. On the other hand, responding too slowly means that some reinforcements may be unnecessarily delayed. Animals learn this from experience. The resultant rate is moderate and maintainable over a long period of time. Its dominant characteristic is its steadiness. In a human example, when a teacher occasionally and randomly praises students, it is a VI schedule. Another example is a store that runs unadvertised specials on a random basis. If they involve a big enough reinforcer to make the effort of frequently coming in to check worth it, they should increase store visitations and produce very steady responding. Note that only occasionally need there be a reinforcer. On the other hand, if all sales are advertised, you do not need to keep coming in to check. If they are done regularly, the schedule becomes FI and you come in only for them, not steadily. I am surprised that more stores do not take advantage of the VI schedule. It may be that, though people come in steadily, they only look to see if there is a bargain and do not buy anything else. In general, however, just getting people into the store is desirable.

Resistance to Extinction. All schedules of reinforcement lead to resistance to extinction. Animals learn to respond in the absence of immediate reinforcement, so that when reinforcement stops, they keep working anyway. The absence of the reinforcement is also perceptually much harder to detect if one has been working on a schedule rather than CRF. The end result is that reinforcements go further. They generate more work, when they are delivered on a schedule, rather than after every response. This suggests that one could start with a one-third schedule, such as in the Deslauriers and Everett (1977) study referred to previously, and gradually increase the ratio without much loss in response.

Stimulus Signals. One final point before we leave the topic of schedules. Stimuli can signal the nature of the reinforcement schedule in effect. For example, Skinner showed that pigeons can learn that the color of a light means a type of schedule, where, perhaps, red means VR, blue means VI, and green means no reinforcement at all. Once they have had a chance to learn this, just changing the color of the light produces an immediate change in the response rate. They speed up with red, slow with blue, and quit with green. In the case of pigeons, however, their responses appear to be automatic and do not indicate a very high level of understanding.

Skinner argues that there is no need to assume that even human behavior is ever above the automatic reflexive level. According to his view, what appears to be choice between responding or not is really the process of selecting the reinforcement that is most desired at the moment. In fact, he argues, we have no choice but rather must respond to the strongest reinforcer at hand. In other words, what appears to be choice is really illusion. This would mean that no animals, including humans, have free will but rather simply react to stimuli in the environment one after the other.

Skinner's view eliminates all personal responsibility for we really have no choices. For example, if people act selfishly, it is only because they did not get conditioned to find thinking of others reinforcing. But we cannot blame their parents instead because they in turn only acted as they were reinforced. Many people, however, who perhaps have been emotionally drained by struggling with hard choices, will find this notion demeaning and depressing, but it appears to be impossible to prove one way or the other. We cannot prove him wrong because the proof is always after the fact. On the other hand, it is important to realize that it is also impossible to prove him right. So far the answer to the question of free will is one of faith, not science.

THE NATURE OF REINFORCEMENT

Simple and Direct

Some products give us pleasure in their use, and no further reinforcement characteristics need be invoked. Mitall and Lee (1989) distinguish two categories that may be important distinctions for marketers. Sometimes the product class gives pleasure (e.g., whirlpool baths), but sometimes it will be a particular brand within that class ("e.g., consider consumer distaste for certain brands of beer even as they enjoy one or more particular brands") (p. 366). For most marketers, the task is to raise the apparent reinforcement value of their brand over the competition. The product class must be introduced to new buyers, if they lack experience with it, before the particular brand can be singled out.

Relativity of Reinforcement

Reinforcers are tied to the specific needs of the person involved. What is one person's reinforcer is even a punishment to someone else. Fortunately, we tend not to be unique, and there are usually a number of people with the same needs if a big enough group is sampled. For example, Schiffman (1971) found that 30% of households, where at least one member was restricting salt intake, tried a new reduced salt product, whereas only 6% of other households did. In this case, salt restriction created reinforcers in the low salt category and clearly made a difference in behavior.

Not only are there differences among people, however, but there are also differences in the same person moment to moment. Reinforcements continually change their values, depending on situational variables. For example, when we are hungry, food reinforcers have increased power. For this reason, you should not go shopping at the supermarket when you are hungry. You may well end up with more impulse items than you intended. Cookies and candies are harder to resist when you are hungry. (If you take your children to the supermarket, be sure your children are not hungry either!) After you have eaten Thanksgiving dinner, the power of food as a reinforcer is low. As another example, consider that we are less fussy about brand and price when we are in a hurry. For this reason, convenience stores can charge higher prices and have more limited stock.

The gestaltists found that stimuli are perceived, not as isolated units, but relative to others around them, and relative to the subject's past experiences. So it is with reinforcers. For example, I may like driving my car until I borrow my friend's newer one, and mine is not as rewarding any more. I knew an automobile dealer who regularly applied this principle. Whenever you took your car into be serviced, he would lend you a brand new one to drive for the few hours yours was being fixed. Of course, the new ones ran smoothly, quietly, were spotlessly clean, and even smelled like new cars. You could not help but entertain thoughts of turning the old one in on one of these new models. Eventually, I did just that. I often wonder how many others he snared the same way.

This principle of relativity is one of the things that keeps us always wanting more than we have. A wealthy woman I knew was always bemoaning the fact that the people in her neighborhood always seemed to have so much more than she did. She was indeed trying to "keep up with the Joneses," but of course, would never be able to. The problem was her own perception, not the Joneses, for she appeared to have fully as much as they. It was rather that after she bought things, they were no longer rewarding to her. I remember one study that I cannot find again, in which it was discovered that a raise in pay at work is seen as extra for only about three weeks. Then, once again it has become the norm.

Some things may be reinforcing to one person, but not to another, because reinforcers may come to have special meanings like all stimuli. Consider a study by Mazis (1975). A law was passed in Miami prohibiting the sale of detergents containing phosphates. When a sample of Miami residents was compared to one from Tampa, which had no such law, the Miami residents rated the detergent more positively. For another example, consider why offers from our friends look more reinforcing than the same offers from our enemies. The fact underscores the value of public relations when selling. Salespeople must be liked before they can sell.

Differences in people mean that they will find different categories of products interesting and worth buying. Things are reinforcing when they fulfill some kind of need. In other words, age, gender, ethnic background, and lifestyle all effect how reinforcing a particular product will be perceived to be. Advertisers who must direct their ads to large groups need to find products that most members of the target group will find reinforcing. The ultimate purpose of psychographic and demographic research is simply finding the right reinforcers that a group values in common.

Perceptual Factors

Part of the marketing game is to put the offer in the terms which look the most reinforcing, so wording and form play a role as we discussed in chapter 4. I received a notice of a sale from a lighting center. It has "1 cent" in big red letters, and says "Buy one lamp for $99 and get a second lamp for only one-cent." Does this sound like a better bargain than saying "Lamps 50% off when you buy two"? We spoke previously of the use of "free gifts" as reinforcers, when of course, they are seldom really free. The way offers are worded makes a huge difference in their perceived value. For example, consider the Discover Card, which claims to pay you 1% for using it. What they mean, of course, is that, if you use it enough, they will deduct 1% from their already high interest rate. The consumers are really getting nothing, but it appears that they are getting a reinforcement for the response of using the card. Clearly, understanding the principles of reasoning and perception, both discussed in earlier chapters, are necessary to evaluate the strength of a reinforcement.

Consider another example. The local bank offers me a free gift, if I sign up for its credit card. This is simple reinforcement at work. The offer is the CS, my response is the CR, the gift is the UCS, and my usage of the gift is the UCR. The intent is that my behavior will be reinforced by the free gift. On the other hand, I may perceive the gift as a trick, and I may not accept it. I might be aware that using the credit card is going to cost me interest payments, the cost of which will more than offset the "free" gifts. In this case the gift is not a reinforcer, and I do not respond. On the other hand, if I do not think it through, perhaps because I am new to this kind of thing, I may accept their free offer. They increase the apparent reward, too, by showing smiling faces getting their free gifts (which is also an illustration of classical conditioning, in that it is attaching positive affect to a stimulus, the gift). Another point, too, is that if I am poor, the gift becomes more valuable to me, and the prospect of buying on credit may be too much to resist. In operant conditioning terms, the reinforcer is much more powerful in this case. I recently received a check in the mail that I could "spend on anything." The amount would simply be placed on a credit card account I was being offered. The credit card APR was more than 20%.

Promotional sales of all kinds involve the same operant conditioning principles. Price really represents the amount of work required to make the response because most of us work for our money. Of course, if I have not worked for my money, perhaps it came through a large inheritance or similar way, then money does not represent as much work to me, and I pay much less attention to it. Hence, for most of us, whenever price is reduced, there is increased motivation to buy, but price can work on both cognitive and affective levels at once. If we intended to buy the item anyway, then to buy when the price is low makes good reasonable sense. On the other hand, to buy an item we do not really need, just because it is a good price, is not really a reasoned response, but an affective one. It may represent a conditioned response to the stimulus of a bargain.

Cognitive Reinforcement: Information-Based

Problems with Drive Reduction.   Not long after the concept of reinforcement appeared, an enormous number of studies began to find out just what makes some things reinforcing. Nearly all studies were done with animals, mostly rats and pigeons. It was hypothesized that food reinforcements, most commonly used with animals, reduce physiological demands which drive the animal to look for food. This was labeled drive reduction, and it was thought that it works for all reinforcements. However, it was not long before studies appeared which could not be explained by drive reduction. For example, animals placed in a complex maze with no reinforcement of any kind still learned how to get around in it. What motivated their learning? The conclusion, bending definitions more than a bit, was that animals have a drive to explore. It was found that monkeys would work at lever pressing, just for a 10 second opportunity to look out into the next room. Was this a curiosity drive? Monkeys seated in front of a board with a variety of complex latches learned to take them apart for no apparent reinforcement. Was this a manipulation drive?

Finding Out.   As more studies of this type appeared, it became clear that inventing new drives to handle each one had little explanatory value. Shortly after, about 1950, research began a major turn toward cognition. When this happened, it was seen that all of these types of reinforcement contain the same element, information gathering. It was hypothesized that a Darwinian principle is involved and that animals do it because it ultimately aids survival. Those animals that do more of it have a better chance to survive and reproduce. For example, if they have been finding out about their environment, they will know where to hide and how to get there in a hurry when needed, and they will know where to look for food.

On the other hand, higher animals, like primates and humans, have much larger cognitive capacities and sometimes seem to play with information just for fun. Though the final theoretical explanations are not all in, we can conclude that sometimes just "finding out" is reinforcing to humans. For example, watching a football or soccer game gains much of its excitement from wondering who is going to win. Reruns lose excitement for this reason. Murder mysteries are not as exciting when we know "who dun it." We want to know how a story came out, if we missed the ending. Have you ever stayed up much later than you should have watching television, just to find out how the story came out? We mentioned under cognitive consistency theory that a tension persists until we can classify things. Here is a case in which we find the ambiguous tension disturbing, as the theory predicts. In the terms of this chapter, resolving ambiguity, finding out, is a reinforcing process.

Recently, Peracchio and Meyers-Levy (1994) confirmed this principle in a study involving advertising that we introduced in chapter 3. They presented ambiguous ads to subjects and found that resolving the ambiguity produces positive affect. The ambiguity was produced by severe cropping, which made pictures hard to understand immediately, or by discrepancies of picture and verbal message, like crystal Pepsi. The demonstrated need to resolve the ambiguities clearly supports the notion that we have a need for information that is as basic as other needs and that satisfying that need acts like other deficits because it is positively reinforcing.

Some types of cognitive reinforcers may be more prevalent in individuals who have higher intelligence or more education, but they are certainly not limited to this group. For example, crossword puzzles are popular across a wide range of individuals. The popular television show "Wheel of Fortune," which involves filling in letters until a familiar phrase is recognized, appeals to a wide range of viewers. In another popular show, "Jeopardy," the reinforcement power of getting the right answer before the contestant is clear. Many games, like Anagrams or Scrabble, involve forming words quickly, and most games involve a certain amount of cognitive skill. Riddles and puzzles of all sorts are perennial favorites that illustrate the power of winning or simply figuring out the solution. One could go on, but these examples will suffice as examples of the reinforcement value of engaging in cognitive activities.

Interactives.   Participation of many kinds seems to be reinforcing, and in some case the reason may be simply finding out. For example, in the museum field, it has been found that participatory devices increase the acquisition and retention of learning (Eason & Linn, 1976; Shettel, 1973) and generally increase an exhibit's appeal (Bitgood, Patterson, & Benefield, 1986). A common type of interactive, for example, asks a question on the outside of a flap or door. You have to lift it to find out the answer. If the question and answer were printed together in the same place, they would be read by far fewer children. Children's museums have reflected this finding and have become heavily interactive. Older types of interactives involved simply pushing a button, but there is no question that the appeal was largely finding out what would happen.

Participation may underlie the effectiveness of the promotions that so frequently come in the mail. For example, consider one from Citibank. Earn free gifts, it says, by enrolling in their free program, and using their credit card instead of cash. Free anything is clearly a reinforcer, but why should the company be interested in your signing up for such a program? What do they get out of it? There may be legal reasons for having someone "enroll in the program," but psychologically, one of the things it does is make the program look like something special and probably makes us use it more. By this principle "free kittens" are not as likely to go as quickly as "kittens, 25 cents." They are also likely to be better cared for if they are not free. Anything we work for is seen as more valuable, possibly because of the perceptual need for consistency, as we discussed with cognitive dissonance theory.

The reason that participation is reinforcing is still not completely clear. Consider, for example, the technique that appears regularly in my junk mail: the inclusion of a sticker to be removed from one location and affixed to another. One from PC Resource Magazine says "FREE" on it in bright red and white. You are to move the sticker to the circle which says "I accept" to get their free first issue in return for trying a subscription. Again, why the sticker? What does the company get from using it? Few people, apparently, can resist moving a sticker. Maybe it goes back to preschool years and the tremendous appeal of sticker books, or maybe its because they look like coins, but they are being used frequently these days. They are also attention-getters and certainly increase participation. One of the technique's main features may be that people do not need to have pen or pencil handy to confirm their response. If they need to write out something or sign their names, they are likely to say, "I'll do it later, when I have a pen," and then, of course, they may never get back to it. Stickers get around this problem very cleverly.

Also, we tend to read what is on the sticker, in this case making sure the would-be consumer gets the message "FREE." Free things are in the nature of reinforcements for no work, and, as outlined in the rules of operant conditioning, minimizing work is desired by everyone. The catch is, of course, that "there are no free lunches," so that the "free issue" is actually paid for in the year's subscription. If you cancel, it is free, but apparently few people actually cancel.

Psychological Reinforcement

Chapter 8 introduced the notion of psychological reinforcements. These arise from a variety of instances in which others are perceived to judge us or where we are evaluating our own worth. A few examples here, however, may clarify the reinforcement nature of these forces.

Direct Psychological Reinforcers. The direct influence of a reinforcer occurs when the satisfaction of a psychological need is produced by the action itself. A number of researchers have studied coupon redemption behavior and have provided evidence that a major part of the motivation (reinforcement) for using coupons comes from the feeling of being a thrifty and smart shopper (Babakus, Tat, & Cunningham, 1988; Price, Feick, & Guskey-Federouch, 1988; Shimp & Kavas, 1984). Schindler (1989) says the feeling state reinforces all price promotions, not just coupons, and concludes that this factor can interact with other motivations and even alter perception. In other words, the reinforcer for the use of coupons and sales is a feeling state not a physical object, an affect based on a psychological need that works directly on the user.

Another type of direct psychological reinforcer is that which gets its power from the way in which it allows people to express their own identities. The possession of an object or a particular brand of object, perhaps, causes one to feel more important or of higher status. Direct reinforcement does not need other people to have its effect. Murray's list of psychological needs in chapter 8 indicates that reinforcers come in many forms.

Indirect Psychological Reinforcers. Psychological reinforcers act indirectly and directly. The indirect effect occurs when the positive feeling state comes to one, not from an individual's own action directly but from someone else's perception of that action. It is revealed when I buy designer jeans. Although I may like the jeans themselves (direct reinforcement), I may also get pleasure from knowing that others will see me in the clothes (indirect) and will infer something about me. Indirect reinforcement is essentially eliciting behaviors from others that are reinforcing to me. In other words, image and status depend to a large extent on the presence of other people for their reinforcing power. To emphasize the psychological component, however, let me point out that sometimes the desired responses of others are only imagined, yet I still may buy the designer jeans. The indirect reinforcement, real or imaginary, must be fairly strong, for we are willing to pay extra for those jeans.

Such status symbols and to an even greater extent conspicuous luxury items are all purchased in part because of their impact on others. They are all meant to tell others something about the owner and give the owner pleasure in the process. Note that the power of these reinforcements ultimately derives from enhancement of ego, which is to say, the perception of increased self-worth that we get from the reactions of others.

The process of eliciting reinforcers from others was raised to a fine art by Dale Carnegie, in his famous book, *How to Win Friends and Influence People* (Carnegie, 1940), which became a sort of salesman's bible. He listed a number of ways to get people to like you. They include smiling, using a person's name, talking about their interests, being a good listener, and finding sincere ways to flatter them. Carnegie's principles soon became effectively utilized by salesmen of all kinds, and his book has gone through umpteen printings. These are, you will recognize, direct psychological reinforcers of others which produce the indirect reinforcer for the initiator, though Carnegie never calls them that. (Skinner called this "mutual reinforcement" and claimed it was the basis of all love relationships, but somehow I want to believe that there is more to love than this!)

Vicarious Operant Conditioning

Observational Learning. Some observational learning goes on in animals, but generally they must respond and actually experience the consequent. This is not necessary in humans. We have many ways of finding out. We can watch and learn. In the early 60s Bandura and his colleagues demonstrated with the now famous Bobo doll experiment that for no apparent reinforcement children would mimic the behavior of adults they had seen punching an enormous inflated clown doll. The probability of their mimicking behavior went up if they had seen the adults rewarded for punching and went down if the children saw the adults scolded (Bandura, Ross, & Ross, 1961). The phenomenon first demonstrated with the Bobo doll, labeled **observational learning**, is sometimes listed as a separate type of learning. More properly, it should be considered a vicarious form of operant conditioning.

In **vicarious conditioning**, we do things because we have seen others rewarded for that behavior. It is an important device in consumer behavior. We buy many items with which we have no experience, and we ask others for their advice or suggestions. This kind of information transmittal is called "word-of-mouth." It changes our behavior to buy the recommended product because we learned that someone else did, not because we ourselves received the reward. As Bandura showed, we learn from the experiences of others. Advertising takes the process one more step and provides us with suitable people to learn from. Testimonials from apparently randomly chosen individuals all testify that the product is superior. Television commercials are particularly effective in showing us others being reinforced for using the product, probably because they come very close to personal experience and are powerful for that reason.

Ten years after his initial Bobo doll demonstration, the principle of vicarious operant conditioning was so well established that Bandura himself provided us with marketing examples in his testimony to the Federal Trade Commission:

As a rule, observed rewards increase and observed punishments decrease imitative behavior. The principle is widely applied in advertising appeals. In positive appeals, following the recommended action results in a host of rewarding outcomes. Smoking a certain brand of cigarettes or using a particular hair lotion wins the loving admiration of voluptuous belles, enhances job performance, masculinizes one's self-concept, tranquilizes irritable nerves, invites social recognition from total strangers, and arouses affectionate reactions in spouses (Bandura, 1971, pp. 21–22, as cited in Mullen & Johnson, 1990).

A few studies have sought to document this modeling effect in real-life situations. For example, Gorn and Florsheim (1985) found that 9- and 10-year-old girls were influenced by TV commercials for lipstick, and they concluded it was because the product was associated with being an adult. Here the reinforcer is an indirect one. In general, older children make more persuasive models for children than same-aged or younger models, but the effect holds only for child-related products, not general items like food (Macklin, 1990). Toys carry an image factor not carried by potatoes, and being seen as older is clearly an image more reinforcing to the young.

Verbal Information about Reinforcers. In the main we are visual creatures, vision is our preferred sense, and therefore, vision is the most powerful. Although visual images are more powerful than verbal statements, we often learn about reinforcers through verbal mechanisms. As humans we can also ask, and we can read. Behaviors that are followed by a reinforcer can obviously be communicated verbally. Most word-of-mouth information is of this type: "That new shampoo really works!" Sales (savings are seen as reinforcing) are generally communicated verbally. For example, "Buy one at regular price, get a second at 50% off." Reading is certainly less powerful than experiencing, so sometimes we do not believe what we read, or we forget it easily. The sign may say "Wet Paint," but we have to touch it to see if it really is. Young children cannot understand verbal reinforcers as well as older ones. They have particular trouble with the type that are worded as propositions, such as, "If you save your money, you can buy something better later." Preschoolers need to actually see the reinforcer happening rather than hearing abstract "If this, then that" type statements. Conversely, however, the effect of seeing is stronger in this age child.

Watching Others and Social Reinforcers. We may see others getting a reward, but watching others may produce reinforcements that are more complex than this. For example, sports events are reinforcing, because we enjoy watching others perform. Concerts have some of the same enjoyment, but there is also a social component, and many activities involve socially based reinforcers. Hearing the music is rewarding, but the live concert has something more, or we would simply be content to play our CDs at home. The feeling of being part of a crowd, part of a "happening," or just being there, are all aspects of it. Being part of a social group or perceiving that I am, as in a beer commercial, is clearly rewarding. On the other hand, watching others may be very passive, as in the classic "couch potato." The reinforcer for this passive behavior may be simply pleasure in the spectacle, or identification, because there is almost no physical participation at all. If the others represent me, as in a high school, college, or even a pro basketball game, then there is clearly something of myself on the line, and I am more involved. We see this when our team wins, and we proclaim "*We* are number one!"

Multiple Reinforcements

Means–Ends Ladders. In our analysis we have tended to speak as if there were only one reinforcer operating at a time. In fact, of course, there are many all the time. An immediate reinforcer may derive its power from what it enables one to reach in the future, not from itself. This structure has been termed means–end relationship, and an example will appear when the student asks her or himself, "Why am I in school today?" There may be very little benefit in the day itself, but being present allows for a better grade on the test, which allows passing the course, which allows getting academic credits, which allows graduation, which allows for a better job, which allows for a better level of living. This is similar to a chain, but the later stages have not yet been experienced. We know they will be there, however, because of our cognitive capacities, particularly verbal symbolism.

In the 80s attempts have been made to apply this structure to consumer motivation. For example, Gutman and Alden (1985) have analyzed adolescents' motivation relative to retail stores and fashion. The technique is called laddering. Any instance in which a respondent links at least two elements together asymmetrically is defined as a ladder. For instance, A causes, produces, or leads to B. They explain the method as follows:

> Let us say that a respondent has told us that she prefers smaller stores to bigger stores.... When asked why she has this preference, she might reply that smaller stores are more apt to have unique merchandise whereas larger stores are more apt to have more ordinary merchandise. When asked whether she prefers unique or ordinary merchandise, our respondent says she prefers unique merchandise because it helps her express her individuality. And when asked why she wants to express her individuality, she replies that she

wants to impress other people. Finally, she says she wants to impress others because it gives her a feeling of self-esteem. Thus, what the laddering procedure tries to do is elicit a string of interrelated elements.... It is not only the elements, but their connections in the consumer's mind that are of importance (Gutman & Alden, 1985, p. 104).

From a sample of 25, Gutman and Alden derived 50 attributes all of which contribute to the reason individuals buy as they do. Although this makes the task of determining motivation extremely complex, it becomes clear that many of the attributes fall into related clusters. Because of the way the questions were structured, 19 of the attributes contributed to the shoppers' determination of high quality. This in turn contributed to a level of 19 practical considerations, such as reducing effort and getting monetary value. Some of these were ends in themselves, such as "fun to shop," "less conflict," "time for other things," "not bored," "wider wardrobe." Most of the factors contributed to the highest level of the 12 attributes that involved self-esteem and self-image. You may recall that these are derivatives from the self-worth concept introduced in chapter 8. This means that although self-esteem is a dominant reinforcer, there are many factors that contribute to the way it is interpreted. The laddering technique should prove valuable in uncovering the multiple layers of motivation within the consumer. One caution should be noted. The technique depends on self-reports, and people are not always aware nor candid about their motivations. This particular study seems to have been successful in creating a climate in which this aspect was minimized.

Competing Reinforcements. Maslow addressed the problem of what happens when two or more reinforcers compete, that is, if we can only have one, which will it be. He did not call them reinforcers, but needs. Yet the satisfaction of a need is what makes reinforcers work, so it amounts to the same thing. He distinguished five main levels, and he argued that each level would have to be satisfied before the next level could be considered. The first, most demanding level is physical needs, such as food, warmth, and shelter. The second level is safety, the third is social needs, and the fourth is ego needs. The highest level is self-actualization, in which we are able to develop and realize our full potential. It is important to remember that these are not steps through which we progress in life, but steps we go up and down all day long. I can move up after breakfast but will find myself back on level one before lunch.

The main application for marketing is in environments where people come for an extended period of time. Only in such a setting do we have control over the whole person to some degree. Such environments include theme parks, museums, exhibit halls, zoos, arboretums, and malls. The main lesson was contained in the chapter on attention, when we noted that transient personal needs can eliminate attention to the occupation at hand. Restrooms, drinking fountains, cafeterias, and simply places to rest, all satisfy competing reinforcers, so that the individual can return to the main task.

When competing reinforcers (products or services) are on the same level, it becomes hard to predict which will dominate at any given moment. Theoretically, it should be that which simply is made to seem the most desirable. Practically, it will be the product or service whose marketers best combine all the principles of perception and psychological motivation for the particular audience.

CHAPTER 11

Culture and Family Influences

THE ROLE OF CULTURE

Culture as Commonalities of Meaning

The collective experiences of a group of people comprises what we call culture. The commonality of their experience gives the objects around them and their relationships commonality of meaning. After comparing a number of definitions from anthropology, Rohner (1984) proposed a definition of culture: "the totality of equivalent and complementary learned meanings maintained by a human population, or by identifiable segments of a population, and transmitted from one generation to the next." (pp. 119–120) Rohner emphasizes the beliefs and values held in common by a group.

In addition to common meanings, others feel that one must also include what Wilke calls "the material elements of culture." (Segall, 1986; Wilke, 1986, p. 131) However, even with major environmental determinants, it is the perception of the environment which transforms it into culture. Hence, one could argue that, even here, all culture is ultimately meaning.

Consumer Goods as Symbols

It is clear that the symbolism of consumer goods was being discussed even before the turn of the century. The idea has grown, so that by 1960 the idea was accepted well enough that many writers advocated a broad symbolic approach to marketing. For example, Sidney Levy wrote:

> The things people buy are seen to have personal and social meanings in addition to their functions. Modern goods are recognized as psychological things, as symbolic of personal attributes and goals, as symbolic of social patterns and strivings (Levy, 1959, p. 410).

Since then, the role of culture in establishing the symbolism behind consumption has gradually become clearer, until today a number of researchers support the viewpoint with considerable evidence. To underscore the relationship we shall draw here on the work of Grant McCracken, one of the more enthusiastic writers, who introduces the topic this way:

> Culture and consumption have an unprecedented relationship in the modern world. No other time or place has seen these elements enter into a relationship of such intense mutuality. Never has the relationship between them been so deeply complicated.
>
> The social sciences have been slow to see this relationship, and slower still to take stock of its significance. They have generally failed to see that consumption is a thoroughly cultural phenomenon.... consumption is shaped, driven, and constrained at every point by cultural considerations. The system of design and production that creates consumer goods is an entirely cultural enterprise. The consumer goods on which the consumer lavishes time, attention, and income are charged with cultural meaning. Consumers use this meaning for entirely cultural purposes. They use the meaning of consumer goods to express cultural categories and principles, cultivate ideals, create and sustain lifestyles, construct notions of the self, and create (and survive) social change. Consumption is thoroughly cultural in character.
>
> The reciprocal truth is, of course, that in Western developed societies culture is profoundly connected to and dependent on consumption. Without consumer goods, modern, developed societies would lose key instruments for the reproduction, representation, and manipulation of their culture. The worlds of design, product development, advertising and fashion that create these goods are themselves important authors of our cultural universe. They work constantly to shape, transform, and vivify this universe. Without them the modern world would almost certainly come undone. The meaning of consumer goods and the meaning creation accomplished by consumer processes are important parts of the scaffolding of our present realities. Without consumer goods, certain acts of self-definition and collective definition in this culture would be impossible (McCracken, 1988).

Culture symbolizes its common meanings, so Jung (1960) felt that culture is mainly a process of symbol formation and symbol usage. It is a representation and communication symbolically of the common relationships we think of as culture. Without those symbols, culture would collapse. In fact, Jung maintained that it has been mainly the process of symbol formation which has led to humankind's development from the primitive to the civilized state.

Thus, our culture consists of our symbols, language, beliefs, and attitudes, shaped by our experiences and environment, usually without our being aware of them. The group beliefs and attitudes appear in terms of what the members value, how they define personal worth, what activities they encourage in each other, what lifestyles they choose and permit, and what products they buy. The perceptual categories that our culture provides us become the very framework on which we organize our phenomenal world (see McCracken, 1988).

The notions of scripts, schemas, inferences, and biases, which we introduced in the early chapters, return here for an encore. Because the experiences of the members of a culture or subculture are so similar, the perceptual frameworks that they use are also similar. This means that one can base motivational appeals on these percepts and have fairly universal acceptance. But it also means that if one crosses cultural lines, such appeals will have to be reevaluated, because consumer goods have cultural meanings that go beyond their personal or utilitarian value. They are meanings unique to some extent to a particular nation or a subgroup of that nation.

Three sources of meaning are important in consumer goods. First, there are cultural meanings that all goods seem to share. Secondly, there are additional specific meanings added to products by advertising, manipulated meanings, if you will. Finally, there are the changes in culture itself that derive from the consumptive process, particularly from advertising, that lead to changing meanings. Let us look at these in turn.

Cultural Meanings

National Values. Our nation is particularly diverse culturally because it has been populated almost entirely by immigrants from all over the world. There are many subcultures, particularly where these immigrants have clustered together with others like themselves. Then, does it make any sense to speak of national characteristics, or the "American culture?" It turns out that it does, because there are many forces to which we are all subject and that shape us similarly, in spite of our neighborhood idiosyncrasies. The problem is exactly the same that psychology in general has in trying to find commonalities in the face of individual differences. Were there no psychological commonalities there would be no psychology, and similarly, were there no national commonalities, there would be no national marketing. When exploring these American traits, however, considerable caution is required, lest we fall into stereo-typing and oversimplification.

Lipset (1963) identified six dimensions by which cultures can be defined. Those that define our culture (with the alternatives in paren-theses) are egalitarian (elitist), performance oriented (tradition ori-ented), materialistic (nonmaterialistic), objective (subjective), intensive/mechanistic (extensive/holistic), and individualistic (collectivistic). These adjectives describe our culture, and they also offer cues to some of the various appeals that are commonly used and why they work.

Pollay (1984) surveyed ads from 1900 to 1980 and found that prac-ticality was the core value most often used. This may include aspects of Lipset's objectivity, materialism, and performance orientation, but it describes an additional value. Others he found frequently used were family, newness, good monetary value, health, sexiness or vanity, wis-dom, and uniqueness. Can these be considered derivatives of Lipset's list, or do they add qualities? Schiffman and Kanuk (1991) compiled a similar list that includes Pollay's practicality and health but adds a number of others: achievement and success, activity, progress, effi-ciency, material comfort, individualism, freedom, external conformity, humanitarianism, and youthfulness (see Table 3). The criteria for inclu-sion in their list were (1) the value must be pervasive; (2) the value must be enduring; and (3) the value must be consumer-related. Their list could possibly be extended even further, particularly considering that any value held by a group can be used as a motivational element in advertis-ing, and, thus, all values are ultimately consumer-related. The point is simply that there are an indefinite number of values on which many members of a particular country will agree. These will all be used at one time or another by advertisers who seek a responsive chord. Some values are used more often than others. Some wax and wane in power, for example, fitness. Fitness is very popular now, but only a few years ago was not.

Our most dominant value is individualism, a value that we often do not realize is particularly strong in our culture, probably because we think it is equally strong in all cultures. Most of us, Native Americans excepted, trace our ancestry back to immigrants who were dissatisfied where they were, and also had the motivation to do something major to correct their situations. They moved themselves and their families from a familiar place to one that was usually very foreign. We revere the independent thinker who questioned the authority of the monarch and the church. Our heroes are the pioneers who carved out their individual homesteads from the wilderness and had to be self-sufficient and practi-cal to survive. Today, by still valuing individualism so highly, our culture makes it correspondingly important for all of us to express and

Table 3 Three Appraisals of the Core Values of the American Culture

From Lipset's (1963) defining characteristics:	From Pollay's (1984) survey of ads:	From Schiffman and Kanuk (1991):
Egalitarian	Practicality	Practicality
Performance oriented	Family	Health
Materialistic	Newness	Achievement and success
Objective	Good monetary value	Activity, progress
Intensive mechanistic	Health	Effciency
Individualistic	Sexiness or vanity	Material comfort
	Wisdom	Individualism
	Uniqueness	Freedom
		External conformity
		Humanitarianism
		Youthfulness

define our individuality. In fact, one could make a case that the strength of our need for individuality gives all of the other core values their power. Because people are individually responsible for their own identities, each feels the need to express that identity in the many dimensions that this list suggests. If we saw that our culture valued those who blend into the group, we would certainly not feel the need to be unique and stand out. We incorporate our culture's values into our personal attitudes, so that many of these same values are found in chapter 8 where they appear as personal ideals. Ultimately, we usually get our sense of self-worth from adopting the values of our culture (or subculture). Thus, the close connection.

We express our values in many ways, but an important way is through the consumer products we buy. Particularly, products used publicly, like clothes and automobiles, become a part of who we are and thus express the values we hold. Marketers know we are looking to express these values and often make it clear that their product does so. Thus, themes based on cultural values have been repeatedly used in advertising because they increase involvement through personal relevance. Consider just a few examples:

> Individualism: ads that use this theme for direct appeal certainly include the now classic Marlboro man. A more recent example is an "istante" (they do not capitalize the first letter) ad in which skinny models with dark, lined eyes are simply labeled, "a class apart." The appeal is clearly to those who feel (or want to feel) different.
>
> Achievement and success: a Lark luggage ad says, "The easy way to handle success," implying that this brand is a symbol of success.

Activity and fitness: a Coca-Cola ad shows a couple in tennis outfits relaxing beside a tennis court and says, "Sometimes the best serve comes after the game." This same company has spent millions sponsoring the Olympic Games, a tie-in that exploits the same theme.

Efficiency: a Lands' End ad that calls attention to the mail order company's new delivery system, says, "Now, we're just two short days away." UPS has used the slogan, "The tightest ship in the shipping business" for some years.

Material comfort: an ad for the Mercury Mountaineer 4-wheel drive truck/auto runs the headline, "When the going gets tough, the tough get comfortable."

The Shifting Design Zeitgeist. Designs come and go, but they influence the whole country at once while they are in vogue. The word "zeitgeist" from the German poet Goethe refers to the spirit of the times. Major happenings in the world come to carry almost universal meanings, so that designers can take their inspirations from them and use them for the latest designs. The notion of a zeitgeist applies well to design, for the same elements often appear in widely different products, and even in different countries at the same time, provoked by a major social or technological change.

Design in the twentieth century has changed markedly in each decade. Each time a new design characteristic sets the tone for what is current and up-to-date. The meaning of older designs begins to change and begins to signal that the object is dated and part of the past, rather than the future. The process took a jump forward with the advent of the first global mass markets in the 20s, which fueled the search, as Horsham says, "for consumer goods and services, the need for positive national and corporate identities, and the desire for a fresh start [after World War I] ... Efficiency and speed came to be seen as watchwords for modernity." (Horsham, 1996)

In the 30s, when aircraft began to carry passengers in any numbers, designers turned to the aircraft as the embodiment of this spirit. Air travel was avant garde. As aircraft became bigger and heavier, streamlining became a necessary consideration, and it was not long before ships and trains were also being streamlined. Streamlining was new, and symbolized the latest thing. Streamlining in automobiles made some sense as an energy conserving measure, but gasoline was so cheap, and speeds so low that the real reason seems to be one of style. Chrysler produced an *Airflow* model in 1934 that was the most streamlined automobile to date, but it did not do well and was discontinued in five years (Bush, 1975). In all likelihood the depression played a major role in its demise as consumers made do with whatever transportation they had. The railroads also sought to attract consumers, and they found the public receptive to streamlining. By 1939, almost every railroad had at least one streamlined passenger train, though the fancy exterior often concealed the same steam powered locomotive inside. All manner of products followed suit, particularly appliances, from refrigerators to toasters, even if there was no need for it. The World's Fair of 1939–40 revealed buildings "of tomorrow" with round corners and curves instead of straight lines. Their interiors featured household and office products that had the same rounded corners. By the 40s the wingfoil and the teardrop shapes were incorporated into products and logos, all in the interest of communicating modernity and because the people of the time came to see these shapes as desirable.

After an extensive interruption because of World War II, design based on the aircraft resumed.

> In 1948 Harley Earl of General Motors took a design detail from the Lockheed P-38 Lightning aircraft and used it on a range of Cadillacs to give them, in his words, "graceful bulk." This design was the tail fin, and it was to dominate US automobile styling throughout the 1950s ... out went any vestige of the old rounded look and in came the angular, streamlined shape." (Powell & Peel, 1996).

The fat tear drop was being slimmed down and "modernized." In the mid-50s the jet engine appeared, and the theme of the jet intake and exhaust ports began to show up on products other than jets, particularly in automobiles in their tail lights and front bumpers, where they signaled a break from the past. Angularity came from the jet's swept wings, and the horizontal V began to appear everywhere, giving new meaning to the popular parabolic curves that had been introduced into architecture as early as the 20s and 30s (Hine, 1986). For example, Chrysler used it as a logo on its Plymouths in the mid-50s, and Speedo still uses it. The V was often transformed into the more curvaceous boomerang, which was widely used and showed up in furniture, fabrics, and accessories in the 50s (Hine, 1986). It can also be found today, for example, as Nike's swoosh logo (Figure 10, p. 194).

Part of this rapid introduction of style was caused by the development of new materials, such as plastics, in the 50s. Plastics made new shapes easy to produce. Then too, lifestyles changed. Symbolizing the postwar prosperity, living moved outdoors, and not only did we see buildings of steel and glass, with picture windows and patios blurring the indoor/outdoor boundary, but the outdoor furniture of the patio moved indoors, and the latest thing became furniture with metal legs and a light airy look. Then, Sputnik went up in 1957, and design moved to the age of rockets signaled by fins. These became ever more swept and exaggerated and reached incredible proportions in the cars of the early 60s.

The sudden oil crises of the 70s forced cars to become smaller and more fuel economical as consumers sought to avoid the long lines that sprang up at the gas pumps. A universal speed limit of 55 mph appeared, and the expansive sweeps of metal gave way to the lighter more efficient box style. Other products followed the new symbol of the day. Refrigerators introduced sharp corners to utilize space better. Just when cars were all looking like variations on the same boring box, the fuel crisis abated. The Ford Taurus went back to curves, combining efficient volume with the streamlining of the 30s, and had outstanding marketing success. Predictably, others followed, though few were so extreme. Honda's low front and Chrysler's cab forward windshield were both copied. The Taurus of today has changed once again. It is ironically reminiscent of the "cars of the future" predicted in the 1939 World's Fair and has elliptical windows. Each change signals a new fashion and relegates the old to the out-of-date category.

Fashion and Style. Clothing shows some of the same characteristics in reflecting the times as other manufactured products. Powell and Peel (1996) summarized some of the ways this occurs. New fabrics give rise to a whole wave of uses, so that clothes are altered to incorporate them, and new styles are born. Synthetic fibers, particularly, revolutionized the industry and changed styles in the process. Nylon produced drip-dry, easy to wash fabrics, and ironing began to disappear in everyday clothes. New dyes produced brighter colors. Orlon and Banlon led to body-hugging clothes and stretch pants. "Stiffened nylon was made into huge petticoats which kept their shape without support and were very light. By the late 1950s most girls had at least one in their wardrobes to wear with their circular skirts." (p. 22)

Social events have also had their fashion impact. For example, the "angry young men" of the 50s preceded nuclear protesters later in the decade and the Vietnam protesters of the 60s. In a parallel trend, clothes first became casual, then counterculture and hip in the 60s. The rise of television at the same time led to more rapid exposure and assimilation of styles by the mass markets, so that changes accelerated. Now, although there are dominant themes (baggy clothes are in at the moment), it also seems that there is much more variety than even 25 years ago. Styles are becoming more individualistic. Everyone used to adopt a basic style and individualize it with accessories. Hemlines were religiously altered every year or so, as fashion moved up or down. Now, even the style is likely to be individualized, and hemlines of every length can be seen on the same city street.

Probably because they are so publicly used and so identified with the individual, cars and clothes are particularly sensitive to style changes, but they are not the only products that reflect momentary shifts in public likes and dislikes. The origins of some motifs are hard to trace. For example, when I was taken with a blue mug with a bright sunflower on it a few years ago, I did not realize I was seeing a fad. One recent writer chronicled the rise of the sunflower motif in the previous five years. She writes that from relative obscurity five years beforehand, now the image of the sunflower is found everywhere. The products she has seen it adorning include wine bottles, boxer shorts, pottery bowls, doormats, jewelry, calendars, greeting cards, notepads, journals, photo albums, plates, lamps, neckties, suspenders, hats, umbrellas, towels, and even perfume (Whittemore, 1996). One could predict that its image may eventually suffer from overexposure, become seen as trite, and gradually disappear again. Those who can predict its replacement will be well situated to capitalize on it.

Judged by Our Possessions. We introduced Veblen's notion of conspicuous consumption in the last chapter as a category of personal psychological need. We bring it back for a reprise to emphasize the social origins of the process. His basic premise, laced with considerable satire, is that for hundreds of years a distinction has been made among types of employment. Manual labor and everyday drudgery are the lot of the inferior classes, whereas the upper classes, particularly chieftains, warriors, and priests have been exempt from such "industrial" employments. As it has evolved, nonindustrial employment has come to include politics, sports, learning, religion, and the nobility. Now, members of these employments, nearly all men, have come to constitute the leisure class. Veblen felt that conspicuous leisure and conspicuous consumption have developed to allow members of this leisure class to identify themselves (Veblen, 1967).

Mason (1981) points out that frugality was considered an economic virtue until 1700, and conspicuous consumption was seen only among the aristocracy.

> After 1700 ... a reasonable demand for luxuries was increasingly seen as a benefit rather than as a handicap to economic and social progress and craftsmen were encouraged to supply this limited market with the goods that it required. (p. 2)

An increasing class of individuals grew wealthy from commerce but, particularly in the United States, did not possess the titles and legitimacy of the aristocracy and needed to establish their place and status in another way.

Adam Smith, writing in 1759, was one of the first to analyze these motivational aspects of conspicuous consumption. Mason (1981) summarizes and comments on Adam Smith's analysis:

> Firstly, conspicuous consumption was a relatively recent (i.e. eighteenth century) phenomenon made necessary only by commercialisation of society and by the increasingly "sophisticated" economic and social system of the time. Secondly, conspicuous consumption was a necessary social phenomenon, ensuring the power of the oligarchy, which, in turn, became a source of social peace and continuity. Ostentatious consumption was therefore seen as not only proper in a stratified society, but indeed as functionally essential. Presumably the conspicuous behavior of the rich is seen as a reinforcement of existing class structures and privileges, and encourages a deference and a belief in the status quo amongst the less fortunate. Finally, Adam Smith saw the ostentatious display of the rich as a good thing, in that it gave incentives to the poor to work hard in the hope of emulating their masters (Mason, 1981, p. 3).

Thus it comes about, Veblen says, that products we purchase symbolize and also service. Veblen included much of what we might call the labor of beautification in his category of "wasted labor," because he felt that standards of beauty were subject to the whim of fashion, and were rarely an innate property of the object. Thus beautification for him often became a rationalization, actually contributing most to the creation of value. Part of the value was what he called the "honorific" element, or the object's symbolic value as an indicator of status. Veblen believed that even articles purchased ostensibly for taste or beauty and even for their utility may contain strong elements of economic display. As Mason so concisely expresses it:

> They were really purchased in order that others will recognize the considerable cost of the product, and will consequently come to admire the individual's ability to find the money to purchase it. The ownership and display of diamonds serves as a good illustration; no matter how outstanding the stones are seen to be, the owner's actual utility in possession may well derive for the greater part from audience reaction to the very high price which must have been paid to obtain them. In cases of this type, taste and cost come to be interrelated and expensiveness comes to be accepted as a tasteful feature of the articles in question, being a mark of 'honorific costliness.' (Mason, 1981, p. 11)

Bourne (1957) called attention to two factors that influence the use of products in the service of conspicuous consumption. The first is whether the product is a luxury or a necessity, and the second is whether it is consumed (that is, used) publicly or privately. Clearly, publicly consumed luxuries are most suited to this function. The aptness of

Mason's particular reference to diamonds in this regard is nicely illustrated by the 1957 cover of *Life* Magazine which shows a close-up of Elizabeth Taylor holding her infant daughter. The actress's left hand is the closest thing to the camera, and its dominant feature is a huge diamond ring that competes with the child for your attention. Clearly a luxury and clearly publicly displayed.

Taking Veblen out of the context of his own work destroys the satire that accompanies his statements, so that he seems more cynical than he is. The appeal, of course, is that he comes so close to the mark. His writing sounds so timely, it is hard to imagine that he anticipated designer jeans by more than a half century. The difficulty with his theory is that he does not offer any way of predicting when status values will dominate over utility. In general, he says they always do, and that is perhaps a bit simplistic.

There is a general tendency in our culture, as Veblen so early noted, to judge people by their possessions. Perhaps it is a by-product of capitalism, but Belk, Bahn, and Mayer (1982) have called this tendency "one of the strongest and most culturally universal phenomena inspired by consumer behavior." (p. 4) Their study looked at the ability of children to recognize the symbolic meanings attached to the owners of different houses and automobiles. They found that the development of this recognition of consumption symbolism is minimal in the preschool years, but emerges before the second grade and is well developed by the sixth grade. A later study suggested that experience with products was a stronger influence in this development than cognitive development or mass media exposure (Belk, Mayer, & Driscoll, 1984).

Recently, Richins (1994) compared high and low materialism in consumers by asking two groups differentiated in this way [using a scale developed earlier (Richins & Dawson, 1992)] what were their most valuable possessions. Her finding supports the social stereotype and shows the link between personal values and consumption. She found that highly materialistic consumers valued most those possessions that are more socially visible and generally named as most valuable things worth $5000 or more. They were more likely than the other group to choose assets (things valued for their worth), transportation, and appearance-related possessions. Less materialistic consumers, on the other hand, listed more privately used, recreational, and less expensive items worth $1000 or less. The possessions they named involved more symbolic and interpersonal associations. The finding was that materialistic consumers were generally less happy with their lives than others. The author notes that this group does not seem to "cultivate pleasurable meanings and experiences." (p. 531) Possessions signaled accomplishments rather than being valued for the pleasure associated with their use. Interestingly, she also found twice as many people 65 or older in the low materialistic group. This suggests that people become more comfortable with their identities in their older years, which in turn implies that identity is an ongoing pursuit and also that eventually most of us come to terms with it.

Manipulated Meanings

By focusing on the cultural meanings of products rather than on their conventional uses and functions, the consumer process is cast in a whole new light. McCracken was one of the first to write of consumption as the process by which meanings are manipulated and moved around in our society. To make this process clear, we will consider three steps in turn that McCracken finds are particularly important: a first step in which meanings are attached to objects; a second step in which the objects transfer their meaning to their owners; and a third step in which the meaning changes as a consequence of these transfers.

Transfer of Meaning to Goods. The transfer of meaning into goods occurs mainly through advertising and fashion. The process transfers both the naturally occurring meanings from the environment and new contrived meanings from designers and advertisers.

Let us take an example from advertising. In New England, the term "colonial" is attached to all manner of styles from furniture to architecture. Under this rubric you can see everything from authentic early New England antiques to cutesy craft items that are clearly twentieth century mass produced. Why are they all called "colonial?" The reason is a matter of cultural meaning.

A major part of New England's cultural identity is derived from the images of the Pilgrims, the Mayflower, and the historical period before the revolution, when the area was an English colony. This period is emphasized in school. Children make pictures of Pilgrims at Thanksgiving and take school trips to the replicas of the Mayflower and Providence Plantations. Thus, New Englanders value their history and heritage, and because they live where so much of it happened, they feel closer to it than people elsewhere. Californians, for instance, feel more connected to the gold rush and the westward movement.

People want symbols of their cultural history to feel that they belong. It is a way of feeling more at home, a way of putting down roots, perhaps of claiming territory. Thus New Englanders are more oriented to the past, whereas New Yorkers, in spite of an equally rich colonial past, have been shaped by the hugeness of their city to take a more urbane track and value style and the latest fashions more. A pottery dealer once told me that business for new handmade pottery was much better south of New York, because north of New York in New England, people want antiques, rather than new things. Likewise, the term "colonial" is valued because of its association with all the qualities New Englanders like in antiques. The word gives some of that meaning to whatever it is attached.

History is always simplified and transformed in the telling to suit the values and ideals of the present culture. In the process it usually loses the harsh edge of reality. Thus "colonial" refers to the best parts of a simpler time, of friendliness, charm, and warmth, certainly not of hardship, adversity, and early death. Advertisers and marketers have picked up the term and apply it widely to add warmth and charm to their products. They may also advertise the product in a picture which includes a fire in a huge fireplace, a braided rug, soft light, and probably some people looking charming.

As we have seen, classical conditioning predicts that whatever product is put into such a setting absorbs some of that charm and attractiveness. Those products that share the most properties with the scene portrayed derive the most conditioned meaning. Lamps and furniture of a similar design pick up more meaning, for instance, than an electrical appliance, because they share more qualities of our concept of colonial. Thus by labeling products "colonial," we are actually invoking two mechanisms. First, we call attention to a common historical connection and assure that the products will be perceived as having this element of similarity, and second, we specifically associate with colonial products the warmth and charm that the word connotes. The point here is that effectiveness of the word "colonial" is a function of the culture of New England and could be expected to have less effectiveness in another culture, for example, in Florida or Southern California. Advertisers must know the cultural characteristics of their market to be most effective. They must give their products the meanings that are most sought after by the local culture.

As McCracken puts it:

> Advertising is a kind of conduit through which meaning is constantly poured in its movement from the culturally constituted world to consumer goods. Through advertising, old and new goods are constantly giving up old meanings and taking on new ones.... To this extent, advertising serves as a lexicon of current cultural meanings (McCracken, 1988, p. 79).

McCracken emphasizes that meanings are continually changing in spatial locations and also across time. The meaning of symbols shifts as

in logos, for example. The logo of a company expresses in a very condensed way a particular meaning that the company seeks for its image,
but it must use culturally relevant terms. If streamlining is seen as new
and up-to-date, then a logo that suggests streamlining is seen that way.
As discussed in chapter 3, even in simple logos we can see how the
design has shifted over the years and how this has subtly changed the
meaning conveyed. Logos are very sensitive to changing taste in design
and must be continually updated to continue to convey the message "we
are a leader" rather than "we are obsolete." On the other hand, too
frequent change destroys the purpose of a consistently recognizable
symbol.

Sometimes, people buy products because of who is using them or
who the endorser is, not because of the meaning attached to the product
directly. Members of the culture notice the adoptions of "opinion
leaders." They tend to follow their lead and adopt the same products.
These opinion leaders are people whom the culture holds in high esteem
because of achievement or celebrity status. When a celebrity uses a
product, some of the meaning of the celebrity transfers to the object. This
happens with endorsements as a part of the advertising transfer of
meaning, but it also happens spontaneously every time a celebrity uses
an identifiable product. With the advent of television, the visibility of
these opinion leaders has increased many fold, and their impact has
increased with it. The adoption of the celebrities' products or habits by a
large segment of the population can change the culture itself.

Transfer of Meaning from Goods to Consumer. After advertisement has put meaning into products, the use of those goods transfers that
meaning to the consumer. Jung relates that even primitive societies used
symbols to transfer power to themselves. This will be particularly true in
a consumer society like ours where the consumer has many alternative
products from which to choose. The role of choice is amplified, and as
discussed before, even the selection of a mundane product, such as
toothpaste, will involve selecting a product that expresses certain meanings, so that in using it the consumer comes to be associated with those
meanings. For example, one toothpaste advertiser may stress "fighting
cavities" or "dentists recommend," and a user of this brand will be seen
as someone aware of health issues. Another brand may stress the appearance of the toothpaste, as a mix of colors or a new taste, and its user is
seen as up with the latest trends and not afraid to try new ideas. Yet
another advertiser may stress that this is "the largest selling brand," and
its user knows people that will see them as normal in the mainstream,
not at all strange.

In other words, in selecting even toothpaste, consumers are made to feel that they are telling something about themselves. In recent years it has been chic to call this "making a statement." The consumers may not actually have the meaning consciously in mind at the time of the purchase, but the meaning is conveyed all the same, whether or not they intend it. These are really just toothpastes, and probably very little distinguishes one from another. But they have been given symbolic meaning by the advertisers, using culturally agreed upon values to do it. Unless significant portions of the culture values "being aware of health issues," or "being open to new ideas," and "being in the mainstream," the advertisers could not have used these as motivators. Toothpaste is a product that is not used publicly, but quite privately, and yet the meaning matters.

The principle is used in every type of product. For a more publicly displayed example, consider the tremendous popularity of designer jeans. These jeans are clearly not bought because they wear better than another brand. The whole point is in the brand label prominently displayed on the wearer's fanny. We see the wearers differently if their labels say Jordache compared to saying Levis. Why? When you compare the price of ordinary versus designer jeans, you can begin to see how much we are willing to pay for the added meanings that products have. In summary, what is happening here is that now the cultural meaning of the products, transferred to the object in step one, is transferred to the consumer.

Changes in Meaning.   A third step also exists in the transfer of meaning in which the meaning changes because of widespread adoption. Fashion, for example, starts with a few and spreads to the many, but the very process changes the meaning. What starts out as a unique and highly individual object quickly becomes pedestrian and common and must, of course, be abandoned by the person who originally chose it because it no longer carries the right message. The meaning of these particular clothes has changed from an upper-class, exclusive symbol to a lower-class, pedestrian symbol. Knowing that this will happen, the opinion leaders will have already moved to a new style. Thus, by its very adoption a fashion symbol changes its meaning. This is the reason that fashion exists in an individualistic society and why it must continually change.

Let us review the transfer of meaning process in fashion. In step one, the designers use symbols of the culture, a few of their own, and, aided by the journalist or advertiser, put meaning into clothes. The meaning might include very high price, one-of-a-kind, and avant garde style, which says that the wearer is rich, tasteful, and unique. In step two, the fashion leaders select from these clothes those that express the meanings they want to associate with themselves. Their ego/self forces are clearly major determinants of this selection, as we discussed in chapter 8. Thus, the celebrity buys the clothes, wears them (probably only once), but is seen by perhaps millions of people. At this point, the clothes have taken on the designer's meanings and now also pick up the meanings associated with the person who is seen wearing them. Then, they become desirable to viewers as a way of associating themselves with the meanings represented, such as affluent, stylish, socially aware, and generally "with it." Then, large numbers of people buy quickly produced copies of the clothes. Speed is essential because the meaning will soon change. Finally, in step three, the meaning changes from avant garde to commonplace because of the large numbers of people wearing the same style clothes. They are in style when purchased but soon go out of style.

Rituals of Transfer of Meaning

The process of transfer of meaning to the individual does not stop with the purchase. McCracken identifies four rituals which go on after the object is acquired. He calls them rituals because they are symbolic actions, culturally agreed upon, that communicate that the properties of an individual have changed. For example, we use rituals, such as bar mitzvah or first communion, to signify symbolically that the individual has discarded the properties of childhood and taken on the property of responsibility. Similarly, "In North America, ritual is used to transfer meaning from goods to individuals ... in four ways. There are exchange, possession, grooming, and divestment rituals." (McCracken, 1988, p. 84)

The **exchange ritual** is essentially the process of gift-giving. Gifts represent the givers and tell the recipients how they are perceived by the givers. The first culturally common element is value, that is, how much the recipient is valued by the giver. A cheap gift suggests that we are not worth much in the eyes of the giver. This is why gifts tend to be of higher quality than purchases made for oneself. Hallmark capitalized on this long ago with the slogan, "For those who care enough to send the very best." In wrestling with the guilt that the slogan engenders, we seem to accept unconsciously the premise that Hallmark actually does represent the "very best."

In addition to value, gifts reveal other elements of the way the recipient is perceived by the giver. For example, if I receive a wild necktie, it suggests that the sender sees me as a person who wears them. If I get a book, the sender must see me as a reader of books. According to McCracken, the giver is inviting the recipient to adopt the symbolic image the gift represents. Thus, gifts from parents often contain elements the parent wishes the child to absorb. Thus, it may not be that the givers do not know who we are or what we like, but rather that they want us to be different. The invitation is sometimes declined, and the item is stored away and never used, or simply discarded, occasionally with accompanying anxiety and guilt.

The question of why someone sent us an inappropriate gift may distract us for some time. Was it us or them? Just how we judge the appropriateness of gifts and the reasons for bad choices depends on several factors, which derive from attribution theory. First is probably the ego strength of the recipient. A threatened ego becomes defensive quickly, assuming that the error was intentional, and reveals itself as anger. It often smolders as resentment, particularly if it cannot be expressed. Second, the recipients's perception of the giver, expressed as expectancies, is important. The giver may be seen as tasteless, self-occupied, or selfish, so that a tasteless gift is not seen as unusual. Thus, we might conclude that the giver made a mistake (if the event is unusual) or is self-centered or insensitive (if it happens often). In the case of children, we will probably excuse it, because of their age, but question their parents' role in the choice. Unless directed, preschoolers often choose toys for adults that they themselves would like to receive, an illustration of their egocentricity or inability to see the world from another's point of view.

Finally, the relationship between the giver and recipient is crucial in determining appropriateness of gifts and even greeting cards. For example, a Christmas card with a printed signature may be seen as acceptable from someone you rarely see or from your company's president, but is generally unacceptable from a close friend, a co-worker, or even your immediate supervisor. In any case, receiving a printed signature says you are part of a large group and even valued less. But on the one hand, that may be accepted, whereas on the other, it is seen as insulting. Humor, too, is a tricky aspect. One person's humor is another's bad taste.

It is not surprising that because of the complex meaning it conveys, the process of choosing gifts involves considerable anxiety for many people. When we consider that a large proportion of annual sales occurs in the few weeks before Christmas/Hanukkah and represents a significant percentage of annual retail revenues, then the importance of gift-giving as a ritual becomes clear. Adding to this all the gifts for other occasions, such as birthdays, weddings, anniversaries, graduations, Mother's Day, Father's Day, and Valentine's Day, just for starters, and then adding the elaborate ritual of wrapping the gift and choosing the card that goes with it, we realize that gift buying is a major portion of consumer spending and deserves study as a separate phenomenon.

By **possession rituals**, McCracken refers to the process of individualizing objects to show that we see them as symbolic of ourselves. "Consumers spend a good deal of time cleaning, discussing, comparing, reflecting, showing off, and even photographing many of their new possessions." (p. 85) Some goods go with us wherever we travel, so that they are particularly important symbols. Clothes and cars are of this type. Notice that, even if you live in a poor neighborhood, you can leave its stigma behind when you go somewhere else, but your car and clothes go with you and must express your new identity, or you carry the image of being poor with you. Hence, transportables always have special importance for identity.

The new car owner, having purchased carefully, is likely to spend considerable time washing, polishing and buffing. A large market devoted to auto accessories allows us to make our particular car look different from all others. One could predict that they have particularly increased appeal to anyone for whom identity or self-esteem are central psychological issues. To young adolescents, particularly males, ownership of the first car symbolizes a major step toward adulthood. Pride in this advance reflects itself in unusually strong tendencies to polish and shine. To be effective, marketers must bear in mind why objects are being bought.

Clothes, too, must be accessorized. This is done with shoes, purses, hats, and with jewelry or scarves. Today the brand name on the item may also be a form of accessorizing, so that all the members of a group may buy the same brands and look down on what they perceive as lesser brands. The process makes a potentially common item unique and personal. In the case of our homes, though they do not go with us, they may be one of our most public possessions. Thus, we may spend many hours decorating and arranging inside and manicuring the lawn outside. The house in these cases clearly represents us and must therefore "make the right statement." Possession rituals are part of the process of preparing objects to be suitable symbols of ourselves.

Grooming rituals involve the same basic idea, but in this case the object is prepared for a particular event or occasion and is often ourselves. Preparing for an evening out, for example, involves clothing and accessory selection, bathing, hair styling, cosmetics, and perfumes. Many of the properties of the grooming products transfer to the consumer in the process. For example, knowing you look your best imparts extra confidence and enthusiasm. Much of this comes from the meanings of the products involved. All of the anxieties noted in earlier chapters come home at this point, and one hopes that the product will really do its thing. Thus, the products used in grooming reflect to the user the meanings put there by advertising. Grooming is often a way of dealing with our insecurities to allay them enough to allow social interaction.

When objects are transferred from one individual to another, **divestment rituals** take place so that the meaning will not become confused. One type involves erasing the meaning of a former owner, as when a house changes hands and the new owners clean and redecorate. A second type happens when one must throw out or give away an object that has become associated with us. Often this process involves emotional components, partly because the object may have come to feel a part of us. We may feel strange about someone wearing our old clothes, for example. "What looks like simple superstition is, in fact, an implicit acknowledgement of the movable quality of the meaning with which goods are invested." (McCracken, 1988, p. 87)

We have condensed McCracken's paper severely here and have not given the many supporting references with which it is supplied. The interested reader should consult the paper directly for a more complete representation of the process of transfer of meaning.

Cultural Changes from the Consumptive Process

All of this moving of meaning around might be expected to have an effect on the culture itself. We have seen how the meaning is continually changing, but the culture itself also undergoes change. The progression of design changes we considered previously has given our environment a different look than it had 70 years ago. The automobile has created a demand for wider, straighter roads and interstates totally removed from the commercial world. Acres and acres of land have been paved over for parking lots. Gasoline stations and dealerships abound. The mall, too, is derived from the advent of the automobile and with it the demise of main street. There is scarcely any part of our lives that does not express an impact of the automobile.

Technology, of course, is the force that permits many of these changes, but technology itself tends to be invisible. It is only when it allows a consumer product change that we feel its impact. For example, the Department of Defense has funded a tremendous amount of research into products and processes that might enhance the national defense, but many products have been "spin-offs" from that industry. The computer was developed during World War II and after by the Department of Defense. It has rapidly moved into the personal consumer product realm and created an almost instant industry that has whole stores springing up overnight to supply software and accessories.

Other changes that have come about in our culture are less obvious. Some of these are psychological. We introduced the notion of the empty self in chapter 8 and the basic unhappiness that a materialistic society fosters. It is essential that consumers feel unfulfilled in many ways so that they will buy the products to correct that feeling. It does not work, of course, because it is essentially an illusion, and it leads to endless consumption. But the effects go further than this because advertising and television teach us unconsciously about the values of society. Until the economists figure out how to separate them, the downside of materialism will continue to accompany the upside of economics. The chief vehicle for transmitting culture, however, is the family, not television. We turn to those dynamics now.

FAMILY DYNAMICS

The Socialization Process

The process "by which young people acquire skills, knowledge, and attitudes relevant to their functioning in the marketplace" was termed **consumer socialization** by Ward (1974). The dominant influence in this process is the mother (Ward, Wackman, & Wartella, 1977). In reviewing the socialization literature, Carlson and Grossbart (1988) found that "Mothers with alternative parental styles differ in communicating with children about consumption, number of consumer socialization goals, restricting and monitoring consumption and media exposure and views on advertising, but do not differ in granting consumption autonomy to children." (p. 77)

Although mothers are the major influence, the type of family and where the family is in the course of its existence are also important. In other words, does this family consist of a newly married couple, a young couple with children, a middle-aged couple, or an older couple whose children have left home? Families gradually change as they move through the life cycle, and considerable research has attempted to determine how consumption varies with our progress through this cycle. Of course, families can take a number of routes, for example, with or without marriage, with or without children, and with or without divorce (see Murphy & Staples, 1979). In general, not surprisingly, spending rises sharply with the transition from the single to the married state, continues to rise though at a slower rate, and declines when the children leave home (see Schaninger & Danko, 1993, and Wilkes, 1995). Today, many families consist of a single parent and any number of children. Children in these situations often find themselves making consumer choices that would be made by one of the parents in two-parent families.

Socioeconomic status level influences consumer learning in children. This was found by Ward, Wackman, and Wartella (1977). They write:

> In general, as social status increases, mothers become more active consumers in terms of using more sources of information and more kinds of information in making consumer decisions. Furthermore, interaction with the child about consumption increases as the mother's social status increases. On the other hand, lower-status parents appear to give their children more opportunities to operate as independent consumers by providing higher income levels and more power in making purchases.... [This] is consistent with a pattern of less frequent communication between low-status mothers and their children, particularly in specific product-request situations, and perhaps indicates less supervision of the children's consumer activities (p. 144).

Intergenerational Influences

Although dramatic changes are taking place in this area, American culture still tends to be based on the nuclear family, consisting of parents and children. Individuals in such societies tend to identify with outsiders, such as peers, more than with family. In contrast in societies based on extended families living together, family influences are much greater (Childers & Rao, 1992). These authors, for example, compared Thailand and the United States and found intergenerational influence higher for nearly all products in Thailand. Within the United States, however, demographic factors have surprisingly little influence on the extent of intergenerational agreement (Moore-Shay & Berchmans, 1996).

Childers and Rao (1992) found that intergenerational influence in the United States varies with the same dimensions as Bourne (1957) had found important in conspicuous consumption, namely, public versus private use and necessities versus luxuries. However, whereas Bourne understandably found the most conspicuous consumption for public luxuries, Childers & Rao found the greatest intergenerational influence for privately used necessities. They comment, "For products used at home the influence of parents on brand choice is marked, perhaps because of the limited opportunity to observe the brand preferences of peers." (p. 206) At the same time, however, one could point out that peers have less opportunity to see the brand being used in privately used products, so that peer influence is also reduced. In other words, if peers cannot observe what you are using, you will not be embarrassed by following parents. Olsen (1993) has pointed out that there may be a deeper level of respect or rebellion that is revealed when children accept or reject the brand choices of their parents. Moreover, one could also note in passing that commonly researchers operationally define intergenerational influence by whether the individual purchases the same brand as the parent. This means that alternative explanations may also be possible, such as the child is influencing the parent or that both are influenced equally by an outside agent. Such interpretations seem less likely in the usual context, but still possible.

Intergenerational influence is greatest for those products of a complex or confusing nature that one begins to need as the move into marriage occurs for the first time. Thus, Woodson, Childers, and Winn (1976) found that 62% of a sample of men in their 20s used the same auto insurance company that their fathers did. The proportion fell to 19% by age 50. These are products that the individual has little opportunity to learn about as a child, yet all of a sudden finds the need for. One might expect that other forms of insurance and probably investments and mortgages also fall in this category.

Child Influences on Parent

Children sometimes do influence parents and not just the other way around. Mangleburg (1990), after reviewing fourteen studies and summarizing their findings, reported that five variables are important in the child's influence. First, she writes that children have more influence on those products for which they are the primary consumer, such as cereals, snacks, toys, and their clothes and school supplies. To a lesser extent studies have also found children's influence in family leisure time activities, such as vacations, movie attendance, eating out, and TV cable subscriptions. Mangleburg points out that a child's personal involvement increases their influence, whereas any increase in financial risk tends to decrease their influence.

The second variable Mangleburg found is the stage in the decision process. A child's influence is greatest at the first, or problem recognition stage, and declines through the information search and decision stages. Thus, children have more influence on brand and color, but little influence in selecting price ranges. For example, young children usually express their influence as a desire for a product (i.e., cereal), often in the supermarket, and in most cases the parent agrees (Atkin, 1978).

The third variable, the characteristics of the parent, is important in determining how much influence a child will have. Generally, children have less influence on traditional and conservative mothers and on all mothers when the child's health or welfare is at stake. Fourth, not surprisingly, older children have more influence than younger children. Mothers of older children are more likely to negotiate with their children about purchases, whereas mothers of younger children are more likely to refuse their children's purchase requests but explain their reasons for doing so (Ward, Wackman, & Wartella, 1977). On the fifth point, however, the literature is apparently mixed, and that concerns the impact of socioeconomic factors on the child's influence. Certainly changes are taking place here. For example, the rise of single parent homes has led to earlier involvement of children with consumer decisions.

Husband and Wife Decisions

Generalizations are difficult to make in the realm of husband-wife decision making. Subcultural factors are important, for instance, how dominant the father is in day-to-day consumer decisions. For example, Webster (1994) found that in families strongly identified with their Hispanic roots, the role of the husband is greater than in other groups, particularly in relation to personal contacts with others outside the family. She also found that, as a family is assimilated into the more general American culture, there is apparently a steady linear movement away from male dominance.

A study by Woodside and Motes (1979) found that joint decision making was common even for items in which one or the other parent is dominant. The main variable determining which parent is likely to maintain control is the type of product. This was borne out by Webster (1994) who found that even in strong Hispanic identifiers, the wife's influence is stronger toward appliances, perhaps because she is the main user.

Persuasion, of course, is a common element in husband-wife decisions. Spiro (1983) found that 88% of couples reported encountering disagreements in purchasing and adopted strategies to cope. Spiro distinguished five groups of people based on the basic strategies that they used in persuasion: (1) low-level influencers (60%) were characterized by only infrequent attempts to influence partners, and their persuasion was done by presenting information to convince; (2) subtle influencers

(20%) added elements of reward or appeals to feelings of closeness; (3) emotional influencers (7%) added elements of emotional display, such as crying, anger, or the silent treatment; (4) combination influencers (10%) used a variety of persuasions equally, but with only moderate frequency; and (5) heavy influencers (3%) used all types frequently. It was likely that a given husband-wife pair both used the same strategy, but they were not aware of doing so. In fact, couples apparently do not agree on just how much influence each has in the relationship. Burns & Hopper (1986) found that both wife's and husband's educational levels and the wife's income and hours worked were important variables in whether they agreed on her influence in purchase decisions. Surprisingly, they also found that years married, husband's income, and their sex role orientation were not factors in their agreement.

When conflicts do arise, however, Moore-Shay and Berchmans (1996) found that discord over financial matters, such as may be triggered by a shortage of money, can have lasting consequences on the children. The children's outlook may reflect anxiety over the ability to control future events. They write, "When conflict about related money matters is evident in the home, children are more pessimistic about their future, more materialistic, and less likely to draw on their parents as consumer role models." (p. 488) Positive outlook, on the other hand, derives from parents who exhibit strong financial management skills.

CHAPTER 12

Developmental Factors

OUR PERSONAL HISTORY
OF AFFECT AND COGNITION

As we grow, we depend more and more on memory. These are not just memories of our education or personal histories, but memories also of everyday things that enable us to understand everything we encounter. For example, we know that without our visual memory, built up by endless visual encounters, our visual world would be simply a kaleido-scope of color and shapes without meaning. The adult is a product of this huge number of experiences, and somewhere we have filed away what things are and whether they are good, bad, or indifferent. What things mean and how we respond to them comes as much from our experience as from the thing itself. It is our past that gives things much of their meaning.

One of the meaning levels that things have is their affective value. As discussed previously, we tag things with their affective value the first time we meet them, so that for adults most things already have affective tags. Children are still encountering many things for the first time. What this means for the advertiser or marketer is that many adults have their minds already made up and become even more "set in their ways," the older they get. The problem of reaching older adults to have them try something new becomes more difficult with age, simply because there is relatively little that really is new.

We travel with an ever increasing store of affective tags that bias most things we encounter, and we are not always aware of the influence. Much of a therapist's work is trying to reveal the source of faulty affective tags that the client put there in childhood but continues to read uncon-sciously as an adult. The same situation must apply to the consumer world, but very little research has ever been done to uncover it. For example, I have always felt a fondness for Plymouth automobiles, though I have never owned one. The reason is that my grandfather drove one, the same one, for 18 years from the time that I was five. I became quite attached to that car, partly because I was also fond of my grandfather. The car and the brand name were affectively tagged as strongly positive early in my life and retain some of that affect to this day.

Then, why it is reasonable to ask, have I never owned a Plymouth? Two reasons come to mind. The first is that although when I was younger I bought used cars that just happened to come my way and today I am more likely to buy a new car based on consumer maintenance reports, neither situation has tended to favor this historical affect. A second, perhaps lesser reason, is that the Plymouths of today have very little connection to that Plymouth of old. They look entirely different. In fact they look like all the other brands, and even the logo has been changed so that it hardly resembles the old one. My affect is attached to a car that no longer exists. Indeed, perhaps Plymouth signifies an old man's car to me, and I certainly do not want to label myself an old man. Oldsmobile concluded that this was happening to a number of its potential buyers when they began using the slogan, "This is not your father's Oldsmobile." Those affective tags, placed there early in life, continue a long time.

Changing Needs

As we move through adulthood, it is obvious that our psychological needs keep changing with the years. Here we need only to stress the point that our sources of affect change along with our psychological needs. For example, when we seek a mate, we are particularly sensitive to appeals to our sexuality, to our appearance to the opposite (usually) sex. Once married for a few years, our interests are elsewhere. Of course, they can return again with death of a spouse or divorce or even a simple midlife crisis. Whenever a significant number of individuals that have the same life situation can be found, a marketing opportunity exists to appeal to their particular affective source.

Changing Values

Values also change. For instance, the sense of newness probably becomes less important in its own right. Adolescents, particularly, want things that are different from their parents to show their separation from them and to establish their independence. Hence, new things have a built-in appeal. As we get older, however, we no longer fight this battle. On the other hand, newness may take on other meanings, perhaps as a means of showing success and material wealth. A new car every year may be important to show the neighbors that we are successful. Eventually newness may become threatening as it signals a world that is no longer familiar and belongs to a younger generation.

INFORMATION PROCESSING IN CHILDREN

Cognitive Development

Much of the interest in the development of children as consumers has focused on their abilities to understand. For example, when do they learn to discriminate between programming and advertising on television, when do they learn that advertising intends to persuade and sell, and when do they learn that money can be saved for future gratification? After an exhaustive review, Ward, Wackman, and Wartella (1977) concluded that "consumer socialization is best understood in terms of children's developing abilities to select, evaluate, and use information relevant to purchasing. We call these abilities "information processing." (p. 19) Both Piagetian and information-processing models have been utilized in recent years, but it is important to understand that the models are not necessarily mutually exclusive. We will look at the major points of each.

The Piagetian Model. Piaget (1969) characterized four distinct stages of child development. Each stage is triggered by a spurt in brain growth and gives the child additional cognitive capacity that enables it to think in more complex ways. He called the first stage, from birth until about age two, the **sensory-motor stage**, and found that it is a time of learning about sensations and mastering basic motor skills. The second stage, from two until about seven (usually second grade), constitutes what Piaget called the **preoperational stage**. In this stage children focus on one dimension of a stimulus and categorize things on the basis of this one dimension. In judging size, for example, they go by the dimension of height, and ignore information about volume. Stage three in Piaget's theory, called the **concrete operational stage**, extends from about age seven to about age twelve (that is, from about grade two to grade six). Children in this stage begin to think in an organized, logical fashion but only with concrete, tangible information that they directly perceive.

Only when they reach the final stage, called the **formal operational stage**, at about age fifteen can they make inferences about things that are totally hypothetical. Concrete references are no longer needed, and they can think abstractly.

The Information-Processing Model. A model of cognitive development that differs somewhat from Piaget is known as the information-processing model. Proponents of this model cite evidence showing that children sometimes can do types of thinking that the Piagetian model would say they cannot do. Sometimes the discrepancy between the models is partly a function of how the cognitive capabilities are measured. For example, Macklin (1983) has shown that when nonverbal measures of their abilities are used, children show more advanced comprehension of commercials than Piagetian theory would predict, as we shall see in a moment.

Roedder (1981) succinctly outlined the difference between the Piagetian model and the information-processing model. Those who favor the information-processing approach have identified three types of processors: limited, cued, and strategic. They see differences based on the ability to transfer information from perception to long-term memory. Although their emphasis is shifted and the source of the differences among the groups is not seen as developmental so much as experiential, the ages of the groups are not unlike Piaget's preoperational, concrete operational, and formal operational stages. The youngest children (limited processors, age seven and under) "cannot use storage and retrieval strategies to enhance learning even when prompted to do so." (p. 145) The children age eight years to 12 (cued processors) can use these strategies but do so only when prompted. The older children (strategic processors, age 13 and older) spontaneously use the skills necessary to store and retrieve information. Proponents of information-processing theory maintain that when children are specifically taught strategies to help in retention, they can think at higher levels. Strategies that aid learning include verbal labeling at the time of presentation, organizational techniques, imagery, and rehearsal (John & Cole, 1986).

Role modeling and communication also play a major part in whether their cognitive abilities are ever actually applied or not. Parents influence the child's consumer behavior by providing role models, interacting with them, and allowing consumptive experiences (Ward, Wackman, & Wartella, 1977). Information-processing theorists maintain that these influences, and other environmental influences, play a larger role than Piaget suggested.

Consumer Aspects

Cognitive Centration. The preoperational child is likely to focus on just one dimension of a situation (called **centration**) and not include other aspects which would alter the meaning of that dimension (Piaget, 1969). Ward, Wackman, and Wartella (1977) call these "lower level" skills and point out that they are based on perceptual (what is in front of them) dominance and are characteristic of younger children. They sampled children from kindergarten, third grade, and sixth grade. They report that, " the youngest children are the most likely to describe just a single element in a commercial (e.g., "there was a man on a horse") or to recall several images but in random fashion. With increased age, children recall more features and relate these features in the proper sequence to represent the story told in the commercial." (p. 56) The focus of young children, in other words, is directed by the stimuli. Strong stimuli and affective stimuli get attention. The children focus on their immediate environment, and one implication is that they are particularly aware of in-store sources. Later they become able to override the stimuli to some extent and focus on essential information. They also become able to attend to a number of stimuli other than the central stimulus, and still get the central idea.

Collins (1970) investigated the extent of centration by using a close simulation of the real world TV situation and found that absorption of the essential content increases from age 8 to 14. Peripheral or incidental learning of other details increases to age 12 and then falls again. A concise explanation is offered by Raju and Lonial (1990):

> Linear increase in central learning shows that the ability to focus on essential information increased with age. The decrease in peripheral learning beyond a certain age suggests that older children are also better at rejecting nonessential information. Preadolescent children, therefore, take in a large amount of information without regard for its value, while older children tend to take in the information more selectively (p. 243).

Of course, such findings are not inconsistent with Piaget, though the information-processing approach focuses more on the importance of environmental factors in the way cognitive differences occur. It is not inconsistent with neurological data that finds that inhibiting sensory inputs in the interest of focusing attention is a function of the cortex of the brain, which continues to develop to the age of 20 or so.

Ward, Wackman, and Wartella (1977) found that a number of other consumer-related cognitive abilities develop gradually with age. Children add on to their skills rather than replacing them. Specifically, they found a movement with age to "higher level" skills that included "(1) the selection of performance attributes in considering a television purchase; (2) comparing brands on the basis of functional characteristics; (3) awareness of a variety of sources of information about new products; (4) awareness of brands; and (5) level of understanding of television advertising." (p. 77)

Affective Centration. Both cognitive development approaches downplay the role of affect in the consumer decision process, but as we discussed previously, the real world is dominated by affective appeals. For example, commercial presentations on television or store displays always show the particular item, often a toy, happily used by one or more other children. Thus, just how much cognitive weighing of choices a child does certainly depends strongly on its age. As their cognitive abilities grow, these abilities are brought to bear more often, but even adults often follow affect rather than cognition. Young children, however, are often disappointed and, I suspect, feel a bit betrayed, when they discover that the happy social group of the commercial does not come with the game.

The affective component of a stimulus, probably the first component to develop, is evolutionarily much older than cognition. In the preoperational child, perception and affect are not separated out into distinct systems (Solley, 1966). Thus, affect dominates perception, and preferences are controlled by simple immediate perceptual components. This means that if the preoperational child likes the look of something or likes the people using something, then it likes the object, no matter what other characteristics it may have. Rust put it this way:

> Children respond globally. They do not have a lot of separate response systems which they somehow try to integrate. They don't distinguish knowing from feeling from acting, or familiarity from liking from intention.... Take a look sometime at the correlations between familiarity and likability ratings over a selection of different products or characters. You will seldom find a coefficient less than 0.90. For most kids, most of the time, liking and knowing are part of the same global response.... They orient to the things they know, not their properties (Rust, 1986, p. 14).

Confirming this, Bahn (1986) found that preoperational children (ages 2-7) base their preferences for products on fewer attributes than concrete operational children and are less consistent in their preferences. What looks like a global response, however, may be a response to a single dominant, affect-laden, feature. In other words, the affect of a single salient feature becomes the affect attached to the whole commercial. Because young children perceive few features, they end up with a single (global) affective response.

All of this means that preoperational children are particularly vulnerable to affect laden advertisements. Later, in the formal operational stage, more subtle cues and perceptual discriminations also trigger affect arousal, and the child eventually can say, "Yes, it looks fun in the ad, but when you get it home it won't be," or "The package is neat, but the stuff is awful." But the preoperational child cannot separate them out.

Reality. When my son was about four, he turned away from the television set and asked, "Is this real?" He wanted a yes or no answer. I cannot remember what I responded, but I began to think about the levels of reality in a television program, and I was not surprised that he was unsure. Story programs vary in time, character, and plot, and each dimension has many levels of reality. For instance, the program can be live (that is, happening now); it can be a tape of something that happened earlier; it can be a reenactment of something that happened earlier or something someone thinks happened earlier, or "based on" something that happened, but has been altered; it can be an enactment of something that never happened, but could have happened, or something that never could have happened. In addition, the characters can also have many levels. The story may be true, but the characters are fictitious. Their dialogue is almost surely made up, but the content may be more or less accurate. They may be cartoon characters, whereas the story is more or less true.

The levels and possibilities go on and on, yet the four-year-old wants a yes or no answer. I remember one three-year-old who tried to peek in the back of the TV set looking for the characters on the screen. Another response I have never forgotten, though unfortunately I cannot remember the source, was from a child who was asked if the Sesame character "Big Bird" was real. Sounding fairly sophisticated, she replied that he was not, but then she added, "It is actually a smaller bird inside."

Raju and Lonial (1990) reviewed a number of studies on children's comprehension of the differences among the characters used in commercials. Not surprisingly, there is a gradual increase in understanding of reality as a function of age. They concluded

> Prospects for confusion on the reality/nonreality dimension are greater for very young children, i.e., those under five years of age.... Findings relating to the use of human versus other characters appear to be equivocal. Very young children under five years may not be able to tell the difference between human, cartoon, and puppet characters. However, children of kindergarten

age appear to have some ability to distinguish between these characters. Verbal ability and a true understanding of animation and the mechanics of TV do not seem to manifest until the fourth grade level (pp. 245–246).

Understanding. The level of reality may shift completely when the commercial comes on, because commercials can also represent multiple levels of reality. Would it be surprising if children were sometimes confused about the reality of the commercial message? Early studies, such as those reviewed by Roedder (1981), led to the conclusion that preoperational children have difficulty understanding the purpose of television commercials and thus are particularly vulnerable to them. The Federal Trade Commission "seriously considered stringent regulations of advertising directed to children under the age of eight." (Macklin, 1987, p. 229) Macklin, however, felt that the earlier results were produced by an overdependence on the Piagetian model which asks preschoolers to articulate their understanding verbally. By using nonverbal methods, she found that by age five, well before age eight, 20–40% understood that a commercial wants you to go to the store and buy the product. Her findings confirm others that although some preschoolers may know the intent of commercials, most do not. But because as many as 40% may understand, Piaget's stage theory is called into question. Even if Piaget's ages are considered means, for 40% to reach a level by age five would require an unreasonably high standard deviation, based on a mean of age eight for that level. In fact, more advanced children begin to understand commercial intent at about age five, and most seem to understand the selling intent by age eight (Brucks, Armstrong, & Goldberg, 1988).

On the other hand, Roberts (1982) pointed out that full comprehension of the intent in commercials requires more than simply knowing that they want you to buy something. It includes an understanding of four additional attributes:

1. that the advertiser and viewer have different perspectives and interests;
2. that the advertiser intends to persuade;
3. that all persuasive messages are, by definition, biased; and
4. that biased messages demand different interpretative strategies than primarily informational, educational, entertainment messages (p. 27).

It seems that preoperational children have not reached understanding on all of these points. For example, one study in which mothers observed their children showed that kindergarten children did not shift their attention away from the program much when a commercial came on, whereas both third and sixth graders showed about a 20% drop in attention to the commercial (Ward, Levinson, & Wackman, 1972). Thus, although preschoolers may be capable of distinguishing the intent of commercials, when specifically asked, in fact they do not pay less attention to them. Note how here attention is being used to measure understanding.

Brand consciousness follows the same course. The average number of brands identified for three types of well-advertised products (gum, gasoline, and soft drinks) was only 0.8 for the preoperationals but rose to 2.4 and 3.3 for two older groups (Ward, Wackman, & Wartella, 1977). As a result of the changing look of families to more single parent families and families with two working parents, a new class of consumer, the latchkey kid, has developed. These children perform more adult roles, such as housework, preparing meals, and doing laundry. In the process they use appliances and products and are more influential in buying, therefore recognizing brands, and forming loyalties earlier. Because their brand loyalties persist for so many years, they are being recognized as a particularly worthwhile advertising market.

Use of Defenses.   In the case of older children, one of the leaders of research on marketing to children, Langbourne Rust (1986), says,"The problem is that there is no assurance that older kids will use more advanced thinking than younger ones. We only know that they can." (p. 14) This analysis echoes the information-processing notion that proper cuing is necessary to evoke cognitive abilities. Supporting this view, one study showed that, in spite of skepticism of commercials, children do not actually use the defenses at their disposal against them (Brucks, Armstrong, & Goldberg, 1988).

Such defenses can be either counterarguments or source derogations (Wright, 1973). Although counterarguments are the most used adult defense, preoperational children do not have the knowledge of products or relevant dimensions to use this defense effectively and find source derogation the only option. Concrete operational children, on the other hand, may have the necessary information for counterarguments, but do not spontaneously use it, unless reminded or cued ahead of time. When cued, however, they do counterargue against commercials. Only the formal operational children can fully marshal counterarguments without cuing while they are actually watching television (Brucks et al., 1988). This means that even eight to twelve year olds are more vulnerable than adults to advertising.

Logic. According to Piagetian theory, logical appeals should be effective only with formal operational children. Logical appeals are what Rust calls "propositions." They state an "if ... then" relationship. "If children get the product, then they will get something else they want: social status, energy, a premium, or whatever." (Rust, 1986, p. 15) Rust points out that this is the kind of advertising that children have the hardest time understanding, and it is also the least effective with them. He says:

> The only effective propositional commercials I have seen for children under the age of 12 or so are premium commercials, where the promise is for something concrete and immediate.... the child most vulnerable to the false proposition is probably the 12 to 14 year old who has just learned to organize parts of life propositionally, and who isn't very good at it yet (Rust, 1986, p. 15).

Drawing Inferences. Macklin (1994b) found that by the time children are seven to eight they can use partial pictures to assist memory, but before that they need the whole picture. This suggests that the constructive abilities of perception arise at about the same time as the concrete operational stage of Piaget. Again this finding suggests that the method of measurement may play a role in the finding. If children in fact do not get their constructive perceptual skills until age seven, then below this age they should show considerable confusion in understanding their visual world. However, they show no evidence of this confusion. It may be that some types of construction arise earlier than other types. The question is clearly a research opportunity.

Belk, Bahn, and Mayer (1982) looked at a different inference, the meaning of products, and the inferences that could be drawn from someone's use of a particular product. Their evidence, gathered from fourth and sixth graders, well along in Piaget's concrete operational stage, supports the development of this inferential ability with age, but, in line with the information-processing approach, suggests that, once into the stage, it is more a function of experience than of cognitive development, as Piagetian theory maintains. Thus, sixth graders, asked to rate a person who owned a product (like a ten-speed bicycle) on the ten qualities of grade, popularity, friendliness, sex, innovativeness, happiness, admirability, wealth, intelligence, and attractiveness, showed stronger stereotypic biases for owners of objects they themselves owned than for owners of other objects. In other words, their own ownership of objects was an important factor along with age. Children of higher social class also make more inferences than children of lower social class on the basis of objects owned.

As a final factor, these researchers found that females hold stronger stereotypes than males for all products on all dimensions, but, contrary to their expectations, females are not more sensitive to clothing cues than to other product categories at either grade level. Although this study does not rule out Piagetian cognitive stages, at least three factors besides cognitive development (product ownership, social class, and gender) strongly influence a child's ability to infer properties about the owners of particular products. In other words, it begins to look as though the Piagetian stage allows the ability, but it takes some experience to develop it.

INFORMATION PROCESSING IN OLDER ADULTS

Cognitive Age Versus Chronological Age

The literature shows that adult processing of information is considerably more variable than children's. The reason is that once the system is in place, it is more a matter of experience and education as to whether the cognitive potential is actually used. The older we are, the more variety can be seen in our personal experiences, and these ultimately create tremendous individual differences, for example, in our cognitive age.

Stephens (1991) provides a good review of the extensive literature on **cognitive age**. She defines it as "the age one perceives one's self to be" and finds the concept as far back as Blau (1956). Milliman and Erffmeyer (1990) report that "when members of this segment are asked how old they think they would be if they did not know their age, about three-quarters of them give an answer that is 75 percent to 80 percent of their chronological age." (p. 31) Although it apparently can apply to any age, clearly it particularly refers to those over 55. Stephens writes:

> Despite advice on how to use the cognitive age concept to gain advertising advantage, only Barak and Gould (1985) have linked cognitive age with variables directly relevant to marketing or advertising. These researchers administered several psychographic scales (based on Wells, 1975) and found that older people who were cognitively young were less likely to be price sensitive, traditional, old-fashioned and a homebody and were more likely to have high morale and self-confidence. In terms of behavior, cognitively young seniors were more likely to dine out frequently and to spend more time watching television and reading books. Cognitive age was unrelated to radio, newspaper, or magazine use (p. 39).

Stephens' own research generally confirmed these data and found young-feeling seniors more likely to own automobiles or vacation homes. She also found "cognitively old senior citizens prefer to wait for others to try new things." (p. 46) She found the average difference between how people felt they looked and their chronological age was 10 years, whereas the difference between their interests and chronological age was 15 years. However, Stephens cautions that

> ... one problem with using cognitive age, by itself, to explain consumers' attitudes and behaviors toward shopping is that its correlations with consumption behaviors and attitudes were rather low and, therefore, explain a low proportion of the variance. Education or income, both of which were linked to cognitive age, might also explain the findings.... People who felt young tended to have significantly higher income. Therefore the willingness of these cognitively young adults to try new things may be a function of feeling less financial risk. Similarly, the cautiousness expressed by cognitively older adults may be due to their more precarious financial situations than to cognitive age (p. 46).

PROCESSING DEFICITS

Sensory Processes

Vision. Kosnik, Winslow, Kline, Rasinski, and Sekuler (1988) surveyed adults from age 18 to 100 and found, consistent with the literature, that older adults reported more difficulty performing a variety of everyday visual activities compared to their younger counterparts. They took longer to carry out visual tasks and had more trouble with glare, dim illumination, and near visual tasks. They had more trouble tracking moving targets and extracting information from those targets, and they had more difficulty locating a target in a cluttered visual scene. These deficiencies affected reading small print, reading signs on moving vehicles, locating signs, and reading signs. They suggest that although Hakkinen (1984) found that most independent elderly persons cope relatively well with even considerably reduced visual acuity, when interest remains high in activities that require good visual acuity, their coping may involve some psychological costs. Their study suggests that slower nervous system processing may be interacting with vision problems to make movement hard to follow.

Other Senses. Stevens (1992) found that the sensitivity of the finger surfaces declines markedly after age 60, but that tremendous variability is evident. This ability would affect particularly the appreciation of texture and qualities of fabric. He concluded that the loss was probably due to a deterioration of the skin receptors, rather than a function of the central nervous system. He also reports that "changes of sensitivity to tastes and smells typically emerge strongly somewhere in the middle years." Food and perfume appreciation would clearly suffer from this particular loss.

Fluid Intelligence

A number of studies have demonstrated differences in the abilities of younger and older adults. For example, John and Cole (1986) cite 21 sources and conclude that "age differences are most likely due to difficulties in acquiring and using new information." (p. 301) They note that this is the part of intelligence called fluid intelligence and find that it declines with age. On the other hand, the other part, crystallized intelligence, that consists of general information, vocabulary, comprehension, arithmetic, and reasoning with familiar material, "... represents an individual's knowledge base [that] remains intact [with age]." (p. 301) Just where in acquiring new information the difficulty lies is not as clear. Their short-term memory capacity shows only modest decline, if any (John & Cole, 1986). Rather, it seems that the elderly do not spontaneously carry processing to a high enough level when they encounter information, but just why is open to discussion. In reviewing the literature, Cole and Houston (1987) found four potential factors in studies which show deficits in the elderly group relative to younger adults at the encoding or storage level of processing, and we will use their framework to expand on these four possibilities and some others.

Measurement Questions. The first factor, expressed by Baltes, Reese, and Lipsitt (1980) is that they can process at higher levels but do not. This, they suggest, could be occurring at the measurement level, because of the school-like nature of many of the tests used to measure the abilities of the older group. The elderly are much farther removed than younger adults from school settings. However, the research of Cole and Houston (1987) did not support this interpretation. They say that although it may be a factor at times, it does not explain the deficits found.

Another measurement problem may be the discrepancy between potential and actuality suggested by Rust relative to children that we introduced previously. Theoretically, nearly everyone should be operating at the formal operational level in their adult years, but this does not always appear to be the case. Tests of various ages measure what we are capable of but not what we actually do day-to-day. For example, many people can read, but prefer to watch television. Thus, although adults can think formally, they may also choose not to do so. Rather, as we have seen in chapter 4, they often prefer to use heuristics instead. John and

Cole (1986) report a number of studies that show the elderly do not use rehearsal, organizational strategies, or retrieval strategies unless instructed to do so. Compounding the measurement problems, they also point out that results vary depending on whether recognition, cued recall, or recall is used as a measure.

Cognitive Speed.   The second factor, represented by Eysenck (1974) and others, is that they simply cannot process deeply, perhaps because of a slowdown in the central nervous system. This view is borne out by Cole and Houston's research and by a considerable literature as well [e.g., John & Cole (1986) cite twelve supporting references]. Johnson and Cobb-Walgren (1994) found a -0.613 correlation between age and cognitive speed after removing gender and educational effects. Further, they found that slower cognitive speed adversely affected advertising recognition and recall responses in both cluttered and uncluttered conditions.

Supporting the notion of a slowdown with age, Phillips and Sternthal report that many of the age differences in learning are reduced or eliminated when pacing is taken into account. When allowed to self-pace material or when the stimuli are slowed in presentation, the elderly are similar to younger adults. The slowdown does not happen at the same age for everyone, and Johnson and Cobb-Walgren (1994) argue that cognitive speed is a better measure of functioning than chronological age: "measures of functional age indicate changes in human functioning and, thus, represent causes of behavior. Chronological age merely acts as a proxy for functional variables." (p. 59)

The increasingly cluttered medium of television should be expected to have a severe impact on commercial absorption by elder viewers. Ads are getting shorter and more frequent. Johnson and Cobb-Walgren (1994) found that this increased clutter did not adversely affect the medium-speed cognitive processors but, oddly, did impact the fast ones and most of all the slower ones. They suggest that faster processors may be responding to the clutter by being more selective in what they watch, cutting down their overall score. Schreiber and Boyd (1980) found that 63% of their sample of elderly saw commercials as "often" or "always" confusing, and "both men and women over 70 were more confused by the difference between commercials and programs than the younger members of the sample." (p. 66) Thus, self-paced media (such as newspapers, and magazines) should be preferred and be more effective than externally paced ones (such as television commercials), and we shall see in a moment that this indeed happens.

Attention Deficit Hypothesis.   Phillips and Sternthal (1977) point out that the elderly are more distractible, which compounds their speed problems. On the other hand, if the elderly have had experience with the issue, they show more efficiency in learning, which compensates to some extent for the loss of speed. The amount of this compensation varies with the extent of social and intellectual resources. There is considerable evidence that our ability to pay attention to stimuli decreases considerably with age, an effect sometimes called the **attention deficit hypothesis**. For example, Rabbitt (1965) found that introducing irrelevant stimuli produces a much greater decrement in the performance of older subjects than in the performance of younger subjects and suggesting that much of the difference is attributable to an attention factor. There is also evidence of a slowdown in the central nervous system that may be contributing to all or most of this effect. If I am still processing stimulus A when stimulus B arrives, I will fail to pay attention properly to B. Although the cause is still not clear, however, the bottom line is a decrease in attention. Phillips and Sternthal (1977) report in their review that an increase in distractibility begins at about age 45. The implications for advertisers, of course, is that commercials must be simpler and slower for older consumers.

Children's attention levels have been measured for commercials. Across the four commercial categories in one study, when compared to the programming, preoperationals (5- to 6-year-olds) and concrete operationals (7- to 9-year-olds) showed similar attention levels to commercials (49% and 47% respectively), whereas the attention of the formal operationals to commercials (12 and older) had dropped to 32% (Ward & Wackman, 1973). This does not mean that the younger groups are processing the commercial message. They are probably paying more attention to the vehicle than to the message, much as infants often pay more attention to the wrapping than to the present.

The kinds of commercials that get their attention also differs across the groups. For the 5- to 6-year-olds toys and games get 70% of their full attention, but attention to toys of the 7- to 9-year-olds falls to 50%. By age 12, attention to toys and games has fallen even further to about 42%. Commercials for personal products, on the other hand, show highest attention (about 57%) for the 7- to 9-year-old group but, surprisingly, only about 2% for the 12 and older group (Ward & Wackman, 1973).

Confusion with age is apparent in other ways. Morrell, Park, and Poon (1990) compared forms of prescription labels, asking younger (18–22) and older (59–85) adults to learn standard information that would appear on the labels of prescription bottles. The younger did better, but the surprising finding was that the older subjects did not benefit from new arrangements that included pictures and icons along with the words. Although the pictorial representation was meant to aid in retention, it apparently confused them because it was seen as more complicated. This study also lends support to the attention deficit hypothesis and suggests that factors other than speed are involved, such as general decline in mental energy much as physical energy declines (Schulz & Ewen, 1993). Still, it is not yet clear whether attention deficits cause cognitive slowdown or cognitive slowdown causes attention deficits, or whether they both result from a loss of mental energy.

Cognitive Organization.   A third factor in **information-processing deficits**, introduced by Craik (1977), is that information is not organized efficiently by the elderly at the time of storage, so it is much harder to retrieve. The elderly, particularly, do not encode distinctively by focusing on unique features of stimuli when encoding. Again, Cole and Houston's (1987) research bears this out. Phillips and Sternthal (1977) suggest this is true only for new information, and that the opposite may be true for material with which they are experienced. The point may be overemphasized because tests used to measure learning are often formats unfamiliar to the elderly. However, these points are not really opposed, for old material would have been organized already when it was stored. New material would require the most organization, and John and Cole (1986) report that "stimulus materials with the most potential for organization produce the greatest differences between young and elderly adults." (p. 301)

Retrieval Cues.   A fourth factor from Lynch and Srull (1982), only slightly different from the third, is that the elderly are less able to self-generate retrieval cues, making retrieval harder for them. This deficiency stems from the same inability to focus on the uniqueness of a stimulus and from a slower speed of cognitive processing. For instance, one of the deficits seen earliest in the aging process is the longer time taken to recall words or names. This slowdown makes words less available at the time of deep processing and leads to fewer semantic connections, in turn, leading to retrieval problems later. Also, slower speed reduces elaboration and rehearsal time (see Wingfield, 1980). Retrieval cues, of course, are particularly important with new material because older material already has some cues supplied from the past.

In general, most studies confirm the information-processing deficits of the elderly. Fewer processing strategies and slower speed also mean that the amount of information, or information load, is a particular problem for the elderly (John & Cole, 1986). Cole and Houston (1987) recommend the use of sensory cues (focused on appearance, such as point-of-purchase) rather than semantic cues (focused on content of the material) for marketers attempting brand recognition with this group. Consistent with this, Mason and Bearden (1978a,b) confirmed that elderly shoppers rely more on physical search, rather than memory, to remind themselves of items needed.

Use of Information Sources

After an extensive review, Phillips and Sternthal (1977) reported two changes with aging that affect exposure to information. First is a shrinkage of the social world, induced by a reduced number and variety of roles one plays because of retirement, loss of spouse, and lessening of contact with children and formal organizations. Second is a common increase in narcissism, a reduction in involvement with others, and a decline in physical energy and abilities. The consequence of these changes is a substitution of television and reading for social contacts, and a marked increase in exposure to television and newspapers after age 60.

However, these authors also report that the elderly are far from isolated, and have frequent contacts with family members. Thus, family is also an important information source for the elderly. They often develop a circle of friends of a similar age because they often live in housing that is over half occupied by older adults.

Shift to Informal Sources.   Sources of information about products fall into two classes: formal and informal. Klippel and Sweeney (1974) provided the distinction: formal includes newspapers, television, and radio advertisements, whereas informal includes friends, neighbors, family, and retail sales representatives. In other words, one-to-one people sources are considered informal. These authors found that over-55s depend on informal sources more than formal. They recommend the use of sampling and in-store demonstrations to reach this group.

Rotter (1954) devised a test to distinguish between "internals," who feel that they have control over their world, and "externals," who feel that their efforts are controlled by fate, chance, or other persons with power. Klippel and Sweeney (1974) noted a difference between aged "internals" and "externals." The latter group places more reliance than the former ·on informal information sources. They also noted that Kleemeier (1963) found that the aged tend to become more "external" with the passage of time, more socially disengaged, and depend more on the word of others. Burnett (1991) confirmed this and found that the affluent elderly (probably more internal than the less affluent) " neither like advertising nor utilize it. In fact, the elderly, both affluent and moderate, tend to exhibit a rather negative attitude toward advertising." (p. 39) The cognitively old are apparently particularly hard to reach, and when they do depend on the media, "They apparently do not seek information for its own sake and probably stick to media vehicles that are known and familiar to them." (Stephens, 1991, p. 46) Thus, Bearden and Mason (1979) found that the elderly lag far behind the national average in the use of the relatively new information sources of open-code dating, nutritional labeling, and unit pricing.

Shift to TV and Newspapers. Schreiber and Boyd (1980) found that "the 'young elderly' (60–70 years of age) were more likely to choose television as the most influential advertising medium than were the older respondents." (p. 67) This may reflect changing interest in product categories as one ages. Elders perhaps are less interested in the categories typically advertised on television. For example, they questioned a representative sample of elderly living in apartment buildings and found that food shopping was their prime consumer concern. Because of this, the authors felt that the presence of coupons in the newspapers might explain why overall 65% reported that newspapers were the most influential in their buying decisions, whereas television was reported by only 22%. The same finding was reported by Gilly and Zeithamal (1985).

Schreiber and Boyd also report a "cut-off point" at age 70 (the study was in 1980, remember) that they believe reflects the time that television was introduced on the market. These people would have been in their 40s when television first appeared. Thus, the age differences they found may reflect experience with television and may not remain constant now for elders. In other words, the result is a cohort effect, rather than an age effect. Similarly, elders today are not likely to rely heavily on the Internet for information. But elders in the future, who knows?

Educational and Affluence Factors. Educational level was a factor in the choice of the most influential advertising medium. Magazines increased as the mentioned source as education increased, and television declined. Men who had at least a high school education watched television mostly between 6 and 8 P.M., perhaps because that is when the evening news was on. Most males who had less than a high school education watched from anywhere from 8 to 12 P.M. "The more educated women also tend to tune in earlier than the less educated women, but a significantly greater number of women than men watch TV all through the evening, regardless of educational level." (p. 65)

The level of education is likely to be highly correlated with income level, so that the two variables are hard to separate. Burnett (1991) found differences very similar to those of education when he looked for differences related to income level. Males who have incomes of more than $30,000 are more likely to read the news, business, travel, and magazine sections of the newspaper than their poorer age mates. Affluent females, on the other hand, are more likely to read the food and lifestyle sections in addition to the news and travel, whereas the less affluent female will read the advertising supplement more. The affluent read news, business, and money, and entertainment magazines, whereas the less affluent read mostly the entertainment magazines. Somewhat surprisingly, television viewing differences among Burnett's groups were "minimal."

Psychological Factor. Davis and French (1989) found a similar variability in the use of information sources and confirmed that the elderly are not a homogeneous group. They identified three types of women (the engaged, autonomous, and receptive), age 60 and over, who differed considerably in their psychographic profiles. The first group, which they called the "engaged" segment, comprised about 25% of their sample. They expressed fairly traditional values and relied heavily on the opinions of others, and on other information sources. They showed a high need to reconfirm self-esteem, a factor that is consistent with their interest in the opinions of others. It is also consistent with their high need for security and their low innovativeness. The second group, called "autonomous," comprised the largest group, some 41%. They did not seek out the advice of friends nor rely on external information sources. They, too, showed a high concern about self-esteem, but did not appear to trust others and so relied heavily on their own personal experience. The third group, labeled "receptive," comprised 34%. They did not feel that advertising insulted their intelligence as the first two groups did, probably reflecting a higher sense of self-esteem and a less threatened outlook overall. Thus, this group was more likely to rely on advertising and not seek friends' advice. This group had the most positive outlook of the groups, again reflecting higher self-esteem, a subject we discussed in chapter 8.

The lowest users of mass information sources were the autonomous group, which made only moderate usage of newspapers and low use of television, generally. The engaged group was particularly high in news usage, both from newspapers and from television, whereas the receptive group was moderate in newspaper usage, but high in the use of television comedies (Davis & French, 1989).

References

Abelson, R. & Miller, J. (1967). Negative persuasion via personal insult. *Journal of Experimental Social Psychology, 3*, 321–333.

A child's primer. (1989, October). *Consumer Reports*, p. 671.

Ad nausea. (1997, September). *Nutrition Action Health Letter, 24*(7), p. 3.

Alesandrini, K. L. (1982). Strategies that influence memory for advertising communications. In R. J. Harris (Ed.). *Information Processing Research in Advertising* (pp. 65–81). Hillsdale, NJ: Erlbaum.

Alpert, J. I., & Alpert, M. I. (1990). Music influences on mood and purchase intentions. *Psychology and Marketing, 7*(2), 109–133.

Allen, C. T., & Janiszewski, C. A. (1989). Assessing the role of contingency awareness in attitudinal conditioning with implications for advertising research. *Journal of Marketing Research, 26*, 30–43.

Allen, C. T., & Madden, T. J. (1985). A closer look at classical conditioning. *Journal of Consumer Research, 12*, 301–315.

Allen, C. T., Machleit, K. A., & Marine, S. S. (1988). On assessing the emotionality of advertising via Izard's Differential Emotions Scale. *Advances in Consumer Research, 15*, 226–231.

Allport, G. W. (1935). Attitudes. In C. Murchison (Ed.), *A Handbook of Social Psychology* (pp. 798–844). Worcester, MA: Clark University Press.

Anand, P., Holbrook, M. B., & Stephens, D. (1988). The formation of affective judgements: The cognitive-affective model versus the independence hypothesis. *Journal of Consumer Research, 15*(December), 386–391.

Anand, P., & Sternthal, B. (1992). The effects of program involvement and ease of message counterarguing on advertising persuasiveness. *Journal of Consumer Psychology, 1*, 225–238.

Anderson, J. R. (1990). *Cognitive psychology and its implications*, 3rd ed. New York: Freeman.

Anderson, N. H. (1965). Averaging versus adding as a stimulus combination rule in impression formation. *Journal of Experimental Psychology, 70*, 394–400.

Antil, J. H. (1984). Conceptualization and operationalization of involvement. *Advances in Consumer Research, 11*, 203–209.

Arenberg, D. (1967). Regression analysis of verbal learning on adult learning at two anticipation intervals. *Journal of Gerontology, 22*, 411–414.

329

Areni, C. S., & Kim, D. (1993). The influence of backgound music on shopping behavior: Classical versus top-forty in a wine store. *Advances in Consumer Research, 20,* 336–340.

Arnold, D. (1993, October 14). Minuteman comes under '90s-style fire. *The Boston Globe,* pp. 1, 14.

Aronson, E., & Carlsmith, J. M. (1963). Effect of the severity of threat on the devaluation of forbidden behavior. *Journal of Abnormal and Social Psychology, 66,* 584–588.

Aronson, E., & Golden, B. W. (1962). The effect of relevant and irrelevant aspects of communicator credibility on attitude change. *Journal of Personality, 30,* 135–146.

Asch, S. E. (1946). Forming impressions of personality. *Journal of Abnormal and Social Psychology, 41,* 258–290.

Atkin, C. K. (1978). Observation of parent-child interaction in supermarket decision-making. *Journal of Marketing, 42,* 41–45.

Babakus, E., Tat, P., & Cunningham, W. (1988). Coupon redemption: A motivational perspective. *Journal of Consumer Marketing, 5*(Spring), 37–43.

Bach, M. J., & Underwood, B. J. (1970). Developmental changes in memory attributes. *Journal of Educational Psychology, 61*(4), 292–296.

Bahn, K. D. (1986). How and when do brand perceptions and preferences first form? A cognitive developmental investigation. *Journal of Consumer Research, 13,* 382–393.

Baltes, P., Reese, H., & Lipsitt, L. (1980). Life span developmental psychology. *Annual Review of Psychology, 31,* 65–110.

Bandura, A. (1969). *Principles of behavior modification.* New York: Holt, Rinehart & Winston.

Bandura, A. (1971 November). *Modeling influences on children.* Testimony to the Federal Trade Commission. (Cited in Mullen & Johnson, 1990.)

Bandura, A., Ross, D., & Ross, S. A. (1961). Transmission of aggression through imitation of aggressive models. *Journal of Abnormal and Social Psychology, 63,* 575–582.

Bandura, A., & Rosenthal, T. L. (1966). Vicarious classical conditioning as a function of arousal level. *Journal of Personality and Social Psychology, 3,* 54–62.

Barak, B., & Gould, S. (1985). Alternative age measures: A research agenda. *Advances in Consumer Research, 12,* 53–58.

Barak, B., & Stern, B. (1985). Women's age in advertising: An examination of two consumer age profiles. *Journal of Advertising Research, 25*(6), 38–47.

Baron, J. (1988). *Thinking and deciding.* Cambridge: Cambridge University Press.

Bartlett, F. C. (1932). *Remembering.* Cambridge: Cambridge University Press.

Batra, R., & Ray, M. L. (1983). Advertising situations: The implications of differential involvement and accompanying affect responses. In R. J. Harris (Ed.), *Information processing research in advertising* (pp. 127–151). Hillsdale, NJ: Erlbaum.

Batra, R., & Ray, M. L. (1986a). Affective responses mediating acceptance of advertising. *Journal of Consumer Research, 13,* 234–249.

Batra, R., & Ray, M. L. (1986b). Situational effects of advertising repetition: The moderating influence of motivation, ability and opportunity to respond. *Journal of Consumer Research, 12,* 432–445.

Batson, C. D., Shaw, L. L., & Oleson, K. C. (1992). Differentiating affect, mood, and emotion. In M. S. Clark (Ed.), *Emotion* (pp. 294–326). Newbury Park, CA: Sage.

Baum, A., Fisher, J. D., & Singer, J. E. (1985). *Social psychology.* New York: Random House.

Baumeister, R. (1987). How the self became a problem: A psychological review of historical research. *Journal of Personality and Social Psychology, 52,* 163–176.

Baumer, F. L. (Ed.). (1952). *Main currents of western thought.* New York: Knopf.

Baxter, P. J. (1991). How children use media and influence purchases. *Journal of Advertising Research, 31*(6), 2–4.

Bearden, W. O., & Mason, J. B. (1979). Elderly use of in-store information sources and dimensions of product satisfaction/dissatisfaction. *Journal of Retailing, 55*(1), 79–91.

Beaumont, J. G. (1982). Studies with verbal stimuli. In J. G. Beaumont (Ed.), *Divided visual field studies of cerebral organization* (pp. 58–86). London: Academic Press.

Beck, M. (1990). Going for the gold. *Newsweek*, April.

Begg, I., & Denny, J. P. (1969). Empirical reconsideration of atmosphere and conversion interpretations of syllogistic reasoning errors. *Journal of Experimental Psychology, 81*, 351–354.

Belch, G. E. (1982). The effects of television commercial repetition on cognitive response and message acceptance. *Journal of Consumer Research, 9*, 56–65.

Belk, R. W. (1988). Possessions and the extended-self. *Journal of Consumer Research, 15*, 139–168.

Belk, R. W., Bahn, K. D., & Mayer, R. N. (1982). Developmental recognition of consumption symbolism. *Journal of Consumer Research, 9*(June), 4–17.

Belk, R. W., Mayer, R., & Driscoll, A. (1984). Children's recognition of consumption symbolism in children's products. *Journal of Consumer Research, 10*(Mar), 386–397.

Berger, S. M. (1962). Conditioning through vicarious instigation. *Psychology Review, 69*, 450–466.

Berlyne, D. E. (1960). *Conflict, arousal, and curiosity*. New York: McGraw-Hill.

Bernal, G., & Berger, S. M. (1976). Vicarious eyelid conditioning. *Journal of Personality and Social Psychology, 34*, 62–68.

Berscheid, E. (1966). Opinion change and communicator-communicatee similarity and dissimilarity. *Journal of Personality and Social Psychology, 4*, 670–680.

Bierley, C., McSweeney, F. K., & Vannieuwkerk, R. (1985). Classical conditioning of preferences for stimuli. *Journal of Consumer Research, 12*, 316–323.

Bitgood, Stephen C. (1995). Visitor circulation: Is there really a right-turn bias? *Visitor Behavior, 10*(1), 5.

Bitgood, S., Patterson, D., & Benefield, A. (Eds.). (1986). Understanding your visitors: Ten factors that influence visitor behavior. *Technical Report of the Psychology Institute, No. 86-60*. Jacksonville, AL: Jacksonville State University, Psychology Institute.

Blair, M. E., & Hatala, M. N. (1992). The use of rap music in children's advertising. *Advances in Consumer Research, 19*, 719–724.

Blair, M. E., & Shimp, T. A. (1992). Consequences of an unpleasant experience with music: A second-order negative conditioning perspective. *Journal of Advertising, 21*(1), 35–43.

Blau, Z. S. (1956). Changes in status and age identification. *American Sociological Review, 21*, 198–203.

Blood, D. J., & Ferriss, S. J. (1993). Effects of background music on anxiety, satisfaction with communication, and productivity. *Psychological Reports, 72*(1), 171–177.

Bornstein, R. F. (1989). Exposure and affect: Overview and meta-analysis of research, 1968–1987. *Psychological Bulletin, 106*(September), 265–284.

Bourne, F. S. (1957). Group influence in marketing and public relations. In R. Lickert & S. P. Hayes (Eds.), *Some applications of behavioral research*. Basel: UNESCO.

Bowers, K. S. (1984). On being unconsciously influenced and informed. In K. S. Bowers & D. Meichenbaum (Eds.), *The unconscious reconsidered* (pp. 227–272). New York: Wiley.

Braun, O. L., & Wicklund, R. A. (1989). Psychological antecedents of conspicuous consumption. *Journal of Economic Psychology, 10*, 161–187.

Brean, H. (1958, March 31). What hidden sell is all about. *Life*, 104–114.

Brehm, J. W. (1956). Post-decision changes in desirability of alternatives. *Journal of Abnormal and Social Psychology*, *52*, 384–389.

Brewer, W. F. (1974). There is no convincing evidence for operant or classical conditioning in adult humans. In W. B. Weimer & D. S. Palermo (Eds.), *Cognition and the symbolic processes* (pp. 1–42). Hillsdale, NJ: Erlbaum.

Brucks, M. (1985). The effects of product class knowledge on information search behavior. *Journal of Consumer Research*, *12*(June), 1–16.

Brucks, M., Armstrong, G. M., & Goldberg, M. E. (1988). Children's use of cognitive defenses against television advertising: A cognitive response approach. *Journal of Consumer Research*, *14*(Mar), 471–482.

Bruner, G. C., II. (1990). Music, mood, and marketing. *Journal of Marketing*, *54*(4), 94–104.

Bryant, W. K. (1988). Durables and wives' employment yet again. *Journal of Consumer Research*, *15*, 37–47.

Bunn, D. W. (1982). Audience presence during breaks in television programs. *Journal of Advertising Research*, *22*, 35–39.

Burke, J. (1992). Children's research and methods: What media researchers are doing. *Journal of Advertising Research*, *32*(1), 1–3.

Burnett, J. J. (1991). Examining the media habits of the affluent elderly. *Journal of Advertising Research*, (October/ November), 33–41.

Burnkrant, R. E., & Sawyer, A. G. (1983). Effects of involvement and message content on information-processing intensity. In R. J. Harris (Ed.), *Information processing research in advertising* (pp. 43–64). Hillsdale, NJ: Lawrence Erlbaum.

Burns, K. (1994). *The making of baseball*. National Public Television, August 16, 1994. Boston: WGBH.

Burns, A. & Hopper, J.A. (1986). An analysis of the presence, stability, and antecedents of husband and wife purchase decision making influence assessment agreement and disagreement. *Advances in Consumer Research*, *13*, 175–180.

Burton, S. & Lichtenstein, D. (1988). The effect of ad claims and ad context on attitude toward the advertisement. *Journal of Advertising*, *17*(1), 3–11.

Bush, D., J. (1975). *The streamlined decade*. New York: George Braziller.

Cacioppo, J. T., & Petty, R. E. (1979). Effects of message repetition and position on cognition response, recall, and persuasion. *Journal of Personality and Social Psychology*, *37*, 97–109.

Carlson, L. & Grossbart, S. (1988). Parental style and consumer socialization of children. *Journal of Consumer Research*, *15*, 77–94.

Carnegie, D. (1940). *How to win friends and influence people*. New York: Pocket Books.

Celsi, R. L., & Olson, J. C. (1988). The role of involvement in attention and comprehension processes. *Journal of Consumer Research*, *15*, 210–224.

Celuch, K. G. & Slama, M. (1995). Cognitive and affective components of A_{ad} in a low motivation processing set. *Psychology and Marketing*, *12*(2), 123–133.

Ceraso, J., & Provitera, A. (1971). Sources of error in syllogistic reasoning. *Cognitive Psychology*, *2*, 400–410.

Chakravarti, D., MacInnis, D., & Nakamoto, K. (1989). Product category perceptions, elaborative processing and brand name extension strategies. *Advances in Consumer Research*, *16*, 123–126.

Chance, P. (1988). *Learning and behavior*, 2nd ed. Belmont, CA: Wadsworth.

Cheesman, J., & Merikle, P. M. (1984). Priming with and without awareness. *Perception and Psychophysics*, *36*, 387–395.

Childers, T. L., & Rao, A. R. (1992). The influence of familial and peer-based reference groups on consumer decisions. *Journal of Consumer Research, 19*, 198–211.

Churchill, G. A., & Surprenant, C. (1982). An investigation into the determinants of customer satisfaction. *Journal of Marketing Research, 19*(4), 491–504.

Ciabattari, J. (1997, September 21). Teens are spending more, saving little. *The Boston Sunday Globe, Parade Magazine*, 14.

Claiborne, C. B., & Sirgy, M. J. (1990). Self-image congruence as a model of consumer attitude formation and behavior: A conceptual review and guide for future research. In B. J. Dunlap (Ed.), *Developments in Marketing Science*, Vol. 13 (pp. 3–7). Cullowhee, NC: Academy of Marketing Science.

Clark, M., & Isen, A. (1982). Toward understanding the relationship between feeling states and social behavior. In A. Hastorf & A. Isen (Eds.), *Cognitive Social Psychology* (pp. 73–108). New York: Elsevier/North Holland.

Clement, C., & Falmagne, R. J. (1986). Logical reasoning, world knowledge, and mental imagery: Interconnections in cognitive processes. *Memory & Cognition, 14*, 299–307.

Cohen, J. B. (1989). An over-extended self? *Journal of Consumer Research, 16*, 125–128.

Cole, C. A., & Gaeth, G. J. (1990). Cognitive and age-related differences in the ability to use nutritional information in a complex environment. *Journal of Marketing Research, 27*(May), 175–184.

Cole, C. A., & Houston, M. J. (1987). Encoding and media effects on consumer learning deficiencies in the elderly. *Journal of Marketing Research, 24*(February), 55–63.

Cole, M., & Scribner, S. (1977). Cross-cultural studies of memory and cognition. In R. V. Vail, Jr. & J. W. Hagen (Eds.), *Perspectives on the development of memory and recognition*. Hillsdale, NJ: Erlbaum.

Collins, W. A. (1970). Learning of media content: A developmental study. *Child Development, 41*, 1133–1142.

Combs, B., & Slovic, P. (1979). Newspaper coverage of causes of death. *Journalism Quarterly, 56*, 832–849.

Coren, S. (1984). Subliminal perception. In R. J. Corsini (Ed.), *Encyclopedia of psychology* (Vol. 3, p. 382). New York: Wiley.

Corteen, R., & Wood, B. (1972). Autonomic responses to shock-associated words in an unattended channel. *Journal of Experimental Psychology, 94*, 308–313.

Craig, K. D., & Weinstein, M. S. (1965). Conditioning vicarious affective arousal. *Psychology Reports, 17*, 955–963.

Craik, F. I. M. (1977). Age differences in human memory. In J. Birren and K. Schaie (Eds.) *The psychology of aging*. New York: Van Nostrand.

Craik, F. I. M., & Lockhart, R. S. (1972). Levels of processing: A framework for memory research. *Journal of Verbal Learning and Verbal Behavior, 11*, 671–684.

Craik, F. I. M., & Watkins, M. J. (1973). The role of rehearsal in short-term memory. *Journal of Verbal Learning and Verbal Behavior, 12*, 599–607.

Cross, H. A., Halcomb, C. G., & Matter, W. W. (1967). Imprinting or exposure learning in rats given early auditory stimulation. *Psychonomic Science, 7*, 233–234.

Cunningham, M. R. (1986). Measuring the physical in physical attractiveness: Quasi-experiments on the sociobiology of female facial beauty. *Journal of Personality and Social Psychology, 50*, 925–935.

Cushman, P. (1990). Why the self is empty. *American Psychologist, 45*, 599–611.

Daoussis, L., & McKelvie, S. J. (1986). Musical preferences and effects of music on a reading comprehension test for extroverts and introverts. *Perceptual and Motor Skills, 62*(1), 283–289.

Davidson, C. W., & Powell, L. A. (1986). The effects of easy-listening background music on the on-task-performance of fifth grade children. *Journal of Educational Research*, *80*(1), 29–33.

Davis, B. & French, W. A. (1989). Exploring advertising usage segments among the aged. *Journal of Advertising Research*, (February/March), 22–29.

Davis, H. L., Hoch, S. J., & Ragsdale, E. K. E. (1986). An anchoring and adjustment model of spousal predictions. *Journal of Consumer Research*, *13*, 25–37.

Dawes, R. M. (1988). *Rational choice in an uncertain world*. San Diego, CA: Harcourt Brace Jovanovich.

Dawson, M. E. (1973). Can classical conditioning occur without contingency learning? *Psychophysiology*, *10*(January), 82–86.

DeBono, K. G., & Snyder, M. (1989). Understanding consumer decision-making processes: The role of form and function in product evaluation. *Journal of Applied Social Psychology*, *19*(5), 416–425.

DeBono, K. G., Kerin, S., Shaker, S., & Shapiro, C. (1992). Pleasant scents and persuasion. *Proceedings and abstracts of the annual meeting of the EPA*. Glassboro, NJ: EPA.

DeFleur, M. L., & Petranoff, R. M. (1959). A television test of subliminal persuasion. *Public Opinion Quarterly*, *23*(Summer), 170–180.

Deslauriers, B. C., & Everett, P. B. (1977). The effects of intermittent and continuous token reinforcement on bus ridership. *Journal of Applied Psychology*, *62*, 369–375.

Dethier, V. G. (1962). *To know a fly*. San Francisco: Holden-Day.

Dion, K. K. (1972). Physical attractiveness and evaluation of children's transgressions. *Journal of Personality and Social Psychology*, *24*, 285–290.

Dion, K. K., Berscheid, E., & Walster, E. (1972). What is beautiful is good. *Journal of Personality and Social Psychology*, *24*, 285–290.

Dipboye, R. L., Fromkim, H. L., & Wiback, K. (1975). Relative importance of applicant, sex, attractiveness, and scholastic standing in evaluation of job applicant resumes. *Journal of Applied Psychology*, *60*, 39–43.

Dixon, S. C., & Street, J. W. (1975). The distinction between self and non-self in children and adolescents. *Journal of the American Genetic Psychology*, *127*, 157–162.

Donohue, T. R., Henke, L. L., & Donohue, W. A. (1980). Do kids know what TV commercials intend? *Journal of Advertising Research*, *20*(5), 51–57.

Douglas, T. (1984). *The complete guide to advertising*. Secaucus, NJ: Chartwell Books.

Douthitt, R. A., & Fedyk, J. M. (1988). The influences of children on family life cycle spending behavior: Theory and applications. *Journal of Consumer Affairs*, *22*, 220–248.

D'Souza, G., & Rao, R. C. (1995). Can repeating an advertisement more frequently than the competition affect brand preference in a mature market? *Journal of Marketing*, *59*(2), 32–42.

Duffy, E. (1962). *Activation and behavior*. New York: Wiley.

Dulany, D. E., Jr., & Eriksen, C. W. (1959). Accuracy of brightness discrimination as measured by concurrent verbal responses and GSRs. *Journal of Abnormal and Social Psychology*, *59*, 418–423.

Eason, L., & Linn, M. (1976). Evaluation of the effectiveness of participatory exhibits. *Curator*, *19*(1), 45–62.

Edell, J. A., & Staelin, R. (1983). The information processing of pictures in print advertisements. *Journal of Consumer Research*, *10*, 45–61.

Ellis, L. (1985). On the rudiments of possessions and property. *Social Science Information*, *24*, 113–143.

Engel, J. F., Blackwell, R. D., & Miniard, P. W. (1986). *Consumer behavior*, 5th ed. Chicago: Dryden Press.

Erdelyi, M. H., & Appelbaum, G. A. (1973). Cognitive masking: The disruptive effect of an emotional stimulus upon the perception of contiguous neutral items. *Bulletin of the Psychonomic Society, 1,* 59–61.

Erikson, E. H. (1956). The problem of ego-identity. *Journal of the American Psychoanalytic Association, 4,* 56–121.

Etaugh, C., & Michals, D. (1975). Effects on reading comprehension of preferred music and frequency of studying to music. *Perceptual and Motor Skills, 41,* 553–554.

Etaugh, C., & Ptasnik, P. (1982). Effects of studying music and post-study relaxation on reading comprehension. *Perceptual and Motor Skills, 55,* 141–142.

Eysenck, M. W. (1974). Age differences in incidental learning. *Developmental Psychology, 10*(June), 936–941.

Eysenck, M. W., & Keane, M. T. (1990). *Cognitive psychology: A student's handbook.* Hillsdale, NJ: LEA.

Falk, J., Koran, J., Dierking, L., & Dreblow, L. (1985). Predicting visitor behavior. *Curator, 28*(4), 249–257.

Fazio, R. H., & Zanna, M. (1981). Direct experience and attitude-behavior consistency. In L. Berkowitz (Ed.), *Advances in experimental social psychology,* Vol. 14, pp. 161–202. New York: Academic Press.

Festinger, L. (1957). *A theory of cognitive dissonance.* Evanston, IL: Row-Peterson.

Festinger, L., & Carlsmith, J. M. (1959). Cognitive consequences of forced compliance. *Journal of Abnormal and Social Psychology, 158,* 203–210.

Fishbein, M., & Ajzen, I. (1972). Attitudes and opinions. *Annual Review of Psychology, 23,* 487–544.

Fishbein, M., & Ajzen, I. (1975). *Belief, attitude, intention, and behavior: An introduction to theory and research.* Reading, MA: Addison-Wesley.

Fischer, M. A. (1985). A developmental study of preference for advertised toys. *Psychology of Marketing, 2,* 3–12.

Fiske, S. T. (1980). Attention and weight in person perception: The impact of negative and extreme behavior. *Journal of Personality and Social Psychology, 38,* 889–906.

Fiske, S. T. (1982). Schema-triggered affect: Applications to social perception. In M. S. Clarke & S. T. Fiske (Eds.), *Affect and cognition: The 17th annual Carnegie symposium on cognition* (pp. 55–78). Hillsdale, NJ: Erlbaum.

Fiske, S. T., & Taylor, S. E. (1991). *Social cognition.* New York: McGraw-Hill.

Fivush, R. (1984). Learning about school: The development of kindergartner's school scripts. *Child Development, 55,* 1697–1709.

Flagg, P. W., Potts, G. R., & Reynolds, A. G. (1975). Instructions and response strategies in recognition memory for sentences. *Journal of Experimental Psychology: Human Learning and Memory, 1,* 592–598.

Florek, W. (1978). *Effects of subliminal stimulation of anxiety and cognitive adaptation.* Unpublished manuscript, St. John's University.

Flugel, J. C. (1930). *The Psychology of Clothes.* London: Hogarth Press, International Psychoanalytic Library.

Fogelson, S. (1973). Music as a distractor on reading-test performance of eighth grade students. *Perceptual and Motor Skills, 36,* 1265–1266.

Forget the people—Just bring on the food. (1992). *Adweek, 33*(41), 17.

Foxman, E. R., Tansuhaj, P. S., & Ekstrom, K. M. (1989). Family members' perceptions of adolescents' influence in family decision making. *Journal of Consumer Research, 15*(Mar), 482–491.

Freedman, J. L., & Fraser, S. C. (1966). Compliance without pressure: The foot-in-the-door technique. *Journal of Personality and Social Psychology, 4,* 195–202.

Freud, S. (1960). *A general introduction to psychoanalysis.* New York: Washington Square Press. (Original work published in 1920).

Friedman, A. (1979). Framing pictures: The role of knowledge in automatized encoding and memory for gist. *Journal of Experimental Psychology: General, 108*, 316–355.

Friestad, M., & Thorson, E. (1986). Emotion-eliciting advertising: Effects on long term memory and judgement. *Advances in Consumer Research, 13*, 111–116.

Gardner, M. P. (1985). Mood states and consumer behavior: A critical review. *Journal of Consumer Research, 12*, 281–300.

Gay, P. (Ed.). (1989). *The Freud reader.* New York: Norton.

Gazzaniga, M. S. (1985). *The social brain: Discovering the networks of mind.* New York: Basic Books.

Geschwind, N., & Galaburda, A. M. (1987). *Cerebral lateralization: Biological mechanisms, associations, and pathology.* Cambridge, MA: MIT Press.

Gest, T. (1992). Product Paranoia. *U.S. News & World Report, 112*(7), 67–69.

Gibson, J. J. (1950). *The perception of the visual world.* Boston: Houghton Mifflin.

Gibson, J. J. (1966). *The senses considered as perceptual systems.* Boston: Houghton Mifflin.

Gilly, M. C., & Zeithamel, V. A. (1985). The elderly and adoption of technologies. *Journal of Consumer Research, 12*(December), 353–357.

Glamser, D. (1990). Mozart plays to empty lot. *USA Today*, August 24, 1990, p. A3.

Goldberg, M. E., & Gorn, G. J. (1974). Children's reactions to advertising: An experimental approach. *Journal of Consumer Research, 1*(September), 69–75.

Gorn, G. J. (1982). The effects of music in advertising on choice behavior: A classical conditioning approach. *Journal of Marketing, 46*, 94–99.

Gorn, G. J., & Florsheim, R. (1985). The effects of commercials for adult products on children. *Journal of Consumer Research, 11*(March), 962–967.

Gorn, G. J., Goldberg, M. E., Chattopadhyay, A., and Litvack, D. (1991). Music and information in commercials: Their effects with an elderly sample. *Journal of Advertising Research*, October/November, 23–32.

Gorn, G. J., Jacobs, W. J., & Mana, M. J. (1987). Observations on awareness and conditioning. In M. Wallendorf & P. F. Anderson (Eds.), *Advances in Consumer Research* (pp. 415–416). Provo, UT: Association for Consumer Research.

Grass, R. C. (1968). Satiation effects of advertising. In the *14th Annual Proceedings.* New York: Advertising Research Foundation.

Greene, A. (1986). The tyranny of melody. *Etc., 43*(3), 285–290.

Greenwald, A. G., & Leavitt, C. (1984). Audience involvement in advertising: Four levels. *Journal of Consumer Research, 11*, 581–592.

Greenwald, A. G., Spangenberg, E. R., Pratkanis, A. R., & Eskenazi, J. (1991). Double-blind tests of subliminal self-help audiotapes. *Psychological Science, 2*, 119–122.

Gregory, W. L., Cialdini, R. B., & Carpenter, K. M. (1982). Self-relevant scenarios as mediators of likelihood estimates and compliance: Does imagining make it so? *Journal of Personality and Social Psychology, 43*, 89–99.

Gresham, L. G., & Shimp, T. A. (1985). Attitude toward the advertisement and brand attitudes. *Journal of Advertising, 14*(1), 10–17.

Groenland, E. A. G., & Schoormans, J. P. L. (1994). Comparing mood-induction and affective conditioning as mechanisms influencing product evaluation and product choice. *Psychology and Marketing, 11*(2), 183–197.

Gulliksen, H. (1927). The influence of occupation upon the perception of time. *Journal of Experimental Psychology, 10*, 52–59.

Gutman, J., & Alden, S. D. (1985). Adolescents' cognitive structures of retail stores and fashion consumption: A means-end chain analysis of quality. In J. Jacoby & J. C. Olson (Eds.), *Perceived quality: How consumers view stores and merchandise* (pp. 99–114). Lexington, MA: Lexington Books.

Hahari, H., & McDavid, J. W. (1973). Name stereotypes and teachers' expectations. *Journal of Educational Psychology, 65,* 222–225.

Hakkinen, L. (1984). Vision in the elderly and its use in the social environment. *Scandanavian Journal of Social Medicine, 35,* 5–60.

Haley, R. I., Richardson, J., & Baldwin, B. M. (1984). The effects of nonverbal communication in television advertising. *Journal of Advertising Research, 24*(August/September), 11–18.

Harrigan, J. A. (1991). Children's research: Where it's been, where it is going. *Advances in Consumer Research, 18,* 11–17.

Harris, R. J. (1977). Comprehension of pragmatic implications in advertising. *Journal of Applied Psychology, 62,* 603–608.

Harris, R. J., & Monaco, G. E. (1978). The psychology of pragmatic implication: Information processing between the lines. *Journal of Experimental Psychology: General, 107,* 1–22.

Harrison, A. A. (1977). Mere exposure. In L. Berkowitz (Ed.), *Advances in Experimental Social Psychology,* Vol. 10. New York: Academic Press.

Hatfield, E., & Sprecher, S. (1986). *Mirror, mirror: The importance of looks in everyday life.* Albany, New York: State University of New York Press.

Haugtvedt, C. P. & Wegener, D. T. (1994). Message order effects in persuasion: An attitude strength perspective. *Journal of Consumer Research, 21,* 205–218.

Havlena, W. J., & Holbrook, M. B. (1986). The varieties of consumption experience: Comparing two typologies of emotion in consumer behavior. *Journal of Consumer Research, 13,* 394–404.

Heider, F. (1946). Attitudes and cognitive organization. *Journal of Psychology, 21,* 107–112.

Hilgard, E. R. (1977). *Divided consciousness: Multiple controls in human thought and action.* New York: Wiley.

Hilliard, O. M., & Tolin, P. (1979). Effect of familiarity with background music on performance of simple and difficult reading comprehension tasks. *Perceptual and Motor Skills, 49,* 713–714.

Hine, T. (1986). *Populuxe.* New York: Knopf.

Hirsch, A. R. (1995). Effects of ambient odors on slot-machine usage in a Las Vegas casino. *Psychology and Marketing, 12*(7), 585–594.

Hirsch, J. S. (1996, May 31). Risk aversion as a behavioral problem. *The Wall Street Journal,* p. C1

Hite, R. E., & Eck, R. (1987). Advertising to children: Attitudes of business vs. consumers. *Journal of Advertising Research, 27*(5), 40–53.

Holbrook, M. B. (1986). Emotion in the consumption experience: Toward a new model of the human consumer. In R. A. Peterson, W. D. Hoyer, & W. R. Wilson (Eds.), *The Role of Affect in Consumer Behavior* (pp. 17–52). Lexington, MA: Heath.

Holbrook, M. B., Chestnut, R. W., Oliva, T. A., & Greenleaf, E.A. (1984). Play as a consumption experience: The roles of emotion, performance, and personality in the enjoyment of games. *Journal of Consumer Research, 11,* 728–739.

Holman, R. H. (1986). Advertising and emotionality. In R. A. Peterson, W. D. Hoyer, & W. R. Wilson (Eds.), *The role of affect in consumer behavior* (pp. 119–140). Lexington, MA: Heath.

Horsham, M. (1996). *'20s & '30s style.* North Dighton, MA: JG Press.

Houston, M. J., Childers, T. L., & Heckler, S. E. (1987). Picture-word consistency and the elaborative processing of advertisements. *Journal of Marketing Research, 24*(November), 359–369.

Hovland, C. I., Harvey, D. J., & Sherif, M. (1957). Assimilation and contrast effects in reactions to communication and attitude change. *Journal of Abnormal and Social Psychology, 55*, 244–252.

Hovland, C. I., Lumsdaine, A. A., & Sheffield, F. D. (1949). *Experiments on mass communication.* Princeton, NJ: Princeton University Press.

Howard, J. A. (1977). *Consumer behavior: Application of theory.* New York: McGraw-Hill.

Hoy, M. G., Young, C. E., & Mowen, J. C. (1986). Animated host-selling advertisements: Their impact on young children's recognition, attitudes, and behavior. *Journal of Public Policy Marketing, 5*, 171–184.

Hudson, J., & Nelson, K. (1983). Effects of script structure on children's story recall. *Developmental Psychology, 19*(4), 625–635.

Insko, C. A., & Oakes, W. F. (1966). Awareness and the conditioning of attitudes. *Journal of Personality and Social Psychology, 4*(November), 487–496.

Isler, L., Popper, E. T., & Ward, S. (1987). Children's purchase requests and parental responses: Result from a diary study. *Journal of Advertising Research, 27*, 28–39.

Izard, C. E. (1977). *Human emotions.* New York: Plenum Press.

Izard, C. E., Nagler, S., Randall, D., & Fox, J. (1965). The effects of affective picture stimuli on learning, perception and the affective values of previously neutral symbols. In S. S. Tomkins & C. E. Izard (Eds.), *Affect, cognition, and personality: Empirical studies* (pp. 42–70). New York: Springer.

Jacoby, L. L., & Dallas, M. (1981). On the relationship between autobiographical memory and perceptual learning. *Journal of Experimental Psychology: General, 3*, 306–340.

Jacoby, L. L., Kelley, C. M., Brown, J., & Jasechko, J. (1989). Becoming famous overnight: Limits on the ability to avoid unconscious influences of the past. *Journal of Personality and Social Psychology, 56*, 326–338.

Janis, I. L., & Frick, F. (1943). The relationship between attitudes toward conclusions and errors in judging logical validity of syllogisms. *Journal of Experimental Psychology, 33*, 73–77.

Janiszewski, C. (1988). Preconscious processing effects: The independence of attitude formation and conscious thought. *Journal of Consumer Research, 15*, 199–209.

Janiszewski, C. (1990). The influence of print advertisement organization on affect toward a brand name. *Journal of Consumer Research, 17*(June), 53–65.

Janiszewski, C., & Warlop, L. (1993). The influence of classical conditioning procedures on subsequent attention to the conditioning brand. *Journal of Consumer Research, 20* (September), 171–189.

Johar, J. S., & Sirgy, M. J. (1991). Value-expressive versus utilitarian advertising appeals: When and why to use which appeal. *Journal of Advertising, 20*(3), 23–33.

John, D. R., & Cole, C. A. (1986). Age differences in information processing: Understanding deficits in young and elderly consumers. *Journal of Market Research, 13*, 297–315.

John, D. R., & Lakshmi-Ratan, R. (1992). Age differences in children's choice behavior: The impact of available alternatives. *Journal of Marketing Research, 29*(2), 216–226.

John, D. R., & Sujan, M. (1990a). Age differences in product categorization. *Journal of Consumer Research, 16*(4), 452–460.

John, D. R., & Sujan, M. (1990b). Children's use of perceptual cues in product categorization. *Psychology and Marketing, 7*(Winter), 277–294.

John, D. R., & Whitney, J. C. (1986). The development of consumer knowledge in children: A cognitive structure approach. *Journal of Consumer Research, 12*, 406–417.

Johnson, R. L., & Cobb-Walgren, C. J. (1994). Aging and the problem of television clutter. *Journal of Advertising Research*, (July/August), 54–62.

Jordan, K. A. (1983). Impact of older models in print advertisements upon the youth market. In the *Proceedings of the Southwestern Marketing Association Conference*. San Antonio, TX: Southwest Marketing Association.

Jung, C. G. (1960). *On the nature of the psyche* (Translated by R. F. C. Hull). Princeton, NJ: Princeton University Press. (From The Collected Works of C. G. Jung, Vol. 8).

Kahle, L. R., Beatty, S. E., & Kennedy, P. (1987). Comment on classically conditioning human consumers. *Advances in Consumer Research*, *14*, 411–414.

Kahneman, D., Knetsch, J. L., & Thaler, R. H. (1990). Experimental tests of the endowment effect and the Coase theorem. *Journal of Political Economy*, *98*, 1325–1348.

Kahneman, D., & Tversky, A. (1979). Prospect theory: An analysis of decision under risk. *Econometrica*, *47*, 263.

Kamins, M. A. (1990). An investigation into the "match-up" hypothesis in celebrity advertising: When beauty may be only skin deep. *Journal of Advertising 19(1)*, 4–13.

Kanner, B. (1992, March 23). On Madison Avenue: Sound effects. *New York*, pp. 12–14.

Katz, D. (1960). The functional approach to the study of attitudes. *Public Opinion Quarterly*, *24*, 163–204.

Kee, D. W., Bell, T. S., & Davis, B. R. (1981). Developmental changes in the effects of presentation mode on the storage and retrieval of noun pairs in children's recognition memory. *Child Development*, *52*, 268–279.

Kellaris, J. J., & Cox, A. D. (1989). The effects of background music in advertising: A reassessment. *Journal of Consumer Research*, *16*, 113–118.

Kellaris, J. J., Cox, A. D., & Cox, D. (1993). The effect of background music on ad processing: A contingency explanation. *Journal of Marketing*, *57*(October), 114–125.

Kellaris, J. J., & Kent, R. J. (1991). Exploring tempo and modality effects on consumer responses to music. *Advances in Consumer Research*, *18*, 243–248.

Kellaris, J. J., & Kent, R. J. (1992). The influence of music on consumers' temporal perceptions: Does time fly when you are having fun? *Journal of Consumer Psychology*, *1*(4), 365–376.

Kellaris, J. J., & Kent, R. J. (1993). An exploratory investigation of responses elicited by music varying in tempo, tonality, and texture. *Journal of Consumer Psychology*, *2*(4), 381–401.

Kelley, H. H. (1950). The warm-cold variable in first impressions of persons. *Journal of Personality*, *18*, 431–439.

Kelly, P., & Soloman, P. J. (1975). Humor in television advertising. *Journal of Advertising*, *4*, 33–35.

Kelman, H. C., & Hovland, C. I. (1953). "Reinstatement" of the communicator in delayed measurement of opinion change. *Journal of Abnormal and Social Psychology*, *48*, 327–335.

Kennedy, J. R. (1971). How program environment affects TV commercials. *Journal of Personality and Social Psychology*, *15*, 344–358.

Kenrick, D. T., & Guitierres, S. E. (1980). Contrast effects and judgements of physical attractiveness: When beauty becomes a social problem. *Journal of Personality and Social Psychology*, *38*, 131–140.

Key, W. B. (1973). *Subliminal seduction: Ad media's manipulation of a not so innocent America*. New York: Prentice-Hall.

Key, W. B. (1976). *Media sexploitation*. Englewood Cliffs, NJ: Prentice-Hall.

Kieras, D. (1978). Beyond pictures and words: Alternative information processing models for imagery effects in verbal memory. *Psychological Bulletin*, *85*, 532–554.

Kiger, D. M. (1989). Effects of music information load on a reading comprehension task. *Perceptual and Motor Skills, 69*(2), 531–534.

Kiselius, J. (1982). The role of memory in understanding advertising media effectiveness: The effect of imagery on consumer decision making. *Advances in Consumer Research, 9*, 183–186.

Kleemeier, R. W. (1963). Attitudes toward special settings for the aged. In R. H. Williams, C. Tibbits, & W. Donahue (Eds.), *Process of Aging*, Vol. 2. New York: Atherton Press.

Klinger, E., Barta, S. G., & Maxeiner, M. E. (1980). Motivational correlates of thought content, frequency and commitment. *Journal of Personality and Social Psychology, 39*, 1222–1237.

Klippel, R. E., & Sweeney, T. W. (1974). The use of information sources by the aged consumer. *The Gerontologist, 14*(April), 163–166.

Knox, R. E., & Inkster, J. A. (1968). Postdecision dissonance at posttime. *Journal of Personality and Social Psychology, 18*, 319–323.

Kohler, W. (1929, 1947). *Gestalt psychology*. New York: Liveright.

Kosnik, W., Winslow, L., Kline, D., Rasinski, K. and Sekuler, R. (1988). Visual changes in daily life throughout adulthood. *Journal of Gerontology: Psychological Sciences, 43*, P63–70.

Kotler, P. (1973). Atmosphere as a marketing tool. *Journal of Retailing, 49*(Winter), 48–64.

Kroeber-Riel, W. (1984). Emotional product differentiation by classical conditioning. *Advances in Consumer Research, 11*, 538–543.

Krugman, H. E. (1965). The impact of television advertising: Learning without involvement. *Public Opinion Quarterly, 29*, 349–356.

Krugman, H. E. (1967). The measuring of advertising involvement. *Public Opinion Quarterly, 23*, 245–253.

Kuiken, D. (Ed.). (1991). *Mood and memory: Theory, research, and applications*. Newbury Park, CA: Sage.

Landy, D., & Aronson, E. (1969). The influence of the character of the criminal and his victim on the decisions of simulated jurors. *Journal of Experimental Social Psychology, 5*, 141–152.

Landy, D., & Sigall, H. (1974). Beauty is talent: Task evaluation as a function of the performer's physical attractiveness. *Journal of Personality and Social Psychology, 29*, 299–304.

Langer, E. J. (1989). *Mindfulness*. Reading, MA: Addison-Wesley.

Lanza, J. (1994). *Elevator music: A sureal history of Muzak, easy-listening and other moodsong*. New York: Picador USA.

Laurent, G., & Kapferer, J. (1985). Measuring consumer involvement profiles. *Journal of Marketing Research, 22*(February), 41–53.

Lazarus, R. S. (1981). A cognitivist's reply to Zajonc on emotion and cognition. *American Psychologist, 36*, 222–223.

Lazarus, R. S. (1984). On the primacy of cognition. *American Psychologist, 39*, 124–129.

Lazarus, R. S. (1991). *Emotion and adaptation*. New York: Oxford University Press.

Lazarus, R. S., & McCleary, R. A. (1951). Autonomic discrimination without awareness: A study of subception. *Psychological Review, 58*, 113–122.

Lears, T. (1983). From salvation to self-realization: Advertising and the therapeutic roots of the consumer culture, 1880–1930. In R. Fox & T. Lears (Eds.), *The culture of consumption: Critical essays in American history, 1880–1980* (pp. 1–38). New York: Pantheon Books.

LeDoux, J. E. (1992). Systems and synapses of emotional memory. In L. R. Squire, N. M.

Weinberger, G. Lynch, & J. L. McGaugh (Eds.), *Memory: Organization and locus of change.* New York: Oxford University Press.

Levey, A. B., & Martin, I. (1983). Part I. Cognitions, evaluations and conditioning: Rules of sequence and rules of consequence. *Advances in Behavioral Research and Therapy, 4,* 181–195.

Levin, J. (1990). Confessions of a soap opera addict. *Northeastern University Alumni Magazine, 15*(5), 18–19.

Levinson, D. J. (1978). *The seasons of a man's life.* New York: Knopf.

Levinson, D. J. (1990). A theory of life structure in adult development. In C. N. Alexander & E. J. Langer (Eds.) *Higher stages of human development: Perspectives on adult growth* (pp. 35–53). New York: Oxford University Press.

Levy, S. (1959). Symbols by which we buy. In L. H. Stockman (Ed.), *Advancing marketing efficiency.* Chicago: American Marketing Association.

Liebert, R. M., & Spiegler, M. D. (1987). *Personality Strategies and Issues,* 5th Ed. Chicago, IL: The Dorsey Press.

Liebman, B. (1997, September). Fraud or find? *Nutrition Action Health Letter, 24*(7), 8–9.

Linder, D. E., Cooper, J., & Jones, E. E. (1967). Decision freedom as a determinant of the role of incentive magnitude in attitude change. *Journal of Personality and Social Psychology, 6,* 245–254.

Lindsay, P. H., & Norman, D. A. (1977). *Human information processing,* 2nd ed. New York: Academic Press.

Lipset, S. (1963). The value patterns of democracy: A case study in comparative values. *American Sociological Review, 28,* 515–531.

Loken, B., Ross, I., & Hinkle, R. L. (1986). Consumer "confusion" of origin and brand similarity perceptions. *Journal of Public Policy and Marketing, 5,* 195–211.

Loudon, D. L., & Della Bitta, A. J. (1984). *Consumer behavior: Concepts and applications.* New York: McGraw-Hill.

Lurie, A. (1981). *The Language of Clothes.* New York: Random House.

Lutz, J. (1994). *Introduction to learning and memory.* Pacific Grove, CA: Brooks/Cole.

Lutz, R. (1986). *Quality is as quality does: An attitudinal perspective on consumer quality judgments.* Presentation to the Marketing Science Institute. Cambridge, MA.

Lynch, J. G., Jr., & Srull, T. K. (1982). Memory and attentional factors in consumer choice: Concepts and research methods. *Journal of Consumer Research, 9*(June), 18–37.

Machleit, K. A., & Wilson, R. D. (1988) Emotional feelings and attitude toward the advertisement: The roles of brand familiarity and repetition. *Journal of Advertising, 17*(3), 27–35.

MacInnis, D. J., Moorman, C., & Jaworski, B. J. (1991). Enhancing and measuring consumers' motivation, opportunity, and ability to process brand information from ads. *Journal of Marketing, 55*(4), 32–53.

MacInnis, D. J., & Park, C. W. (1991). The differential role of characteristics of music on high and low involvement consumers' processing of ads. *Journal of Consumer Research, 18*(September), 161–173.

Macklin, C. M. (1983). Do children understand TV ads? *Journal of Advertising Research, 23*(1), 63–70.

Macklin, M. C. (1986). Classical conditioning effects in product/character pairings presented to children. *Advances in Consumer Research, 13,* 198–203.

Macklin, M. C. (1987). Preschoolers' understanding of the informational function of television advertising. *Journal of Consumer Research, 14*(Sept), 229–239.

Macklin, M. C. (1988). The relationship between music in advertising and childrens' responses: An experimental investigation. In S. Hecker & D. W. Stewart (Eds.), *Non-verbal communication in advertising* (pp. 225–252). Lexington, MA: Heath.

Macklin, M. C. (1990).The influence of model age on children's reactions to advertising stimuli. *Psychology and Marketing, 7*(4), 295–310.

Macklin, M. C. (1994a). The impact of audiovisual information on children's product-related recall. *Journal of Consumer Research, 21*(1), 154–164.

Macklin, M. C. (1994b). The effects of an advertising retrieval cue on young children's memory and brand evaluations. *Psychology and Marketing, 11*(3), 291–311.

Malloy, J. T. (1988). *John T. Malloy's new dress for success.* New York: Warner Books.

Malone, J. C. (1990). *Theories of learning: A historical approach.* Belmont, CA: Wadsworth.

Mandler, G. (1982). The structure of value: Accounting for taste. In M. S. Clark & S. T. Fiske (Eds.), *Affect and cognition: The 17th annual Carnegie symposium* (pp. 3–36). Hillsdale, NJ: Erlbaum.

Mandler, J. M., & DeForest, M. (1979). Is there more than one way to recall a story? *Child Development, 50,* 886–889.

Mangleburg, T. F. (1990). Children's influence in purchase decisions: A review and critique. *Advances in consumer research, 17,* 813–825.

Markiewicz, D. (1974). Effects of humor on persuasion. *Sociometry, 37,* 407–422.

Markin, R. J., Lillis, C. M., & Narayana, C. L. (1976). Social-psychological significance of store space. *Journal of Retailing, 52,* 43–54.

Markus, H. R., & Nurius, P. (1986). Possible selves. *American Psychologist, 41*(9), 954–969.

Mason, R. S. (1981). *Conspicuous consumption: A study of exceptional consumer behavior.* New York: St. Martin's Press.

Mason, J. B. & Bearden, W. O. (1978a). Profiling the shopping behavior of elderly consumers. *The Gerontologist, 18*(5), 454–461.

Mason, J. B., & Bearden, W. O. (1978b). Elderly shopping: Behavior and marketplace perceptions. In R. S. Fraz, R. M. Hopkins, and A. Toma (Eds.), *Proceedings Southern Marketing Association.* Lafayette, LA: Southern Marketing Association.

Mason, R. S. (1981). *Conspicuous consumption: A study of exceptional consumer behavior.* New York: St. Martin's Press.

Masten, D. L. (1988, December 5). Logo's power depends on how well it communicates with target market. *Marketing News,* p. 20.

Matlin, M. W. (1989). *Cognition,* 2nd ed. Fort Worth: Holt, Rinehart & Winston.

Mazis, M. B. (1975). Antipollution measures and psychological reactance theory: A field experiment. *Journal of Personality and Social Psychology, 31,* 654–660.

Mazis, M. B., Ringold, D. J., Perry, E. S., & Denman, D. W. (1992). Perceived age and attractiveness of models in cigarette advertisements. *Journal of Marketing, 56*(January), 22–37.

McClelland, D. C. (1951). *Personality.* New York: Holt, Rinehart & Winston.

McClelland, D. C. (1976). *The achieving society,* 2nd ed., New York: Irvington.

McCracken, G. (1988). *Culture and consumption.* Bloomington, IN: Indiana University Press.

McElrea, H., & Standing, L. (1992). Fast music causes fast drinking. *Perceptual and Motor Skills, 75*(2), 362.

McGuire, W. J. (1976). Some internal psychological factors influencing consumer choice. *Journal of Consumer Research, 2*(March), pp. 302–319.

McNeal, J. (1969). An exploratory study of the consumer behavior of children. In J. U. McNeal (Ed.), *Dimensions of consumer behavior* (pp. 255–275). New York: Appleton-Century-Crofts.

McNeal, J. (1992). Marketing to children means communicating in a special language. *Advertising Age, 63*(35), 21.

McSweeney, F. K., & Bierley, C. (1984). Recent developments in classical conditioning. *Journal of Consumer Research, 11,* 619–631.

Medin, D. L., & Ross, B. (1992). *Cognitive psychology.* Fort Worth, TX: Harcourt Brace Jovanovich.

Mehrabian, A., & Russell, J. A. (1974). *An approach to environmental psychology.* Cambridge, MA: MIT Press.

Melton, A. (1933). Some behavior characteristics of museum visitors. *Psychological Bulletin, 30,* 720–721.

Melton, A. (1935). Problems of installation in museums of art. *American Association of Museums Monograph* (New Series No. 14). Washington, DC: American Association of Museums.

Meyers-Levy, J., & Tybout, A. M. (1989). Schema congruity as a basis for product evaluation. *Journal of Consumer Research, 16,* 39–54.

Milburn, M. A. (1991). *Persuasion and politics: The social psychology of public opinion.* Pacific Grove, CA: Brooks/Cole.

Miller, L. K., & Schyb, M. (1989). Facilitation and interference by background music. *Journal of Music Therapy, 26*(1), 42–54.

Miller, N., Maruyama, G., Beaber, R. J., & Valone, K. (1976). Speed of speech and persuasion. 30.*Journal of Personality and Social Psychology, 34,* 615–624.

Milliman, R. E. (1982). Using background music to affect the behavior of supermarket shoppers. *Journal of Marketing, 46*(3), 86–91.

Milliman, R. E. (1986). The influence of background music on the behavior of restaurant patrons. *Journal of Consumer Research, 13*(2), 286–289.

Milliman, R. E. (1988). The sweet sound of profits. *Restaurant Management, 2*(7), 53–54.

Milliman, R. E., & Erffmeyer, R. C. (1990). Improving advertising aimed at seniors. *Journal of Advertising Research,* (December 1989/ January 1990), 31–36.

Mitchell, A. A. (1979). Involvement: A potentially important mediator of consumer behavior. *Advances in Consumer Research, 6,* 191.

Mitchell, A. A. (1981). The dimensions of advertising involvement. *Advances in Consumer Research, 8,* 25–30.

Mitchell, A. A. (1986). The effect of verbal and visual components of advertisements on brand attitudes and attitude toward the advertisement. *Journal of Consumer Research, 13*(June), 12–23.

Mitchell, A. A. and Olson, J. C. (1981). Are product attribute beliefs the only mediator of advertising effects on brand attitudes? *Journal of Marketing Research, 18*(August), 318–332.

Mittal, B. (1987). A framework for relating consumer involvement to lateral brain functioning. *Advances in Consumer Research, 14,* 41–45.

Mittal, B. (1988). The role of affective choice mode in the consumer purchase of expressive products. *Journal of Economic Psychology, 9,* 499–524.

Mittal, B., & Lee, M. (1989). A causal model of consumer involvement. *Journal of Economic Psychology, 10*(3), 363–389.

Mollay, J. T. (1988). *New dress for success.* New York: Warner Books.

Moore-Shay, E. S., & Berchmans, B. M. (1996). The role of the family environment in the development of shared consumption values: An intergenerational study. *Advances in Consumer Research, 23,* 484–490.

Morgan, H. (1987). *Symbols of America.* New York: Penguin Books.

Morgan, L. A. (1985). The importance of quality. In J. Jacoby & J. Olson (Eds.), *Perceived quality* (pp. 61–64). Lexington, MA: Lexington Books.

Morrell, R.W., Park, D. C., & Poon, L. W. (1990). Effectas of labeling techniques on memory and comprehension of prescription information in young and old adults. *Journal of Gerontology, 45*, 166–172.

Morris, W. N. (1992). A functional analysis of the role of mood in affective systems. In M. S. Clark (Ed.), *Emotion* (pp. 256–293). Newbury Park, CA: Sage.

Morrison, B. J., & Dainoff, M. J. (1972). Advertisement complexity and viewing time. *Journal of Marketing Research, 9*(November), 396–400.

Moschis, G. P., & Moore, R. L. (1979). Decision making among the young: A socialization perspective. *Journal of Consumer Research, 6*(Sept), 1979.

Mowrer, O. H. (1960). *Learning theory and behavior*. New York: Wiley.

Mullen, B., & Johnson, C. (1990). *The psychology of consumer behavior*. Hillsdale, NJ: Erlbaum.

Muncy, J. A., & Hunt, S. D. (1984). Consumer involvement: Definitional issues and research directions. *Advances in Consumer Research, 11*, 193–196.

Murphy, P. & Staples, W. (1979). A modernized family life cycle. *Journal of Consumer Research, 6*, 12–22.

Murray, H. A. (1938). *Explorations of personality*. New York: Oxford.

Nahemow, L. (1963). *Persuasibility, social isolation and conformity among residents of a home for aged*. Unpublished doctoral dissertation, Columbia University.

Neely, K. (1990). Judas Priest gets off the hook. *Rolling Stone*, (October 4), 39.

Nelson, K. (1986). *Event knowledge: Structure and function in development*. Hillsdale, NJ: Erlbaum.

Nelson, S. A. (1980). Factors influencing young children's use of motives and outcomes as moral criteria. *Child Development, 51*, 823–829.

Nielson, S. L., & Sarason, S. G. (1981). Emotion, personality, and selective attention. *Journal of Personality and Social Psychology, 41*, 945–960.

Nisbett, R. E., & Ross, L. (1980). *Human inference: Strategies and shortcomings of social judgement*. Englewood Cliffs, NJ: Prentice-Hall.

Nisbett, R. E., & Wilson, T. D. (1977). Telling more than we can know: Verbal reports on mental processes. *Psychological Review, 84*, 231–259.

Nord, W. R., & Peter, J. P. (1980). A behavior modification perspective on marketing. *Journal of Marketing, 44*, 36–47.

Northcraft, G. B., & Neale, M. A. (1986). Opportunity costs and the framing of resource allocation decisions. *Organizational Behavior and Human Decision Processes, 39*, 84–97.

Obermiller, C. (1985). Varieties of mere exposure: The effects of processing style and repetition on affective responses. *Journal of Consumer Research, 12*(June), 17–30.

Ogilvy, D. (1985). *Ogilvy on advertising*. New York: Vintage Books.

Olds, J. (1956). Pleasure centers in the brain. *Scientific American, 195*, 105–116.

Olney, T.J., Holbrook, M.B., & Batra, R. (1991). Consumer responses to advertising: The effects of ad content, emotions, and attitude toward the ad on viewing time. *Journal of Consumer Research, 17*, 440–453.

Olsen, B. (1993). Brand loyalty and lineage: Exploring new dimensions for research. *Advances in Consumer Research, 20*, 575–579.

Olshavsky, R. W. (1985). Perceived quality in consumer decision making: An integrated theoretical perspective. In J. Jacoby & J. Olson (Eds.), *Perceived quality* (pp. 3–29). Lexington, MA: Lexington Books.

Olshavsky, R. W., & Granbois, D. H. (1979). Consumer decision-making—Fact or fiction? *Journal of Consumer Research, 6*, 93–100.

Olson, J. G., & Jacoby, J. (1972). Cue utilization in the quality perception process. In M. Venkatesan (Ed.), *Proceedings of the Third Annual Conference of the Association for Consumer Research* (pp. 167–179). Iowa City, IA: Association for Consumer Research.

Ornstein, R. E. (1969). *On the experience of time.* Baltimore: Penguin Books.

Oscamp, S. (1977). *Attitudes and opinions.* Englewood Cliffs, NJ: Prentice-Hall.

Osgood, C. E., Suci, G. J., & Tannenbaum, P. H. (1957). *The measurement of meaning.* Urbana, IL: University of Illinois Press.

Packard, V. (1957). *The hidden persuaders.* New York: Pocket Books.

Page, M. M. (1969). Social psychology of a classical conditioning of attitudes experiment. *Journal of Personality and Social Psychology, 11,* 177–186.

Papalia, D. E., & Olds, S. W. (1996). *Human development,* 3rd ed. New York: McGraw-Hill.

Park, C. W., & Young, S. M. (1986). Consumer response to television commercials: The impact of involvement and background music on brand attitude formation. *Journal of Marketing Research, 23*(February), 11–24.

Pavlov, I. P. (1927). *Conditioned reflexes.* Oxford: Oxford University Press.

Pearsall, E. R. (1989). Differences in listening comprehension with tonal and atonal background music. *Journal of Music Therapy, 26*(4), 188–197.

Peracchio, L. A. (1990). Designing research to reveal the young child's emerging competence. *Psychology and Marketing, 7*(Winter), 257–276.

Peracchio, L. A. (1992). How do young children learn to be consumers? A script-processing approach. *Journal of Consumer Research, 18*(4), 425–440.

Peracchio, L. A., & Meyers-Levy, J. (1994). How ambiguous cropped objects in ad photos can affect product evaluations. *Journal of Consumer Research, 21,* 190–204.

Petty, R. E., & Cacioppo, J. T. (1981). *Attitudes and persuasion: Classic and contemporary approaches.* Dubuque, IA: Wm. C. Brown.

Petty, R. E., Cacioppo, J. T., & Schumann, D. (1983). Central and peripheral routes to advertising effectiveness: The moderating role of involvement. *Journal of Consumer Research, 10,* 135–146.

Pezdek, K., & Stevens, E. (1984). Children's memory for auditory and visual information on television. *Developmental Psychology, 20*(2), 212–218.

Piaget, J. (1936). *La naissance de l'intelligence chez l'enfant.* Neuchatel et Paris: Delachau et Niestle.

Piaget, J. (1969). *The mechanisms of perception.* London: Routledge and Kegan Paul.

Phillips, L. W., & Sternthal, B. (1977). Age differences in information processing: A perspective on the aged consumer. *Journal of Marketing Research, 14*(November), 444–457.

Plous, S. (1993). *The psychology of judgment and decision making.* New York: McGraw-Hill.

Plutchik, R. (1984). Emotion. In K. Scherer & P. Ekman (Eds.), *Approaches to emotion.* Hillsdale, NJ: Erlbaum.

Poetzl, O. (1960). The relationship between experimentally induced dream images and indirect vision [Monograph No. 7]. *Psychological Issues, 2,* 41–120. (Originally published 1917).

Pollay, R. W. (1984). The identification and distribution of values manifest in print advertising 1900–1980. In R. E. Pitts, Jr., and A. G. Woodside (Eds.), *Personal values and consumer psychology.* Lexington, MA: Lexington Books.

Posner, M. I., & Snyder, C. R. R. (1975). Attention and cognitive control. In R. L. Solso (Ed.), *Information processing and cognition.* Hillsdale, NJ: Erlbaum.

Powell, P. & Peel, L. (1996). *'50s & '60s style.* North Dighton, MA: JG Press.

Pratkanis, A. R., & Greenwald, A. G. (1989). A sociocognitive model of attitude structure and function. In L. Berkowitz (Ed.), *Advances in experimental social psychology*, Vol. 22, (pp. 245–285). New York: Academic Press.

Pratkanis, A. R., Greenwald, A. G., Leippe, M. R., & Baumgardner, M. H. (1988). In search of reliable persuasion effects: III.The sleeper effect is dead. Long live the sleeper effect. *Journal of Personality and Social Psychology, 54*, 203–218.

Prelinger, E. (1959). Extension and structure of the self. *Journal of Psychology, 47*(January), 13–23.

Price, L. L., Feick, L. F., & Guskey-Federouch, A. (1988). Couponing behaviors of the market maven: Profile of a super-couponer. *Advances in Consumer Research, 15*, 354–359.

Queenan, J. (1993, October 25). Classical gas. *Forbes*, pp. 214–215.

Rabbitt, P. (1965). An age decrement in the ability to ignore irrelevant information. *Journal of Gerontology, 20*(April), 233–238.

Rachlin, H. (1989). Judgment, decision, and choice: A cognitive/behavioral synthesis. New York: Freeman.

Raju, P. S., & Lonial, S. C. (1990). Advertising to children: Findings and implications. In *Current issues & research in advertising*, Vol. 12 (pp. 231–274). Ann Arbor, MI: University of Michigan.

Razran, G. (1940). Conditioned response changes in rating and appraising sociopolitical slogan. *Psychological Bulletin, 37*, 481.

Razren, G. (1938). Conditioning away social bias by the luncheon technique. *Psychological Bulletin, 35*, 693.

Reber, A. S. (1993). *Implicit learning and tacit knowledge: An essay on the cognitive unconscious*. New York: Oxford.

Reeves, R. (1961). *Reality in advertising*. New York: Knopf.

Rescorla, R. A. (1967). Pavlovian conditioning and its proper control procedures. *Psychological Review, 74*, 71–80.

Rescorla, R. A. (1988). Pavlovian conditioning: It's not what you think it is. *American Psychologist, 43*(3), 151–160.

Richins, M. L. (1994). Special possessions and the expression of material values. *Journal of Consumer Research, 21*, 522–533.

Richins, M. L., & Dawson, S. (1992). A consumer values orientation for materialism and its measurement: Scale development and validation. *Journal of Consumer Research, 19*, 303–316.

Riecken, G., & Samli, A. C. (1981). Measuring children's attitudes toward television commercials: Extension and replication. *Journal of Consumer Research, 8*(June), 57–61.

Riecken, G., & Yavas, U. (1990). Children's general, product and brand-specific attitudes toward television commercials: Implications for public policy and advertising strategy. *International Journal of Advertising, 9*(2), 136–148.

Ries, A., & Trout, J. (1986). *Positioning: The battle for your mind*. New York: Warner Books.

Roberts, D. F. (1982). Children and commercials: Issues, evidence, interventions. *Prevention in Human Services, 2*(1–2), 19–35.

Roberts, L. (1992). Affective learning, affective experience: What does it have to do with museum education? In A. Benefield, S. Bitgood, & H. Shettel (Eds.), *Visitor studies*: Vol. 4, *Theory, research, and practice* (pp. 162–168). Jacksonville, AL: The Center for Social Design.

Robertson, T. S., & Rossiter, J. R. (1974). Children and commercial persuasion. *Journal of Consumer Research, 1*(June), 13–20.

Robertson, T. S., Zielinski, J., & Ward, S. (1984). *Consumer behavior*. Glenview, IL: Scott, Foresman.

Roedder, D. L. (1981). Age differences in children's responses to television advertising: An information-processing approach. *Journal of Consumer Research, 8*(September), 144–153.

Rogers, C. R. (1959). A theory of therapy, personality, and interpersonal relationships, as developed in the client-centered framework. In S. Koch (Ed.), *Psychology: A study of a science*, Vol. 3, New York: McGraw-Hill.

Rogers, T. B., Kuiper, N. A., & Kirker, W. S. (1977). Self-reference and the encoding of personal information. *Journal of Personality and Social Psychology, 35*, 677–688.

Rohner, R. (1984). Toward a conception of culture for cross-cultural psychology. *Journal of Cross-Cultural Psychology, 15*, 111–138.

Rosenbaum, L., & Rosenbaum, W. (1975). Persuasive impact of a communicator where groups differ in apparent re-orientation. *Journal of Psychology, 89*, 189–194.

Rosenberg, M. J. (1965). Some content determinants of intolerance for attitudinal inconsistency. In S. S. Tomkins & C. E. Izard (Eds.), *Affect, cognition, and personality: Empirical studies* (pp. 130–147). New York: Springer.

Rosenfeld, P., Giacalone, R. A., & Tedeschi, J. T. (1983). Cognitive dissonance vs. impression management. *Journal of Social Psychology, 120*, 203–211.

Rossi, A. (1984). Gender and parenthood. *American Sociological Review, 49*, 1–19.

Rotter, J. B. (1954). *Social learning and clinical psychology.* New York: Prentice-Hall.

Rozelle, R. M. (1968). Meaning established by classical conditioning: Failure to replicate. *Psychological Reports, 22*, 889–895.

Runyon, K. E., & Stewart, D. W. (1987). *Consumer behavior and the practice of marketing*, 3rd ed. Columbus: Merrill.

Russell, J. A. (1979). Affective space is bipolar. *Journal of Personality and Social Psychology, 37*, 345–356.

Russell, J. A., & Mehrabian, A. (1977). Evidence for a three-factor theory of emotions. *Journal of Research in Psychology, 11*, 273–294.

Rust, L. (1986). Children's advertising: How it works, how to do it, how to know if it works. *Journal of Advertising Research, 26*(Aug/Sept), 13–15.

Sabini, J. (1992). *Social psychology.* New York: W. W. Norton.

Sawyer, A. G. (1974). The effects of repetition: Conclusions and suggestions about experimental laboratory research. In G. D. Hughes & M. L. Ray (Eds.), *Buyer/Consumer information processing* (pp. 190–219). Chapel Hill, NC: University of North Carolina Press.

Schachter, S., & Singer, J. E. (1962). Cognitive, social, and physiological determinants of emotional state. *Psychological Review, 69*, 379–399.

Schaninger, C. M., & Danko, W. D. (1993). A conceptual and empirical comparison of alternative life cycle models. *Journal of Consumer Research, 19*, 580–594.

Schiffman, L. G. (1971). Sources of information for the elderly. *Journal of Advertising Research, 11*(5), 33–37.

Schiffman, L. G., & Kanuk, L. L. (1994). *Consumer behavior*, 5th ed. Englewood Cliffs, NJ: Prentice Hall.

Schindler, R. M. (1989). The excitement of getting a bargain: Some hypotheses concerning the origins and effects of smart-shopper feelings. *Advances in Consumer Research, 16*, 447–453.

Schlenker, B. R. (1982). Translating actions into attitudes: An identity-analytic approach to the explanation of social conduct. In L. Berkowitz (Ed.), *Advances in experimental social psychology*, Vol. 15, (pp. 193–247). New York: Academic Press.

Schlosberg, H. (1954). Three demensions of emotion. *Psychological Review, 61*, 81–88.

Schreiber, E. S., & Boyd, D. A. (1980). How the elderly perceive television commercials. *Journal of Communication, 30*(4), 61–70.

Schroeder, H. W. (1993). Preference for and meaning of arboretum landscapes. *Visitor Behavior, VIII*(1), 13–14.

Schulz, R., & Ewen, R. B. (1993). *Adult development and aging: Myths and emerging realities.* New York: Macmillan.

Schwartz, B., & Reisberg, D. (1991). *Learning and memory.* New York: W. W. Norton.

Screven, C. G. (1976). Exhibit evaluation—goal-referenced approach. *Curator, 19*(4), 271–290.

Sears, D. O., Freedman, J. L., & Peplau, L. A. (1985). *Social Psychology,* 5th ed. Englewood Cliffs, NJ: Prentice-Hall.

Segall, M. H. (1986). Culture and behavior: Psychology in global perspective. In M. R. Rosenzweig & L. W. Porter (Eds.), *Annual review of psychology,* Vol. 37, (pp. 523–564). Palo Alto, CA: Annual Reviews.

Serrell, B. (1983). *Making exhibit labels: A step-by-step guide.* Nashville, TN: American Association for State and Local History.

Sherif, M., & Hovland, C. I. (1961). *Social judgement.* New Haven: Yale University Press.

Shettel, H. (1973). Exhibits: Art form or educational medium? *Museum News, 52,* 32–41.

Shevrin, H., & Fritzler, D. E. (1968). Visual evoked response correlates of unconscious mental processes. *Science, 161,* 295–298.

Shifren, I. E. (1981). The interaction between hemispheric preference and the perception of subliminal auditory and visual symbiotic gratification stimuli. Unpublished doctoral dissertation, St. John's University.

Shimp, T. A. (1991). Neo-Pavlovian conditioning and its implications for consumer theory and research. In T. S. Robertson & H. H. Kassarjian (Eds.), *Handbook of consumer behavior* (pp. 162–187). Englewood Cliffs, NJ: Prentice-Hall.

Shimp, T. A., & Kavas, A. (1984). The theory of reasoned action applied to coupon usage. *Journal of Consumer Research, 11*(December), 795–809.

Shimp, T. A., Hyatt, E. M., & Snyder, D. J. (1991). A critical appraisal of demand artifacts in consumer research. *Journal of Consumer Research, 18*(December), 273–283.

Shimp, T. A., Stuart, E. W., & Engle, R. W. (1991). A program of classical conditioning experiments testing variations in the conditioned stimulus and context. *Journal of Consumer Research, 18*(June), 1–12.

Shrank, J. (1977). *Snap, crackle and popular taste.* New York: Dell.

Silverman, L. H. (1983). The subliminal psychodynamic activation method: Overview and comprehensive listing of studies. In J. Masling (Ed.), *Empirical studies of psychoanalytical theories:Vol.1. Psychoanalytic perspectives on psychopathology* (pp. 69–100). Hillsdale, NJ: Analytic Press, distributed by Erlbaum.

Sirgy, M. J. (1982). Self-concept in consumer behavior: A critical review. *Journal of Consumer Research, 9*(December), 287–300.

Slovic, P., & Lichtenstein, S. (1971). Comparison of Bayesian and regression approaches to the study of information processing in judgment. *Organizational Behavior and Human Performance, 6,* 649–744.

Smetana, J. G., & Adler, N. E. (1980). Fishbein's value X expectancy model: An examination of some assumptions. *Personality and Social Psychology Bulletin, 6,* 89–96.

Smith, P. C., & Curnow, R. (1966). 'Arousal hypothesis' and the effects of music on purchase behavior. *Journal of Applied Psychology, 50,* 255–256.

Snyder, M. (1974). The self-monitoring of expressive behavior. *Journal of Personality and Social Psychology, 30,* 526–537.

Snyder, M. (1989). Selling image versus selling products: Motivational foundations of consumer attitudes and behavior. *Advances in Consumer Research, 16,* 306–311.

Sogin, D. W. (1988). Effects of three different musical styles of background music on coding by college-age students. *Perceptual and Motor Skills, 67,* 275–280.

Solley, C. M. (1966). Affective processes in perceptual development. In A. H. Kidd & J. L. Rivoire (Eds.), *Perceptual development in children* (pp. 275–304). New York: International Universities Press.

Solso, R. L. (1995). *Cognitive psychology,* 4th ed. Boston: Allyn and Bacon.

Spence, D. P. (1964). Conscious and preconscious influences on recall: Another example of the restricting effects of awareness. *Journal of Abnormal and Social Psychology, 68,* 92–99.

Sperling, G. (1960). The information available in brief visual presentations. *Psychological Monographs, 74*(11, No. 498).

Spiro, R. L. (1983). Persuasion in family decision-making. *Journal of Consumer Research, 9,* 393–402.

Sproles, G. B., & Burns, L. D. (1994). *Changing appearances: Understanding dress in contemporary society.* New York: Fairchild.

Staats, A. W. (1969). Experimental demand characteristics and the classical conditioning of attitudes. *Journal of Personality and Social Psychology, 11,* 187–192.

Staats, A. W., & Staats, C. K. (1958). Attitudes established by classical conditioning. *Journal of Abnormal and Social Psychology, 57,* 37–40. (Reported in *Chance,* 1988, p. 64.)

Staats, A. W., & Staats, C. K. (1959). Effect of number of trials on the language conditioning of meaning. *Journal of General Psychology, 61*(October), 211–223.

Staats, C. K., & Staats, A. W. (1957). Meaning established by classical conditioning. *Journal of Experimental Psychology, 54,* 74–80. (Reported in *Chance,* 1988, p. 64).

Stanton, H. E. (1975). Music and test anxiety: Further evidence for an interaction. *British Journal of Educational Psychology, 45,* 80–82.

Stephens, N. (1991). Cognitive age: A useful concept for advertising? *Journal of Advertising, 20*(4), 38–48.

Stephens, N., & Warrens, R. A. (1984). Advertising frequency requirements for older adults. *Journal of Advertising Research, 23*(6), 23–32.

Stern, B. L., & Resnik, A. (1978). Children's understanding of a televised commercial disclaimer. In C. J. Subhash (ed.), *Research frontiers in marketing: Dialogues and directions* (pp. 332–336). Chicago: American Marketing Association.

Sternthal, B., & Craig, C. S. (1973). Humor in advertising. *Journal of Marketing, 37,* 12–18.

Stevens, J. C. (1992). Aging and spatial acuity of touch. *Journal of Gerontology: Psychological Sciences, 47,* P35–40.

Stratton, V. N., & Zalanowski, A. (1984). The effect of background music on verbal interaction in groups. *Journal of Music Therapy, 21*(1), 16–26.

Stuart, E. W., Shimp, T. A., & Engle, R. W. (1987). Classical conditioning of consumer attitudes: Four experiments in an advertising context. *Journal of Consumer Research, 14,* 334–348.

Stutts, M. A., & Hunnicutt, G. G. (1987). Can young children understand disclaimers in television commercials? *Journal of Advertising, 16,* 41–46.

Sullivan, G. L. (1990). Music format effects in radio advertising. *Psychology and Marketing, 7*(2), 97–108.

Susman, W. (1973). *Culture as history: The transformation of American society in the twentieth century.* New York: Pantheon Books.

Swartzentruber, D., & Bouton, M. E. (1992). Context sensitivity of conditioned suppression following preexposure to the conditioned stimulus. *Animal Learning and Behavior, 20*(2), 97–108.

Tannen, D. (1990). *You just don't understand: Women and men in conversation*. New York: Ballantine Books.

Taylor, S. E., Fiske, S. T., Etcoff, N. L., & Ruderman, A. J. (1978). Categorical and contextual bases of person memory and stereotyping. *Journal of Personality and Social Psychology, 36*, 778–793.

Tedeschi, J. T., Lindskold, S., & Rosenfeld, P. (1985). *Introduction to social psychology*. St. Paul: West.

Thaler, R. (1980). Toward a positive theory of consumer choice. *Journal of Economic Behavior and Organization, 1*, 39–60.

Thaut, M. H., & de l'Etoile, S. K. (1993). The effects of music on mood state-dependent recall. *Journal of Music Therapy, 30*(2), 70–80.

Tinbergen, N. (1951). *The study of instinct*. Oxford: Clarendon Press.

Tom, G. (1995). Classical conditioning of unattended stimuli. *Psychology and Marketing, 12*(1), 79–87.

Troutman, C., Michael, R., & Shanteau, J. (1976). Do consumers evaluate products by adding or averaging attribute information? *Journal of Consumer Research, 3*, 101–106.

Tuan, Y. (1980). The significance of the artifact. *Geographical Review, 70*(4), 462–472.

Tulving, E. (1962). Subjective organization in free recall of "unrelated" words. *Psychological Review, 69*, 344–354.

Tulving, E. (1983). *Elements of episodic memory*. Oxford: Oxford University Press.

Tversky, A. (1972). Elimination by aspects: A theory of choice. *Psychological Review, 79*, 281–299.

Tversky, A., & Kahneman, D. (1973). Availability: A heuristic for judging frequency and probability. *Cognitive Psychology, 4*, 207–232.

Tversky, A., & Kahneman, D. (1974). Judgment under uncertainty: Heuristics and biases. *Science, 185*, 1124–1131.

Vaughn, K. B., & Lanzetta, J. T. (1980). Vicarious instigation and conditioning of facial expressive and autonomic responses to a model's expressive displays of pain. *Journal of Personality and Social Psychology, 38*, 909–923.

Veblen, T. (1967). *The theory of the leisure class*. New York: Penguin Books. (Originally published in 1899 by Macmillan).

Venn, J. R., & Short, J. G. (1973). Vicarious classical conditioning of emotional responses in nursery school children. *Journal of Personality and Social Psychology, 28*, 249–255.

Vokey, J. R., & Read, J. D. (1985). Subliminal messages: Between the devil and the media. *American Psychologist, 40*, 1231–1239.

Wakshlag, J. J., Reitz, R. J., & Zillman, D. (1982). Selective exposure and acquisition of information from educational television programs as a function of appeal and tempo of background music. *Journal of Educational Psychology, 74*(5), 666–677.

Walster, E., & Festinger, L. (1962). The effectiveness of "overheard" persuasive communications. *Journal of Abnormal and Social Psychology, 65*, 395–402.

Warah, R. (1986). Brand recall as a function of the presence of a person in the ad. Unpublished manuscript. Boston: Suffolk University, Psychology Department.

Ward, S. (1974). Consumer socialization. *Journal of Consumer Research, 1*, 1–14.

Ward, S., Levinson, D., & Wackman, D. (1972). Children's attention to television advertising. In E. Rubenstein (Ed.), *Television and social behavior*, Vol. 4 (pp. 491–516). Washington, DC: GPO.

Ward, S., & Wackman, D. (1973). In P. Clarke (Ed.), *New models for mass communication research* (p. 139). Beverley Hills, CA: Sage.

Ward, S., Wackman, D. B., & Wartella, E. (1977). *How children learn to buy: The development of information-processing skills*. Beverley Hills, CA: Sage.

Watson, J. B., & Rayner, R. (1920). Conditioned emotional reactions. *Journal of Experimental Psychology, 3*, 1–4.

Webb, R. C. (1962). Perception of two visual stimuli presented in rapid succession. Unpublished Masters Thesis, Brown University, Providence.

Webb, R. C. (1993). The relevance of the consumer behavior literature to the visitor studies field: The case of involvement. *Visitor Studies: Theory, research, and practice* Vol. 6.(pp. 7–19). Jacksonville, AL: The Visitor Studies Association.

Webb, R. C. (1994). *The wiles and worries of getting attention.* Paper presented at Annual Conference of Visitor Studies Association, Raleigh, NC.

Webster, C. (1994). Effects of Hispanic ethnic identification on marital roles in the purchase decision process. *Journal of Consumer Research, 21*, 319–331.

Weiskrantz, L. (1986). *Blindsight: A case study and its implications.* Oxford: Oxford University Press.

Weiskrantz, L. (1990). Blindsight. In M. W. Eysenck (Ed.), *The Blackwell dictionary of cognitive psychology.* Oxford: Blackwell.

Wells, W. D. (1975). Psychographics: A critical review. *Journal of Marketing Research, 12*(May), 196– 213.

White, R. W. (1959). Motivation reconsidered: The concept of competence. *Psychological Review, 66*, 297–333.

White, R. W., & Watt, N. F. (1981). *The abnormal personality,* 5th ed. New York: Wiley.

Whittemore, K. (1996). How a weed once scorned became the flower of the hour. *Smithsonian, 27*(5), 52–58.

Wilhelm, R. (1956). Are subliminal commercials bad? *Michigan Business Review, 8*(January), p. 26.

Wilke, W. L. (1986). *Consumer behavior.* New York: Wiley.

Wilkes, R. E. (1995). Household life-cycle changes, transitions, and product expenditures. *Journal of Consumer Research, 22*, 27–42.

Wilson, T. D., Lisle, D. J., Kraft, D., & Wetzel, C. G. (1989). Preferences as expectation-driven inferences: Effects of affective expectations on affective experience. *Journal of Personality and Social Psychology, 56*, 519–530.

Wingfield, A. (1980). Attention, levels of processing, and state dependent recall. In L. W. Poon et al. (Eds.) *New directions in memory and aging.* Hillsdale, NJ: Erlbaum.

Wolf, R. H., & Weiner, F. (1972). Effects of four noise conditions on arithmetic performance. *Perceptual and Motor Skills, 35*, 928–930.

Woltman, R. M. (1993). A sense of place within the space. *Visitor Studies: Theory, research and practice,* Vol. 6 (pp. 24–27). Jacksonville, AL: The Visitor Studies Association.

Woodrow, H. (1951). Time perception. In S. S. Stevens (Ed.), *Handbook of experimental psychology* (pp. 1224–1236). New York: Wiley.

Woodside, A. G. & Motes, W. H. (1979). Perceptions of marital roles in consumer decision processes for six products. In Beckwith et al. (Eds.) *American Marketing Association Proceedings* (pp. 214–219). Chicago: American Marketing Association.

Woodson, L. G., Childers, T. L. & Winn, P. R. (1976). Intergenerational influences in the purchase of auto insurance. In W. Locander (Ed.), *Marketing looking outward: 1976 business proceedings* (pp. 43–49). Chicago: American Marketing Association.

Worts, D. (1992). Visitor-centered experiences. In A. Benefield, S. Bitgood, & H. Shettel (Eds.), *Visitor studies: Theory, research, and practice* Vol. 4. (pp. 156–161). Jacksonville, AL: The Center for Social Design.

Wright, P. L. (1973). The cognitive processes mediating acceptance of advertising. *Journal of Marketing Research, 10*(February), 53–62.

Wundt, W. (1902). *Outlines of psychology,* 2nd ed. (C. H. Judd, Trans.). Leipzig: Engelmann.

Yalch, R., & Spangenberg, E. (1990). Effects of store music on shopping behavior. *Journal of Consumer Marketing, 7*(2), 55–60.

Yerkes, R. M., & Dodson, J. D. (1908). The relation of strength of stimulus to rapidity of habit-formation. *Journal of Comparative and Neurological Psychology, 18*, 459–482.

Zajonc, R. B. (1968). Attitudinal effects of mere exposure. *Journal of Personality and Social Psychology Monographs, 9*(pt.2), 1–28.

Zajonc, R. B. (1980). Feeling and thinking: Preferences need no inferences. *American Psychologist, 35*, 151–175.

Zajonc, R. B. (1984). On the primacy of affect. *American Psychologist, 39*, 117–123.

Zajonc, R. B. (1986). Basic mechanisms of preference formation. In R. A. Peterson, W. D. Hoyer, & W. R. Wilson (Eds.), *The role of affect in consumer behavior: Emerging theories and applications* (pp. 1–16). Lexington, MA: Lexington Books.

Zajonc, R. B., & Markus, H. (1982). Affective and cognitive factors in preferences. *Journal of Consumer Research, 9*(September), 123–131.

Zajonc, R. B., & Markus, H. (1985). Must all affect be mediated by cognition? *Journal of Consumer Research, 12*, 363–364.

Zanna, M. P. (1989). Attitude-behavior consistency: Fulfilling the need for cognitive structure. *Advances in Consumer Research, 16*, 318–320.

Zanna, M. P., & Rampel, J. K. (1988). Attitudes: A new look at an old concept. In D. Bar-Tal & A. Kruglanski (Eds.), *The social psychology of knowledge.* New York: Cambridge University Press.

Zeithamel, V. A. (1988). Consumer perceptions of price, quality, and value: A means-end model and synthesis of evidence. *Journal of Marketing, 52*(July), 2–22.

Zeithamel, V. A. (1987). Defining and relating price, perceived quality, and perceived value. Working paper. Cambridge, MA: Marketing Science Institute. (Report No. 87–101).

Zuckerman, P., Ziegler, M., & Stevenson, H. W. (1978). Children's viewing of television and recognition memory of commercials. *Child Development, 49*, 96–104.

Zuckoff, M. (1995, July 2). Kicking the connection. *The Boston Sunday Globe*, pp. 65–66.

Index